FIELDS

OF VISION

readings

about

culture,

race,

and

ethnicity

Edited by

Elizabeth J. Stieg
Centennial College

Toronto

For my mother—E.J.S.

National Library of Canada Cataloguing in Publication Data

Main entry under title:
   Fields of vision : readings about culture, race, and ethnicity

ISBN 0-13-089054-5

   1. Ethnicity in literature. 2. Cultural relations in literature.
3. Multiculturalism in literature. 4. Race relations in literature.
I. Stieg, Elizabeth J., 1952–

PN6071.R23F53 2002   820.8′0355   C2001-902106-2

Copyright © 2002 Pearson Education Canada Inc., Toronto, Ontario

For permission to reproduce copyright material, we gratefully acknowledge the copyright holders listed on pages 407–10, which are considered an extension of the copyright page.

ISBN 0-13-089054-5

Vice President, Editorial Director: Michael Young
Editor-in-Chief and Acquisitions Editor: David Stover
Marketing Manager: Sharon Loeb
Developmental Editor: Lise Creurer
Production Editor: Avivah Wargon
Copy Editor: Pam Young
Proofreaders: Cheryl Cohen, Patricia Thorvaldson
Production Manager: Wendy Moran
Page Layout: Debbie Kumpf
Art Director: Mary Opper
Interior Design: Sarah Battersby
Cover Design: Sarah Battersby
Cover Images: Photodisc

1 2 3 4 5   06 05 04 03 02

Printed and bound in Canada.

Prentice
Hall

contents

part i: the roots of identity

part ii: finding a voice: the issue of language

part iii: migrants' tales

part iu: race relations and the struggle for justice

part u: the idea of home— real and imagined

preface

Fields of Vision is a collection of literature that focusses on cross-cultural experience. It reflects the issues that arise from living in a pluralistic society in which "race" (whether or not cultural critics see this as a legitimate concept, it is certainly a popular one), culture and ethnicity are just as often what separates an individual from others as they are a bond with a larger community. The collection offers a wide variety of perspectives from people of different ethnic and cultural backgrounds and thus reflects the diversity of attitude and experience that is present in our own increasingly multi-cultural society. It is an international anthology, containing writing from India and Africa, Australia and the Caribbean, in short, pretty much wherever English is a major language, but it also directly reflects Canadian experience since approximately one third of the authors either live or have lived in Canada.

The anthology is divided into five thematic sections, each of which is followed by a series of questions inviting readers to draw connections between and among the works. While the organization of the selections reflects what I perceive to be their leading ideas, it should not obscure the fact that many authors deal with several of the themes identified. As I have worked on the book, some pieces have wandered from one section to another because it seemed to me that they had more to say about a different theme or idea than I had at first realized. As a result, some of the questions reflect the complex concerns of the authors by directing the reader's attention to selections other than those in the section dealing specifically with the theme under discussion.

Many of the authors found here are well known, while others are clearly less so. Each section thus begins with a biographical introduction that provides information about the author's life and major literary concerns as well as an overview of the critical response to his/her work. Because many of these writers have been viewed in the context of postmodernist or postcolonial fiction, I have provided some theoretical background and explanation for these terms (particularly in the general introduction, but also, where relevant, throughout the text). Glosses are also provided for some of the allusions and non-English passages in the texts themselves. Each selection is followed by a list of resources—both print and Web—which can be consulted for further information about authors or their literary contexts.

I owe a huge debt of gratitude to the staff at Pearson Education Canada—especially to David Stover, Lise Creurer, Sharon Loeb, Sarah Battersby, Avivah Wargon—and my copy editor, Pam Young, proofreader, Cheryl Cohen, and researcher, David Baughan. I thank Soraya Erian Dokainish, Alexandra MacLennan and David McCarthy, who helped shape the text with their productive feedback as reviewers. I am also particularly grateful to Maureen Coleman, who gave so much time and thought to reviewing the work throughout development and who was the source of so many good ideas. My deepest gratitude goes to my husband, whose support—both intellectual and emotional—made this book possible.

Elizabeth Stieg

introduction

The title of this collection of international writing comes from the science of ophthalmology. A visual field test is used by ophthalmologists to measure the extent and accuracy of peripheral vision; in other words, it attempts the scientific measurement of how well one sees. A friend of mine who has been myopic (short-sighted) from birth once speculated that ophthalmology was a conspiracy to make everyone see in the same way. She bought the glasses prescribed for her because they made her life easier, but she retained the conviction that her own unaided vision was more interesting and personal, more authentic somehow, than the vision she was capable of when using glasses that "normalized" her perception. Without glasses, her field of vision was particular; with them, it was (more or less) standard.

Like the prescriptive lenses my friend so much resented, our cultures provide us with a more or less standardized way of seeing things. Our culture, with its values, beliefs, approaches, rituals, ways of interpreting the world and behavioural expectations, seems to us "normal," "natural" in a way that other cultures do not—rather like the way we think of our manner of speaking as being without accent, while others speaking the same language but using a different mode of pronunciation are perceived as having particular regional or national accents. Our field of vision is unconsciously deemed accurate; alternative visions thus seem exotic, anomalous, "other." Those who ignore the fact that their cultures constitute as particular (and as arbitrary) a way of interpreting the world and determining behaviour as any other, who insist that their visual field or mode of perception is the absolute against which every other is measured, are called **ethnocentric (Eurocentric** if their culture is European)—that is, they see their ethnicity, their cultural lenses, as central, while all others are deviations. When this attitude is embodied in a state policy of imposing one culture or way of understanding the world on people who belong to another, it is called **cultural imperialism**.

"Otherness is a fundamental category of human thought," wrote Simone de Beauvoir in her feminist study of the position of women, *The Second Sex* (1952). Noting that the concepts of "duality, alternation, opposition, and symmetry" characterize human interpretations of the world, she remarks that "we find in consciousness itself a fundamental hostility toward every other consciousness; the subject can be posed only in being opposed—he sets himself up as the essential as opposed to the other, the inessential, the object" (xvii). In fact of course, as she points out, the concept of the "other" is relative. In any human relationship, we become in some sense the other to those who perceive us. The imperialist powers justified domination and exploitation of other lands by portraying the inhabitants as "others" who would benefit from exposure to a superior culture; the powers themselves were "the other, the inessential, the object" to those they sought to control.

Scholars and cultural critics have argued that the effectiveness with which imperialist nations have imposed their own cultures on subject or colonized peoples has been less a function of their ability to control the economies of other states than of their ability to dominate what Ashcroft et al. refer to as "the means of representation": "Economic, political and military dominance enabled the dissemination of European ideas through the powerful agencies of education and publishing. But it was the power of imperial discourse rather than military or economic might that confirmed the hegemony [domination] of imperialism in the late nineteenth century" (*Key Concepts* 127). By dominating the "means of representation"—newspapers, books of history, religion, philosophy, literature, and eventually, films, as well as the educational curriculum—the colonizers were able to impose their "corrective" cultural lenses on others.

In a seminal book called *Orientalism*, Edward Said describes the process whereby European and, more recently, American colonial powers have generated texts that categorize and define the East (the Orient of Said's title) in reductive, simplistic and Euro-centred terms. Said points to books such as the *Description de l'Egypte*, written by the team of scholars Napoleon took to Egypt to uncover the secrets of the mysterious East: "Egyptian or Oriental history as history possessing its own coherence, identity and sense" is displaced by "world history, a euphemism for European history" (86). The *Description* was published (in twenty-three volumes) between 1809 and 1828, but it and other European texts like it shaped the European understanding of the East throughout the nineteenth century and, as Said demonstrates, its stereotypes and misinformation continue to make appearances in twentieth-century (and presumably, twenty-first century) discussions of Islam and the Middle East.

Modern psychology has demonstrated that perception—everything from literally seeing something to understanding an idea or concept—is a function of both the nature of the stimulus (for example, the table in front of you) and the characteristics of the perceiver. Important factors affecting the act of perception include the past experience, the motivation and readiness to respond to stimulus, and the mood or emotional state of the perceiver. No two people experience reality in precisely the same way because "each individual perceives in terms of those aspects of the situation which have special significance for him [or her]"(Chaplin 352) and interprets them in accordance with what he or she has already learned. The past experience of any individual includes the influence of his or her culture. If the transmitters of cultural attitudes—the media, books, educational systems—suggest to generations of Europeans that "Orientals" are exotic, mysterious, emotional (not rational, like Europeans), self-indulgent "others," it becomes difficult for individual Europeans to see beyond these stereotypes. If we are ourselves the "other" in the culture in which we live, if we are for example women, people of colour, homosexuals, it can be very difficult to perceive ourselves without the cultural lens that reduces us to stereotypes.

One of the things this book aims to do is to afford its readers opportunities to perceive the world through different eyes, different cultural lenses, in the belief that each perspective has something of value to offer and that no one has a monopoly on truth. Beyond simply expanding and enriching our awareness, exposure to alternative perspectives can give us a greater understanding of each other and ideally, greater tolerance. As Henry Louis Gates, Jr. observes in the introduction to *Loose Canons,*

> Ours is a . . . world profoundly fissured by nationality, ethnicity, race, class, and gender. And the only way to transcend those divisions—to forge, for once, a civic culture that respects both differences and commonalities—is through education that seeks to comprehend the diversity of human culture. Beyond the hype and the high-flown rhetoric is a pretty homely truth: There is no tolerance without respect—and no respect without knowledge. (xv)

Many of the diverse perspectives on offer here have only recently begun to attract a world audience. They present **counter-hegemonic** positions, that is, positions that oppose or counter the interpretations found in traditional Eurocentric texts. Many of them can be seen to belong, therefore, to a category that literature critics in the late 1970s began to identify as **postcolonial**.

According to a definition Ashcroft et al. put forward in 1998, post-colonial literature deals with "the political, linguistic and cultural experience of societies that were . . . European colonies" (*Key Concepts* 186). A decade earlier the same authors had suggested that postcolonial writers, whether from Africa or Canada, India or Australia, share "themes and recurrent structural and formal patterns" (*Empire* 29). Arun Mukherjee summarizes the themes that these and other postcolonial critics discern in all postcolonial fiction as follows: "issues of identity, hybridity, creolization [both of the latter terms refer to mixed forms—for example, native narrative structures or mythic elements, combined with the structures of the colonizing culture], language, subversion of imperial texts [texts produced by the colonizing, European cultures], parody and mimicry . . ." (8). Noting that much postcolonial theory "claims that the major theme of literatures from postcolonial societies is discursive resistance to the now-absent colonizer" (18), Mukherjee argues that this view of postcolonial fiction is reductive. She asserts that a substantial amount of the literature in the period following the collapse of the European empires is not related to these themes and focusses instead on problems and experience intrinsic to the societies being described, having nothing (or very little) to do with the impact of colonization, the loss of a pre-colonial identity or language, or the experience of being oppressed by a foreign power (8). Her argument should make us wary of finding only the patterns that the academic cultural lens reveals to us.

Another "ism" that is often associated with many of the authors who appear here is **postmodernism**, itself often linked to ideas about postcolonial writing. Postmodernism is (not surprisingly) a development of **modernism**, which is a collection of ideas about culture and society that was most influential between 1910 and 1930. The great modernist literary figures include Virginia Woolf, James Joyce, T.S. Eliot, and Franz Kafka. In its rejection of the conventions of the nineteenth century, modernism moved away from realism in art, rejecting distinctions between high and low (or popular) forms of art and among genres, mixing poetry with prose, documentary with fiction, and incorporating parody, irony and pastiche— a "literary patchwork formed by piecing together extracts from various works by one or several authors" (Thrall et al. 342). It emphasized the partial and fragmented nature of human experience and perception and thus led to the creation of fiction with fragmented, discontinuous narrative structures—that is, the action of a story may weave back and forth through time with no clear chronological progression.

Postmodernism inherited many of the leading ideas and techniques of **modernism**—both see human experience, history and perception as essentially fragmented and often meaningless. But, according to most critics, while modernism views this fragmentation and loss of meaning as tragic and strives to create works of art that will restore a sense of wholeness and meaning, postmodernism views the same phenomena as something to be celebrated or played with artistically. Theorist François Lyotard argues that the goal of modernism is stability and order and, to this end, modernists create what he calls "grand narratives" or "master narratives" which explain the development of a society's practices and beliefs. All information is subordinated to the "grand narrative" that interprets (and selects) it. Thus a "grand narrative" of the United States might be about the ultimate triumph of democracy and its power to enable human society to achieve perfection (see Klages 4).

Postmodernism takes some of the techniques of modernism further, giving rise to movements such as "magical realism" or the fantastic, dreamlike worlds of authors like Kincaid and Okri. It also addresses itself to the deconstruction of the "grand narratives" of modernism, believing they simply mask the real instabilities of any social structure and the inherent subjectivity and partialness of any human perception. Since the "grand narratives" are largely the product of politically and economically dominant societies or empires, postmodernism's championing of individual narratives that are local and particular as opposed to claiming to be global or universal, allies it with the narratives of postcolonial writers, themselves often seen as engaged in critiquing the "grand narratives" of their former colonizers. For example, when Chinua Achebe writes about the fatuity of the British myth of the savagery and ignorance of Africans, he is deconstructing a "grand narrative" that justified British control in Nigeria by arguing that it brought civilization to a people who had none. Similarly, Mudrooroo's presentation of the colonizing of Australia by white Europeans from the perspective of the native people acts as a corrective to the European narrative that depicts the Aborigines as one more obstacle to be overcome in a heroic, white adventure.

Recognizing the relative nature of truth, postmodernism privileges the particular—what is manifestly true for one person or group may be entirely false for another. It tends to focus on the minority view, the distinctive perspective of the disenfranchised and hitherto unheard rather than that of the "mainstream" which claims its truths as universal. (This is one reason that postmodernism has been so attractive to feminists.) Viewing reality and human experience as fundamentally strange and unstable, postmodernism gives rise to fictions that are fantastic rather than realistic. In its fondness for mixed forms, for creating hybrids that borrow from a variety of sources, postmodernism also allies itself with postcolonial writing in which not only literary forms but also languages are mixed to produce both structural hybrids and linguistic Creoles.

Not all of the works in this book will fit easily into the categories of postcolonialism and postmodernism, however the concepts can deliver insight into the nature of the fictional worlds found here. James Baldwin's writing, for example, does not conform readily to postmodernist criteria. Neither can Baldwin be seen, strictly speaking, as a postcolonial writer though he certainly voices a minority perspective, since the United States has been for so long itself an empire that it is not considered to be, in any meaningful sense, a postcolonial society. In spite of this, the concept of postcolonialism is useful in understanding his work, since he clearly shares a collection of concerns and issues with many writers who are the products of former colonies. Ultimately, these concepts are themselves lenses that are useful for revealing some aspects of the phenomena we are studying (in this case, a body of literature) while perhaps obscuring or distorting others. As Mukherjee points out, the terminology of much postcolonial discourse with its broad references to "the colonized peoples" and "the oppressed" can obscure "the internal hierarchies and divisions in these societies" (18–19), ethnic and class divisions that predate the colonial period and continue to plague countries long after it.

Yet there is a common thread running through the pieces gathered here: in one way or another, they are all concerned with the intersections of cultures, with life on the borderlines of different cultural realities. In *The Location of Culture*, Homi Bhabha asserts that "what is . . . politically crucial, is the need to . . . focus on those moments or processes that are produced in the articulation of cultural differences." It is the points at which cultures meet, where one culture may define itself against another but be, nonetheless, influenced by it, that provide the opportunity for developing a new sense of identity and for "defining the idea of society itself" (1–2). There can be few places in the world where such opportunities do not exist. Whether we live in a post-colonial country, have migrated from one culture to another, or were born and remain in a country that is the destination of those migrations, our states have altered both individually and collectively. It is no longer possible for most of us to define ourselves in terms of a homogeneous nation with a unitary culture and tradition. Increasingly, in a world linked by technology and travel, we have become the "global village" that Marshall McLuhan predicted.

If there is a danger in all of this, it lies in what cultural critics have called the "Coca-Cola-ization" of culture: the looming possibility that corporate culture will overtake particular regional and ethnic culture and everywhere will look like everywhere else. Even worse, perhaps, is the possibility that we will all end up using the same cultural lenses to look at the world. Literature provides an important defence against this tendency. Each original work of imagination, each carefully thought-out essay, provides us with a valuable individual perspective, a more particular lens through which human experience can be viewed and, when we read authors whose backgrounds and experience are very different from our own, an opportunity to transcend stereotypes of the "other."

The principal reason for the inclusion of the selections found here is their excellence. They are the work of powerful and exciting authors, most of whom have international reputations, and they all have something important to say about the nature of human identity and relationships in an era of massive migration and profound change. In his essay "Imaginary Homelands," Salman Rushdie argues for greater freedom for contemporary writers to utilize the cultural traditions of the whole world (rather than limiting themselves to what is "their" inherited tradition). Pointing to the diverse international influences acknowledged by major novelists, Rushdie asserts "we are inescapably international writers." He concludes his essay with an image from a novel by American author Saul Bellow, in which the central character, hearing a dog barking, "imagines that the barking is the dog's protest against the limit of dog experience. 'For God's sake,' the dog is saying, 'open the universe a little more!' And because Bellow is, of course, not really talking about dogs, or not only about dogs, I have the feeling that the dog's rage, and its desire, is also mine, ours, everyone's. 'For God's sake, open the universe a little more!'" More than anything else, the selections contained in *Fields of Vision* are intended to open the universe a little more.

References

Ashcroft, Bill, Gareth Griffiths and Helen Tiffin. *The Empire Writes Back: Theory and Practice in Post-Colonial Literatures*. London: Routledge, 1989.

———. *Key Concepts in Post-Colonial Studies*. London: Routledge, 1998.

Bhabha, Homi. *The Location of Culture*. London: Routledge, 1994.

Chaplin, J.P. *Dictionary of Psychology*. New York: Dell, 1968.

de Beauvoir, Simone. *The Second Sex*. New York: Alfred A. Knopf, 1952.

Gates, Henry Louis, Jr. *Loose Canons: Notes on the Culture Wars*. New York and Oxford: Oxford UP, 1992.

Klages, Mary. *Postmodernism*. Online at
www.colorado.edu/English/ENGL2012Klages/pom.html

Mukherjee, Arun. *Postcolonialism: My Living*. Toronto: TSAR, 1998.

Said, Edward. *Orientalism*. New York: Pantheon Books, 1978.

———. *Culture and Imperialism*. New York: Knopf /Random House, 1993.

Thrall, William Flint, Addison Hibbard and C. Hugh Holman. *A Handbook to Literature*. New York: Odyssey P, 1960.

Other Sources and Weblinks

Bahri, Deepika. "Introduction to Postcolonial Studies." *Postcolonial Studies* at Emory.
www.emory.edu/ENGLISH/Bahri/Intro.html

———. "Orientalism."
www.emory.edu/ENGLISH/Bahri/Orientialism.html

[p a r t   o n e]

the
roots of
identity

C anadian philosopher and political scientist Charles Taylor has
argued that the concept of identity as we currently understand it
is a relatively recent phenomenon. In traditional hierarchical
societies, an individual's identity was determined by his or her
social position and the roles and responsibilities that were
related to it. This identity was recognized and acknowledged by everyone
since it was based on categories built into the fabric of the society.

The rise of Romanticism at the end of the eighteenth century brought
about fundamental changes in the ways in which people defined
themselves and understood their identities, both as individuals and as parts
of collectives. These changes were the results of two seminal ideas which
Taylor believes led to the modern formulation of the nature of human
identity. The first idea, which found its most popular articulation in the
writings of Jean-Jacques Rousseau, is the notion that instead of looking
without for moral guidance—to a hierarchical society and Church—people
should look within themselves and listen to the voice of nature. Rejecting
society as corrupt and unjust, Rousseau emphasised the inward nature of
identity and the importance of, in Taylor's words, "recovering authentic
moral contact with ourselves" (1994:29).

The second idea Taylor associates with Johann Gottlob Herder, who
argued that each of us is possessed of a unique identity, a way of being
human that is uniquely ours, and that our life task is to discover what that

is and to be true to it. Herder believed this was true not only of individuals but also of ethnic groups, of peoples. A people should be true to its unique collective self, to its culture. Only in this way would it be able to make a significant contribution to the world. Thus Herder opposed colonialism, which deprived the colonized peoples of their freedom to develop and express their own cultures. As Taylor points out, these ideas—that identity is inward, that it is unique for each person and for each people, and that it is related to an individual's ethnic or racial origins—were new ideas and they have exerted a powerful influence on modern thinking.

Writing about what he calls "The Politics of Recognition," Taylor argues that the demand for recognition expressed by "minority or **'subaltern'** groups" is made more sharply because of a belief in a link between recognition and identity. He summarizes: "The thesis is that our identity is partly shaped by recognition or its absence, often by the misrecognition of others, and so a person or group of people can suffer real damage, real distortion, if the people or society around them mirror back to them a confining or demeaning or contemptible picture of themselves" (25). This thesis and the concomitant belief in the necessity of establishing an independent and positive identity are important ideas which figure prominently in contemporary writing by women, native peoples, people of colour and gay writers. They also constitute a major theme in the literature of former colonies, what has been called post-colonial literature—that is, literature which offers a critical evaluation of the impact of colonialism and asserts a different non-colonial or anti-colonial perspective. In *Colonial and Postcolonial Literature*, Elleke Boehmer observes that her book's preoccupation with writers' exploration of the nature of identity, their "need to achieve an independent sense of being in the world," is characteristic of its time period (8). While other themes, concerns and ideas may be of equal or greater importance in literature from the former colonies and that produced by minority writers, ours is a period during which a great deal of attention has been focussed on the issue of identity, perhaps because, as Taylor observes, it is an issue which we believe (influenced by Rousseau and Herder) is central to achieving a meaningful existence for individuals, groups and nations.

The works that follow explore a variety of ideas and issues and many could as easily find a home in one of the other sections as in this one, but each contributes an important and interesting perspective on the issue of identity, sometimes echoing the beliefs expressed by Rousseau and Herder and those found in the contemporary pursuit of recognition. Identity is explored in terms ranging from the broadly cultural and emphatically political (Achebe's argument that the African writer has a responsibility to

---

subaltern, which literally means "of inferior rank" (*Oxford English Dictionary*), is a term employed by postcolonial theorists to refer to groups of people who have been denied access to power within their society. Such groups could include peasants, workers, colonized peoples, and, in many societies, women.

educate his readers by providing a positive sense of African identity), to the individual and personal (the narrator of Hodgins' story is engaged in an essentially private quest for a sense of who he is, where he belongs). More often, though, the personal *is* political, as Gloria Steinem observed, and the establishing of identity is both an inward journey and a negotiation conducted in a social and political context.

Works Cited

Boehmer, Elleke. *Colonial and Postcolonial Literature*. Oxford: Oxford University Press, 1995.

Taylor, Charles. "The Politics of Recognition." *Multiculturalism: Examining the Politics of Recognition*. Ed. Amy Gutman. Princeton: Princeton University Press, 1994. 25–73.

Derek Walcott

N obel Prize–winning author Derek Walcott was born in St. Lucia, a Caribbean island that passed repeatedly from French to British control before becoming, finally, a British colony in 1814. While a majority of the island's residents are Roman Catholic and speak a French-based "patwa," Walcott himself was raised in a Protestant, English-speaking household. His mother was a teacher at a Methodist school who recited extended passages of Shakespeare and encouraged him in his writing career by contributing $200 for the private publication of his first collection of verse when he was eighteen. Walcott was educated at the University College of the West Indies in Jamaica and subsequently worked as a journalist in Trinidad where he founded the Trinidad Theatre Workshop in 1959, serving as its director until 1977. In 1962, his first major collection of poems, *In a Green Night*, was published in Britain, establishing his international reputation. It has been followed by further collections of poetry and plays as well as by a number of literary essays and reviews. His most recent work, *The Bounty* (1997), is an elegy for his mother and the poet John Clare.

Walcott's poetry is stylistically intricate and sophisticated, dense with allusions to English (and other Western) literary works. He has been accused of being "out of touch with the currents of everyday life," "not West Indian enough" (Walder 125); in the words of the fictional narrator of "The Schooner Flight," "I wasn't black enough for their pride" (*Collected Poems* 6). Yet many of his poems incorporate a number of Creole dialects, the French "patwa" of St. Lucia as well as the English Creoles of Jamaica and Trinidad. In his poetry, he has dealt with the painful history of the West Indies and celebrated its popular culture. West Indian poet and scholar Mervyn Morris writes:

The accusers get stuck with allusions to world literature or with stylistic influences. Poems which happen to be about death, love, evil, art, the loss of faith, are not relevant enough for those who find compassion or complex ambiguity decadent luxuries in our emerging society, and call instead for poems which speak stridently of politics, class and race. Poems are fine if they are black enough. Walcott has written many poems about race, but usually they are exploratory enough to displease the propagandists. (178–79)

Walcott's complicated sense of identity is related to his concept of history. The product of mixed ancestry (African, Dutch and British), he has called himself a "hybrid" or "mongrel." In "A Far Cry from Africa," he presents the painful struggle to reconcile his European with his African inheritance in terms of an impossible choice between "Africa and the English tongue I love." Ultimately he has refused the choice, seeing history, his own ancestral history and the larger history of peoples and nations, not as the inescapable burden of a painful and narrowly defining past but as a vehicle for understanding and liberation.

Works Cited

Morris, Mervyn. "Walcott and the Audience for Poetry." *Critical Perspectives on Derek Walcott*. Ed. Robert Hamner. Washington, D.C.: Three Continents Press, 1993. 174–92.

Walcott, Derek. *In a Green Night*. Jonathan Cape: London, 1962.

Walder, Dennis. *Post-Colonial Literatures in English: History, Language, Theory*. Oxford: Blackwell, 1998.

Other Sources and Weblinks

Bradley, Heather. "In the Spirit of Homer: Constructing National Identity by Reconstructing Individual Histories."

authors.about.com/arts/cs/caribbeanauthors/index_2html

almaz.com/nobel/literature/1992a.html

Lefkowitz, Mary. "Bringing Him Back Alive." *The New York Times* 7 Oct. 1990: Sect. 7: 1.

www.nytimes.com

A Far Cry from Africa

A wind is ruffling the tawny pelt
Of Africa, Kikuyu°, quick as flies
Batten upon the bloodstreams of the veldt.
Corpses are scattered through a paradise.
But still the worm, colonel of carrion, cries:
'Waste no compassion on these separate dead'
Statistics justify and scholars seize
The salients of colonial policy.
What is that to the white child hacked in bed?
To savages, expendable as Jews?

Threshed out by beaters, the long rushes break
In a white dust of ibises° whose cries
Have wheeled since civilization's dawn
From the parched river or beast-teeming plain;
The violence of beast on beast is read
As natural law, but upright man
Seeks his divinity with inflicting pain.
Delirious as these worried beasts, his wars
Dance to the tightened carcass of a drum,
While he calls courage still, that native dread
Of the white peace contracted by the dead.

Again brutish necessity wipes its hands
Upon the napkin of a dirty cause, again
A waste of our compassion, as with Spain.°
The gorilla wrestles with the superman.

I who am poisoned with the blood of both,
Where shall I turn, divided to the vein?
I who have cursed
The drunken officer of British rule, how choose
Between this Africa and the English tongue I love?
Betray them both, or give back what they give?
How can I face such slaughter and be cool?
How can I turn from Africa and live?

Kikuyu: the largest tribal group in Kenya; many joined the insurgent organization called the Mau Mau in the 1950s to drive the British colonists from their land. By 1960, most of the leaders had been captured or killed and the state of emergency was lifted.

ibis: graceful wading bird, found in tropical regions of America and Africa

Spain: a reference to the Spanish Civil War in the 1930s in which the Fascist party, led by General Franco, defeated the leftist coalition of the Popular Front. For the politically engaged youth of the period, the loss of democracy in Spain was tragic and many had volunteered to fight on the side of the Popular Front.

Chinua Achebe

i nternationally acclaimed author Chinua Achebe has played an
important role in the development of modern African culture. He was
born in 1930 in Ogidi, an Ibo° village in Nigeria. The son of a teacher
and Christian missionary, Achebe received his primary education at a
school run by the Church Missionary Society. He graduated from high
school just after the opening of University College in Ibadan, which he
entered in 1948 on a science scholarship, intending to study medicine. After
his first year, however, he switched to arts, studying English, history and
comparative religion.

Observing that education in Nigeria during the colonial period° was
entirely European in focus, Achebe has remarked: "You didn't really study
too much of your own things. Your own things were more or less not fit for
education" (Lewis 190). For colonized peoples, this resulted in the loss of a
sense of their own history and traditional culture, the loss of an African
perspective. In the fifties, when Achebe was in university, the growing
independence movement in Nigeria led to the questioning of European
political and cultural authority. He describes his experience of maturing

The **Ibo** (or Igbo) people constitute one of Nigeria's largest ethnic groups. Possessing a
strong sense of cultural and political unity, they were instrumental in gaining Nigerian
independence from Britain in 1960. During the struggle for political power in Nigeria which
followed the country's becoming a republic in 1963, many of the Ibo people who had
migrated to northern Nigeria were killed. Becoming increasingly concerned about their
position, the Ibo seceded from Nigeria and proclaimed the independent Republic of Biafra in
July of 1967. The ensuing conflict between Nigeria and secessionist Biafra, referred to as the
Nigerian Civil War, ended with the capitulation of Biafra in January of 1970.

The **colonial period** in Nigeria lasted from approximately 1906 (by which time Britain had
consolidated its control over the country) to 1960, when Nigeria achieved independence.
During this period, the British had control over most aspects of Nigerian life including
government, the economy and education. An important part of colonization was the
conversion of the inhabitants to Christianity, a process undertaken by missionaries from
Europe who established church schools as well as churches.

intellectually while at Ibadan as a reassessment of what he had read and the recognition that all he had been exposed to were colonial narratives "written by white people about us . . . what I'm talking about is encountering the colonial ideology" (Lewis 183).

> When I had been younger, I read these books about the good white man, you know, wandering into the jungle, and savages were after him. And I would instinctively be on the side of the white man . . . In the university I suddenly saw that these books had to be read in a different light. Reading *Heart of Darkness*, for instance, which was a very, very highly praised book and which is still highly praised, I realized that I was one of those savages jumping up and down on the beach. (Qtd. in Rooke 20)

Achebe's critically acclaimed first novel, *Things Fall Apart* (1958), can be seen as a response to the experience of reading European (mis)representations of Africans and the African experience. The novel describes the arrival of European colonizers and missionaries in the nineteenth century from the perspective of the Ibo people. In doing so, it affirms the existence of a developed and complex culture prior to European contact. In subsequent novels and essays Achebe has continued to contribute to the creation of an anti-colonialist canon, arguing vigorously against not only the racism of colonialism, but also against the internalized racism that afflicts colonized peoples with a sense of inferiority.

> Achebe sees himself as working in the context of the Ibo oral tradition in which stories, myths and folktales fulfill religious, social and educational purposes. He observes that, contrary to the Western belief that "art should be accountable to no one," in fact, "art is, and always was, at the service of man" and "any good story, any good novel, should have a message, should have a purpose." Seeing himself as a link in the tradition of oral storytellers and poets gives him "that sense of connectedness of being part of things that are eternal like the rivers, the mountains, and the sky, and creation myths about man and the world. The beginning was a story; it is the story that creates man, then man makes other stories, you see." (Lewis 182)

Achebe has produced five novels and several volumes of short stories, poetry and essays. In addition, he is the founder of *Okike*, a Nigerian literary journal, and has edited a number of anthologies of African literature. He has worked as a broadcaster and teacher and has been an active participant in the politics of his country, acting as a diplomat for Biafra during the Nigerian Civil War. The recipient of numerous honorary degrees and literary awards, Achebe currently occupies the Charles P. Stevenson, Jr., Chair in Literature at Bard College in New York State.

Works Cited

Achebe, Chinua. *Hopes and Impediments: Selected Essays*. New York: Doubleday, 1980.

Lewis, Gordon. Interview with Gordon Lewis, 1995. *Conversations with Chinua Achebe*. Ed. Bernth Lindfors. Jackson: University Press of Mississippi, 1997. 185–197.

Rooke, Constance, and Leon Rooke, eds. *The Writer's Path*. Scarborough: ITP Nelson, 1998.

Weblinks

Postcolonial Literature in Africa
landow.stg.brown.edu/post/achebe/achebio.html

Postcolonial Studies @ Emory
www.emory.edu/English/Bahri/Contents.html#Authors

The Novelist as Teacher

Writing of the kind I do is relatively new in my part of the world and it is too soon to try and describe in detail the complex of relationships between us and our readers. However, I think I can safely deal with one aspect of these relationships which is rarely mentioned. Because of our largely European education our writers may be pardoned if they begin by thinking that the relationship between European writers and their audience will automatically reproduce itself in Africa. We have learnt from Europe that a writer or an artist lives on the fringe of society—wearing a beard and a peculiar dress and generally behaving in a strange, unpredictable way. He is in revolt against society, which in turn looks on him with suspicion if not hostility. The last thing society would dream of doing is to put him in charge of anything.

All that is well known, which is why some of us seem too eager for our society to treat us with the same hostility or even behave as though it already does. But I am not interested now in what writers expect of society; that is generally contained in their books, or should be. What is not so well documented is what society expects of its writers.

I am assuming, of course, that our writer and his society live in the same place. I realize that a lot has been made of the allegation that African writers have to write for European and American readers because African readers where they exist at all are only interested in reading textbooks. I don't know if African writers always have a foreign audience in mind. What I do know is that they don't have to. At least I know that I don't have to. Last year the pattern of sales of *Things Fall Apart* in the cheap paperback edition was as follows: about 800 copies in Britain; 20,000 in Nigeria; and about 2,500 in all other places. The same pattern was true also of *No Longer at Ease*.

Most of my readers are young. They are either in school or college or have only recently left. And many of them look to me as a kind of teacher. Only the other day I received this letter from Northern Nigeria:

Dear C. Achebe,

I do not usually write to authors, no matter how interesting their work is, but I feel I must tell you how much I enjoyed your editions of *Things Fall Apart* and *No Longer at Ease*. I look forward to reading your new edition *Arrow of God*. Your novels serve as advice to us young. I trust that you will continue to produce as many of this type of books. With friendly greetings and best wishes.

Yours sincerely,

I. BUBA YERO MAFINDI

It is quite clear what this particular reader expects of me. Nor is there much doubt about another reader in Ghana who wrote me a rather pathetic letter to say that I had neglected to include questions and answers at the end of *Things Fall Apart* and could I make these available to him to ensure his success at next year's school certificate examination. This is what I would call in Nigerian pidgin "a how-for-do" reader and I hope there are not very many like him. But also in Ghana I met a young woman teacher who immediately took me to task for not making the hero of my *No Longer at Ease* marry the girl he is in love with. I made the kind of vague noises I usually make whenever a wise critic comes along to tell me I should have written a different book to the one I wrote. But my woman teacher was not going to be shaken off so easily. She was in deadly earnest. Did I know, she said, that there were many women in the kind of situation I had described and that I could have served them well if I had shown that it was possible to find one man with enough guts to go against custom?

I don't agree, of course. But this young woman spoke with so much feeling that I couldn't help being a little uneasy at the accusation (for it was indeed a serious accusation) that I had squandered a rare opportunity for education on a whimsical and frivolous exercise. It is important to say at this point that no self-respecting writer will take dictation from his audience. He must remain free to disagree with his society and go into rebellion against it if need be. But I am for choosing my cause very carefully. Why should I start waging war as a Nigerian newspaper editor was doing the other day on the "soulless efficiency" of Europe's industrial and technological civilization when the very thing my society needs may well be a little technical efficiency?

My thinking on the peculiar needs of different societies was sharpened when not long ago I heard an English pop song which I think was entitled *"I Ain't Gonna Wash for a Week."* At first I wondered why it should occur to anyone to take such a vow when there were so many much more worthwhile resolutions to make. But later it dawned on me that this singer belonged to the same culture which in an earlier age of self-satisfaction had blasphemed and said that cleanliness was next to godliness. So I saw him in a new light—as a kind of divine administrator of vengeance. I make bold to say, however, that his particular offices would not be required in my society because we did not commit the sin of turning hygiene into a god.

Needless to say, we do have our own sins and blasphemies recorded against our name. If I were God I would regard as the very worst our acceptance—for whatever reason—of racial inferiority. It is too late in the day to get worked up about it or to blame others, much as they may deserve such blame and condemnation. What we need to do is to look back and try and find out where we went wrong, where the rain began to beat us.

Let me give one or two examples of the result of the disaster brought upon the African psyche in the period of subjection to alien races. I remember the shock felt by Christians of my father's generation in my village in the early 1940s when for the first time the local girls' school performed Nigerian dances at the anniversary of the coming of the gospel. Hitherto they had always put on something Christian and civilized which I believe was called the Maypole dance. In those days—when I was growing up—I also remember that it was only the poor benighted heathen who had any use for our local handicraft, e.g., our pottery. Christians and the well-to-do (and they were usually the same people) displayed their tins and other metalware. We never carried water pots to the stream. I had a small cylindrical biscuit-tin suitable to my years while the older members of our household carried four-gallon kerosene tins.

Today, things have changed a lot, but it would be foolish to pretend that we have fully recovered from the traumatic effects of our first confrontation with Europe. Three or four weeks ago my wife, who teaches English in a boys' school, asked a pupil why he wrote about winter when he meant the harmattan.° He said the other boys would call him a bushman if he did such a thing! Now, you wouldn't have thought, would you, that there was something shameful in your weather? But apparently we do. How can this great blasphemy be purged? I think it is part of my business as a writer to teach that boy that there is nothing disgraceful about the African weather, that the palm tree is a fit subject for poetry.

Here then is an adequate revolution for me to espouse—to help my society regain belief in itself and put away the complexes of the years of denigration and self-abasement. And it is essentially a question of education, in the best sense of that word. Here, I think, my aims and the deepest aspirations of my society meet. For no thinking African can escape

harmattan: a desiccating, dust-laden wind of Africa and the Middle East

the pain of the wound in our soul. You have all heard of the "African personality"; of African democracy, of the African way to socialism, of negritude, and so on. They are all props we have fashioned at different times to help us get on our feet again. Once we are up we shan't need any of them anymore. But for the moment it is in the nature of things that we may need to counter racism with what Jean-Paul Sartre has called an anti-racist racism, to announce not just that we are as good as the next man but that we are much better.

The writer cannot expect to be excused from the task of re-education and regeneration that must be done. In fact, he should march right in front. For he is, after all—as Ezekiel Mphahlele says in his *African Image*—the sensitive point of his community. The Ghanaian professor of philosophy, William Abraham, puts it this way:

> Just as African scientists undertake to solve some of the scientific problems of Africa, African historians go into the history of Africa, African political scientists concern themselves with the politics of Africa; why should African literary creators be exempted from the services that they themselves recognize as genuine?

I for one would not wish to be excused. I would be quite satisfied if my novels (especially the ones I set in the past) did no more than teach my readers that their past—with all its imperfections—was not one long night of savagery from which the first Europeans acting on God's behalf delivered them. Perhaps what I write is applied art as distinct from pure. But who cares? Art is important, but so is education of the kind I have in mind. And I don't see that the two need be mutually exclusive. In a recent anthology a Hausa° folk tale, having recounted the usual fabulous incidents, ends with these words:

> They all came and they lived happily together. He had several sons and daughters who grew up and helped in raising the standard of education of the country.

As I said elsewhere, if you consider this ending a naïve anticlimax then you cannot know very much about Africa.

Leeds University, 1965

Hausa: an African ethnic group living chiefly in North Nigeria and South Niger; most are Muslim farmers

Michelle Cliff

lthough she was born in Kingston, Jamaica, in 1946, Michelle Cliff has spent much of her life in the United States. She received a B.A. in European History in 1969 from Wagner College and worked in New York for the publisher W.W. Norton before moving to England, where she studied at the Warburg Institute (University of London), and received an M. Phil. in Comparative Historical Studies of the Renaissance in 1974.

A "white Creole" (a Jamaican of mostly white ancestry) and a gay woman, Cliff is centrally concerned with issues of identity and with the ways in which racism, sexism and homophobia shape an individual's sense of herself. In poetry, fiction and non-fiction, she has explored the hybrid nature of her own identity and in doing so, that of Jamaica, which is characterised by a similarly complex, Creole identity and also possesses no single, clear point of origin, no simple linear narrative.

Cliff's first book, the semi-autobiographical *Claiming an Identity They Taught Me to Despise* (1980), presents the story of a Jamaican woman of mixed ancestry who chooses to affirm her Black heritage in defiance of her family's attempts to persuade her to "Forget about your great-grandfather with the darkest skin" and "Blend in." The identity she attempts to construct for herself is one which incorporates all of the disparate strands of her ancestry and family history, the Black slaves as well as the white slave-owners. Critic Carole Boyce Davies has observed:

> The creoleness that is essentially Caribbean identity is the necessity of accepting all facets of experience, history and personhood in the definition of the self . . . Cliff integrates these into a consciousness of her own identities. Personal history, family history and a people's history and culture all converge. (Davies 116,122–23)

The selection included here is a polemical exploration and affirmation of identity in which Cliff exposes the injustice and exploitation of British colonialism and the politics of colour and privilege that are its legacy.

Works Cited

Davies, Carole Boyce. *Black Women, Writing and Identity: Migrations of the Subject.* London: Routledge, 1994.

Kaplan, Caren. "Deterritorializations: The Rewriting of Home and Exile in Western Feminist Discourse." *Cultural Critique.* 6 (Spring 1987): 188–96.

Other Sources and Weblinks

Biddle, Arthur W. et al., eds. "Michelle Cliff." *Global Voices.* Englewood Cliffs, N.J.: Prentice Hall, 1995. 68.

Bloom, Harold, ed. 1997. *Caribbean Women Writers.* Philadelphia: Chelsea House, 1997. 32.

If I Could Write This in Fire, I Would Write This in Fire

1

We were standing under the waterfall at the top of Orange River. Our chests were just beginning to mound—slight hills on either side. In the center of each were our nipples, which were losing their sideways look and rounding into perceptible buttons of dark flesh. Too fast it seemed. We touched each other, then, quickly and almost simultaneously, raised our arms to examine the hairs growing underneath. Another sign. Mine was wispy and light-brown. My friend Zoe had dark hair curled up tight. In each little patch the riverwater caught the sun so we glistened.

The waterfall had come about when my uncles dammed up the river to bring power to the sugar mill. Usually, when I say "sugar mill" to anyone not familiar with the Jamaican countryside or for that matter my family, I can tell their minds cast an image of tall smokestacks, enormous copper cauldrons, a man in a broad-brimmed hat with a whip, and several dozens of slaves—that is, if they have any idea of how large sugar mills once operated. It's a grandiose expression—like plantation, verandah, out-building. (Try substituting farm, porch, outside toilet.) To some people it even sounds romantic.

Our sugar mill was little more than a round-roofed shed, which contained a wheel and woodfire. We paid an old man to run it, tend the fire, and then either bartered or gave the sugar away, after my grandmother had taken what she needed. Our canefield was about two acres of flat land next to the river. My grandmother had six acres in all—one donkey, a mule, two cows, some chickens, a few pigs, and stray dogs and cats who had taken up residence in the yard.

Her house had four rooms, no electricity, no running water. The kitchen was a shed in the back with a small pot-bellied stove. Across from the stove was a mahogany counter, which had a white enamel basin set into it. The only light source was a window, a small space covered partly by a wooden shutter. We washed our faces and hands in enamel bowls with cold water carried in kerosene tins from the river and poured from enamel pitchers. Our chamber pots were enamel also, and in the morning we carefully placed them on the steps at the side of the house where my grandmother collected them and disposed of their contents. The outhouse was about thirty yards from the back door—a "closet" as we called it—infested with lizards capable of changing color. When the door was shut it was totally dark, and the lizards made their presence known by the noise of their scurrying through the torn newspaper, or the soft shudder when they dropped from the walls. I remember most clearly the stench of the toilet, which seemed to hang in the air in that climate.

But because every little piece of reality exists in relation to another little piece, our situation was not that simple. It was to our yard that people came with news first. It was in my grandmother's parlor that the Disciples of Christ held their meetings. Zoe lived with her mother and sister on borrowed ground in a place called Breezy Hill. She and I saw each other almost every day on our school vacations over a period of three years. Each morning early—as I sat on the cement porch with my coffee cut with condensed milk—she appeared: in her straw hat, school tunic faded from blue to gray, white blouse, sneakers hanging around her neck. We had coffee together, and a piece of hard-dough bread with butter and cheese, waited a bit and headed for the river. At first we were shy with each other. We did not start from the same place.

There was land. My grandparents' farm. And there was color.

(My family was called *red*. A term which signified a degree of whiteness. ("We's just a flock of red people," a cousin of mine said once.) In the hierarchy of shades I was considered among the lightest. The countrywomen who visited my grandmother commented on my "tall" hair—meaning long. Wavy, not curly.

I had spent the years from three to ten in New York and spoke—at first—like an American. I wore American clothes: shorts, slacks, bathing suit. Because of my American past I was looked upon as the creator of games. Cowboys and Indians. Cops and Robbers. Peter Pan.

(While the primary colonial identification for Jamaicans was English, American colonialism was a strong force in my childhood—and of course continues today. We were sent American movies and American music. American aluminum companies had already discovered bauxite on the island and were shipping the ore to their mainland. United Fruit bought our bananas. White Americans came to Montego Bay, Ocho Rios, and Kingston for their vacations and their cruise ships docked in Port Antonio and other places. In some ways America was seen as a better place than England by many Jamaicans. The farm laborers sent to work in American agribusiness came home with dollars and gifts and new clothes; there were few who mentioned American racism. Many of the middle class who emigrated to Brooklyn or Staten Island or Manhattan were able to pass into the white American world—saving their blackness for other Jamaicans or for trips home; in some cases, forgetting it altogether. Those middle-class Jamaicans who could not pass for white managed differently—not unlike the Bajans in Paule Marshall's *Brown Girl, Brownstones*—saving, working, investing, buying property. Completely separate in most cases from Black Americans.)

I was someone who had experience with the place that sent us triple features of B-grade westerns and gangster movies. And I had tall hair and light skin. And I was the granddaughter of my grandmother. So I had power. I was the cowboy, Zoe was my sidekick, the boys we knew were Indians. I was the detective, Zoe was my "girl," the boys were the robbers. I was Peter Pan, Zoe was Wendy Darling, the boys were the lost boys. And the terrain around the river—jungled and dark green—was Tombstone, or Chicago, or Never-Never Land.

This place and my friendship with Zoe never touched my life in Kingston. We did not correspond with each other when I left my grandmother's home.

I never visited Zoe's home the entire time I knew her. It was a given: never suggested, never raised.

Zoe went to a state school held in a country church in Red Hills. It had been my mother's school. I went to a private all-girls school where I was taught by white Englishwomen and pale Jamaicans. In her school the students were caned as punishment. In mine the harshest punishment I remember was being sent to sit under the *lignum vitae* to "commune with nature." Some of the girls were out-and-out white (English and American), the rest of us were colored—only a few were dark. Our uniforms were blood-red gabardine, heavy and hot. Classes were held in buildings meant to re-create England: damp with stone floors, facing onto a cloister, or quad as they called it. We began each day with the headmistress leading us in English hymns. The entire school stood for an hour in the zinc-roofed gymnasium.

Occasionally a girl fainted, or threw up. Once, a girl had a grand mal seizure. To any such disturbance the response was always "keep singing." While she flailed on the stone floor, I wondered what the mistresses would do. We sang "Faith of Our Fathers," and watched our classmate as her eyes rolled back in her head. I thought of people swallowing their tongues. This student was dark—here on a scholarship—and the only woman who came forward to help her was the gamesmistress, the only dark teacher. She kneeled beside the girl and slid the white web belt from her tennis shorts, clamping it between the girl's teeth. When the seizure was over, she carried the girl to a tumbling mat in a corner of the gym and covered her so she wouldn't get chilled.

Were the other women unable to touch this girl because of her darkness? I think that now. Her darkness and her scholarship. She lived on Windward Road with her grandmother; her mother was a maid. But darkness is usually enough for women like those to hold back. Then, we usually excused that kind of behavior by saying they were "ladies." (We were constantly being told we should be ladies also. One teacher went so far as to tell us many people thought Jamaicans lived in trees and we had to show these people they were mistaken.) In short, we felt insufficient to judge the behavior of these women. The English ones (who had the corner on power in the school) had come all this way to teach us. Shouldn't we treat them as the missionaries they were certain they were? The creole Jamaicans had a different role: they were passing on to those of us who were light-skinned the creole heritage of collaboration, assimilation, loyalty to our betters. We were expected to be willing subjects in this outpost of civilization.

The girl left school that day and never returned.

After prayers we filed into our classrooms. After classes we had games: tennis, field hockey, rounders (what the English call baseball), netball (what the English call basketball). For games we were divided into "houses"—groups named for Joan of Arc, Edith Cavell, Florence Nightingale, Jane Austen. Four white heroines. Two martyrs. One saint. Two nurses. (None of us knew then that there were Black women with Nightingale at Scutari.) One novelist. Three involved in white men's wars. Two dead in white men's wars. *Pride and Prejudice.*

Those of us in Cavell wore red badges and recited her last words before a firing squad in W.W.I: "Patriotism is not enough. I must have no hatred or bitterness toward anyone."

Sorry to say I grew up to have exactly that.

Looking back: To try and see when the background changed places with the foreground. To try and locate the vanishing point: where the lines of perspective converge and disappear. Lines of color and class. Lines of history and social context. Lines of denial and rejection. When did we (the light-skinned middle-class Jamaicans) take over for *them* as oppressors? I need to see when and how this happened. When what should have been reality was overtaken by what was surely unreality. When the house nigger became master.

"What's the matter with you? You think you're white or something?"

"Child, what you want to know 'bout Garvey for? The man was nothing but a damn fool."

"They not our kind of people."

Why did we wear wide-brimmed hats and try to get into Oxford? Why did we not return?

Great Expectations: a novel about origins and denial, about the futility and tragedy of that denial, about attempting assimilation. We learned this novel from a light-skinned Jamaican woman—she concentrated on what she called the "love affair" between Pip and Estella.

Looking back: Through the last page of *Sula*. "And the loss pressed down on her chest and came up into her throat. 'We was girls together,' she said as though explaining something." It was Zoe, and Zoe alone, I thought of. She snapped into my mind and I remembered no one else. Through the greens and blues of the riverbank. The flame of red hibiscus in front of my grandmother's house. The cracked grave of a former landowner. The fruit of the ackee which poisons those who don't know how to prepare it.

"What is to become of us?'

We borrowed a baby from a woman and used her as our dolly. Dressed and undressed her. Dipped her in the riverwater. Fed her with the milk her mother had left with us: and giggled because we knew where the milk had come from.

A letter: "I am desperate. I need to get away. I beg you one fifty-dollar."

I send the money because this is what she asks for. I visit her on a trip back home. Her front teeth are gone. Her husband beats her and she suffers blackouts. I sit on her chair. She is given birth control pills which aggravate her "condition." We boil up sorrel and ginger. She is being taught by Peace Corps volunteers to embroider linen mats with little lambs on them and gives me one as a keepsake. We cool off the sorrel with a block of ice brought from the shop nearby. The shopkeeper immediately recognizes me as my grandmother's granddaughter and refuses to sell me cigarettes. (I am twenty-seven.) We sit in the doorway of her house, pushing back the colored plastic strands which form a curtain, and talk about Babylon and Dred. About Manley and what he's doing for Jamaica. About how hard it is. We walk along the railway tracks—no longer used— to Crooked River and the post office. Her little daughter walks beside us and we recite a poem for her: "Mornin' buddy/Me no buddy fe wunna/Who den, den I saw?" and on and on.

I can come and go. And I leave. To complete my education in London.

2

Their goddam kings and their goddam queens. Grandmotherly Victoria spreading herself thin across the globe. Elizabeth II on our TV screens. We stop what we are doing. We quiet down. We pay our respects.

1981: In Massachusetts I get up at 5 a.m. to watch the royal wedding. I tell myself maybe the IRA will intervene. It's got to be better than starving themselves to death. Better to be a kamikaze in St. Paul's Cathedral than a hostage in Ulster. And last week Black and white people smashed storefronts all over the United Kingdom. But I really don't believe we'll see royal blood on TV. I watch because they once ruled us. In the back of the cathedral a Maori woman sings an aria from Handel, and I notice that she is surrounded by the colored subjects.

To those of us in the commonwealth the royal family was the perfect symbol of hegemony.° To those of us who were dark in the dark nations, the

hegemony: leadership or predominance over others, especially the dominance of one state or culture over another

prime minister, the parliament barely existed. We believed in royalty—we were convinced in this belief. Maybe it played on some ancestral memories of West Africa—where other kings and queens had been. Altars and castles and magic.

The faces of our new rulers were everywhere in my childhood. Calendars, newsreels, magazines. Their presences were often among us. Attending test matches between the West Indians and South Africans. They were our landlords. Not always absentee. And no matter what Black leader we might elect—were we to choose independence—we would be losing something almost holy in our impudence.

WE ARE HERE BECAUSE YOU WERE THERE

BLACK PEOPLE AGAINST STATE BRUTALITY

BLACK WOMEN WILL NOT BE INTIMIDATED

WELCOME TO BRITAIN . . . WELCOME TO SECOND-CLASS CITIZENSHIP

(slogans of the Black movement in Britain)

Indian women cleaning the toilets in Heathrow airport. This is the first thing I notice. Dark women in saris trudging buckets back and forth as other dark women in saris—some covered by loosefitting winter coats—form a line to have their passports stamped.

The triangle trade: molasses/rum/slaves. Robinson Crusoe was on a slave-trading journey. Robert Browning was a mulatto. Holding pens. Jamaica was a seasoning station. Split tongues. Sliced ears. Whipped bodies. The constant pretense of civility against rape. Still. Iron collars. Tinplate masks. The latter a precaution: to stop the slaves from eating the sugar cane.

A pregnant woman is to be whipped—they dig a hole to accommodate her belly and place her face down on the ground. Many of us became light-skinned very fast. Traced ourselves through bastard lines to reach the duke of Devonshire. The earl of Cornwall. The lord of this and the lord of that. Our mothers' rapes were the things unspoken.

You say: But Britain freed her slaves in 1833. Yes.

Tea plantations in India and Ceylon. Mines in Africa. The Cape-to-Cairo Railroad. Rhodes scholars. Suez Crisis. The white man's bloody burden. Boer War. Bantustans. Sitting in a theatre in London in the seventies. A play called *West of Suez*. A lousy play about British colonials. The finale comes when several well-known white actors are machine-gunned by several lesser-known Black actors. (As Nina Simone says: "This is a show tune but the show hasn't been written for it yet.")

The red empire of geography classes. "The sun never sets on the British empire and you can't trust it in the dark." Or with the dark peoples. "Because of the Industrial Revolution European countries went in search of markets and raw materials." Another geography (or was it a history) lesson.

Their bloody kings and their bloody queens. Their bloody peers. Their bloody generals. Admirals. Explorers. Livingstone. Hillary. Kitchener. All the bwanas°. And all their beaters, porters, sherpas. Who found the source of the Nile. Victoria Falls. The tops of mountains. Their so-called discoveries reek of untruth. How many dark people died so they could misname the physical features in their blasted gazetteer. A statistic we shall never know. Dr. Livingstone, I presume you are here to rape our land and enslave our people.

There are statues of these dead white men all over London.

An interesting fact: The swear word "bloody" is a contraction of "by my lady"—a reference to the Virgin Mary. They do tend to use their ladies. Name ages for them. Places for them. Use them as screens, inspirations, symbols. And many of the ladies comply. While the national martyr Edith Cavell was being executed by the Germans in 1915 in Belgium (called "poor little Belgium" by the allies in the war), the Belgians were engaged in the exploitation of the land and peoples of the Congo.

And will we ever know how many dark peoples were "imported" to fight in white men's wars. Probably not. Just as we will never know how many hearts were cut from African people so that the Christian doctor might be a success—i.e., extend a white man's life. Our Sister Killjoy observes this from her black-eyed squint.

Dr. Schweitzer—humanitarian, authority on Bach, winner of the Nobel Peace Prize—on the people of Africa: "The Negro is a child, and with children nothing can be done without the use of authority. We must, therefore, so arrange the circumstances of our daily life that my authority can find expression. With regard to Negroes, then, I have coined the formula: 'I am your brother, it is true, but your elder brother.'" (*On the Edge of the Primeval Forest,* 1961)

They like to pretend we didn't fight back. We did: with obeah°, poison, revolution. It simply was not enough.

"Colonies . . . these places where 'niggers' are cheap and the earth is rich." (W.E.B. DuBois, "The Souls of White Folk")

A cousin is visiting me from Cal Tech where he is getting a degree in engineering. I am learning about the Italian Renaissance. My cousin is recognizably Black and speaks with an accent. I am not and do not—unless I am back home, where the "twang" comes upon me. We sit for some time in a bar in his hotel and are not served. A light-skinned Jamaican comes over to our table. He is an older man—a professor at the University of London. "Don't bother with it, you hear. They don't serve us in this bar." A run-of-the-mill incident for all recognizable Black people in this city. But for me it is not.

Henry's eyes fill up, but he refuses to believe our informant. "No, man, the girl is just busy." (The girl is a fifty-year-old white woman, who may just

bwana: master, boss; from African language of Swahili

obeah: African Caribbean magico-religion; practised in West Africa and in the West Indies

be following orders. But I do mention this. I have chosen sides.) All I can manage to say is, "Jesus Christ, I hate the fucking English." Henry looks at me. (In the family I am known as the "lady cousin." It has to do with how I look. And the fact that I am twenty-seven and unmarried—for all they know, unattached. They do not know that I am really the lesbian cousin.) Our informant says—gently, but with a distinct tone of disappointment—"My dear, is that what you're studying at the university?"

You see—the whole business is very complicated.

Henry and I leave without drinks and go to meet some of his white colleagues at a restaurant I know near Covent Garden Opera House. The restaurant caters to theatre types and so I hope there won't be a repeat of the bar scene—at least they know how to pretend. Besides, I tell myself, the owners are Italian *and* gay; they *must* be halfway decent. Henry and his colleagues work for an American company which is paying their way through Cal Tech. They mine bauxite from the hills in the middle of the island and send it to the United States. A turnaround occurs at dinner: Henry joins the white men in a sustained mockery of the waiters: their accents and the way they walk. He whispers to me: "Why you want to bring us to a battyman's° den, lady?" I keep quiet.

We put the white men in a taxi and Henry walks me to the underground station. He asks me to sleep with him. (It wouldn't be incest. His mother was a maid in the house of an uncle and Henry has not seen her since his birth. He was taken into the family. She was let go.) I say that I can't. I plead exams. I can't say that I don't want to. Because I remember what happened in the bar. But I can't say that I'm a lesbian either—even though I want to believe his alliance with the white men at dinner was forced: not really him. He doesn't buy my excuse. "Come on, lady, let's do it. What's the matter, you 'fraid?" I pretend I am back home and start patois° to show him somehow I am not afraid, not English, not white. I tell him he's a married man and he tells me he's a ram goat. I take the train to where I am staying and try to forget the whole thing. But I don't. I remember our different skins and our different experiences within them. And I have a hard time realizing that I am angry with Henry. That to him—no use in pretending—a queer is a queer.

1981: I hear on the radio that Bob Marley° is dead and I drive over the Mohawk Trail listening to a program of his music and I cry and cry and cry. Someone says: "It wasn't the ganja° that killed him, it was poverty and working in a steel foundry when he was young."

I flash back to my childhood and a young man who worked for an aunt I lived with once. He taught me to smoke ganja behind the house. And to

battyman: faggot in Jamaican

patois: Jamaican dialect

Bob Marley: Jamaican reggae performer and songwriter who brought reggae to a worldwide audience. A committed Rastafarian and proponent of non-violent opposition to racism, Marley created music that was both popular and profoundly political.

ganja: marijuana

peel an orange with the tip of a machete without cutting through the skin—"Love" it was called: a necklace of orange rind the result. I think about him because I heard he had become a Rastaman. And then I think about Rastas.

We are sitting on the porch of an uncle's house in Kingston—the family and I—and a Rastaman comes to the gate. We have guns but they are locked behind a false closet. We have dogs but they are tied up. We are Jamaicans and know that Rastas mean no harm. We let him in and he sits on the side of the porch and shows us his brooms and brushes. We buy some to take back to New York. "Peace, missis."

There were many Rastas in my childhood. Walking the roadside with their goods. Sitting outside their shacks in the mountains. The outsides painted bright—sometimes with words. Gathering at Palisadoes Airport to greet the Conquering Lion of Judah. They were considered figures of fun by most middle-class Jamaicans. Harmless—like Marcus Garvey.°

Later: white American hippies trying to create the effect of dred° in their straight white hair. The ganja joint held between their straight white teeth. "Man, the grass is good." Hanging out by the Sheraton pool. Light-skinned Jamaicans also dred-locked, also assuming the ganja. Both groups moving to the music but not the words. Harmless. "Peace, brother."

3

My grandmother: "Let us thank God for a fruitful place."

My grandfather: "Let us rescue the perishing world."

This evening on the road in western Massachusetts there are pockets of fog. Then clear spaces. Across from a pond a dog staggers in front of my headlights. I look closer and see that his mouth is foaming. He stumbles to the side of the road—I go to call the police.

I drive back to the house, radio playing "difficult" piano pieces. And I think about how I need to say all this. This is who I am. I am not what you allow me to be. Whatever you decide me to be. In a bookstore in London I show the woman at the counter my book and she stares at me for a minute, then says: "You're a Jamaican." "Yes." "You're not at all like our Jamaicans."

Encountering the void is nothing more nor less than understanding invisibility. Of being fogbound.

Then: It was never a question of passing. It was a question of hiding. Behind Black and white perceptions of who we were—who they thought we were. Tropics. Plantations. Calypso. Cricket. We were the people with the musical voices and the coronation mugs on our parlor tables. I would be whatever figure these foreign imaginations cared for me to be. It would be so simple to

---

Marcus Garvey: 1887–1940, one of the most important Black leaders of the 1920s; born in Jamaica but moved to the United States, where he promoted the idea of a Black homeland in Africa in which Blacks would be free to pursue their own culture without white oppression

dred: a natural lock of hair traditionally worn by Rastafarians

let others fill in for me. So easy to startle them with a flash of anger when their visions got out of hand—but never to sustain the anger for myself.

It could become a life lived within myself. A life cut off. I know who I am but you will never know who I am. I may in fact lose touch with who I am.

I hid from my real sources. But my real sources were also hidden from me.

Now: It is not a question of relinquishing privilege. It is a question of grasping more of myself. I have found that in the real sources are concealed my survival. My speech. My voice. To be colonized is to be rendered insensitive. To have those parts necessary to sustain life numbed. And this is in some cases—in my case— perceived as privilege. The test of a colonized person is to walk through a shantytown in Kingston and not bat an eye. This I cannot do. Because part of me lives there—and as I grasp more of this part I realize what needs to be done with the rest of my life.

Sometimes I used to think we were like the Marranos—the Sephardic Jews forced to pretend they were Christians. The name was given to them by the Christians, and meant "pigs." But once out of Spain and Portugal, they became Jews openly again. Some settled in Jamaica. They knew who the enemy was and acted for their own survival. But they remained Jews always.

We also knew who the enemy was—I remember jokes about the English. Saying they stank. saying they were stingy. that they drank too much and couldn't hold their liquor. that they had bad teeth. were dirty and dishonest. were limey bastards. and horse-faced bitches. We said the men only wanted to sleep with Jamaican women. And that the women made pigs of themselves with Jamaican men.

But of course this was seen by us—the light-skinned middle class—with a double vision. We learned to cherish that part of us that was them—and to deny the part that was not. Believing in some cases that the latter part had ceased to exist.

None of this is as simple as it may sound. We were colorists and we aspired to oppressor status. (Of course, almost any aspiration instilled by Western civilization is to oppressor status: success, for example.) Color was the symbol of our potential: color taking in hair "quality," skin tone, freckles, nose-width, eyes. We did not see that color symbolism was a method of keeping us apart: in the society, in the family, between friends. Those of us who were light-skinned, straight-haired, etc., were given to believe that we could actually attain whiteness—or at least those qualities of the colonizer which made him superior. We were convinced of white supremacy. If we failed, we were not really responsible for our failures: we had all the advantages—but it was that one persistent drop of blood, that single rogue gene that made us unable to conceptualize abstract ideas, made us love darkness rather than despise it, which was to be blamed for our failure. Our dark part had taken over: an inherited imbalance in which the doom of the creole was sealed.

I am trying to write this as clearly as possible, but as I write I realize that what I say may sound fabulous, or even mythic. It is. It is insane.

Under this system of colorism—the system which prevailed in my childhood in Jamaica, and which has carried over to the present—rarely will dark and light people co-mingle. Rarely will they achieve between themselves an intimacy informed with identity. (I should say here that l am using the categories light and dark both literally and symbolically. There are dark Jamaicans who have achieved lightness and the "advantages" which go with it by their successful pursuit of oppressor status.)

Under this system light and dark people meet in those ways in which the light-skinned person imitates the oppressor. But imitation goes only so far: the light-skinned person becomes an oppressor in fact. He/she will have a dark chauffeur, a dark nanny, a dark maid, and a dark gardener. These employees will be paid badly. Because of the slave past, because of their dark skin, the servants of the middle class have been used according to the traditions of the slavocracy. They are not seen as workers for their own sake, but for the sake of the family who has employed them. It was not until Michael Manley° became prime minister that a minimum wage for houseworkers was enacted—and the indignation of the middle class was profound.

During Manley's leadership the middle class began to abandon the island in droves. Toronto. Miami. New York. Leaving their houses and businesses behind and sewing cash into the tops of suitcases. Today—with a new regime—they are returning: "Come back to the way things used to be" the tourist advertisement on American TV says. "Make it Jamaica again. Make it your own."

But let me return to the situation of houseservants as I remember it: They will be paid badly, but they will be "given" room and board. However, the key to the larder will be kept by the mistress in her dresser drawer. They will spend Christmas with the family of their employers and be given a length of English wool for trousers or a few yards of cotton for dresses. They will see their children on their days off: their extended family will care for the children the rest of the time. When the employers visit their relations in the country, the servants may be asked along—oftentimes the servants of the middle class come from the same part of the countryside their employers have come from. But they will be expected to work while they are there. Back in town, there are parts of the house they are allowed to move freely around; other parts they are not allowed to enter. When the

---

Michael Manley: prime minister of Jamaica 1972–80 and again 1989-92. As the leader of the socialist People's National Party, he followed a leftist political agenda establishing close relations with Cuba, nationalizing industry, and denouncing U.S. imperialism. His efforts to ensure greater economic fairness for labourers and the poor did not endear him to the affluent middle class.

family watches the TV the servant is allowed to watch also, but only while standing in a doorway. The servant may have a radio in his/her room, also a dresser and a cot. Perhaps a mirror. There will usually be one ceiling light. And one small square louvered window.

A true story: One middle-class Jamaican woman ordered a Persian rug from Harrod's in London. The day it arrived so did her new maid. She was going downtown to have her hair touched up, and told the maid to vacuum the rug. She told the maid she would find the vacuum cleaner in the same shed as the power mower. And when she returned she found that the fine nap of her new rug had been removed.

The reaction of the mistress was to tell her friends that the "girl" was backward. She did not fire her until she found that the maid had scrubbed the Teflon from her new set of pots, saying she thought they were coated with "nastiness."

The houseworker/mistress relationship in which one Black woman is the oppressor of another Black woman is a cornerstone of the experience of many Jamaican women.

I remember another true story: In a middle-class family's home one Christmas, a relation was visiting from New York. This woman had brought gifts for everybody, including the housemaid. The maid had been released from a mental institute recently, where they had "treated" her for depression. This visiting light-skinned woman had brought the dark woman a bright red rayon blouse and presented it to her in the garden one afternoon, while the family was having tea. The maid thanked her softly, and the other woman moved toward her as if to embrace her. Then she stopped, her face suddenly covered with tears, and ran into the house, saying, "My God, I can't, I can't."

We are women who come from a place almost incredible in its beauty. It is a beauty which can mask a great deal and which has been used in that way. But that the beauty is there is a fact. I remember what I thought the freedom of my childhood, in which the fruitful place was something I took for granted. Just as I took for granted Zoe's appearance every morning on my school vacations—in the sense that I knew she would be there. That she would always be the one to visit me. The perishing world of my grandfather's graces at the table, if I ever seriously thought about it, was somewhere else.

Our souls were affected by the beauty of Jamaica, as much as they were affected by our fears of darkness.

There is no ending to this piece of writing. There is no way to end it. As I read back over it, I see that we/they/I may become confused in the mind of the reader: but these pronouns have always co-existed in my mind. The Rastas talk of the "I and I"—a pronoun in which they combine themselves with Jah. Jah is a contraction of Jahweh and Jehovah, but to me always sounds like the beginning of Jamaica. I and Jamaica is who I am. No matter how far I travel—how deep the ambivalence I feel about ever returning. And Jamaica is a place in which we/they/I connect and disconnect—change place.

Matt Cohen

b orn in Kingston, Ontario in 1942, Matt Cohen spent much of his childhood in Ottawa before attending the University of Toronto, where he studied political theory. He received a B.A. in 1964 and a master's degree in 1965. He worked briefly as a lecturer in the sociology of religion at McMaster University before becoming a full-time writer in 1968. A prolific and versatile writer, Cohen produced poetry and short stories, literary criticism, children's books and both experimental fiction and more traditional novels. He was twice nominated for the Governor General's Award before winning it in 1999 for *Elizabeth and After*. He died a few weeks after accepting the award.

Discussing the relationship between his Jewish heritage and his writing, Cohen remarked, "I didn't decide to be a Jewish writer. It's something that happened." His parents were products of very different Jewish traditions, his mother coming from a family of committed Zionists° who were relatively secular in outlook, while his father's family were Orthodox, strictly observant Jews. In an interview given when he was in his late forties, Cohen described his own Jewish education as "minimum" and "half-hearted" but observed that at about the age of thirty:

> I realized that questions about my identity as a Jew were totally unresolved
> and that I simply wasn't going to be able to discard them. But neither
> could I become a strictly religious Jew. So I was left with this half-loaf, as
> it were. Yet these questions have turned out to be far more important than
> I thought at the time.

Zionists: Jews who support the reconstitution of a Jewish national state in Palestine

Jewishness for me has become a lot more interesting. In a sense it is partly an obsession which I'm trying to work through in my writing; I pursue it because I have no choice. It's also partly a lens—a changing lens—through which I see the world, and finally it is something that I keep exploring and learning about. (Butovsky 177)

Most of Cohen's early fiction is set in the countryside north of Kingston and four of his major works (the "Salem" novels) deal with the people who live in what George Woodcock has called their "obsolescent decadence" in a small farming community where they struggle with the poverty that has become endemic to small-scale agriculture. In 1983 Cohen published a collection of short stories called *Café Le Dog,* which Woodcock describes as "transitional," observing that it demonstrates "the manifest veering of Cohen's interests and his growing acceptance of the need . . . to give voice to his Jewish inheritance" (Woodcock 48). Cohen's shift in focus to Jewish themes in succeeding novels evoked widespread critical bewilderment, a sense, he remarked, "that I had betrayed my Canadianness by writing about being Jewish." Yet it also brought him a larger readership and a greater international reputation.

In a 1999 interview with Eleanor Wachtel, critic Lyn Van Leuven observed that in his mature work, Cohen has been interested in exploring two very powerful themes: death and guilt (2). Both themes are present in "Racial Memories," which also explores the difficulty inherent in the process of establishing (and accepting) identity.

Works Cited

Butovsky, Mervin. 1990. "An Interview by Mervin Butovsky." Hutcheon, Linda, and Marion Richmond, eds. *Other Solitudes*. Toronto: Oxford University Press, 1990. 172–178.

Wachtel, Eleanor. "The Worlds of Matt Cohen: An Interview with Lyn Van Leuven." *The Arts Today*. CBC Radio. 17 August 1999. **infoculture.cbc.ca/archives/bookswr/-04121999-mattcohen.html**

Woodcock, George. *Matt Cohen and His Works*. Toronto: ECW Press, 1985.

Other Sources

Mills, John. "Two Novels by Matt Cohen." *The Canadian Novel. Vol. 4: Present Tense*. Ed. John Moss. Toronto: NC Press, 1985. 135–144.

Racial Memories

The beard of my grandfather was trimmed in the shape of a spade. Black at first, later laced liberally with white, it was also a flag announcing to the world that here walked an orthodox Jew. Further uses: an instrument of torture and delight when pressed against the soft ticklish skin of young children, a never empty display window for the entire range of my grandmother's uncompromising cuisine. To complement his beard my grandfather—indoors and out—kept his head covered. His indoor hats were *yarmulkahs*° that floated on his bare and powerful skull; the hats he wore outside had brims which kept the sun away and left the skin of his face a soft and strangely attractive waxy white. White, too, were his square-fingered hands, the moons of his nails, his squarish slightly-gapped teeth, the carefully washed and ironed shirts my grandmother supplied for his thrice-daily trips to the synagogue. A typical sartorial moment: on the day before his seventieth birthday I found him outside on a kitchen stepladder wearing slippers but no socks, his suit-pants held up by suspenders, his white shirt complete with what we used to call bicep-pinchers, his outdoors hat—decked out in style, in other words, even though he was sweating rivers while he trimmed the branches of his backyard cherry trees.

Soon after I met him, I began remembering my grandfather. Especially when I lay in bed, the darkness of my room broken by the thin yellow strip of light that filtered through the bottom of my door. Staring at the unwavering strip I would try to make it dance. 'Be lightning,' I would say. 'Strike me dead; prove that God exists.' And then I would cower under my sheets, waiting for the inevitable. That was when I would remember my grandfather. Standing alone with him in the big synagogue in Winnipeg, the same synagogue where he must have sought God's guidance in dealing with Joseph Lucky, looking up at the vaulted ceilings, holding his hand as he led me up the carpeted aisle to the curtained ark where the Torah was kept.

And then he showed me the words themselves. God's words. Indecipherable squiggles inked onto dried skin not so different from the tough dry calluses on my grandfather's palms.

Also full of words was the high bulging forehead of my grandfather. Everything he said to me in English, which he spoke in a gently accented cadence I had difficulty understanding, he would repeat in Hebrew, which I couldn't understand at all. Cave-man talk, I would think, listening to the guttural sounds. He showed me, too, the separate section where the women sat. I was amazed at this concept of the women being put to one side, just as

yarmulkah: a small skullcap worn by Orthodox and Conservative Jewish males for prayer and ceremonial occasions. Some strongly religious Jews wear one at all times, following the traditional Jewish practice of keeping the head covered.

later I was to be amazed to discover that when women had 'the curse' they spent their nights in their own dark beds, left alone to bleed out their shame.

My great-great Uncle Joseph, the one after whom I was named, served in the cavalry of the Russian czar. This is true, and I still have a photograph of a bearded man in full uniform sitting on a horse in the midst of a snowy woods. After two years, during which he was promoted once and demoted twice, my ancestor deserted and made his way across Europe to a boat which took him to Montreal. From there he caught a train on which, the story goes, he endeared himself to a wealthy Jewish woman who owned a large ranch in Alberta. We could pause briefly to imagine the scene: minor-key *War and Peace* played out against a background of railway red velvet, cigar smoke, and a trunk filled with souvenirs. Unfortunately the lady was married, so my uncle ended up not in the castle but out on the range, riding wild mustangs. (Also, it has been claimed, singing Yiddish folk songs to the animals as they bedded down beneath their starry blankets.)

And then my Uncle Joseph struck it rich. Sitting around the campfire one night, he reinvented the still with the help of an old horse trough and a few length of hose. All this is according to my father; he was the historian-in-exile, but that is another story. The rest of the family claims he was only trying to make barley soup. Maybe that explains how my uncle became known as Joseph Lucky.

Having made his fortune and his name, Joseph Lucky began sending money to the relatives. We've all heard about those Russian Jews: semi-Cro-Magnon types covered in beards, furs, dense body hair, living without flush toilets or electricity in a post-feudal swamp of bone-breaking peasants, child-snatching witches and wicked landowners. Having helped his blood relations through the evolutionary gate of the twentieth century—to say nothing of destroying the racial purity of his adopted homeland—my uncle asked only one thing in return: that the newcomers settle in Winnipeg, well away from his field of operations. When they got established, he came to pay a visit. By this time the wealthy Jewess had died and, because of a jealous husband, my uncle Joseph had moved on from his life on the range to 'business interests.' Another photograph I possess: Joseph Lucky standing on the Winnipeg train platform, winter again, wearing matching fur coat and hat and framed by two enormous suitcases which my father tells me were made from 'soft brown leather you could eat.'

This was before the First World War, before my father was born. Also before the War was my uncle's demise. What had happened was that for causes unknown he was put in jail. After a few months he wrote to his nephew, my grandfather. The letter was written in Yiddish, using Hebrew characters—the same formula which my grandmother employed to torture my mother decades later. I've seen the letter; my grandfather showed it to me when I was a child. He opened the envelope and out blew the smell which made a permanent cloud in my grandparents' house, a permanent storm-cloud to be exact, always threatening to rain down the pale greenish soup that my grandmother claimed was all her frail stomach could support.

My grandfather was a strong man. Once, when a neighbour's shed was burning down, he carried out two smoke-damaged pigs. The image of my grandfather, wearing his inevitable satin waistcoat and box *yarmulkah*, walking down the street with a sow over each shoulder, has never seemed improbable to me. I can imagine him, too, poring over the letter from his benefactor. Caught between his duty to help a relative, his distaste for my uncle's way of life and his own poverty. According to my father, my grandfather never answered the letter. Instead, after waiting two weeks he gathered what cash he could and took a train for Edmonton. When he arrived he discovered Joseph Lucky had died of blood poisoning and that his body had been claimed by someone whose name had not been recorded. My grandfather always feared that his delay had killed Joseph Lucky. That is why my father felt obliged to give me his name. Also because, he always insisted, Joseph Lucky had likely died not of food poisoning at all, but had been bribed away from the jail (body claimed by an 'unrecorded stranger'!—who could believe that?) by a rich client and spent the rest of his days happily riding some faraway range.

'If you could credit a Jewish cowboy . . . ,' my mother would protest and shake her head. But that was where Joseph Lucky was lucky, I didn't have to be told. Somehow he had escaped being Jewish, wiggled out from under his fate and galloped off into that carefree other world where you were not under a life sentence or, to be more exact, perhaps you were under a life sentence of mortality (even an assimilated Jew finds it hard to believe in Heaven) but you had been promoted to a different part of the sentence: instead of being the object, you were the subject.

'Did you hear the one about the rabbi's wife?'

'No,' I say. We are lying in the centre of the school football field, six of us in a circle, face to face with our bodies extended like the spokes of a wagon-wheel. It is late September, a cool heart-breaking twilight. At the word 'rabbi' my stomach has suddenly tensed up and my hipbones start to press against the hard ground

'This sausage salesman comes to the door . . . Are you sure you haven't heard it?' The five of us are the offensive backfield of our high-school football team: the wheel of which I am the only Jewish spoke.

'I'm sure,' I say. I look up over at the boy who is talking. The fullback. A power runner known as Willy 'Wild Bill' Higgins. He's the one we need when it's late afternoon. November, and gusts of cold rain are sweeping down the river valley and turning us into sodden little boys who want to go home. That's when Wild Bill—it's me who gave him the name—drives forward with his cleats spitting out gobs of mud, knees pumping up into the face of anyone crazy enough to tackle him.

'All right,' he says. 'forget it. Don't get your cock in a knot.'

All evening, over my homework, I'm left wondering. Something to do with circumcision no doubt. Animal sex? Two weeks ago a girl I asked to a dance told me her father wouldn't let her go out with a Jew. I'm at my sixth school in ten years but I still can't get used to breaking the ice. Can't get used to the fact that it never breaks.

At eleven o'clock the phone rings. It's another spoke of the wheel—a small spoke, like me. 'Don't let dickface get you down,' he says. The first thing I think is how glad I am that this is happening over the telephone, so my friend can't see my eyes swelling up with unwanted tears.

Idiot, I say to myself. *Thin-skinned Jew*. 'Doesn't matter,' I say aloud. 'Except that maybe I missed a good joke.'

Peter Riley laughs. He's a skinny Irish kid whose father has lung cancer. Sometimes, after school, I go home with him and we sit in the living room with his father, feeding him tea and watching him die. 'She says she only eats kosher,' Peter Riley says.

I start a fake laugh, then stop.

'Not funny?'

'Not funny to me.'

'Join the club,' Peter Riley says.

'What club?'

'You name it.'

'The Wild Bill Fan Club,' I say, a little chunk of the past—another school, another group of boys—jumping unbidden out of my mouth.

Leonard lived above the garage attached to the house my grandfather bought after he moved to Toronto to be nearer the brothers, sisters, aunts, uncles, cousins, etc. The spider's web of relatives in Toronto didn't include my own parents: they had already learned their lesson and were hiding out in Ottawa, on their way to greener fields. As a gesture of family solidarity, however, they had sent me to the University of Toronto. There I was not only to carry my parents' proud banner in the world of higher learning, but to act as unofficial delegate and/or sacrifice. Leonard, not a relative but a paying boarder, was also at the university; ten years older than I, he had the exalted status of a graduate student in religious philosophy. 'He doesn't eat kosher,' my grandmother confided to me in the kitchen, 'you can tell by his smell, but he goes to *shul* every morning and he doesn't make noise.'

In a room with my grandparents, Leonard was so well-behaved and courteous that he hardly seemed to exist. Once out of sight, however, he became the main subject of my grandmother's conversation. 'Did you see how he wiped his mouth?' she always began, as though she had spent the whole time doing nothing but watching Leonard compulsively snatch at the napkin. And then Laura, a cousin slightly older than I who had sealed her reputation by going to a drive-in at age fourteen with a married man (self-made, rich from vending-machine concessions), would point out that once again the insides of Leonard's nostrils were flaming red because—she had seen him at it through his window—every night he spent an hour yanking out his nasal hairs in order to combat his other urges.

'Wanna see my place?' Leonard invited, while we were drinking tea after a sabbath lunch.

I followed him out the back door, along a path worn through the grass, and we arrived at the metal stairway leading up the outside of the garage to Leonard's room. Immediately I found myself thinking this arrangement was ideal because it allowed Leonard to come and go as he pleased, even bringing company with him if he wanted. Or could. An unlikely possibility I thought, following the shiny seat of Leonard's grey-and-black checked trousers up the final steps.

The first thing I noticed was the mirror where Leonard was reported to carry on with his nose. It hung above a dresser from which the drawers jutted out, each one overflowing. The cartoon chaos of the room continued. Piled over every available surface were dirty clothes, newspapers and magazines, empty pop bottles, wrappings from candy-store food. Even the desk of the graduate philosopher was a tower of babble—unsteady stacks of library books interspersed with sheaves of folded paper. Ostentatiously draped over the back of the chair was a strangely mottled towel. Stepping closer I saw that the towel was, in fact, heavily stained with blood.

'War wounds,' Leonard said.

At lunch I had already noticed Leonard's soft white fingers, his unmuscled arms blotched with freckles and covered with a sparse layer of white-orange fur.

'They're crazy for it then. Ever notice?'

I shook my head.

'Read Freud. The power of taboo. Close your eyes. Imagine it. You're in the dark with the woman of your dreams. The smell of sweat and blood. Smells so strong you can taste it. Get up from the bed and your dick is dripping with it.'

My eyes weren't closed. I was looking at Leonard. His eyes were boring straight into my face. 'You some kind of a pervert?'

Leonard looked puzzled. Encouraged. I continued with a further inspiration: 'If you didn't pick your nose, it wouldn't bleed.'

Leonard shook his head. 'You're going to study philosophy, kid, you need to have an open mind. I told you the truth.'

'Don't make me laugh. No woman in her right mind would come into this rat's nest for more than five minutes.'

At which point Laura opened the door, came and stood by Leonard's chair, practically sticking her chest in his face while he patted her bum. 'Isn't this great? Look, we're going to drive you into town and then we'll pick you up later for dinner. Isn't this place unbelievable?'

Laura and Leonard are halfway up the greys, exactly at centre ice. From where I line up on defence I can see the steam billowing from their styrofoam cups of coffee. They grin at me. 'Go get 'em,' Leonard shouts and his voice echoes in the empty arena. This is intra-mural hockey, a house-league game taking place close to midnight. The only other spectators are a few couples who have discovered that the shadowed corners of the varsity rink are good for more than watching hockey.

My legs are tired. There are lines of pain where the blades of the skates, which don't quite fit me, press into the bones of my feet. One of my shoulders has already begun to ache as the result of a collision against the boards. Peter Riley looks back at me. He is our centre. A quick skater with dozens of moves and a hard wrist-shot, he is the only one who really knows how to play. The rest of us make up a supporting cast, trying to feed him the puck and to protect our goalie, a non-skating conscript whose main virtue is that he has the courage to buckle on his armour, slide across the ice in his galoshes and risk his life.

Most games we just give the puck to Peter and he scores with tricky unstoppable shots. Now we're in the finals and they've got the strategy to beat us. Two, sometimes, three, players shadow Peter, sandwiching him every time he tries to dart forward The rest of us are often left in the open but compared to these other bigger, stronger players, we are ineffectual midgets. Somehow, however, our goalie has risen to the occasion. With a couple of minutes to go in the game we are only one goal behind.

The referee looks back at us. I bend over my stick. My rear end is sore from numerous forced landings. Riley winks at me and then nods his head for good measure. I know what this signal—our only signal—is supposed to mean: when the puck is dropped he will gain control—then I am to skate by at full speed so that he can feed it to me and send me in.

As the puck bounces on the ice I'm already driving forward, and by the time I've crossed centre ice the puck—via Riley—has arrived at my stick. I'm alone, the crowd of two is screaming. I'm going as fast as I can but I can hear the ice being chewed up behind me, long powerful strides gaining on my short choppy ones. The hollow ominous sound of steel carving ice, Laura's amazingly loud voice—I lift my stick back preparing to blast the puck before I'm overtaken—and then something has hooked my ankles and I'm sliding belly-down.

No whistle so I'm up again. Peter has somehow recovered the puck from the corner and is waiting for me to get in front of the net. This time I'm going to shoot on contact, no waiting: again my stick goes back. Then I'm swinging it forward, towards the puck, already feeling the sweet perfect impact of the hard rubber on the centre of my blade, already seeing the net billow with the tying goal. Suddenly the curtain comes down. A blast to my forehead so intense that I lose consciousness falling to the ice. Get up dazed, glove held to my head. Start skating again, vision foggy, towards the puck, until I see that everyone else has stopped, and my glove and hockey stick are covered with red, that the clouding of my vision isn't dizziness but a veil of blood over my eye. Leonard and Laura are rushing towards me.

There are words, too. 'Jew, Eat it Jew,' I thought I heard someone say. The words are rattling in my head like pebbles in a gourd but I'm too confused to know who put them there. Laura's got a handkerchief out of her purse, it's soaked in perfume, soft white cloth with a pink stitched border. The pebbles are still rattling in my skull and I can't stand them, have to do something about them, twist away from Laura and skate towards the big boy with blood on his hockey stick.

But Peter Riley is already there. When the boy hears me coming, turns towards me, Riley twists—twists and straightens his legs as he sends an uppercut deep into the unpadded belly. Mine enemy collapses to the ice retching. His team prepares to rush ours. By now I have felt my cut with my bare finger: a small gash above the left eyebrow that opens and closes every time I move the muscles in my face.

Before anything can happen there is a sharp blast of the whistle. The referee, who is also the Dean of Men and who hands out suspensions for fighting—from the university, not just from hockey—is holding the puck and standing bent over the spot where he wants play to begin again.

'Sir,' Riley says, 'one of our players is bleeding.'

'Have his friends take him to the hospital.'

As I'm clumping along the wooden gangway, Laura's scented hanky pressed to my wound, Leonard is calling my dean a 'Jew-baiting bastard, an anti-Semitic son-of-a-bitch who would have spent his afternoons cracking open teeth to get at their gold fillings'.

By three o'clock in the morning, when I am sharing a mickey of rye with Peter Riley, my wound has been reduced to a small throbbing slice covered by a neat white patch. And Riley is telling me that the dean shook his hand as he left the dressing room.

As I fall asleep, the words are still with me. I am lying in the dark. The first time I heard such words, such words said by other than my own, I was ten years old. I was in a new school that year, but friends had come quickly and life seemed suddenly to have grown wide and easy. Then one day late in the fall, my friends turned on me. There were three of them. 'Jew,' one of them said. 'Jew,' said the other two. We had been standing in a vacant lot on the way home from school. Talking about nothing. One of them pushed me. A nothing push, not really a punch, something I wasn't sure whether or not to ignore.

'Jews are Christ-killers,' one of them said.

'Christ-killers,' the others repeated. The words unfamiliar to all of us.

Now I can see they didn't know what to do. Something their parents had said would have put them up to this, probably without intending anything specific.

There were more shoves. I shoved back. 'Christ-killer,' they were saying, still trying to convince themselves. 'Run,' one of them said.

'No.'

'Run,' said the biggest one. He slapped me across the face, knocking my glasses to the grass. When I bent to pick them up, he covered them with his foot. I reached anyway. As I pulled them out from his shoe he stamped on my hand.

'Run.'

I held my glasses tightly. The other two boys, the ones I had thought were my friends, had backed away. Without my glasses their faces were foggy and distorted. I put my glasses on. My friends had pebbles in their hands.

'Run.'

I ran, hating myself from the first step. As I did a shower of rocks fell gently on my back. One boy, the biggest, chased me. I was smaller but faster. I vaulted over the fence—clearing it the way I'd had to in order to become a member of the club they had invented—the Wild Bill Fan Club— then ran to the back door as the one boy still chased after me. As I opened the door, he reached in. To grab? To punch? A reflex action? I slammed the door on his hand.

For a week I walked back and forth from school alone. Stomach broiling. At night I couldn't wait to be in bed, alone, lights out. Then finally the world of fear I'd been containing all day in my belly could expand, spread out, swallow the make-believe theatre of pretend-niceness that surrounded me during the day. In the dark, instead of daring God to show himself as I used to, I listened for the sound of convoy tracks on the road, knocks at the door, policemen's boots on the stairs. And if they weren't going to come? I eventually had to ask myself. Did that mean that in this new world there was safety after all? That my great-great Uncle Joseph Lucky truly had led us out of the wilderness and into the promised land?

One afternoon recess, during the compulsory all-school no-rules soccer game, mine enemy was delivered. Head down, dribbling the ball forward at full speed, running straight at me while being chased by fifty screaming boys. An hour later we were standing on either side of the door of the principal's office. Him with scratched cheeks from the gravel he fell into when I tripped him, plus a swollen lip from the only punch I had managed to land; me with a bloody nose and ribs rearranged from the fight-ending bearhug.

I still remember the principal's suit. A blue-grey plaid too long for his short legs, worn cuffs, lapels sporting a maple leaf pin. In his hands, very small, was a thick strap. Without comment he reddened our palms. Then we were out in the hall again, the door closed behind us. No handshakes, no words of mutual consolation, no smiles. But by the time the school day had finished, the underground telegraph had turned us into folk heroes, victims, and survivors of the principal's best, warmly united members of the Wild Bill Fan Club once more.

I am in Laura's bedroom. Laura is in her dressing gown, then takes it off to try on her dress. Laura encased in sterile white brassiere and panties surrounded by tanned skin. The body is untouched, an uninhabited countryside, a national park waiting for its first visitor; but her face is the city. A long curved jaw stubbornly set. Lips painted what Peter Riley called 'North Toronto Red.' Brown eyes, Jewish eyes, eyes which I knew my friend found sympathetic and embracing, but which to me looked hardened with all the calculations they had made.

I am in Laura's bedroom because I have been delegated the task no one wants. Why me? Instead of, for example, my father? The explanation for this lies in other stories, stories too long and intertwined to tell, stories not about Joseph Lucky and Laura and Leonard, but stories about my parents. Most of all my father who had decided by now to complete his escape and was residing (with my mother, of course—herself a subject not to be broached without lengthy explanations) in Sydney, Australia where he was attempting to unknot the city's bus schedules.

'This is crazy, I'm supposed to talk you out of marrying my best friend.'

'So talk me out.'

'He's a shit. His father's dead and his mother drinks too much. So does he. His brother is a lawyer and makes deals with politicians. His sister goes to church on Sundays. Five years from now he'll be screwing his secretary. How's that?'

'You can do better.'

'He's a Catholic. Secretly he hates Jews but he hasn't got the guts to say it. He's marrying you in order to destroy you. When you have children he'll drag them down the basement to a priest he has hidden in the furnace and baptize them.'

'At least we'll have a house.'

'Tell me,' I suddenly say. As if I'm thinking about it for the first time, and maybe I am. 'Why *are* you marrying outside? Really why?'

Laura looks at me. For a second it seems that my question has truly surprised her, cracked the shell. Then I realize that she's only waiting for me to back down. 'I love him,' she says. Her voice is so wooden as she pronounces this formula that I can't help believing her.

'But answer my question.'

'Crazy boy.'

She crosses the room to where I am sitting on her bed. Bends over me and kisses the scar above my eyebrow. Then my lips. A slow kiss that leaves me bathed in her taste and scent. 'I couldn't marry a Jew. It would be like incest, if you know what I mean. Did I ever show you this? Grandpa gave it to me.'

Dear Nephew,

You will remember me. I am your wicked uncle, Joseph Lucky. A few years ago I came to visit you and the rest of those whom you call your family. As always, I brought gifts. As always, they were greedily snatched and then scorned. His money is dirty, they would like to say, since they have none. You alone wrote to thank me. I kept your letter, nephew, because I, a childless old man, wanted to dream about what might be possible. I imagined such things, nephew, as bringing you to live with me and making you a partner in my various enterprises. That is the letter I should have written you because you might have been the one to change my fate. Too late now. Now I am in jail, starving because despite everything you might have heard about me I refuse to eat anything but kosher food. To tell the truth, even the smell of pork chops is enough to turn this old stomach. Nephew, I beg you to come and see that I am released, or at least fed. When you arrive I will give you the name of a lawyer who can arrange things.

Love from your fond Uncle—

'What about the other letter? The one my father has?'

'There were lots of letters. Each one written as through the others had somehow failed to arrive. Not all of them were sent to Grandpa either.'

'And when he went to Edmonton?'

'He never went. No one did. They let him die because they were ashamed of him.' Laura puts on her dressing gown and lights a cigarette. 'You think Peter's cousins are on their knees right now? Begging Peter not to marry me?'

'They should be.'

An hour later I am at Leonard's. Stiffening the spine so that I can report the failure of my mission to my grandparents. 'You are the outsider,' Leonard is explaining to me, 'the perennial third man. You think it's because of your shiny metal mind. Forget it. You're outside because you're a Jew. And that's why Laura is marrying your friend. She grew up being outside and now she wants to be sure she'll be outside forever. Except that she won't because ten years from now the whole world will be people like you and Laura, people trying to get away from themselves. And you know what will happen then? Laura will decide she's unhappy. She'll start to drink or have an affair or run away to a kibbutz° in Israel. The next time you see her, middle-aged, she'll say that she wasted ten years of her life. She'll ask you why you let her get married.'

'Why did I?'

'Because you want to do the same thing.'

Leonard was dressed in his *shul*-going suit. Black without stripes or flecks. Shiny seat bottom. Pockets padded with *yarmulkahs* and hankies just in case someone needed an extra. Soon we would be going to the bride's house, which was where the wedding would take place—under the supervision of a Unitarian minister who didn't seem to believe anything overly offensive.

'And you? I thought you were the one who was so hot for her.'

After my grandfather's first heart attack Leonard had evolved from paying boarder to man of the house. Now he even had a job—as a history teacher at the Orthodox Synagogue Hebrew Day School. Leonard the responsible citizen was heavier, jowled and his hair was turning a dull grey at the temples. And then he smiled. With the memory of whatever had transpired between him and Laura, I thought at first, though what could have linked this prematurely middle-aged perpetual bachelor to the ripe and bursting Laura was hard to imagine. 'Never,' Leonard said. 'I promised myself years ago to a young woman of strong character who takes care of her mother in Vancouver.'

'And when did you meet her?'

'The summer I went to study in New York. She was on the Holocaust° committee.'

kibbutz: a communal settlement or farm in Israel

Holocaust: the attempted elimination of European Jews by the Nazis under Adolf Hitler during the Second World War. More than six million Jews were murdered.

'How romantic.'

Leonard gave me a look I hadn't seen since the day he explained his bloody shirt. 'You're a fool. Helen is the perfect woman for me in every way.' He turned to his desk. In his student days it had been heaped with scholarly texts. But since the summer in New York, the philosophical treatises had been pushed aside first to make room for bulky volumes on the Holocaust and then, more recently, for the history primers he needed for his job. From a drawer stuffed with letters he pulled a picture of a squarish-looking woman with a young smile and a surprising splash of freckles across her nose. 'When her mother dies—'

My grandparents are waiting for me in their parlour. Like Leonard, like my grandfather, like Laura's own father waiting resignedly at home, I am dressed in a suit. An almost new suit, in fact, the one I bought a few months ago when I graduated from law school. Eventually I will wear the same suit, the same white shirt, the same gold cuff-links to my grandfather's funeral. The cuff-links were his gift to me on my Bar Mitzvah°. On that occasion, a few weeks after my thirteenth birthday, I had needed new thick-heeled shoes to push me over the five-foot mark. One sideburn had started to grow, but not the other, and this unequal hormonal outburst had been accompanied by the very unmasculine swelling of one of my nipples. For some reason this swollen nipple ached when I sang, especially when my voice cracked in public, which it did dozens of times during the painful delivery of my *moftar°*. Afterwards my grandfather, his breath thick with rye, had delivered me a bristly kiss and pinched my arm so lovingly that I carried the bruise for a month.

Now they are sitting stiffly and waiting, elderly patients bracing themselves for the bad news. Stubborn but helpless. I beg them to at least come to the reception, for Laura's sake. This is the compromise everyone has been hoping for—avoiding the wedding but joining the celebration.

My grandfather is looking placidly about the room. His most recent attack seems to have taken away his electricity. He is perpetually serene, almost vacant. Even his shining and muscular skull seems to have lost its power; now the skin is greyer, listless. I try to imagine what might be going on inside. Weather?

My grandmother is twisting her hands. Everything considered, she has big diamonds. 'We'll go,' she announces. 'The mother of those bastard children was born a Jew and so the children can still be rescued, God willing, after the father has left.'

'Assimilated,' Leonard says. He pronounces the word slowly, savouring, then repeats it. First he stares at me—a Leonard who has emerged in the

---

Bar Mitzvah: the onset of a young man's religious and legal maturity, at age thirteen, usually marked by a ceremony. The female equivalent is called Bat Mitzvah, and is attained at either age twelve or thirteen.

moftar: the last portion of the day's Torah reading, traditionally read by the person being honoured on a day such as the Bar Mitzvah.

ten years since his own marriage, a Daddy Leonard with a rounded bulldog face, muscular cheeks, blue eyes that have spent so many long nights poring over his Holocaust documents that they have turned the skin surrounding them into dark crater-holes—then he swings his head to Laura for confirmation. She nods. Laura whom I've known forever. Laura who is prettier than ever, but whose face seems more angular because she decided to replace her contact lenses with glasses when she started taking Hebrew lessons again.

I am sitting by the window. It's still open, a souvenir from the golden warmth of the October afternoon. Now it's evening and a cold breeze sucks at the back of my neck, but no one is thinking about the heartbreak of Indian summer.

Laura is kneeling on the floor. Her floor, the floor of the living room of her and Peter Riley's North Toronto house. While she kneels she staples posters to sticks. NAZI JEW KILLER the posters all read.

'I can't believe how *assimilated* you are,' Leonard says, pleased with himself now that he has found the word for me. 'How *typical*. I won't say you're a coward. When it comes to being punched in the face, you're ready. When they call for volunteers to get baked, you'll probably run to the train. *Bravo*. But ask you to stick your neck out and stand up for yourself—all of a sudden you turn into a lawyer for some Jew-baiting creep.'

'Listen to yourself,' I say. 'You're filled with hate. Do you think Jews are the only people in the world who have ever been killed? Even during the Second World War there were three million Poles who died. Gypsies were sent to concentration camps too. Do you think the Holocaust gave the Jews some sort of moral credit card? Do we get to trade our dead for Palestinians? Is it one for one or do Chosen People get a special rate of exchange?'

'I have never killed anyone. But I am proud of my people when they defend themselves.'

'Violence poisons,' I say.

'God is violent,' Leonard comes back.

Bang-clack, bang-clack, goes Laura's stapler. Now she's finished her signs, a dozen of them. In a few minutes it will be time to carry them out to the family-size station-wagon. While the 'family'—twin four-year-old daughters—sleeps, Peter is to babysit. And while Peter babysits, Laura and Leonard are to drive the signs out to the airport, where Leonard has been tipped off that an East German cabinet minister someone claims was once a concentration-camp guard is to arrive for intergovernmental trade discussions.

Laura and Leonard stand up.

'I'll go with you,' I say.

Leonard's face breaks open. 'I knew you would.' He moves forward, hugs me. All those years living above my grandparents and now he smells like they used to—the same food, the same soap, the same sickly sweet lemon furniture polish. I can't help smiling, thinking about Leonard's youth as I knew it: tortured nasal passages, a white towel soaked with what he claimed was menstrual blood.

We stand around for a moment while Leonard phones home. At the other end, apparently saying little, is his woman of perfect character, the devoted Helen who has borne him four children and seems to make a virtue of obeying Leonard. They live in the main house now—my grandparents left it to them—and the room above the garage is consecrated to books and pamphlets detailing the attempted destruction of the Jews. Lately they've added slides, films, one of those roll-up white screens with little sprinkles on the surface. You know what I mean.

We all drag the posters out the front door to the waiting station-wagon. A few leaves crackle and drift in the cool breeze. Lights are on in all the houses around us. It's the moment when children have gone to bed, tables have been cleared, televisions have been turned on or attaché cases opened. We're on the lawn waiting for Peter to open the back hatch when a neighbour walking his dog stops to talk.

The subject of conversation is, of course, the weather, the growing possibility of snow, the desire to spend one last weekend at the cottage. Only while the neighbour is agonizing over his big decision—whether or not to dig trenches so that he can keep the cottage water turned on until Christmas—does he notice the NAZI JEW KILLER signs. He says he is going to dig the trenches after all, if the weather is good, you have to think of the future, and besides he has always wanted his children to share his own dream, a white Christmas in the country.

At the airport a small band of the faithful were waiting on the fifth floor of the parking garage. We got out of the car, distributed the signs. According to Leonard's information, the former concentration guard was due on an Air Canada flight from London. The plan was to meet him at the Passenger Arrivals gate.

There were ten of us. Too many, with our NAZI JEW KILLER signs, to fit into a single elevator. Laura went with the first group—Leonard too—so I was left with four strangers to descend in the second shift. One of those strangers became you, but only later. Sharing our elevator were two passengers with suitcases. At first they paid no attention—then, reading our signs, they shrank back.

By the time we had left the elevator and were walking towards the Arrivals gate, Leonard's group was surrounded by airport security officials and police. We raised our own signs and began to approach them. But before we could be noticed Leonard had gotten into a shouting match with one of the officials. 'Never lose your temper needlessly,' Leonard had lectured us in the Riley living room. But, as Laura told me later, Leonard had already called his friends at the television station and promised a confrontation. When photographers with television cameras on their shoulders and assistants carrying portable lights began to run towards the struggling group, Leonard turned towards them. Soon, the official forgotten, he had positioned himself in front of one of the cameras to make a speech about a country that denied its own citizens free expression while protecting foreign 'criminals against humanity.' Then there was one of those incidents that is not supposed to happen, a relic from other countries, other eras: just as Leonard was working himself to a climax, a policeman smashed his truncheon into the back of his head, sending him falling face forward onto the floor.

Later that night I could watch myself on the television news as I entered the circle of light, knelt above Leonard and turned him over so I could see on his face, running with blood, a half-smile of triumph. You weren't in the picture. 'Communist,' shouted a voice from off-camera, but no one laughed.

Driving to the liquor store Peter Riley and I are already drunk. Actually, we have been drinking all afternoon. It's the kind of day that deserves drinking, a Toronto December special that is cold but snowless, a gritty colourless day that merges pavement and sky. Peter's shirt is open. The tuft of red hair at the base of his neck has gone to flat silver; silver too is the colour of the red mop that used to peek out the holes and edge of his football helmet. To heighten the effect he's wearing a leather jacket left over from our university days; U of T 66 is blazoned across the back in white. Looking at him, at myself slumped uncomfortably beneath the seat belt, I am reminded of the men Peter Riley and I used to go and watch during the summer in Ottawa, fat and powerful men with big paunches and thick arms who played evening softball at the high school diamond. Strong but graceless, able to swat the ball a mile, but stumbling around the bases in slow motion, the evening athletes had always seemed an awesome joke to us. 'Battles of the dinosaurs,' we called their games, delighting in their strength, the kaleidoscope of grunts and sweat and beer-fed curses.

At the liquor-store parking lot we climb out of the car and stand, side by side, looking up at the clouds. We aren't two baseball players, I am thinking, among other things; we are two middle-aged lawyers, partners in a small firm. We are tense, over-tired, mind-fatigued businessmen taking a day off to drink ourselves into oblivion because it's the only cure we know for the fact that while eating lunch we reminded each other that Leonard had died exactly six weeks before. Not that either of us had ever considered ourselves admirers of Leonard. Still.

'Among other things' includes the sound of the dirt falling onto Leonard's coffin, his family's uncontrolled grief, the talk at the funeral about another martyr to anti-Semitism. You were present, silent, beautiful, though your face was pinched with cold. We started walking towards each other at the same time and before we had even told each other our names, I was asking you for your telephone number. Also at the funeral were the wide circle I see once every few years at such events. Aunts, uncles, cousins at various removes who have come not because they think of Leonard as a martyr or support his politics but because they remember Leonard as the faithful boarder who helped my grandparents through their old age, the daily *shul*-goer who, even when my grandfather was eighty years old, patiently shepherded him back and forth to the synagogue.

Some of the aunts, the uncles, the cousins at various removes are themselves getting old now. Short stocky men and women in their seventies, eighties, even the old shrunken survivor who was born in the last century. Many of them, not all, were born in Russia and came out of the mythic peasant crucible to Canada where they gradually adorned themselves in suits, jewellery, houses, coats, stock-market investments until finally, at this group funeral portrait, they could be seen literally staggering under the weight of their success.

I find myself looking at Peter Riley's open shirt again. 'For Christ's sake, do up the buttons, you'll get arrested.'

'Undo yours,' Peter Riley says. 'In the name of the Wild Bill Fan Club, I finally dare you to undo your buttons.'

'For Christ's sake,' I say again, this time wondering why on this occasion it is Christ I invoke—Leonard must have been right. An occasion, to be precise, on which Peter Riley and I have already emptied one bottle of scotch, to say nothing of a few beer chasers, and now find ourselves at 4:33 P.M. in front of the Yonge Street liquor store in search of a refill. Near the liquor store is a shop where we can buy newspapers, mix, cigarettes, ice, candies. Even twenty years ago, when we were under-age, we went there to buy Coke for our rum.

'I'll go to the liquor store,' I say, 'you get the other.'

The scotch hits me while I am alone in the heated display room. 'The last of the big drinkers I am not' is the sentence that comes into my mind—spoken by my father. But my father is dead, possibly along with whatever part of me is his son. 'Never shit on your own doorstep,' my father also told me. Translation: you can go to bed with non-Jewish girls, but don't bring them home. I move down the counter and settle on a bottle of *The Famous Grouse* scotch whisky. When I present my order the cashier makes a point of staring at my unbuttoned shirt. He has straight oiled hair into which each plastic tine of the comb has dug its permanent trench. My age or older. Skin boiled red by repeated infusions of the product he is selling. Looks a bit like Wild Bill near the end, I finally decide, but not enough for me to tell him about the fan club. I look into his eyes. Tough guy. He doesn't flinch. Meanwhile the store is empty, we could go on staring like this forever. 'I'm having an identity crisis,' I imagine saying to him, 'I mean I was born Jewish but I don't feel comfortable carrying Nazi Jew Killer signs.'

That night I dream about the hearse, a sleek powerful limousine. You aren't in the dream but the rest of us are. We're sitting behind the driver: Laura in the centre, Peter Riley and I surrounding. Behind us is the coffin and its presence somehow makes us even smaller than we are, reminding us that Death is the queen bee and we humans are just worker bees keeping Death supplied. It is nighttime, the time of night when time does not exist.

The hearse is carrying us down University Avenue. Wide, empty, stately, the street conducts us to the American Embassy where there is one other car, an ambulance with its rotating light winking 'He's nuts' into the sky. The attendants, bored, are leaning against the ambulance and talking to the lone policeman.

Crouched on all fours, his weight on his knees and hands, Leonard is howling like a dog at the closed door of the American Embassy.

When he sees us he interrupts to wink, then turns back to his howling. After listening for a while I realize that his howl is in fact controlled, a merely moderate howl you can howl until dawn or at least until newspaper reporters arrive. I turn to relay this news to Laura and Peter Riley, but as I turn I see they have been transformed into the ambulance attendants, while I have somehow ended up on my knees, baying at the door. When Leonard tries to arrest me I leap at his throat, bringing him to the ground and tearing at him until I wake myself up with my screams.

At the funeral the men took turns throwing shovelfuls of earth on the coffin. Into the silence small stones and earth rattled against the dull wood. I couldn't help listening. I couldn't help watching, I couldn't help crying at the thought of Leonard dead. At some point I discovered you were still standing beside me. Anonymous in your black coat, bare fingers gripping each other in the frozen air, thin black shoes with the toes pressed together. When the service was over we walked towards the parking lot, climbed into my car, drove to a hotel.

Now this hotel is my train. You are my benefactress, wealthy in the dark cream skin that you inhabit, the mysterious odours of your mysterious places, your eyes that becalm everything they see. Under your protection we ride our wild animals into the twilight. Until beneath our starry blankets we find a way to sleep—out on the range, in this room which hovers in an otherwise unmarked universe, which exists for no other purpose than the mutual exploration of mutual desire. *Assimilated,* as Leonard used to say; against our non-existent will we have been assimilated into this compromised situation—two unrecorded strangers claiming each other with words sight touch smell until we raise spark enough to join our foreign bodies.

Jack Hodgins

ack Hodgins was born in 1938 on Vancouver Island. He studied English literature at the University of British Colombia, graduating in 1960 with a Bachelor of Education. While at UBC, he took a course in creative writing from poet Earle Birney, which confirmed him in his resolve to become a published writer. While working as an English teacher at a high school in Nanaimo, Hodgins continued to write but it was not until 1968 that he began to be published. His short stories appeared in a number of small literary magazines but it was the publication of his first novel, *The Invention of the World*, in 1977, that brought him significant critical attention and commercial success. In 1979 he published *The Resurrection of Joseph Bourne*, which won the Governor General's Literary Award for English Language Fiction and provided him with sufficient recognition and encouragement to enable him to become a full-time writer. His most recent novel, *Broken Ground* (1998), has been widely acclaimed; it presents the experiences of a group of soldiers dealing with their painful memories of the First World War.

"The Lepers' Squint" anticipates many of the concerns and themes of Hodgins' later work, particularly *The Invention of the World*, in which he explores the limitations of Old World history and myth and the need to break out of their controlling patterns. In a passage articulating what critic Frank Davey calls "the novel's most resonant idea" (Davey 31), one of the characters muses "Myth . . . like all the past, real or imaginary, must be acknowledged" but not necessarily believed in, for "[w]hen you begin to disbelieve in [myth] you can begin to believe in yourself" (Hodgins 314). For Hodgins, then, the quest for identity would seem to begin with the deconstruction of the patterns of the past.

Works Cited

Davey, Frank. "Disbelieving Story: A Reading of The Invention of the World." *The Canadian Novel. Vol. 4: Present Tense.* Ed. John Moss. Toronto: NC Press, 1985. 29–44.

Hodgins, Jack. *The Invention of the World.* Toronto: Macmillan, 1977.

Weblink

"Jack Hodgins." *Northwest Passage Author Profiles.*
www.nwpassages.com/bios/hodgins.asp

The Lepers' Squint

Today, while Mary Brennan may be waiting for him on that tiny island high in the mountain lake called Gougane Barra, Philip Desmond is holed up in the back room of this house at Bantry Bay, trying to write his novel. A perfect stack of white paper, three black nylon-tipped pens, and a battered portable typewriter are set out before him on the wooden table. He knows the first paragraph already, has already set it down, and trusts that the rest of the story will run off the end of it like a fishing line pulled by a salmon. But it is cold, it is so cold in this house, even now in August, that he presses both hands down between his thighs to warm them up. It is so cold in this room that he finds it almost impossible to sit still, so damp that he has put on the same clothes he would wear if he were walking out along the edge of that lagoon, in the spitting rain and the wind. Through the small water-specked panes of the window he can see his children playing on the lumpy slabs of rock at the shore, beyond the bobbing branches of the fuchsia hedge. Three children; three red quilted jackets; three faces flushed up by the steady force of the cold wind; they drag tangled clots of stinking seaweed up the slope and, crouching, watch a family of swans explore the edges of a small weedy island not far out in the lagoon.

A high clear voice in his head all the while insists on singing to him of some girl so fair that the ferns uncurl to look at her. The voice of an old man in a mountain pub, singing without accompaniment, stretched and stiff as a rooster singing to the ceiling and to the crowd at the bar and to the neighbours who sit around him. *The ferns uncurled to look at her, so very fair was she, was her hair as bright as the seaweed that floats in from the sea.* But here at Ballylickey the seaweed is brown as mud and smells so strong your eyes water.

Mrs. O'Sullivan is in the next room, Desmond knows, in her own room, listening. If he coughs she will hear. If he sings. She will know exactly the moment he sets down his next word on that top sheet of paper. Mrs. O'Sullivan is the owner of this house, which Desmond rented from home through the Borde Failte people before he discovered that she would live in it with them, in the centre of the house, in her two rooms, and silently listen to the life of his family going on around her. She is a tall dry-skinned old woman with grey finger-waves caged in blue hair-net, whose thick fingers dig into the sides of her face in an agony of desire to sympathize with everything that is said to her. "Oh I know I know I know," she groans. Last night when Desmond's wife mentioned how tired she was after the long drive down from Dublin, her fingers plucked at her face, her dull eyes rolled up to search for help along the ceiling: "Oh I know I know I know." There is no end to her sympathy, there is nothing she doesn't already know. But she will be quiet as a mouse, she promised, they won't know she is here.

"Maybe she's a writer," Desmond's wife whispered to him, later in bed. "Maybe she's making notes on us. Maybe she's writing a book called *North Americans I Have Eavesdropped On.*"

I can't live with someone listening to me breathe," Desmond said. "And I can't write with someone sitting waiting."

"Adjust," his wife said, and flicked at his nose. She who could adjust to anything, or absorb it.

On this first day of his novel Desmond has been abandoned by his wife, Carrie, who early this morning drove the car in to Cork. There are still, apparently, a few Seamus Murphy statues she hasn't seen, or touched. "Keep half an eye on the kids," she said before she left. Then she came back and kissed him and whispered, "Though if you get busy it won't matter. I'm sure Mrs. O'Sullivan won't miss anything." To be fair, to be really fair, he knows that his annoyance is unjustified. He didn't tell her he intended to work today, the first day in this house. She probably thinks that after travelling for six weeks through the country he'll rest a few more days before beginning; she may even believe that he is glad to be rid of her for the day, after all those weeks of unavoidable closeness. She certainly knows that with Mrs. O'Sullivan in the house no emergency will be overlooked, no crisis ignored.

Desmond, now that his hands have warmed a little, lifts one of the pens to write, though silently as possible, as if what he is about to do is a secret perversion from which the ears of Mrs. O'Sullivan must be protected. But he cannot, now, put down any new words. Because if the novel, which has been roaring around in his head all summer and much longer, looking for a chance to get out, should not recognize in the opening words the crack through which it is to spring forth, transformed into a string of words like a whirring fishline, then he will be left with all that paper to stare at, and an unmoving pen, and he is not ready to face that. Of course he knows the story, has seen it all in his mind a hundred times as if someone else had gone to the trouble of writing it and producing it as a movie just for him. But he has never been one for plunging into things, oceans or stories, and prefers to work his way in gently. That opening paragraph, though, is only a paragraph after all and has no magic, only a few black lifeless lines at the top of the paper. So he writes his title again, and under it his name, Barclay Philip Desmond. Then he writes the opening paragraph a second time, and again under that, and again, hoping that the pen will go on by itself to write the next words and surprise him. But it does not happen, not now. Instead, he discovers he is seeing two other words which are not there at all, as if perhaps they are embedded, somehow, just beneath the surface of the paper.

Mary Brennan.

Desmond knows he must keep the name from becoming anything more than that, from becoming a face too, or the pale scent of fear. He writes his paragraph again, over and over until he has filled up three or four pages. Then, crumpling the papers in his hand, he wonders if this will be one of those stories that remain forever in their authors' heads, driving them mad, refusing to suffer conversion into words.

It's the cold, he thinks. Blame it on the bloody weather. His children outside on the rocky slope have pulled the hoods of their jackets up over their heads. Leaves torn from the beech tree lie soaked and heavy on the grass. At the far side of the lagoon the family of swans is following the choppy retreating tide out through the gap to the open bay; perhaps they know of a calmer inlet somewhere. The white stone house with red window frames in its nest of bushes across the water has blurred behind the rain, and looks more than ever like the romantic pictures he has seen on postcards. A thin line of smoke rises from the yellowish house with the gate sign *Carrigdhoun*.

But it is easier than writing, far easier, to allow the persistent day-dreams in, and memory. That old rooster-stiff man, standing in the cleared-away centre of the bar in Ballyvourney to pump his song out to the ceiling, his hands clasping and unclasping at his sides as if they are responsible for squeezing those words into life. The ferns uncurled to see her, he sings, so very fair was she. Neighbours clap rhythm, or stamp their feet. Men six-deep at the bar-counter continue to shout at each other about sheep, and the weather. With hair as bright as the seaweed that floats in from the sea.

"'Tis an island of singers sure!" someone yells in Desmond's ear "An island of saints and paupers and bloody singers!"

But Desmond thinks of Mary Brennan's hot apple-smelling breath against his face: "Islands do not exist until you have loved on them." The words are a Caribbean poet's, she explains, and not her own. But the sentiment is adaptable. The ferns may not uncurl to see the dark brown beauty of her eyes, but Desmond has seen men turn at her flash of hair, the reddish-brown of gleaming kelp. Turn, and smile to themselves. This day while he sits behind the wooden table, hunched over his pile of paper, he knows that she is waiting for him on a tiny hermitage island in a mountain lake not far away, beneath the branches of the crowded trees. Islands, she had told him, do not exist until you've loved on them.

Yesterday, driving south from Dublin across the Tipperary farmland, they stopped again at the Rock of Cashel so that Carrie could prowl a second time through that big roofless cathedral high up on the sudden limestone knoll and run her hands over the strange broken form of St. Patrick's Cross. The kings of Munster lived there once, she told him, and later turned it over to the church. St. Patrick° himself came to baptize the king there, and accidentally pierced the poor man's foot with the point of his heavy staff.

"There's all of history here, huddled together," she said, and catalogued it for him. "A tenth-century round tower, a twelfth-century chapel, a thirteenth-century cathedral, a fourteenth-century tower, a fifteenth-century castle, and . . ." she rolled her eyes, "a twentieth-century tourist shop."

But it was the cross itself that drew her. Originally a cross within a frame, it was only the central figure of a man now, with one arm of the cross and a thin upright stem that held that arm in place. Rather like a tall narrow pitcher. There was a guide this second time, and a tour, and she pouted when he insisted they stick to the crowd and hear the official truths instead of making guesses or relying on the brief explanations on the backs of postcards. She threw him a black scowl when the guide explained the superstition about the cross: that if you can touch hand to hand around it you'll never have another toothache as long as you live. Ridiculous, she muttered; she'd spent an hour the last time looking at that thing, marvelling at the beautiful piece of sculpture nature or time or perhaps vandals had accidentally made of it, running her hands over the figures on the coronation stone at its base and up the narrow stem that supported the remaining arm of the cross.

He was more curious, though, about the round swell of land which could be seen out across the flat Tipperary farms, a perfect green hill crowned with a circle of leafy trees. The guide told him that after one of the crusades a number of people returned to Ireland with a skin disease which was mistaken for leprosy and were confined to that hill, inside that circle, and forbidden to leave it. They were brought across to Mass here on Sundays, she said, before leading him back inside the cathedral to show a small gap in the stones far up one grey wall of the empty Choir. "The poor lepers, a miserable lot altogether as you can imagine, were crowded into a little room behind that wall," she said, "and were forced to see and hear through that single narrow slit of a window. It's called the Lepers' Squint, for obvious reasons."

Afterwards, when the crowd of nuns and priests and yellow-slickered tourists had broken up to walk amongst the graves and the Celtic crosses or to climb the stone steps to the round tower, Desmond would like to have spoken to one of the priests, perhaps the short red-faced one, to say, "What do you make of all this?" or "Is it true what she told us about that fat arch-bishop with all his wives and children?" But he was intimidated by the black suit, that collar, and by the way the priest seemed always to be

---

St. Patrick (385–461): saint and missionary credited with the Christianizing of Ireland

surrounded by nuns who giggled like schoolgirls at the silly jokes he told, full of words Desmond couldn't understand. He would go home without ever speaking to a single member of the one aristocracy this country still permitted itself.

But while he stood tempted in the sharp wind that howled across the high hump of rock the guide came over the grass to him. "'Tis certain that you're not American as I thought first," she said, "for you speak too soft for that. Would you be from England then?"

"No," he said. And without thinking: "We're from Vancouver Island."

"Yes?" she said, her eyes blank. "And where would that be now."

"A long way from here," he said. "An island, too, like this one, with its own brand of ruins."

"There's a tiny island off our coast," he said, "where they used to send the lepers once, but the last of them died a few years ago. It's a bare and empty place they say now, except for the wind. There are even people who believe that ghosts inhabit it."

But then there were people, too, who said he was crazy to take the children to this country. It's smaller than you think, they said. You'll hear the bombs from above the border when you get there. What if war breaks out? What if the IRA decides that foreign hostages might help their cause? What about that bomb in the Dublin department store?

Choose another country, they said. A warmer safer one. Choose an island where you can lie in the sun and be waited on by smiling blacks. Why pick Ireland?

Jealousy, he'd told them. Everyone else he knew seemed to have inherited an "old country," an accent, a religion, a set of customs, from parents. His family fled the potato famine° in 1849 and had had five generations in which to fade out into Canadians. "I don't know what I've inherited from them," he said, "but whatever it is has gone too deep to be visible."

They'd spent the summer travelling; he would spend the fall and winter writing.

His search for family roots, however, had ended down a narrow hedged-in lane: a half tumbled stone cabin, stony fields, a view of misty hills, and distant neighbours who turned their damp hay with a two-tined fork and knew nothing at all of the cabin's past.

"Fled the famine did they?" the old woman said. "'Twas many a man did that and was never heard from since."

The summer was intended as a literary pilgrimage too, and much of it was a disappointment. Yeats's castle tower near Coole had been turned into a tourist trap as artificial as a wax museum, with cassette recorders to listen to as you walk through from room to room, and a souvenir shop to sell you books and postcards; Oliver Goldsmith's village was not only deserted, it had

---

potato famine: The Irish potato famine of the late 1840s (when crop after crop of potatoes, the mainstay of the Irish diet, rotted in the fields because of disease), was responsible for mass starvation. Between a million and a half and two million destitute people fled Ireland. Many came to North America.

disappeared, the site of the little schoolhouse nothing more than a potato patch and the parsonage just half a vine-covered wall; the James Joyce museum only made him feel guilty that he'd never been able to finish *Ulysses,* though there'd been a little excitement that day when a group of women's libbers crashed the male nude-bathing beach just behind the tower.

A man in Dublin told him there weren't any live writers in this country. "You'll find more of our novelists and poets in America than you'll find here," he said. "You're wasting your time on that."

With a sense almost of relief, as though delivered from a responsibility (dead writers, though disappointing, do not confront you with flesh, as living writers could, or with demands), he took the news along with a handful of hot dogs to Carrie and the kids, who had got out of the car to admire a statue. Watching her eat that onion and pork sausage "hot dog" he realized that she had become invisible to him, or nearly invisible. He hadn't even noticed until now that she'd changed her hair, that she was pinning it back; probably because of the wind. In the weeks of travel, in constant too-close confinement, she had all but disappeared, had faded out of his notice the way his own limbs must have done, oh, thirty years ago.

If someone had asked, "What does your wife look like?" he would have forgotten to mention short. He might have said dainty but that was no longer entirely true; sitting like that she appeared to have rounded out, like a copper Oriental idol: dark and squat and yet fine, perhaps elegant. He could not have forgotten her loud, almost masculine laugh of course, but he had long ago ceased to notice the quality of her speaking voice. Carrie, his Carrie, was busy having her own separate holiday, almost untouched by his, though they wore each other like old comfortable unnoticed and unchanged clothes.

"A movie would be nice," he said. "If we could find a babysitter."

But she shook her head. "We can see movies at home. And besides, by the evenings I'm tired out from all we've done, I'd never be able to keep my eyes open."

After Cashel, on their way to the Bantry house, they stopped a while in the city of Cork. And here, he discovered, here after all the disappointments, was a dead literary hero the tourist board hadn't yet got ahold of. He forgot again that she even existed as he tracked down the settings of the stories he loved: butcher shops and smelly quays and dark crowded pubs and parks.

The first house, the little house where the famous writer was born, had been torn down by a sports club which had put a high steel fence around the property, but a neighbour took him across the road and through a building to the back balcony to show him the Good Shepherd Convent where the writer's mother had grown up, and where she returned often with the little boy to visit the nuns. "If he were still alive," Desmond said, "if he still lived here, I suppose I would be scared to come, I'd be afraid to speak to him." The little man, the neighbour, took off his glasses to shine them on a white handkerchief. "Ah, he was a shy man himself. He was back here a few years before he died, with a big crew of American fillum people, and he was a friendly man, friendly enough. But you could see he was a shy man too, yes. 'Tis the shy ones sometimes that take to the book writing."

Carrie wasn't interested in finding the second house. She had never read the man's books, she had never read anything at all except art histories and museum catalogues. She said she would go to the park, where there were statues, if he'd let her off there. She said if the kids didn't get out of the car soon to run off some of their energy they would drive her crazy, or kill each other. You could hardly expect children to be interested in old dead writers they'd never heard of, she said. It was no fun for them.

He knew as well as she did that if they were not soon released from the backseat prison they would do each other damage. "I'll go alone," he said.

"But don't be long. We've got a good ways to do yet if we're going to make it to that house today."

So he went in search of the second house, the house the writer had lived in for most of his childhood and youth and had mentioned in dozens of his stories. He found it high up the sloping streets on the north side of the river. Two rows of identical homes, cement-grey, faced each other across a bare sloping square of dirt, each row like a set of steps down the slope, each home just a gate in a cement waist-high wall, a door, a window. Somewhere in this square was where the barefoot grandmother had lived, and where the lady lived whose daughter refused to sleep lying down because people died that way, and where the toothless woman lived who between her sessions in the insane asylum loved animals and people with a saintly passion.

The house he was after was half-way up the left-hand slope and barely distinguishable from the others, except that there was a woman in the tiny front yard, opening the gate to come out.

"There's no one home," she said when she saw his intentions. "They weren't expecting me this time, and presumably, they weren't expecting you either."

"Then it is the right house?" Desmond said. Stupidly, he thought. Right house for what? But she seemed to understand. "Oh yes. It's the right house. Some day the city will get around to putting a plaque on the wall but for the time being I prefer it the way it is. My name, by the way," she added, "is Mary Brennan. I don't live here but I stop by often enough. The old man, you see, was one of my teachers years ago."

She might have been an official guide, she said it all so smoothly. Almost whispering. And there was barely a trace of the musical tipped-up accent of the southern counties in her voice. Perhaps Dublin, or educated. Her name meant nothing to him at first, coming like that without warning. "There would be little point in your going inside anyway, even if they were home," she said. "There's a lovely young couple living there now but they've redone the whole thing over into a perfectly charming but very modern apartment. There's nothing at all to remind you of him. I stop by for reasons I don't begin to understand, respect perhaps, or   inspiration, but certainly not to find anything of him here."

In a careless, uneven way, she was pretty. Even beautiful. She wore clothes—a yellow skirt, a sweater—as if they'd been pulled on as she'd hurried out the door. Her coat was draped over her arm, for the momentary blessing of sun. But she was tall enough to get away with the sloppiness and had brown eyes which were calm, calming. And hands that tended to behave as if they were helping deliver her words to him, stirring up the pale scent of her perfume. He would guess she was thirty, she was a little younger than he was.

"Desmond," he said. "Uh, Philip Desmond."

She squinted at him, as if she had her doubts. Then she nodded, consenting. "You're an American," she said. "And probably a writer. But I must warn you. I've been to your part of the world and you just can't do for it what he did for this. It isn't the same. You don't have the history, the sense that everything that happens is happening on top of layers of things which have already happened. Now I saw you drive up in a motor car and I arrived on a bus so if you're going back down to the city centre I'll thank you for a ride."

Mary Brennan, of course. Why hadn't he known? There were two of her books in the trunk of his car. Paperbacks. Desmond felt his throat closing. Before he'd known who she was she hadn't let him say a word, and now that she seemed to be waiting to hear what he had to offer, he was speechless. His mind was a blank. All he could think of was *Mary Brennan* and wish that she'd turned out to be only a colourful eccentric old lady, something he could handle. He was comfortable with young women only until they turned out to be better than he was at something important to him. Then his throat closed. His mind pulled down the shades and hid.

All Desmond could think to say, driving down the hill towards the River Lee, was: "A man in Dublin told me there was no literature happening in this country." He could have bitten off his tongue. This woman *was* what was happening. A country that had someone like her needed no one else.

She would not accept that, she said, not even from a man in Dublin. And she insisted that he drive her out to the limestone castle restaurant at the mouth of the river so she could buy him a drink there and convince him Dublin was wrong. Inside the castle, though, while they watched the white ferry to Swansea slide out past their window, she discovered she would rather talk about her divorce, a messy thing which had been a strain on everyone concerned and had convinced her if she needed convincing that marriage was an absurd arrangement. She touched Desmond, twice, with one hand, for emphasis.

Oh, she was a charming woman, there was no question. She could be famous for those eyes alone, which never missed a detail in that room (a setting she would use, perhaps, in her next novel of Irish infidelity and rebellion?) and at the same time somehow returned to him often enough and long enough to keep him frozen, afraid to sneak his own glances at the items she was cataloguing for herself. "Some day," she said, "they will have converted all our history into restaurants and bars like this one, just as I will have converted it all to fiction. Then what will we have?"

And when, finally, he said he must go, he really must go, the park was pretty but didn't have all that much in it for kids to do, she said, "Listen, if you want to find out what is happening here, if you really do love that old man's work, then join us tomorrow. There'll be more than a dozen of us, some of the most exciting talent in the country, all meeting up at Gougane Barra . . . you know the place, the lake in the mountains where this river rises . . . it was a spot he loved."

"Tomorrow," he said. "We'll have moved in by then, to the house we've rented for the winter."

"There's a park there now," she said. "And of course the tiny hermitage island. It will begin as a picnic but who knows how it will end." The hand, a white hand with unpainted nails, touched him again.

"Yes," he said. "Yes. We've been there. There's a tiny church on the island, he wrote a story about it, the burial of a priest. And it's only an hour or so from the house, I'd guess. Maybe. Maybe I will."

"Oh you must," she said, and leaned forward. "You knew, of course, that they call it Deep-Valleyed Desmond in the songs." She drew back, biting on a smile.

But when he'd driven her back to the downtown area, to wide St. Patrick's Street, she discovered she was not quite ready yet to let him go. "Walk with me," she said, "for just a while," and found him a parking spot in front of the Munster Arcade where dummies dressed as monks and Vikings and Celtic warriors glowered at him from behind the glass.

"This place exists," she said, "because he made it real for me. He and others, in their stories. I could never write about a place where I was the first, it would panic me. I couldn't be sure it really existed or if I were inventing it."

She led him down past the statue of sober Father Matthew and the parked double-decker buses to the bridge across the Lee. A wind, coming down the river, brought a smell like an open sewer with it. He put his head down and tried to hurry across.

"If I were a North American, like you," she said, "I'd have to move away or become a shop girl. I couldn't write."

He was tempted to say something about plastering over someone else's old buildings, but thought better of it. He hadn't even read her books yet, he knew them only by reputation, he had no right to comment. He stopped, instead, to lean over the stone wall and look at the river. It was like sticking his head into a septic tank. The water was dark, nearly black, and low. Along the edges rats moved over humps of dark shiny muck and half-buried cans and bottles. Holes in the stone wall dumped a steady stream of new sewage into the river. The stories, as far as he could remember, had never mentioned this. These quays were romantic places where young people met and teased each other, or churchgoers gathered to gossip after Mass, or old people strolled. None of them, apparently, had noses.

Wind in the row of trees. Leaves rustling. Desmond looked at her hands. The perfect slim white fingers lay motionless along her skirt, then moved suddenly up to her throat, to touch the neck of her sweater. Then the nearer one moved again, and touched his arm. Those eyes, busy recording the street, paused to look at him; she smiled. Cataloguing me too? he thought. Recording me for future reference? But she didn't know a thing about him.

"I've moved here to work on a book," he said.

Her gaze rested for a moment on the front of his jacket, then flickered away. "Not about here," she said. "You're not writing about *this* place?" She looked as if she would protect it from him, if necessary, or whisk it away.

"I have my own place," he said. "I don't need to borrow his."

She stopped, to buy them each an apple from an old black-shawled woman who sat up against the wall by her table of fruit. Ancient, gypsy-faced, with huge earrings hanging from those heavy lobes. Black Spanish eyes. Mary Brennan flashed a smile, counted out some silver pieces, and picked over the apples for two that were red and clear. The hands that offered change were thick and wrinkled, with crescents of black beneath the nails. They disappeared again beneath the shawl. Desmond felt a momentary twinge about biting into the apple, vague memories of parental warnings. You never know whose hands have touched it, they said, in a voice to make you shudder in horror at the possibilities and scrub at the skin of fruit until it was bruised and raw.

Mary Brennan, apparently, had not been subjected to the same warnings. She bit hugely. "Here," she said, at the bridge, "here is where I'm most aware of him. All his favourite streets converge here, from up the hill. Sunday's Well, over there where his wealthy people live. And of course Blarney Lane. If you had the time we could walk up there, I could show you. Where his first house was, and the pub he dragged his father home from."

"I've seen it," Desmond said, and started across the bridge. She would spoil it all for him if he let her.

But she won him again on the way back down the other side with her talk of castles and churches. Did he know, she asked, the reason there was no roof on the cathedral at Cashel? Did he know why Blackrock Castle where they'd been a half-hour before was a different style altogether than most of the castles of Ireland? Did he know the origin of the word "blarney"?

No he did not, but he knew that his wife would be furious if he didn't hurry back to the park. They passed the noise of voices haggling over second-hand clothes and old books at the Coal Market, they passed the opera house, a tiny yellow book store. She could walk, he saw, the way so many women had forgotten how to walk after high-heeled shoes went out, with long legs and long strides, with some spring in her steps as if there were pleasure in it.

"Now you'll not forget," she said at his car, in his window. "Tomorrow, in Deep-Valleyed Desmond where the Lee rises." There was the scent of apple on her breath. Islands, she leaned in to say, do not exist until you've loved on them.

But today, while Mary Brennan waits on that tiny island for him, Philip Desmond is holed up in the back room of this house at Bantry Bay, trying to write his novel. His wife has taken the car to Cork. When she returns, he doesn't know what he will do. Perhaps he'll get into the car and drive up the snaking road past the crumbling O'Sullivan castle into the mountains, and throw himself into the middle of that crowd of writers as if he belongs there. Maybe he will make them think that he is important, that back home he is noticed in the way that Mary Brennan is noticed here, that his work matters. And perhaps late at night, when everyone is drunk, he will lead Mary Brennan out onto the hermitage island to visit the oratory, to speak in whispers of the stories which had happened there, and to lie on the grass beneath the trees, by the quiet edge of the lake. It is not, Desmond knows, too unthinkable. At a distance.

The piece of paper in front of him is still blank. Mrs. O'Sullivan will advertise the laziness of writers, who only pretend they are working when they are actually dreaming. Or sleeping. She will likely be able to tell exactly how many words he has written, though if he at the end of this day complains of how tired he is, she will undoubtedly go into her practised agony. He wonders if she too, from her window, has noticed that the tide had gone out, that the lagoon is empty of everything except brown shiny mud and seaweed, and that the nostril-burning smell of it is penetrating even to the inside of the house, even in here where the window hasn't been opened, likely, in years. He wonders, too, if she minds that the children, who have tired of their sea-edge exploring, are building a castle of pebbles and fuchsia branches in the middle of her back lawn. The youngest, Michael, dances like an Indian around it; maybe he has to go to the bathroom and can't remember where it is. While his father, who could tell him, who could take him there, sits and stares at a piece of paper.

For a moment Desmond wonders how the medieval masses in the cathedral at Cashel must have appeared to the lepers crowded behind that narrow hole. Of course he has never seen a Mass of any kind himself, but still he can imagine the glimpses of fine robes, the bright colours, the voices of a choir singing those high eerie Latin songs, the voice of a chanting priest, the faces of a few worshippers. It was a lean world from behind that stone wall, through that narrow hole. Like looking through the eye of a needle. The Mass, as close as they were permitted to get to the world, would be only timidly glimpsed past other pressed straining heads. For of course Desmond imagines himself far at the back of the crowd.

("Yes?" the guide said. "And where would that be now?"

"A long way from here," he said. "An island, too, like this one, with its own brand of ruins. You've never heard of it though it's nearly the size of Ireland?"

"I have, yes. And it's a long way you've come from home."

"There's a tiny island just off our coast where they used to send the lepers, but the last of them died there a few years ago. It's a bare and empty place they say now, except for the wind. There are even people who believe that ghosts inhabit it.")

What does the world look like to a leper, squinting through that narrow hole? What does it feel like to be confined to the interior of a circle of trees, at the top of a hill, from which everything else can be seen but not approached? Desmond likes to think that he would prefer the life of that famous fat archbishop, celebrating Mass in the cathedral and thinking of his hundred children.

Somewhere in the house a telephone rings. Desmond hasn't been here long enough to notice where the telephone is, whether it is in her part of the house or theirs. But he hears, beyond the wall, the sudden rustling of clothes, the snap of bones, the sound of feet walking across the carpet. Why should Mrs. O'Sullivan have a phone? There are so few telephones in this country that they are all listed in the one book. But her footsteps return, and he hears behind him the turning of his door handle, the squeal of a hinge. Then her voice whispering: "Mr. Desmond? Is it a bad time to interrupt"

"Is it my wife?"

No it is not. And of course Desmond knows who it is. Before he left the castle-restaurant she asked for his address, for Mrs. O'Sullivan's name, for the name of this village.

"I'm sorry, Mrs. O'Sullivan," he said. "Tell her, tell them I'm working, they'll understand. I don't want to be disturbed, not just now anyway."

He doesn't turn to see how high her eyebrows lift. He can imagine. Working, she's thinking. If that's working. But when she has closed the door something in him relaxes a little—or at least suspends its tension for a while—and he writes the paragraph again at the top of the page and then adds new words after it until he discovers he has completed a second. It is not very good; he decides when he reads it over that it is not very good at all, but at least it is something. A beginning. Perhaps the dam has been broken.

But there is a commotion, suddenly, in the front yard. A car horn beeping. The children run up the slope past the house. He can hear Carrie's voice calling them. There is a flurry of voices and then one of the children is at the door, calling, "Daddy, Daddy, come and see what Mommy has!"

What Mommy has, he discovers soon enough, is something that seems to be taking up the whole back seat, a grey lumpy bulk. And she, standing at the open door, is beaming at him. "Come help me get this thing out!" she says. There is colour in her face, excitement. She has made another one of her finds.

It is, naturally, a piece of sculpture. There is no way Desmond can tell what it is supposed to be and he has given up trying to understand such things long ago. He pulls the figure out, staggers across to the front door, and puts it down in the hall.

"I met the artist who did it," she says. "He was in the little shop delivering something. We talked, it seemed, for hours. This is inspired by the St. Patrick's Cross, he told me, but he abstracted it even more to represent the way art has taken the place of religion in the modern world."

"Whatever it represents," Desmond says, "we'll never get it home."

Nothing, to Carrie, is a problem. "We'll enjoy it here, in this house. Then before we leave we'll crate it up and ship it home." She walks around the sculpture, delighted with it, delighted with herself.

"I could have talked to him for hours," she says, "we got along beautifully. But I remembered you asked me to have the car home early." She kisses him, pushes a finger on his nose. "See how obedient I am?"

"I said that?"

"Yes," she says. "Right after breakfast. Some other place you said you wanted to go prowling around in by yourself. I rushed home down all that long winding bloody road for you. On the wrong side, I'll never get used to it. Watching for radar traps, for heaven's sake. Do you think the gardai have radar traps here?

But Desmond is watching Mrs. O'Sullivan, who has come out into the hall to stare at the piece of sculpture. Why does he have this urge to show her his two paragraphs? Desmond doesn't even show Carrie anything until it is finished. Why, he wonders, should he feel just because she sits there listening through the wall that she's also waiting for him to produce something? She probably doesn't even read. Still, he wants to say, "Look. Read this, isn't it good? And I wrote it in your house, only today."

Mrs. O'Sullivan's hand is knotting at her throat. The sculpture has drawn a frown, a heavy sulk. "'Tis a queer lot of objects they've been making for the tourists, and none of them what you could put a name to."

"But oh," Carrie says, "he must be nearly the best in the country! Surely. And this is no tourist souvenir. I got it from an art shop in Cork."

Mrs. O'Sullivan's hand opens and closes, creeps closer to her mouth. "Oh," she says. "Cork." As if a lot has been explained. "You can expect anything at all from a city. Anything at all. There was people here staying in this house, 'twas last year yes, came back from Cork as pleased as the Pope with an old box of turf they had bought. They wanted to smell it burning in my fire if you don't mind. What you spend your money on is your own business, I told them, but I left the bogs behind years ago, thank you, and heat my house with electricity. Keep the turf in your car so."

Carrie is plainly insulted. Words struggle at her lips. But she dismisses them, apparently, and chooses diversion. "I'll make a pot of tea. Would you like a cup with us, Mrs. O'Sullivan? The long drive's made me thirsty."

And Mrs. O'Sullivan, whose role is apparently varied and will shift for any occasion, lets her fingers pluck at her face. "Oh I know I know I know!" Her long brown-stockinged legs move slowly across the patterned carpet. "And Mr. Desmond, too, after his work. I was tempted to take him a cup but he shouldn't be disturbed I know.

" Work?" Carrie says. "Working at what?"

"I started the novel," Desmond says.

''You have? Then that's something we should celebrate. Before you go off wherever it is you think you're going."

"It's only a page," Desmond says. "And it's not very good at all, but it's a start. It's better than the blank paper."

Like some children, he thinks, he's learned to make a virtue out of anything. Even a page of scribble. When he'd be glad to give a thousand pages of scribble for the gift of honesty. Or change. Or even blindness of a sort. What good is vision after all if it refuses to ignore the dark?

Because hasn't he heard, somewhere, that artists—painters—deliberately create frames for themselves to look through, to sharpen their vision by cutting off all the details which have no importance to their work?

He follows the women into the kitchen, where cups already clatter onto saucers. "Maybe after tea," he says, "I'll get a bit more done."

Pretending, perhaps, that the rest of the world sits waiting, like Mrs. O'Sullivan, for the words he will produce. Because his tongue, his voice, has made the decision for him. Desmond knows that he may only sit in front of that paper for the rest of that day, that he may only play with his pen—frustrated—until enough time has gone by to justify his coming out of the room. To read one of the books he's bought. To talk with Carrie about her shopping in Cork, about her sculptor. To play with the children perhaps, or take them for a walk along the road to look for donkeys, for ruins. Desmond knows that the evening may be passed in front of the television set, where they will see American movies with Irish commercials, and will later try to guess what *an nuacht* is telling them about the day's events, and that he will try very hard not to think of Mary Brennan or of the dozen Irish writers at Cougane Barra or of the tiny hermitage island which the famous writer loved. Deep-Valleyed Desmond. He knows that he could be there with them, through this day and this night, celebrating something he'd come here to find; but he acknowledges, too, the other. That words, too, were invented perhaps to do the things that stones can do. And he has come here, after all, to build his walls.

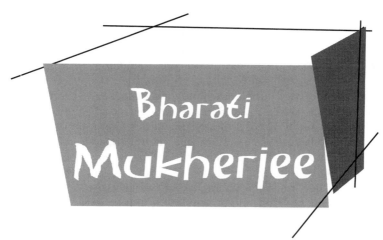

Bharati Mukherjee

I don't think of myself as a postcolonial person stranded on the out shores of the collapsed British Empire. I haven't thought of myself as a postcolonial since I finished co-authoring, with my husband Clark Blaise, *Days and Nights in Calcutta*. Writing my half of that book was my way of thinking who I was, where I was, where I'd rather be.

When I first arrived [in North America] . . . I thought of myself as a Bengali rather than as an Indian. You were who you were because of the language and dialect you spoke, the location of the village of your male ancestors, the family and religion you were born into.

I'm an American writer of Bengali-Indian origin . . . I experience, simultaneously, the pioneer's capacity to be shocked and surprised by the new culture, and the immigrant's willingness to de-form and re-form that culture.

—Bharati Mukherjee, quoted in *Jouvert*

bharati Mukherjee was born in 1940, into a wealthy family living in Calcutta. In 1947, she moved with her family to England where her father was working. The family returned to India in 1951. There, Mukherjee attended the University of Calcutta, graduating with a B.A. in 1959, and the University of Baroda, earning an M.A. in English and ancient Indian culture in 1961. In the same year, she left India to attend the University of Iowa. She received a Master's of Fine Art in creative writing in 1963 and a Ph.D. in English and comparative literature in 1969. It was at the University of Iowa Writer's Workshop that she met fellow writer Clark Blaise, whom she married after a brief courtship. She has held teaching posts at universities across Canada and the United States and is currently Distinguished Professor of English at the University of California, Berkeley. Her writing has brought her critical recognition and awards, including a National Endowment for the Arts Grant (1986), and the National Book Critics Circle Award for Fiction for *The Middleman and Other Stories* (1988). *Days and Nights in Calcutta* (1977), from which this excerpt is taken, was written with her husband (each providing an individual perspective) about their trip to India after a fire destroyed their Montreal house.

Describing her childhood, Mukherjee has written: "My identity was viscerally connected with ancestral soil and genealogy. I was who I was because I was Dr. Sudhir Lal Mukherjee's daughter, because I was a Hindu Brahmin, because I was Bengali-speaking, and because my *desh*—the Bengali word for homeland—was an East Bengal° village called Faridpur" (Mukherjee 1). As a foreign student in the United States who fully intended to return to India, she remained rooted in her Bengali/Indian identity, but "the five-minute [marriage] ceremony in the lawyer's office suddenly changed me into a transient with conflicting loyalties to two very different cultures" (1). She spent the first years of her marriage feeling like an exile, estranged from both the culture she had left and the one in which she found herself. After fourteen years in Canada which she describes as "particularly harsh" because of the racism she encountered, Mukherjee and her family moved to the United States, where she has made the transition from exile to being an "immigrant in a country of immigrants" (Pradhan 2). She defines herself as "American," rejecting the hyphenated identity so common in North America.

Mukherjee's biographer, Fakrul Alam, has identified the focus of her fiction as the "phenomenon of migration, the status of new immigrants, and the feeling of alienation often experienced by expatriates" (qtd. in Pradhan 1) as well as the difficulties faced by Indian women both within traditional Indian society and in the West. Mukherjee's own sense of identity has brought her a great sense of strength and freedom:

> I maintain that I am an American writer of Indian origin, not because I'm ashamed of my past, not because I'm betraying or distorting my past, but because my whole adult life has been lived here, and I write about the people who are immigrants going through the process of making a home here. . . . I write in the tradition of immigrant experience rather than nostalgia and expatriation . . . the luxury of being a U.S. citizen for me is that I can define myself in terms of things like my politics, my sexual orientation or my education. (qtd. in Pradhan 2)

Works Cited

Alam, Fakrul. *Bharati Mukherjee*. New York: Twayne Publishers, 1996.
Chen, Tina, and S.X. Goudie. "Holders of the World: An Interview with Bharati Mukherjee." *Jouvert* 1.1 (1997).
 152.1.96.5/jouvert/v1i1/bharat.htm
Mukherjee, Bharati. "American Dreamer." *Mother Jones*.
 www.motherjones.com/mother_jones/JF97/mukherjee.html
Pradhan, Shilpi. "Bharati Mukherjee."
 www.emory. Edu/ENGLISH/Bahri/Mukherjee.htm

Bengal: state in east India, divided at the time of Partition (the division of India into India and Pakistan); Calcutta is the capital of West Bengal; East Bengal, with a Muslim majority, became part of Pakistan

Days and Nights in Calcutta
[excerpt]

It was not yet a time for emergency measures. It was a year of protest marches and labor strikes and of heartbreaking letters in local newspapers. It was a year for predicting horrendous famine and economic collapse. Street people knifed each other over minor irritations. Housewives complained of food shortages and adulteration; neurasthenic women spread newfangled ideas about dust pollution and nervous tension. Students rebelled against irrelevant syllabi and poorly devised examinations; in some examination halls, they knifed to death defenseless proctors. Cities changed their characters: placid Ahmedabad°, where Gandhi was still revered, staged a memorable riot, while unruly Calcutta preserved a fragile calm. In Bombay some literate young ex-untouchables read *Soul on Ice°*, formed an America-inspired militant group called the Dalit° [Oppressed] Panthers, wrote angry poems, and battled with the police, who, they claimed, were recruited from higher castes. In Kerala° women members of a volunteer defense force wore men's uniforms and undertook night patrols. In Orissa° one million people were devastated by floods. The Guru Maharaj-ji° was said to have been harassed by skeptical customs officials at an Indian airport. Rich young Indians drinking cappuccino at the Sheraton-Oberoi in Bombay were heard to concede that the American Hare Krishna chaps might have some spiritual insight to offer India, after all. The Prime Minister, Mrs. Gandhi, went on an official trip to Canada and saw snow on mountaintops in Banff National Park. No, it was not yet the time for excessive measures. It was still a time for gossip and innuendo.

Ahmedabad: India's largest inland industrial centre; Gandhi lived there for a time

Soul on Ice: by Eldridge Cleaver, an American Black Panther who resisted the movement's later rejection of violence—see note in Gates' "What's in a Name?"

Dalit: formerly referred to as the Harijans (children of God) or untouchables; people at the lowest level of or entirely excluded from Hinduism's caste system. After centuries of discrimination because of their assumed "polluting" effect on others, they have been granted the right to education, employment and representation in the government. The Dalit Panthers are a militant group in Bombay.

Kerala: a state at the southern tip of India

Orissa: a state in India on the Bay of Bengal

Guru Maharaj-ji: a *guru* is a spiritual guide or teacher; *Maharaj* is the traditional designation for a ruler

It is, of course, America that I love. Where history occurs with the dramatic swiftness and interest of half-hour television shows. America is sheer luxury, being touched more by the presentation of tragedy than by tragedy itself. History can be dealt with in thirty-second episodes; I need not suffer its drabness and continuum. If I give him thirty minutes, John Chancellor will provide neat beginnings, ends, and middles; he will guide me to my catharsis. When he bids me good night, I have been ennobled. There is so much less confusion in America.

In India, history is full of uninterpreted episodes; there is no one to create heroes and define our sense of loss, of right and wrong, tragedy and buffoonery. Events have no necessary causes; behavior no inevitable motive. Things simply *are*, because that is their nature.

Going to India was Clark's idea. I was surprised by his enthusiasm. Prior to this, India had been a place to send the family on summer vacations so that he could have undisturbed time for writing. He had shown little curiosity to learn Bengali; he had, in fact, seemed bored by my endless stories of a tribal childhood. In cynical moments I had joked that going to India was for him a bizarre death wish. Then in the space of three months, he had broken his hand, we had lost our house in a fire and our car in a three-vehicle crash on a quiet street. Suddenly, Calcutta seemed less terrifying. India, I warned, would be the fourth and fatal accident.

For my part, going to India was simpler than going anywhere else, simpler even than staying in Montreal. I knew the rules in India (I hoped I still remembered them); there, I felt it would be possible to control my destiny better. In Canada I was helpless and self-absorbed. Ours was the only house on the block to suffer the embarrassment of a major fire. Fires occurred to poor, or to careless, people. I was personally not to blame (I was anxious for my neighbors to understand that, at least); I had been at the department meeting; the baby-sitter, cooking french fries for my five-year-old, Bernard, had permitted the fire to start and spread. But we cannot escape the consequences of our most banal ambitions, and so there we were, homeless, petless, and plantless, though, thank God, not childless, on a subzero February afternoon. I was going to India, then, because I was tired and irritable and because I thought of myself as a careless person on a callous continent. In India I would relearn the precautions taken by a people fluent in self-protection.

Of course I had other reasons for going to India. I was going because I had discovered that while changing citizenships is easy, swapping cultures is not.

For a Commonwealth citizen like me, becoming Canadian took no more than five minutes in an unpretentious office. A maternal French-Canadian official insisted over my protests that Indian citizens were British subjects. In the end I undid the work of generations of martyred freedom fighters, pledged loyalty to the British Queen, and became a Canadian citizen. But in Canada I feel isolated, separate in the vastness of this underpopulated country. I cannot bring myself to snowshoe or ski. Unspoiled nature terrifies me. I have not yet learned the words to the national anthem. I tell myself I shall never make friends here, though, in truth, I am lying; I am unlikely to make friends in any country. In Canada I am both too visible and too invisible. I am brown; I cannot disappear in a rush-hour Montreal crowd. The media had made me self-conscious about racism. I detect arrogance in the slow-footedness of salesclerks. At lunch, in the Faculty Club, I am not charmed when colleagues compliment me for not having a "singsong" accent. I am tired of being exotic, being complimented for qualities of voice, education, bearing, appearance, that are not extraordinary.

But if as a citizen I am painfully visible, I cannot make myself visible at all as a Canadian writer. The literary world in Canada is nascent, aggressively nationalistic, and self-engrossed. Reviewers claim that my material deals with Indians usually in India, and because my publisher is American, my work is of no interest to Canadian writers and readers. In Canada I am the wife of a well-known Canadian writer who "also writes," though people often assume it is in Bengali. In order to be recognized as an India-born Canadian writer, I would have to convert myself into a token figure, write abusively about local racism and make Brown Power fashionable. But I find I cannot yet write about Montreal. It does not engage my passions. It is caught up in passion all its own, it renders the Asian immigrant whose mother tongue is neither French nor English more or less irrelevant. Montreal merely fatigues and disappoints. And so I am a late-blooming colonial who writes in a borrowed language (English), lives permanently in an alien country (Canada), and publishes in and is read, when read at all, in another alien country, the United States. My Indianness is fragile; it has to be professed and fought for, even though I look so unmistakably Indian. Language transforms our ways of apprehending the world; I fear that my decades-long use of English as a first language has cut me off from my *desh*.

In those weeks of preparation, of applying for American Express cards and of packing an enormous shipping trunk with typing paper, color film, two-ply toilet paper, deodorant, dental floss—all the exotica of North America—I realized that though my usurpation of English had forced me to act as if I were rational and analytic, it had not destroyed completely my susceptibility to magic. To be a Hindu is to believe in magic; it is to see madmen as visionaries and prophets. The trip seemed to have detonated an energy which I had spent years restraining and disguising. Perhaps the broken hand, the fire, and the collision were the result of this unleashed mental energy. Perhaps I was a fool to think that the trip to India was to be simply a fourth event in a chain of disastrous events. In any case, in those weeks, while friends talked to us of modern India with its tiresome problems of overpopulation and hunger, I thought of the India of derelict temple friezes, embodying in plaster or stone derelict wisdom.

I thought particularly of a temple relief from Deoghar, Bihar (an area crowded with skeletons in maps of global starvation). I had not seen the temple relief itself, only a plate of it in a book about Indian art written by Heinrich Zimmer, whose work had not been brought to my attention as a schoolgirl in Calcutta because the missionary school I attended taught no Indian history, culture, art, or religion.

The plate of the temple relief showed the god Vishnu asleep on a multiheaded serpent. Above the reclining chief god were other, lesser divine manifestations, seated on lotuses or winged bulls. At Vishnu's feet sat his spouse, goddess Lakshmi, dutifully massaging the god's tired calf muscles. Below, separated from all the gods by a wall of serpentine coils, were mythological human figures.

I was entranced not by craftsmanship but by the inspired and crazy vision, by the enormity of details. Nothing had been excluded. As viewer, I was free to concentrate on a tiny corner of the relief, and read into the shape of a stone eyelid or stone finger human intrigues and emotions. Or I could view the work as a whole, and see it as the story of Divine Creation. For me, it was a reminder that I had almost lost the Hindu instinct for miraculous transformation of the literal. Not only was Vishnu the chief god, but the serpent supporting Vishnu was also the god Vishnu, given a magical, illusory transformation. My years abroad had made me conscious of ineradicable barriers, of beginnings and endings, of lines and definitions. And now, the preparation for the visit to India was setting off an explosion of unrelated images. Reptile, lotus, flying bull, gods, and heroes: All functioned simultaneously as emblem and as real.

As a very small child, before I learned to read, I used to listen to my grandmother (my father's mother) reciting ancient stories from the puranas°. But after I started missionary school in earnest, the old gods and goddesses and heroes yielded to new ones, Macbeth and Othello, Lord Peter Wimsey and Hercule Poirot°. I learned, though never with any ease, to come and go talking of Michelangelo, to applaud wildly after each scene in school productions of *Quality Street*, and to sing discreetly as a member of the chorus in *The Gondoliers°*. School exposed me to too much lucidity. Within its missionary compound, multiheaded serpents who were also cosmic oceans and anthropomorphic gods did not stand a chance of survival. My imagination, therefore, created two distinct systems of cartography.° There were seas like the Dead Sea which New Testament characters used as a prop to their adventures and which the nuns expected us to locate on blank

puranas: a group of eighteen epics, a direct offshoot of the Mahabharata (the classical epic of India and the longest single poem in the world); probably composed between 200 B.C. and 200 A.D. by bardic (oral) poets and later revised by priests

Lord Peter Wimsey and Hercule Poirot: heroes of English detective fiction

The Gondoliers: one of a number of popular nineteenth-century English operettas written by Sir William Schwenck Gilbert and Sir Arthur Sullivan

cartography: map-making

maps of Asia Minor. And then there were the other seas and oceans, carved in stone on walls of temples, bodies of water that did not look like water at all and which could never be located on maps supplied by the school.

The mind is no more than an instrument of change. My absorptive mind has become treacherous, even sly. It has learned to dissemble and to please. Exquisitely self-conscious by its long training in the West, it has isolated itself from real snakes and real gods. But the snakes and gods remain, wailing to be disturbed during incautious sabbaticals.

Identity

I had been away from Calcutta for fourteen years. My parents no longer lived there and I had never written letters, nor even sent birthday cards, to friends and relatives during this period. Yet after all these years, their first question invariably was: "Has Calcutta changed very much?" And my response was what I knew they wanted to hear: "No, it's just the way I remember it." Then it was their turn to smile benevolently at me and whisper: "You know, you might have a Canadian husband and kids, but you haven't changed much either." I was not lying, merely simplifying, when I agreed with friends I had not seen since our missionary school days that nothing had changed. Because in Calcutta, "change" implies decline and catastrophe; friendship is rooted in the retention of simplicity. The fact that after fourteen years away I was still judged "simple" was the greatest compliment my friends and relatives could bestow.

I was born in Ballygunge, a very middle-class neighborhood of Calcutta, and lived the first eight years of my life in a ground-floor flat on a wide street sliced in half by shiny tram tracks. The flat is still rented by my *jethoo*°; the tram tracks still shine through the mangy blades of grass in the center of the street; and the trams are still owned by British shareholders most of whom have never seen Calcutta. Ballygunge remains, in these small, personal terms, a stable society. Wars with China and Pakistan, refugee influxes from Assam, Tibet, Bangla Desh, and Bihar, Naxalite political agitations: Nothing has wrenched out of recognizable shape the contours of the block where I grew up.

In those first eight years, though I rarely left Ballygunge, I could not escape the intimations of a complex world just beyond our neighborhood. I saw the sleek white trams (perhaps never sleek nor white) and I associated them with glamour and incredible mobility. My own traveling was limited to trips to the *mamabari*° a few blocks away, and to school which was in the no man's land between Ballygunge and the European quarters. These trips we accomplished by rickshaw. My mother had a tacit agreement with one of the pullers at the nearby rickshaw stand, and whenever he saw her approaching with her three little daughters, he would drag his vehicle over at a trot. Rickshaws were familiar—the same puller and the same route over back

jethoo: an extended family
mamabari: the maternal home

streets with light traffic. Only trams promised journeys without destination. And sometimes trams promised drama. While swinging on the rusty iron gate that marked the insides and outsides of properties but was not intended to keep trespassers out, I had seen a man (a pickpocket, I was later told by an older cousin) flung bodily out of a moving tram by an excited crowd. And once I had seen the heaving body of a run-over cow on the tracks just in front of our house. The cow had drawn a larger crowd than the pickpocket. The head had not been completely severed from the body; I think now that a fully severed head might have been less horrible. I saw it as an accident, cruel, thrilling, unnecessary, in a city where accidents were common.

I saw processions of beggars at our front door, even Muslim ones, and it was often the job of us small children to scoop out a measure of rice from a huge drum in my widowed grandmother's vegetarian kitchen and pour it into the beggars' pots. I was too little to lean over the edge of the drum and fill the scoop, and for that I was grateful. The beggars terrified me. I would wait for them to cluster at our front door, but when they were actually there, I would hide behind my older cousin Tulu (now a geneticist in Hamburg), who would issue efficient commands to the beggars to stop fighting among themselves and to hold out their sacks and pots. It is merely a smell that I now recall, not the hungry faces but the smell of starvation and of dying. Later, my mother, a powerful storyteller, told me how millions had died in the 1943 Bengal famine—she did not care about precise statistics, only about passion—and how my father had personally organized a rice-gruel kitchen in our flat. I had no concept of famine; I only knew that beggars were ugly and that my father was a hero.

As a child in Ballygunge, I did not completely escape World War II. My mother told me later, especially after we had been to war movies at the Metro Cinema, that there had been periodic air-raid sirens in the fields just beyond the landlord's palm trees, and that my father had set aside a small room as air-raid shelter for the forty-odd people who were living at the flat at the time. She remembered the tins of imported crackers, the earthenware pitchers of water, the bed-rolls, and the complaints of the younger uncles who felt that tea made on a hot plate in the shelter did not taste as good as tea made on the regular open stove. She said she had not been frightened at all during the raids, not even after the bombing of the Kidderpore docks°, and that sometimes instead of rushing to the shelter at the first wail of the siren, she had settled us in, then raced to the street to admire beautiful formations of the Japanese planes. The Japanese, she insisted, meant us Indians no harm. She talked of prewar Japanese hawkers who had come to the front gate with their toys and silks. I did not see the Japanese planes. I do not remember the sirens. But in the last year of the war, as I was sitting in the first-floor balcony of the *mamabari* on Southern Avenue, I saw a

Kidderpore docks: docks on the river Hoogly in the port of Calcutta that have been in operation since 1893

helmeted soldier on a motorcycle swerve around a car, then crash into a stalled truck. His body was flung high (all the way up to the level of the second-floor windows, my aunts said), before it splattered against the sidewalk. That is my only memory of the war: street children scurrying after the dead soldier's helmet. My aunts said that the solider must have been drunk, that all soldiers were drunk and crude. I was shocked that a soldier who was drunk could also be Indian. I had never seen a drunk person.

And immediately after the war, when many British-owned Wolseleys, Rovers, and Austins bore gigantic white V's° on their hoods, I became aware of signs of violence of another sort. Funeral processions for teen-age freedom fighters passed our house. At the head of these processions were bullet-ridden bodies laid out on string beds and covered over with flowers. In those days, we thought of them as freedom fighters° and martyrs but called them "anarchists" and "terrorists" for we had accepted the terminology of the British without ever understanding or sharing their emotions. Later still, during the communal riots between Hindus and Muslims at the time of Partition, I saw from the roof (where we always rushed at the first signal of a possible invasion of our block) giggling young men loot a store and carry off radios and table fans. This was comic, but I knew that in other parts of the city, looters were vandalizing households and murdering everyone in sight. A week later, my father and the workers in his pharmaceutical plant were besieged by a Muslim group and had to be rescued by troops. The event might have been tragic for our family—and in fact, three workers were killed by the rioters before the troops arrived—but my father delivered the account with so much elegance and wit that I have never been able to picture it as a riot.

It is that Ballygunge which has not changed. It is still possible for my parents' separate families to continue renting the flats they have lived in since I was born, to conduct discreet and fairly stable middle-class lives, although each year the periphery of violence draws a little closer to the center.

I cannot claim that same stability in Montreal. In the last ten years I have moved at least five times, perhaps more. The few women I claim to know have undergone several image changes. They seem to have tired of drugs, of radical politics, of women's movements. Two have taken lesbian lovers. Two others have discarded their lesbian lovers. One rents a high school boy. To me they seem marvelously flamboyant. I envy them their nervous breakdowns, their violent self-absorption, their confident attempts to remake themselves. Having been born in pre-Independence India, and having watched my homeland change shape and color on schoolroom maps, then having discarded that homeland for another, I know excess of passion leads only to trouble. I am, I insist, well mannered, discreet, secretive, and above all, pliable.

gigantic white V's: celebrating the Allies' victory over the Axis powers in the Second World War

freedom fighters . . . anarchists: people fighting for Indian independence from the British

As I told and retold, to friends and family, the story of our fire and car crash in the first months of our visit, I realized that it was not plot that fascinated me, but coincidence. I think there is such a thing as a Hindu imagination; everything is a causeless, endless muddle. What oddity of fate or personality had brought one particular twenty-six-year-old Québecoise baby-sitter far from her home to my kitchen in English Westmount on Thursday, February 22, 1973, so that she could start heating Crisco oil for Bernie's french fries, lose herself in daydreams, and inadvertently set the house on fire? I could not remember how many fire trucks had been on the scene, nor how long it had taken to put out the fire. I could remember the squelch and crackle of freezing water on our queen-sized mattress, frozen cedar shavings in a smoke-blackened gerbil cage, the sticky black mess where the kitchen telephone had hung, and sticky white mess where the stove and refrigerator had stood.

What mysterious design had trapped me, safety belt unfastened, in the passenger seat of our Volvo on Thursday, April 4, so that a housewife in a station wagon, missing a stop sign, could cause me to crack the windshield with my head? Those few details spread out in my imagination, obliterating everything else. But there was no regret. A strange acceptance and then relief at the swift disposal of sentimental baggage acquired over almost ten years; I was pained only by what neighbors must have thought of us; we were careless young people playing at professions. We couldn't afford competent help, and we paid the price.

But my mother, from whom I learned very early the persuasiveness of oral literature, has a more communal Hindu imagination. On the first night Clark and I spent in Chembur in 1973, after the children had finally fatigued themselves to sleep in strange hot beds, and after we had told all we could about the fire and collision, my mother gave us her version of the story of our fire.

She told us that she had had premonitions. Did I remember that she was given to premonitions? So, my mother continued, she had had premonitions of danger and had worried herself sick over our well-being. And a week prior to receiving news of our fire, there had been a fire in Chembur, a colossal fire at the nearby Esso refinery. Plans had been made to evacuate everyone from the general neighborhood, including my parents and other residents of Calico Colony. And my mother had stood at the open windows of her bedroom overlooking the crazy distant flames, and she had panicked. Not because she had been afraid for herself, for at fifty-odd years she had long been preparing to die, but because she felt *we* were in danger, that we in Montreal were vastly unhappy. And in a week our letter had explained the mystery. She had sensed our danger through mental telepathy. Though we had been oceans apart, she had shared our misery. That was the point of her story. Drama and detail did not concern her. Nor causality, nor sequence: What mattered was her oneness with our suffering. It was as though we were figures in the same carving and the oceans that separated us were but an inch or two of placid stone. This is, quite simply, the way I perceive as well. In Deoghar several time sequences coexist in what appears to be a single frieze. *In the eye of God,* runs another quote from Zimmer, *mountain ranges rise and fall like waves on the ocean.*

Clark wanted to know how many tanks had exploded and how many rupees' worth of damage had been assessed. My mother did not know. She could not respond to his logical method of reconstruction. He separated the peripheral elements from the central, then forced such a swift, dramatic pace on the haphazard event of our fire that hearing him recount it moved me in ways that the event itself had not.

And, unlike me, my mother did not isolate details for their metaphoric content. For her the incident was indivisible from the general functioning of the universe; mental telepathy was possible in a world that fused serpent and God without self-destructing.

I often thought back to that story of mental telepathy when I later heard other Hindus—barristers, bank managers, sports writers, businessmen—confide to Clark and me that though they considered themselves rational, modern men, they believed in healers, palmistry, astrology, and miracles. Our talks with these men inevitably concluded with a reference to Sai Baba, the young South Indian saint, who, we heard, produced holy ash, vermilion powder, lockets, and even diamond rings out of thin air. For the West, the educated Hindu's belief in telepathy and psychokinetic energy may seem intellectually dishonest. But I am convinced that such beliefs have more to do with radically different ways of telling a story than with underdeveloped logic. Hindus entrust much less of the universe to logical explanation—and dismissal—than do Europeans. Belief in magic, miracles, and myth still causes very little conflict, even among successful scientists and businessmen.

On that first night in Chembur, I did not dispute my mother's claim of mental telepathy. I heard it as a call from a portion of my brain that I thought had long ago been stilled. But because talk of miracles, magic, and telepathy made me uncomfortable, I tried to deflect the mood; I chattered instead about the charred percale sheets and towels, the waterlogged suitcases full of my silk saris and photographs from my decade-long married life.

"At least I didn't have to worry too much about packing," I joked as my father poured me my second gin and lime cordial.

Intimations

My life, I now realize, falls into three disproportionate parts. Till the age of eight I lived in the typical joint family, indistinguishable from my twenty cousins, indistinguishable, in fact, from an eternity of Bengali Brahmin girls. From eight till twenty-one we lived as a single family, enjoying for a time wealth and confidence. And since twenty-one I have lived in the West. Each phase required a repudiation of all previous avatars; an almost total rebirth.

Prior to this year-long stay in India, I had seen myself as others saw me in Montreal, a brown woman in a white society, different, perhaps even special, but definitely not a part of the majority. I receive, occasionally, crazy letters from women students at McGill accusing me of being "mysterious," "cold," "hard to get to know," and the letter writers find this mysteriousness offensive. I am bothered by these letters, especially by the aggressive desire of students to "know" me. I explain it as a form of racism. The unfamiliar is frightening; therefore I have been converted into a "mystery." I can be invested with powers and intentions I do not possess.

Adrienne Rich

C ritic Deborah Pope calls Adrienne Rich "one of the most eloquent, provocative voices on the politics of sexuality, race, language, power, and women's culture." A celebrated poet, essayist and editor of lesbian-feminist journals, Rich has also played an important role as a political activist, fighting racism, homophobia and social injustice.

Adrienne Rich was born in 1929, in Baltimore, Maryland, to affluent and intellectual parents. In 1951, she graduated from Radcliffe College and won the Yale Younger Poets Prize for her first book of poetry, *A Change of World*. Two years later, she married Harvard economist Alfred Conrad and, over the next five years, produced three sons, an experience she later described as "radicalizing." In the years that followed, Rich became increasingly engaged in the process of critically examining the nature of her roles as woman and artist. She also became more politically involved both with her husband in the movement opposing American involvement in Viet Nam and as a participant in the women's movement. In 1976, she published *Of Woman Born: Motherhood as Experience and Institution*, a consideration of the nature of motherhood in terms of anthropology, political and medical history and her own personal experience, together with the mythology which has developed around the idea of the role of the mother. As a teacher of remedial English in the SEEK program which was designed to help disadvantaged students entering college, Rich became increasingly sensitive to the issues surrounding language and its relationship to power. Deborah Pope remarks that Rich has presented herself in her poetry as "the seer with the burden of 'verbal privilege' and the weight of moral imagination, who speaks for the speechless, records for the forgotten . . ." (2)

In *Stealing the Language*, her book about American women's poetry, Alicia Ostriker observes that "the central project of the women's poetry movement is a quest for autonomous self-definition" (59). For Adrienne Rich, this quest begins with a re-examination of the past, what she calls "re-vision." In her 1971 essay "When We Dead Awaken: Writing as Re-vision" she writes, "[u]ntil we can understand the assumptions in which we are drenched we cannot know ourselves" (2045). In her long poem, "Sources" (written, as she says below, in 1960 but published in 1983), Rich asks herself "From where does your strength come, you Southern Jew? / split at the root, raised in a castle of air?" (qtd. in Gilbert and Gubar 2023). In the essay below, written more than twenty years after "Sources," she continues the process of exploring the split, "re-visioning" her history and the often conflicting facets of her self, to reveal an identity which, for all its difficulty and complexity, is consciously chosen and willingly affirmed.

Works Cited

Gilbert, Sandra M., and Susan Gubar, eds. "Adrienne Rich." *The Norton Anthology of Literature by Women: The Tradition in English*. New York: W. W. Norton, 1985. 2044–2056.

Ostriker, Alicia. *Stealing the Language*. Boston: Beacon Press, 1986.

Pope, Deborah. "Rich's Life and Career." *The Oxford Companion to Women's Writing in the United States*. Ed. Elizabeth Ammons et al. New York: Oxford University Press, 1995.
    www.english.uiuc.edu/maps/poets/m_r/rich/rich.html

Rich, Adrienne. "When We Dead Awaken." Reprinted in *The Norton Anthology of Literature by Women: The Tradition in English*. Ed. Sandra M. Gilbert and Susan Gubar. New York: W. W. Norton, 1985. 2044–2056.

Weblinks

www.poets.org/LIT/poet/arichtst.html

www.bostonphoenix.com/archive/1in10/99/06/RICH.html

Split at the Root: An Essay on Jewish Identity

For about fifteen minutes I have been sitting chin in hand in front of the typewriter, staring out at the snow. Trying to be honest with myself, trying to figure out why writing this seems to be so dangerous an act, filled with fear and shame, and why it seems so necessary. It comes to me that in order to write this I have to be willing to do two things: I have to claim my father, for I have my Jewishness from him and not from my gentile mother; and I have to break his silence, his taboos; in order to claim him I have in a sense to expose him.

And there is, of course the third thing: I have to face the sources and the flickering presence of my own ambivalence as a Jew; the daily, mundane anti-Semitisms of my entire life.

These are stories I have never tried to tell before. Why now? Why, I asked myself sometime last year, does this question of Jewish identity float so impalpably, so ungraspably around me, a cloud I can't quite see the outlines of, which feels to me to be without definition?

And yet I've been on the track of this longer than I think.

In a long poem written in 1960, when I was thirty-one years old, I described myself as "Split at the root, neither Gentile nor Jew,/Yankee nor Rebel." I was still trying to have it both ways: to be neither/nor, trying to live (with my Jewish husband and three children more Jewish in ancestry than I) in the predominantly gentile Yankee academic world of Cambridge, Massachusetts.

But this begins, for me, in Baltimore, where I was born in my father's workplace, a hospital in the Black ghetto, whose lobby contained an immense white marble statue of Christ.

My father was then a young teacher and researcher in the department of pathology at the Johns Hopkins Medical School, one of the very few Jews to attend or teach at that institution. He was from Birmingham, Alabama; his father, Samuel, was Ashkenazic°, an immigrant from Austria-Hungary, and his mother, Hattie Rice, a Sephardic° Jew from Vicksburg, Mississippi. My grandfather had had a shoe store in Birmingham, which did well enough to allow him to retire comfortably and to leave my grandmother income on his death. The only souvenirs of my grandfather, Samuel Rich, were his ivory flute, which lay on our living-room mantel and was not to be played with; his thin gold pocket watch, which my father wore; and his Hebrew prayer book, which I discovered among my father's books in the course of reading my way through his library. In this prayer book there was a newspaper clipping about my grandparents' wedding, which took place in a synagogue.

My father, Arnold, was sent in adolescence to a military school in the North Carolina mountains, a place for training white southern Christian gentlemen. I suspect that there were few, if any, other Jewish boys at Colonel Bingham's, or at "Mr. Jefferson's university" in Charlottesville, where he studied as an undergraduate. With whatever conscious forethought, Samuel and Hattie sent their son into the dominant southern WASP culture to become an "exception," to enter the professional class. Never, in describing these experiences, did he speak of having suffered—from loneliness, cultural alienation, or outsiderhood. Never did I hear him use the word *anti-Semitism*.

Ashkenazic: adj. form of Ashkenazim: Jews of Eastern or Central Europe

Sephardic: adj. form of Sephardim: Jews of Spanish or north African ancestry. There are differences in religious practice and law between the two groups with the Sephardic Jews being, on the whole, more secular in orientation.

It was only in college, when I read a poem by Karl Shapiro beginning "To hate the Negro and avoid the Jew / is the curriculum," that it flashed on me that there was an untold side to my father's story of his student years. He looked recognizably Jewish, was short and slender in build with dark wiry hair and deep-set eyes, high forehead and curved nose.

My mother is a gentile. In Jewish law I cannot count myself a Jew. If it is true that "we think back through our mothers if we are women" (Virginia Woolf)—and I myself have affirmed this—then even according to lesbian theory, I cannot (or need not?) count myself a Jew.

The white southern Protestant woman, the gentile, has always been there for me to peel back into. That's a whole piece of history in itself, for my gentile grandmother and my mother were also frustrated artists and intellectuals, a lost writer and a lost composer between them. Readers and annotators of books, note takers, my mother a good pianist still, in her eighties. But there was also the obsession with ancestry, with "background," the southern talk of family, not as people you would necessarily know and depend on, but as heritage, the guarantee of "good breeding." There was the inveterate romantic heterosexual fantasy, the mother telling the daughter how to attract men (my mother often used the word "fascinate"); the assumption that relations between the sexes could only be romantic, that it was in the woman's interest to cultivate "mystery," conceal her actual feelings. Survival tactics of a kind, I think today, knowing what I know about the white woman's sexual role in the southern racist scenario. Heterosexuality as protection, but also drawing white women deeper into collusion with white men.

It would be easy to push away and deny the gentile in me—that white southern woman, that social christian. At different times in my life I have wanted to push away one or the other burden of inheritance, to say merely *I am a woman; I am a lesbian.* If I call myself a Jewish lesbian, do I thereby try to shed some of my southern gentile white woman's culpability? If I call myself only through my mother, is it because I pass more easily through a world where being a lesbian often seems like outsiderhood enough?

According to Nazi logic, my two Jewish grandparents would have made me a *Mischling°, first-degree*—nonexempt from the Final Solution.

The social world in which I grew up was christian virtually without needing to say so—christian imagery, music, language, symbols, assumptions everywhere. It was also a genteel, white, middle-class world in which "com-mon" was a term of deep opprobrium. "Common" white people might speak of "niggers"; *we* were taught never to use that word—*we* said "Negroes" (even as we accepted segregation, the eating taboo, the assumption that Black people were simply of a separate species). Our language was more polite, distinguishing us from the "rednecks" or the lynch-mob mentality.

Mischling: half-breed

But so charged with negative meaning was even the word "Negro" that as children we were taught never to use it in front of Black people. We were taught that any mention of skin color in the presence of colored people was treacherous, forbidden ground. In a parallel way, the word "Jew" was not used by polite gentiles. I sometimes heard my best friend's father, a Presbyterian minister, allude to "the Hebrew people" or "people of the Jewish faith." The world of acceptable folk was white, gentile (christian, really), and had "ideals" (which colored people, white "common" people, were not supposed to have). "Ideals" and "manners" included not hurting someone's feelings by calling her or him a Negro or a Jew—naming the hated identity. This is the mental framework of the 1930s and 1940s in which I was raised.

(Writing this, I feel dimly like the betrayer: of my father, who did not speak the word; of my mother, who must have trained me in the messages; of my caste and class; of my whiteness itself.)

Two memories: I am in a play reading at school of *The Merchant of Venice.* Whatever Jewish law says, I am quite sure I was *seen* as Jewish (with a reassuringly gentile mother) in that double vision that bigotry allows. I am the only Jewish girl in the class, and I am playing Portia. As always, I read my part aloud for my father the night before, and he tells me to convey, with my voice, more scorn and contempt with the word "Jew": "Therefore, Jew . . ." I have to say the word out, and say it loudly. I was encouraged to pretend to be a non-Jewish child acting a non-Jewish character who has to speak the word "Jew" emphatically. Such a child would not have had trouble with the part. But *I* must have had trouble with the part, if only because the word itself was really taboo. I can see that there was a kind of terrible, bitter bravado about my father's way of handling this. And who would not dissociate from Shylock in order to identify with Portia? As a Jewish child who was also a female, I loved Portia—and, like every other Shakespearean heroine, she proved a treacherous role model.

A year or so later I am in another play, *The School for Scandal,* in which a notorious spendthrift is described as having "many excellent friends . . . among the Jews." In neither case was anything explained, either to me or to the class at large, about this scorn for Jews and the disgust surrounding Jews and money. Money, when Jews wanted it, had it, or lent it to others, seemed to take on a peculiar nastiness; Jews and money had some peculiar and unspeakable relation.

At this same school—in which we had Episcopalian hymns and prayers, and read aloud through the Bible morning after morning—I gained the impression that Jews were in the Bible and mentioned in English literature, that they had been persecuted centuries ago by the Wicked Inquisition, but that they seemed not to exist in everyday life. These were the 1940s, and we were told a great deal about the Battle of Britain, the noble French Resistance fighters, the brave, starving Dutch—but I did not learn of the resistance of the Warsaw ghetto until I left home.

I was sent to the Episcopal church, baptized and confirmed, and attended it for about five years, though without belief. That religion seemed to have little to do with belief or commitment; it was liturgy that mattered, not spiritual passion. Neither of my parents ever entered that church, and my father would not enter *any* church for any reason—wedding or funeral. Nor did I enter a synagogue until I left Baltimore. When I came home from church, for a while, my father insisted on reading aloud to me from Thomas Paine's *The Age of Reason*—a diatribe against institutional religion. Thus, he explained, I would have a balanced view of these things, a choice. He—they—did not give me the choice to be a Jew. My mother explained to me when I was filling out forms for college that if any question was asked about "religion," I should put down "Episcopalian" rather than "none"—to seem to have no religion was, she implied, dangerous.

But it was white social christianity, rather than any particular christian sect, that the world was founded on. The very word *Christian* was used as a synonym for virtuous, just, peace-loving, generous, etc., etc.[1] The norm was christian: "religion: none" was indeed not acceptable. Anti-Semitism was so intrinsic as not to have a name. I don't recall exactly being taught that the Jews killed Jesus—"Christ killer" seems too strong a term for the bland Episcopal vocabulary—but certainly we got the impression that the Jews had been caught out in a terrible mistake, failing to recognize the true Messiah, and were thereby less advanced in moral and spiritual sensibility. The Jews had actually allowed *moneylenders in the Temple* (again, the unexplained obsession with Jews and money). They were of the past, archaic, primitive, as older (and darker) cultures are supposed to be primitive; christianity was lightness, fairness, peace on earth, and combined the feminine appeal of "The meek shall inherit the earth" with the masculine stride of "Onward, Christian Soldiers."

Sometime in 1946, while still in high school, I read in the newspaper that a theater in Baltimore was showing films of the Allied liberation of the Nazi concentration camps. Alone, I went downtown after school one afternoon and watched the stark, blurry, but unmistakable newsreels. When I try to go back and touch the pulse of that girl of sixteen, growing up in many ways so precocious and so ignorant, I am overwhelmed by a memory of despair, a sense of inevitability more enveloping than any I had ever known. Anne Frank's diary and many other personal narratives of the Holocaust were still unknown or unwritten. But it came to me that every one of those piles of corpses, mountains of shoes and clothing had contained, simply, individuals, who had believed, as I now believed of myself, that they were intended to live out a life of some kind of meaning, that the world possessed some kind of sense and order; yet *this* had happened to them. And I, who believed my life was intended to be so interesting and meaningful, was connected to those dead by something—not just mortality but a taboo name, a hated identity. Or was I—did I really have to be? Writing this now, I feel belated rage that I was so impoverished by the family and social

---

[1] In a similar way the phrase "That's white of you" implied that you were behaving with the superior decency and morality expected of white but not of Black people.

worlds I lived in, that I had to try to figure out by myself what this did indeed mean for me. That I had never been taught about resistance, only about passing. That I had no language for anti-Semitism itself.

When I went home and told my parents where I had been, they were not pleased. I felt accused of being morbidly curious, not healthy, sniffing around death for the thrill of it. And since, at sixteen, I was often not sure of the sources of my feelings or of my motives for doing what I did, I probably accused myself as well. One thing was clear: there was nobody in my world with whom I could discuss those films. Probably at the same time, I was reading accounts of the camps in magazines and newspapers; what I remember were the films and having questions that I could not even phrase, such as *Are those men and women "them" or "us"?*

To be able to ask even the child's astonished question *Why do they hate us so?* means knowing how to say "we." The guilt of not knowing, the guilt of perhaps having betrayed my parents or even those victims, those survivors, through mere curiosity—these also froze in me for years the impulse to find out more about the Holocaust.

1947: I left Baltimore to go to college in Cambridge, Massachusetts, left (I thought) the backward, enervating South for the intellectual, vital North. New England also had for me some vibration of higher moral rectitude, of moral passion even, with its seventeenth-century Puritan self-scrutiny, its nineteenth-century literary "flowering," its abolitionist righteousness, Colonel Shaw and his Black Civil War regiment depicted in granite on Boston Common. At the same time, I found myself, at Radcliffe, among Jewish women. I used to sit for hours over coffee with what I thought of as the "real" Jewish students, who told me about middle-class Jewish culture in America. I described my background—for the first time to strangers—and they took me on, some with amusement at my illiteracy, some arguing that I could never marry into a strict Jewish family, some convinced I didn't "look Jewish," others that I did. I learned the names of holidays and foods, which surnames are Jewish and which are "changed names"; about girls who had had their noses "fixed," their hair straightened. For these young Jewish women, students in the late 1940s, it was acceptable, perhaps even necessary, to strive to look as gentile as possible; but they stuck proudly to being Jewish, expected to marry a Jew, have children, keep the holidays, carry on the culture.

I felt I was testing a forbidden current, that there was danger in these revelations. I bought a reproduction of a Chagall portrait of a rabbi in striped prayer shawl and hung it on the wall of my room. I was admittedly young and trying to educate myself, but I was also doing something that *is* dangerous: I was flirting with identity.

One day that year I was in a small shop where I had bought a dress with a too-long skirt. The shop employed a seamstress who did alterations, and she came in to pin up the skirt on me. I am sure that she was a recent immigrant, a survivor. I remember a short, dark woman wearing heavy glasses, with an accent so foreign I could not understand her words. Something about her presence was very powerful and disturbing to me. After marking and pinning up the skirt, she sat back on her knees, looked up at me, and asked in a hurried whisper: "You Jewish?" Eighteen years of training in assimilation sprang into the reflex by which I shook my head, rejecting her, and muttered, "No."

What was I actually saying "no" to? She was poor, older, struggling with a foreign tongue, anxious; she had escaped the death that had been intended for her, but I had no imagination of her possible courage and foresight, her resistance—I did not see in her a heroine who had perhaps saved many lives, including her own. I saw the frightened immigrant, the seamstress hemming the skirts of college girls, the wandering Jew. But I was an American college girl having her skirt hemmed. And I was frightened myself, I think, because she had recognized me ("It takes one to know one," my friend Edie at Radcliffe had said) even if I refused to recognize myself or her, even if her recognition was sharpened by loneliness or the need to feel safe with me.

But why should she have felt safe with me? I myself was living with a false sense of safety.

There are betrayals in my life that I have known at the very moment were betrayals: this was one of them. There are other betrayals committed so repeatedly, so mundanely, that they leave no memory trace behind, only a growing residue of misery, of dull, accreted self-hatred. Often these take the form not of words but of silence. Silence before the joke at which everyone is laughing; the anti-woman joke, the racist joke, the anti-Semitic joke. Silence and then amnesia. Blocking it out when the oppressor's language starts coming from the lips of one we admire, whose courage and eloquence have touched us: *She didn't really mean that; he didn't really say that.* But the accretions build up out of sight, like scale inside a kettle.

1948: I come home from my freshman year at college, flaming with new insights, new information. I am the daughter who has gone out into the world, to the pinnacle of intellectual prestige, Harvard, fulfilling my father's hopes for me, but also exposed to dangerous influences. I have already been reproved for attending a rally for Henry Wallace and the Progressive party. I challenge my father: "Why haven't you told me that I am Jewish? Why do you never talk about being a Jew?" He answers measurably, "You know that I have never denied that I am a Jew. But it's not important to me. I am a scientist, a deist. I have no use for organized religion. I choose to live in a world of many kinds of people. There are Jews I admire and others whom I despise, I am a person, not simply a Jew." The words are as I remember them, not perhaps exactly as spoken. But that was the message. And it contained enough truth—as all denial drugs itself on partial truth—so that it remained for the time being unanswerable, leaving me high and dry, split at the root, gasping for clarity, for air.

At that time Arnold Rich was living in suspension, waiting to be appointed to the professorship of pathology at Johns Hopkins. The appointment was delayed for years, no Jew ever having held a professional chair in that medical school. And he wanted it badly. It must have been a very bitter time for him, since he had believed so greatly in the redeeming power of excellence, of being the most brilliant, inspired man for the job. With enough excellence, you could presumably make it stop mattering that you were Jewish; you could become the *only* Jew in the gentile world, a Jew so "civilized," so far from "common," so attractively combining southern gentility with European cultural values that no one would ever confuse you with the raw, "pushy" Jews of New York, the "loud, hysterical" refugees from eastern Europe, the "overdressed" Jews of the urban South.

We—my sister, mother, and I—were constantly urged to speak quietly in public, to dress without ostentation, to repress all vividness or spontaneity, to assimilate with a world which might see us as too flamboyant. I suppose that my mother, pure gentile though she was, could be seen as acting "common" or "Jewish" if she laughed too loudly or spoke aggressively. My father's mother, who lived with us half the year, was a model of circumspect behavior, dressed in dark blue or lavender, retiring in company, ladylike to an extreme, wearing no jewelry except a good gold chain, a narrow brooch, or a string of pearls. A few times, within the family, I saw her anger flare, felt the passion she was repressing. But when Arnold took us out to a restaurant or on a trip, the Rich women were always tuned down to some WASP level my father believed, surely, would protect us all—maybe also make us unrecognizable to the "real Jews" who wanted to seize us, drag us back to the *shtetl*, the ghetto, in its many manifestations.

For, yes, that *was* a message—that some Jews would be after you, once they "knew," to rejoin them, to re-enter a world that was messy, noisy, unpredictable, maybe poor—"even though," as my mother once wrote me, criticizing my largely Jewish choice of friends in college, "some of them will be the most brilliant, fascinating people you'll ever meet." I wonder if that isn't one message of assimilation—of America—that the unlucky or the un-achieving want to pull you backward, that to identify with them is to court downward mobility, lose the precious chance of passing, of token existence. There was always within this sense of Jewish identity a strong class discrimination. Jews might be "fascinating" as individuals but came with huge unruly families who "poured chicken soup over everyone's head" (in the phrase of a white southern male poet). Anti-Semitism could thus be justified by the bad behavior of certain Jews; and if you did not effectively deny family and community, there would always be a remote cousin claiming kinship with you who was the "wrong kind" of Jew.

I have always believed his attitude toward other Jews depended on who they were. . . . It was my impression that Jews of this background looked down on Eastern European Jews, including Polish Jews and Russian Jews, who generally were not as well educated. This from a letter written to me recently by a gentile who had worked in my father's department, whom I had asked about anti-Semitism there and in particular regarding my father. This informant also wrote me that it was hard to perceive anti-Semitism in Baltimore because the racism made so much more intense an impression: *I would almost have to think that blacks went to a different heaven than the whites, because the bodies were kept in a separate morgue, and some white persons did not even want blood transfusions from black donors.* My father's mind was predictably racist and misogynist; yet as a medical student he noted in his journal that southern male chivalry stopped at the point of any white man in a streetcar giving his seat to an old, weary Black woman standing in the aisle. Was this a Jewish insight—an outsider's insight, even though the outsider was striving to be on the inside?

Because what isn't named is often more permeating than what is, I believe that my father's Jewishness profoundly shaped my own identity and our family existence. They were shaped both by external anti-Semitism and my father's self-hatred, and by his Jewish pride. What Arnold did, I think, was call his Jewish pride something else: achievement, aspiration, genius, idealism. Whatever was unacceptable got left back under the rubric of Jewishness or the "wrong kind" of Jews—uneducated, aggressive, loud. The message I got was that we were really superior: nobody else's father had collected so many books, had traveled so far, knew so many languages. Baltimore was a musical city, but for the most part, in the families of my school friends, culture was for women. My father was an amateur musician, read poetry, adored encyclopedic knowledge. He prowled and pounced over my school papers, insisting I use "grownup" sources; he criticized my poems for faulty technique and gave me books on rhyme and meter and form. His investment in my intellect and talent was egotistical, tyrannical, opinionated, and terribly wearing. He taught me, nevertheless, to believe in hard work, to mistrust easy inspiration, to write and rewrite; to feel that I *was* a person of the book, even though a woman; to take ideas seriously. He made me feel, at a very young age, the power of language and that I could share in it.

The Riches were proud, but we also had to be very careful. Our behavior had to be more impeccable than other people's. Strangers were not to be trusted, nor even friends; family issues must never go beyond the family; the world was full of potential slanderers, betrayers, *people who could not understand.* Even within the family, I realize that I never in my whole life knew what my father was really feeling. Yet he spoke— monologued—with driving intensity. You could grow up in such a house mesmerized by the local electricity, the crucial meanings assumed by the merest things. This used to seem to me a sign that we were all living on some high emotional plane. It was a difficult force field for a favored daughter to disengage from.

Easy to call that intensity Jewish; and I have no doubt that passion is one of the qualities required for survival over generations of persecution. But what happens when passion is rent from its original base, when the white gentile world is softly saying "Be more like us and you can be almost one of us"? What happens when survival seems to mean closing off one emotional artery after another? His forebears in Europe had been forbidden to travel or expelled from one country after another, had special taxes levied on them if they left the city walls, had been forced to wear special clothes and badges, restricted to the poorest neighborhoods. He had wanted to be a "free spirit," to travel widely, among "all kinds of people." Yet in his prime of life he lived in an increasingly withdrawn world, in his house up on a hill in a neighborhood where Jews were not supposed to be able to buy property, depending almost exclusively on interactions with his wife and daughters to provide emotional connectedness. In his home, he created a private defense system so elaborate that even as he was dying, my mother felt unable to talk freely with his colleagues or others who might have helped her. Of course, she acquiesced in this.

The loneliness of the "only," the token, often doesn't feel like loneliness but like a kind of dead echo chamber. Certain things that ought to don't resonate. Somewhere Beverly Smith writes of women of color "inspiring the behavior" in each other. When there's nobody to "inspire the behavior, "act out of the culture, there is an atrophy, a dwindling, which is partly invisible.

Sometimes I feel I have seen too long from too many disconnected angles: white, Jewish, anti-Semite, racist, anti-racist, once-married, lesbian, middle-class, feminist, exmatriate southerner, *split at the root*—that I will never bring them whole. I would have liked, in this essay, to bring together the meanings of anti-Semitism and racism as I have experienced them and as I believe they intersect in the world beyond my life. But I'm not able to do this yet. I feel the tension as I think, make notes: *If you really look at the one reality, the other will waver and disperse.* Trying in one week to read Angela Davis° and Lucy Davidowicz°; trying to hold throughout to a feminist, a lesbian, perspective—what does this mean? Nothing has trained me for this. And sometimes I feel inadequate to make any statement as a Jew; I feel the history of denial within me like an injury, a scar. For assimilation has affected *my* perceptions; those early lapses in meaning, those blanks, are with me still. My ignorance can be dangerous to me and to others.

Yet we can't wait for the undamaged to make our connections for us; we can't wait to speak until we are perfectly clear and righteous. There is no purity and, in our lifetimes, no end to this process.

This essay, then, has no conclusions: it is another beginning for me. Not just a way of saying, in 1982 Right Wing America, *I, too, will wear the yellow star.* It's a moving into accountability, enlarging the range of accountability. I know that in the rest of my life, the next half century or so, every aspect of my identity will have to be engaged. The middle-class white girl taught to trade obedience for privilege. The Jewish lesbian raised to be a heterosexual gentile. The woman who first heard oppression named and analyzed in the Black Civil Rights struggle. The woman with three sons, the feminist who hates male violence. The woman limping with a cane, the woman who has stopped bleeding are also accountable. The poet who knows that beautiful language can lie, that the oppressor's language sometimes sounds beautiful. The woman trying, as part of her resistance, to clean up her act.

Angela Davis: American political activist who supported Marxism and the rights of women and Blacks. A philosophy professor at the University of California, she wrote *Women, Race, and Class* (1981) and *Women, Culture, and Politics* (1989).

Lucy S. Davidowicz: wrote about anti-Semitism and the slaughter of the Jews by the Nazis during the Second World War in *The War against the Jews 1933–1945* (1979)

Olive Senior

[W]e have become so caught up in the 'satellite culture' that our true indigenous cultures—which just began to be explored at the time of independence—are being swept away or ignored. And you wonder, who are we going to be down the road if we don't have something of our own to cling to?

One of the things I want my writing to do is to paint to the world a picture of Caribbean people as real people, because a lot of people, the images they have of us are real stereotype images.

—Olive Senior, quoted in *Sunday Guardian*

born in 1941 to peasant farmers in rural Jamaica—"really in the bush," as she told writer Lisa Allen-Agnostini—Olive Senior attended school in Montego Bay and later worked for Jamaica's main newspaper, *The Daily Gleaner*, in Kingston. She left Jamaica to study journalism at Ottawa's Carleton University, graduating in 1967. For many years, she worked as the editor of *Jamaica Journal* and as the managing director of the Institute of Jamaica Publications Ltd. She has been awarded the Institute of Jamaica Centenary Medal for Creative Writing and the Commonwealth Prize for Fiction for her first collection of short stories, *Summer Lightning* (1987). In addition to her poetry and short fiction, Senior is the author of several works of non-fiction, including a Jamaican encyclopedia: *A-Z of Jamaican Heritage* (1984; she was recently working on a revision). She currently lives in Toronto but she has worked as writer-in-residence and visiting professor of creative writing at a number of universities in Canada and the United States.

In both her stories and poetry, Senior describes the landscape, culture and history of Jamaica, exploring the tensions between rural and urban life, between old ways and new ones. A recurring theme is the impact of British colonialism on Jamaican society. Senior believes it is important for those writing in a region "still working out a definition of its own essence" to present the serious concerns of their societies. Stories written simply to entertain "are the product of places like the U.S. where writers can afford that luxury" (Allen-Agnostini 2).

In both poetry and stories, Senior has proven herself adept at re-creating the rhythms of Jamaican patois and interweaving it with Standard English. In a review of Senior's most recent story collection, *Discerner of Hearts*, Carrol Fleming describes the stories as "exquisitely wrought," and remarks on the transforming power of language in Senior's fiction: "Her characters become real through speech, through their efforts to talk sense about an unjust world. The stories seem to offer language itself, the communicative act, as balm, as recompense" (1).

Works Cited

Allen-Agnostini, Lisa. "Olive Senior: An Embodiment of Conflict." *Sunday Guardian*. 12 March 2000: 19.
   www.nalis.gov.tt/Biography/bio_OLIVESENIOR

Fleming, Carrol. "Olive Senior, Discerner of Hearts."
   rps.uvi.edu/CaribbeanWriter/volume11/discernerofhearts.html

Other Sources and Weblinks

Benson, Eugene, and L.W. Conolly. *The Encyclopedia of Post-Colonial Literatures in English*. Vol. 2. New York: Routledge, 1994. 1436–7.
   www.humbolt.edu/~wjh4/olivebio.htmlcrit.html

Markham, E.A., ed. *The Penguin Book of Caribbean Short Stories*. London: Penguin, 1996.

"Olive Senior: Biography." *Commonwealth Resource Centre*. Dec. 1999.
   www.commonwealth.org.uk/resource/litcol/commonplaces/Senior/ seniorbio.htm"

Colonial Girls School

Borrowed images
willed our skins pale
muffled our laughter
lowered our voices
let out our hems
dekinked our hair
denied our sex in gym tunics and bloomers
harnessed our voices to madrigals
and genteel airs
yoked our minds to declensions in Latin
and the language of Shakespeare

Told us nothing about ourselves
There was nothing about us at all

How those pale northern eyes and
aristocratic whispers once erased us
How our loudness, our laughter
debased us

There was nothing left of ourselves
Nothing about us at all

Studying: *History Ancient and Modern*
Kings and Queens of England
Steppes of Russia
Wheatfields of Canada

There was nothing of our landscape there
Nothing about us at all

Marcus Garvey° turned twice in his grave.
'Thirty-eight was a beacon. A flame.
They were talking of desegregation
in Little Rock, Arkansas. Lumumba°
and the Congo. To us: mumbo-jumbo.
We had read Vachel Lindsay's °
vision of the jungle

Feeling nothing about ourselves
There was nothing about us at all

Months, years, a childhood memorising
Latin declensions
(For our language
—'bad talking'—
detentions)

Finding nothing about us there
Nothing about us at all

So, friend of my childhood years
One day we'll talk about
How the mirror broke
Who kissed us awake
Who let Anansi° from his bag

For isn't it strange how
northern eyes
in the brighter world before us now

Pale?

Marcus Garvey: See note in Michelle Cliff, "If I Could Write This in Fire, . . ." p. 22

Lumumba: Patrice Lumumba (1925-61) was president of the Congolese National Movement and active in the drive for the independence of the Congo from Belgium. When the independent Republic of the Congo was declared (June 1960), he became its first premier and minister of defence.

Vachel Lindsay: (1879-1931) American poet seen as modern troubadour—romantic, wandering reciter of poetry

Anansi: Caribbean trickster figure, something like Coyote in Amerindian folklore

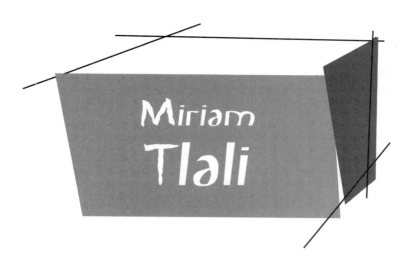

Miriam Tlali

born in Johannesburg in the early 1930s, Miriam Tlali grew up in South Africa during the period when its policy of racial segregation and white supremacy hardened into apartheid with the election in 1948 of the National Party. Under apartheid, people were classified into three major racial groups: white, Bantu or Black Africans, and Coloured—people of mixed descent. A fourth category, Asians (largely Indians and Pakistanis), was added later. An individual's place of residence, education and job prospects were determined by his or her membership in a particular racial category and virtually any social contact between races was prohibited by law. The group who suffered the greatest hardships and were the most restricted in their choices were Black Africans. Coloured people and Asians enjoyed considerably more freedom and economic and educational opportunities (hence, in the story, Velani's uncle's interest in being thought "coloured" instead of Black). With the advent of apartheid, Tlali, a student at the University of the Witwatersrand, was obliged to withdraw when the institution decided to exclude Black students. She subsequently studied at Roma University in Lesotho, but financial difficulties forced her to quit before graduating.

A stint as a clerk/typist in Johannesburg furnished Tlali with the material for her semi-autobiographical novel *Muriel at Metropolitan,* which was published in 1975, the first novel published in South Africa by a Black woman. Her second novel, *Amandla* (1982), is about the Black Johannesburg satellite city of Soweto and was banned by the apartheid regime almost immediately upon publication. It was followed in 1989 by the publication in Britain of *Soweto Stories* (titled *Footprints in the Quag°: Stories and Dialogues from Soweto* in its South African edition). This is where "Metamorphosis," the story that follows, first appeared. In addition to her fiction, Tlali has worked as a journalist, contributing columns and interviews

Quag: a quagmire or bog

to the radical arts journal *Staffrider,* and as the editor of a literary magazine for women called *Straight Ahead International.*

Like much of Tlali's fiction, "Metamorphosis" is set in Soweto, where she has lived for much of her life. She was born in Dorfontein and grew up in Sophiatown. The Native Resettlement Act of 1954 called for the demolition of Sophiatown to enable the creation of a white suburb. Despite the efforts of local protestors, Sophiatown was razed in 1955 and its Black residents relocated to Soweto. Comprising an area of roughly sixty-four square kilometres, Soweto (the name is an acronym for South Western Townships) was characterised by its extreme poverty, its paucity of public services and its high crime rate. (The police, concerned only with crime affecting whites, left it virtually unpoliced.) Developed in the 1940s to accommodate Black workers in the local gold mines, it became the home for the majority of the Black population of Johannesburg. In 1976, Soweto was the site of a violent uprising which began as a protest by students against the use of the Afrikaans° language in schools. The protest spread to other Black urban areas and broadened its focus to become a revolt against the government's policy of apartheid. More than six hundred people were killed when the army was called in to quell the riots. The Soweto riots became a byword in the growing campaign to overthrow apartheid rule.

Works Cited

"Apartheid." *Microsoft Encarta Online Encyclopedia 2000.* **encarta.msn.com. 1997–2000 Microsoft Corporation.**

"Huddleston, Trevor." *Microsoft Encarta Online Encyclopedia 2000.* **encarta.msn.com**

Oosthuizen, Ann, ed. *Sometimes When It Rains.* London and New York: Pandora, 1987.

Weblinks

"Miriam Tlali."
www.arts.uwa.edu.au/AFLIT/TlaliFR.html
www.his.no/aud/hum/afrika.htm

Afrikaans: developed from Dutch, one of two official languages of apartheid South Africa— the other was English.

Metamorphosis

The narrow streets tapered even more towards the west where the sunken sun had left a beautiful golden glow barely visible in the grey smog. Velani noticed the crimson ardour only because he—out of impulse—had decided to remain seated in his Volkswagen Golf. One never really noticed the setting sun's beauty in Soweto. He shut his eyes and tried to listen to the music from the car radio.

He was waiting. He looked around. His car was parked near the gate of house No. 2249. In this township of Mapetla there were no numbers on the doors. They had been erased with white paint. The houses were faceless, mute matchboxes, Velani thought, smiling. The comrades had done a perfect job of it. It was amazing how these youths thought of everything to befuddle the system. If he had been a stranger and did not know his uncle's house, he would have been completely at a loss as to which one of the rows of similar matchboxes on either side of the dusty road it was. His wife, Mavis, a district nurse, had often spoken of developments in and around the townships but he had never really taken everything seriously. All she said had been just a lot of woman-talk. Even at the spot which he frequented, the Suzzie's Haunt, people had alluded casually to 'incidents' but he always thought there were more serious matters a man could think of. He recalled that Mavis had once said that it was important for the struggle that we be one thing, no one should be labelled 'good' or 'bad' by the authorities, that injury to the one must be injury to the next. 'After all,' they say, 'we are all black; we all belong to the soil. Besides, we are all oppressed. An attack on the one must be an attack on all.'

Velani tried to listen to the music but the kids in the street were excited. They were frolicking around, jumping and chasing one another. He looked through the window and clicked his tongue loudly. He shut the window and closed his eyes. It was becoming dark and he was sitting there waiting for his mother—affectionately known as Aunt Tillie (for Matilda)—and his sister Tembi. He spoke to himself: 'Waiting . . . Ngisalindile namanje°, I'm still waiting even now. You always have to wait for abantu bes'fazane, womenfolk. They never seem to get over what they are doing. It doesn't matter whether it's talking, washing their faces, exchanging greetings, even praying . . . I bet they're on their knees right now, praying "Nkulunkul'

Ngisalindile namanje: in "Tsotsi Taal," a blending of languages used by the comrades during the uprisings against the apartheid regime: "I am waiting even now" N.B. In South Africa—especially in the Gauteng Province in and around Soweto (where the resistance movements against apartheid usually excelled in their intensity) —the dialect known as "tsotsi-taal" is generally spoken by the youth. This dialect is a concoction of many of the African languages and it also has many words and phrases borrowed from (mainly) Afrikaans—a language that originated from (mainly) Dutch and English. Hence "taal" is an Afrikaans word meaning "language," and the youth who speak this concocted language are referred to as "tsotsi's."

olungile-e-e-eyo. . . Nkulunkul' olungile-e-eyo!" (merciful God . . . merciful God!). He shook his head vigorously. And this was Friday mind you, he thought regretfully; Friday, the day on which he and the 'MaGents' would normally be 'in conference,' enjoying good music, chatting the night away over a c-o-o-l beer.

It was his own fault, Velani thought regretfully. What on earth had made him go via his mother's house anyway? Somehow his dear mother never seemed to hesitate to send him off on one errand or another. On this day, he had tried to dissuade her. He had emphasized, 'You know, Ma, that I never refuse to drive you to U-Malume (Uncle's place). But *today* . . . it's not safe to drive to Deep Soweto, surely you *know* that Ma. Moreover, travelling there with two abantu bes'fazane . . . If you were *men*, yes: but abantu bes'fazane . . . He shook his head . . . 'Hayi, hayi, hayi.'

To which his mother replied, 'But Velie, you rarely ever come except in the late hours. In fact, this time you're early. And you *know* that unless you drive me to U-Malume's place I can never hope to see him. Besides, I don't think I can have a good night's sleep when a message came this morning that your Uncle Bafana is very ill indeed. Who knows what can happen? Even *he* would rush here if he received news that I was on the brink of . . .' She dared not mention 'Death,' no: not her beloved brother Bafana. She had pleaded, 'Please my son, drive me there. Your sister Tembi can help me walk.'

Velani tried to drive his point home. He added, smiling, 'But you three are the ones . . . Your daughter-in-law Mavis, your daughter Tembi and *you*, Ma . . . You three are the ones always speaking about ama-necklace°, a-Makabasa, ama-Comrades yonke lento° and now . . .'

His mother interjected, waving apologetically, 'Velie, Bafana is my own brother, my mother's and my father's only other living child. His end is near; I can feel it. You don't seem to realize that it's only the two of us left now. When he goes, I'll be left alone.'

Tembi, who had been busy in the bedroom, was now standing at the entrance to the dining room, listening and smiling. She anticipated what Velani was going to say and the two were amused. He said, 'Why Ma always says "only the two of us are left" I don't know. Doesn't Ma also have another brother in Eldorado Park'? What about *him*? Just the other day I passed at the coloured township with a friend of mine who wanted to have his car panel beaten by Uncle Boetie—Uncle Mbuti to be correct. Isn't he also your very own mother's and father's son? Why do you always exclude him as if he doesn't exist?'

Ama-necklace: During the Soweto uprisings of the 1970s and 80s, it was common practice for the activists to eliminate the "sell-outs" or "traitors" (who operated amongst the Africans for the system of apartheid) by putting tyres round their necks and setting them alight. The practice was known as "necklacing." N.B. "Ama" is an Nguni prefix that denotes plurality. Therefore, "i-necklace" means one necklace, and "ama-necklace" means two or more or many necklaces.)

"a-Makabasa, ama-Comrades yonke lento": Kabasas (or vigilantes), comrades, all these "things."

Aunt Tillie's two children were relieved that in spite of their mother's sadness, there was a smile on her face as she replied, 'You two know the answer to that one. I have told you on many occasions that it is because we all have to remember always to refer to him as Uncle Boetie McCabel and not Mbuti Mkhabela. He does not want to be exposed and known as unyana ka Mkhabela (son of Mkhabela). That, as you very well know, would take the bread out of his mouth. In this country, it is only the fairer ones who eat, don't you know?'

The three were now ready to go, Tembi following her brother on whose arm their mother was leaning. As she clung to the strong biceps of her son, Aunt Tillie felt safe and she moved slowly and confidently over the uneven bricks of the pathway leading to the Volksie. When she was seated comfortably on the back seat, Velani took the travelling rug Tembi was holding and tucked it gently around his mother's knees. He smiled into his mother's face. It was a strong, stoic and steadfast face which, to both her children, never seemed to yield to the vicissitudes of life and the inevitable hazards of ageing.

The radio blared away and Velani listened and watched as the red arm on the car-watch ticked the seconds on and on. His boot tapped almost unconsciously to the rhythm of the song and he kept his eyes closed. When the music stopped, he opened his eyes and looked through the windscreen into the thick grey smog which competed with the dotted heaps of garbage, ash and rubbish of every description. The unsightly mounds formed a screen on the narrow end of the road where a short while ago he had watched the rosy hue of the setting sun. Velani clicked his tongue again and kept his eyes focused on the faintly illuminated dashboard. The record had stopped. Velani wished that the rather too enthusiastic announcer would stop his remarks and let the bands play on without stopping. He stretched his arm, clicking his tongue once more. He reached for the dial-knob and moved the needle from so-called Radio Zulu to so-called Radio Bophuthatswana°. He scoffed loudly, 'These howlers should be fired!'

On Radio Bop a drumming thumping hit was playing and Velani smiled as he twisted his torso, rolling his eyes dreamily in sheer ecstasy. The boredom he had experienced a while ago seemed to wear away.

When Velani opened his eyes again, the sun had gone completely, leaving the sky dull and murky, with the thick smog hanging as if suspended in mid-air from some invisible frame. He knew that no breeze would clear the dense menace.

It was quite dark outside in the street now, and the people kept passing. Their footsteps were more brisk. Velani could only just make out from their obscure silhouettes that they were men, women and children. He remembered that it was Friday, and on Friday night people hurry home to

Bophuthatswana: one of the Black "homelands" established by the apartheid state to segregate Black people and ensure they had no access to the political process. The "homelands" tended to be arid wastes on which it was almost impossible to farm effectively.

the safety of their matchboxes. Only the brave and daring ones remain. The footsteps were awkward and now and again Velani could hear a woman's voice groan, 'Ichu-u-u!' as she stumbled, apparently knocking her toes against a stone. The rocky roads had been eroded by the rains into uneven footpaths and the jutting rocks were everywhere, merging with the wire fences on what should have been pavements but were now sloping irregular banks.

There was a loud thud on the window and Velani started. The knock was so close that it felt like it was from inside his own head. The dark figures on both sides of the car were peering eagerly. A quick glance around made Velani realize at once that the car was in fact completely surrounded by a number of youths. Most of them were wearing balaclavas with brims lowered over their eyebrows. Velani was shaken, but something within him told him that there was no need to fear, that he was not going to be intimidated because he was not born yesterday. He switched off the radio and asked furiously, 'What's the matter?'

There were several hard taps on all four side windows, and impatient shouts of, 'Vula, bula, bula!'

'What is it?' Velani asked.

'Vula, vula! Open the window or we break all of them!'

The youths meant business but Velani was no Mafikizolo. He would not give in to their demands. He looked around and asked, 'Why?'

Some of them replied, 'We would like to borrow your car. We have to attend a vigil of one of our boys who was shot dead by the police in Emdeni. Are you going to give us the car or not? Just open and let us in. You can drive us there if you want. Open!'

'No; I won't!' Velani shouted back, determined to hold his ground.

The car rocked uncomfortably on to one side and he felt his stomach fold into a knot. His heart beat faster and the sweat ran down his temples and forehead. There was an even louder chorus from outside: 'Open!'

This was real trouble. Had his ancestors turned their backs on *him*, Velani, who was never a coward? But even if he tried to fight the mob he would never overpower them. They were too many. They were wielding knives, sharp instruments and iron bars. He just could not understand it. The stark shocking reality of what he had up to then only imagined was happening to *him*; he, Velani, a 'clever' of Soweto . . . No, it can't. Not to *him*. He shouted stubbornly, 'I won't open!'

Again the car rocked uneasily as if it were resting on foam; and his entrails felt like they were suspended in a jelly-like fluid. He felt sick. What was he to do? According to what he knew, from what he heard from his wife, his mother and his sister, in fact all those who made it their business to attend the people's meetings, no right-thinking comrades would do that, not to *him*. Wasn't he a well-known clever with all the power of a real man? He *had* to be a man. He challenged them, 'Do what you like; I won't open!'

Crash! came the violent sound. Velani looked back and saw that the rear window was now a mosaic of broken glass. In the centre was a gaping hole as big as the fist of a full-grown man where a heavy steel bar had landed. The bloodshot vicious eyeballs of one of the assailants peered at him through the window next to him. He pointed a clenched menacing fist at Velani, threatening, 'Sizak'nyova thi-ina, grootman uyezwa? Uyacu-u-uga ne?'°

A whistle . . . a whistle . . . If only he could sound a loud SOS. Call someone, everybody, anybody to come to his assistance. Had his mother, his sister, his wife, all those who attended the people's meetings not warned him to carry a whistle wherever he went? And *that* he thought was only woman-talk . . . sheer cowardice. But now he had to act. His life, his beloved Volksie . . . All these thoughts raced through his mind in a flash. He *had* to do something. In that state of uncertainty and fear, his manly thumb groped for the hooter and pressed it down . . . hard. The car came down with a clamorous bang, and only then did he realize that the youths were going to turn it over.

His call had aroused people inside nearby houses. Doors and windows were flung open. Tembi was the first one to emerge, from his uncle's home nearby. Her shrill voice pierced through the dark night, making an urgent appeal for help. Whistle sounds from windows all around permeated through the thick smog, sending alarm signals in all directions.

Velani knew that it was the women—mothers, sisters, wives—who were blowing the whistles. At that moment he seemed to hear the voice of his wife sound the resolve of the people in distress: 'The system does not care. All they want is to exploit us. They will never go out of their way to protect us. Stand together and fight as one. They are guarding the borders and hunting for so-called terrorists like you look for a needle in a haystack. Blackman, you're on your own. Only *you* can root out the evil in our midst and its hired lackeys who are only there to confuse the people: to distract them from the real enemy . . .'

It was bad for the marauding youths. Velani watched them still in a state of complete paralysis and shock. They sauntered away in all directions, some dropping their weapons as they scaled over the dilapidated fences into the adjoining streets and vanished.

'Cowards!' Velani cursed, spitting through the window which he had now opened to assure the converging people that *he*, Velani, was safe and sound.

'Soweto is a jungle. I don't know what you want there. You should come to Eldorado Park. We coloureds here are safe!'

Velani remembered the words of hope his uncle had often whispered to him when he paid him a business call. None of Boetie McCabel's neighbours and friends had ever suspected that he was in fact an African who, according to the South African divide-and-rule laws, should have

---

"Sizak'nyova thi-ina, grootman uyezwa? Uyacu-u-uga ne?": "we will kill you, big man, why are you so stubborn?"

been in Soweto. Who could have known that he was Mbuti Mkha-bela? On his not-so-frequent visits to his uncle in Eldorado Park, Velani had been like all McCabel's African customers from Soweto. From a struggling start, Uncle Boetie's panelbeaters had flourished over the twenty-five years in that township. Only his fair-skinned wife had known the secret and she had vowed to keep it from anyone's 'prying' ears.

Very often now, while he lay in bed thinking, Velani became increasingly uneasy. All right, he had fitted on a new rear window to his Volksie . . . But what of the future? He was a traveller and often he did not sleep at home. The fences surrounding his house were not so good either. It would cost a fortune to erect good ones. The people were not paying rent. To do that would be to risk getting a necklace. The signs were all over . . . 'YOU PAY, WE BURN.' Who would risk that? Perhaps it was a good thing to leave Soweto and go to Eldorado Park after all.

Once while he lay awake in bed with his mind besieged by these thoughts, he patted his wife Mavis's shoulder gently to make a suggestion to her. She had just fallen asleep lightly. She grunted, 'Hm?' Her eyelids already heavy, she asked, 'What's the matter?'

At least Mavis was willing to listen. Velani thought, his mind already excited by what he had to tell her. He asked, 'What if we pack up everything and go to Eldorado, May?'

Mavis was now fully awake. She replied, 'Velie, are you dreaming? Eldorado is somewhere in North America. Where have you ever heard of someone leaving Soweto to go and live so far away . . . even if one were crazy enough to think he or she could afford the plane ticket, let alone get a passport from the Boers°?'

Velani answered anxiously, 'No. I mean the Eldorado next to us; next to Soweto, on the other side of Kliptown, May, please. Things are so difficult for us here now. Look, the car, the house, everything.'

'Heyi wena, are you crazy, what's wrong with you anyway? Why do you think you can run away from the struggle?'

Mavis shook her head in disbelief. Somehow she felt grateful. 'At least he is worried,' she said to herself. That silly suggestion he had made meant that he was restless. How long had she wished that Velani would stop floating around in a cloud of self-deception and concern himself with what was happening? He would never even listen to what she had to say whenever she came from the people's meetings. She sighed, 'The struggle is everywhere, Vene.'

'But the people in Eldorado lead normal lives. They pay rent, electricity bills and water. Their houses still have the numbers. Everything is going on smoothly.'

'So you think if you do that—run away to Eldorado—you'll be safe? Okay, you want a house with a number so that the police, the army, the

Boers: a Dutch word meaning "farmers"; the descendants of Dutch settlers who intermarried with other European colonists; the primary speakers of Afrikaans

council messengers can spot you easily. You want to eat, sleep and drink in their safe hands . . . What about those who cannot run away? Do you think you can build an island of comfort and safety around you when everyone else is oppressed? Not even the Boers still think they can.'

But Velani's coloured uncle's voice haunted him, and the harder he tried to forget it now of late, the more it goaded him: 'Leave that Soweto and come to Eldorado. The Immigration Control Laws°, the 101 (a)s, (b)s. (c)s are all suspended. They are scrapped for good. You can live anywhere you like now. Save your neck and your property. Come to our coloured township. Come to Eldorado.'

Velani could not remember when he finally fell asleep.

Whether Velani's ancestors had turned their backs towards him, he did not know. It had happened again. His beloved Volksie had gone—grabbed from him at gunpoint. This time he decided that he would take his uncle's advice.

It had been seven months since he had last spoken to his Eldorado uncle. The fact that Uncle Boetie had not even bothered to attend the funeral of his own brother Bafana in Mapetla, Soweto, had made him bitter towards him. If Eldorado made him insensitive towards his own people then it was not worth living there. Perhaps Mavis was right after all. That was before the whole 'ibadi' (bad luck) happened again.

But now it had happened. His nice little Volksie had gone, taken from him by an unscrupulous mob of youngsters in broad daylight. Where did they get the guns from anyway? He had been chatting away at Suzzie's Haunt and some time late in the afternoon, he decided to go to S'godiphola. In the bare veld overlooking the township he saw the youths who came into the road blocking him from passing. Something within him told him to run straight into them, but his dazed mind would not think straight. He slowed down when something inside him snapped with anger. He thought that if they attacked him outside, then he had a good chance of confusing them. It was only after he had slowed down that he realized they were armed.

It was the next day. Velani could think clearly. He asked Mavis to go to work and leave him to his thoughts. If he were left alone, he would be able to figure out just how it happened.

He sat alone, his mind putting the pieces together.

After the no-good hoodlums had knocked him unconscious, they sped off in his Volksie leaving him lying there. Some good Samaritan—also a regular customer at Suzzie's Haunt—recognized him and picked him up. With some of their friends, they decided to take Velani first to the police station to report the loss of his car. When he, Velani, had regained consciousness, he pleaded with his friends that he would rather go and report the matter to the police than go home 'on foot' to face his wife Mavis. They immediately rushed him to the nearby Moroka Police Station.

Immigration Control Laws: clauses dictating precisely where Black people could/could not live

Never in his life had Velani seen so many people lined up in a small room waiting to be served. All of them had lost their cars. They all had sad stories to tell. Even sobbing women were there. Some of them had also been raped. It is only when you have your personal share of pain that you know what it is like to be pierced. Velani listened. His sense of loss had made him sober. He wondered how it was still possible for some of these people to speak about the pain at all, with their hearts still bleeding. He listened, absent-minded. The two men next to him, with homemade bandages tied around injured limbs, one an elbow and another his shin, rattled on in whispers. 'A friend of mine had his car interfered with and pushed away right out of his yard, mind you; and he could do nothing! They were armed, so what could he do?'

The other confirmed, nodding all the time, 'I *know*. Others are hijacked at intersections. And when you come to report here they tell you that there are no policemen to come to your aid, that they are short of them. I'm not surprised. How can they be everywhere? Zambia, Malawi, Zimbabwe, Botswana, the Bantustans, Swaziland, Lesotho, the border—all over . . . What are they—an octopus?'

'It is dangerous these days to stop at a robot. Even when it is red, just dash on!'

Some sat looking hopefully at the official on the other side of the desk. The bespectacled policeman looked up at the rows of anxious, exhausted faces while he kept reaching for dockets. He seemed polite and Velani wondered what had happened . . . He was thinking . . . A so-called 'kaffer-konstabel' polite? Never . . . or was it in keeping with the so-called reform process? . . . So this was what they meant by 'reform', eh? It was a rather annoying revelation; especially because he kept on reiterating to one complainant after another, 'We can only try to do our best, but we cannot make promises that you'll get your cars. Soweto is bad. Most of you I know have no insurance cover. Too many cars are stolen. The thieves work fast. They use false number plates and they spray the cars almost immediately. It is difficult to spot any stolen car from the descriptions you give . . . We are your friends. We are here to protect your property and your lives.'

The whole rhetoric sounded meaningless and hollow. The sad people's eyes and ears were open, but they remained stern and unimpressed. Velani knew that he would never see his car again. It was gone for good. He could feel it in his blood.

Velani knew what he would do. He would ring his Eldorado uncle and ask for advice. Perhaps he was right after all. What was the use of staying in Soweto? Who cares what happens to people in Soweto anyway? Certainly not the police or the so-called councillors or the lawmakers in Pretoria.

As he sat alone, thinking, he became more and more certain that Boetie McCabel was in fact his best adviser. He only had had the common sense to look into the problem facing the blacks—especially the Africans—and arriving at the best solution to it. Escape . . . escape from the jungle and draw closer to the well-provided-for world, the privileged one.

He reached for the telephone receiver and dialled the number impatiently, his brow sweating with excitement. It was the voice of a woman—possibly Mrs. McCabel which answered, 'Hello, kan ek u help?'

Velani replied, 'It's Mkhabela here, Ma'am. Can I speak to Mr. McCabel please?'

'Just hold on please, I'll call him . . . Boetie!' she yelled, placing the receiver on the table. McCabel rushed from the kitchen into the lounge.

Velie recognized his uncle's voice immediately. He whispered into the receiver, 'Hello, it's Velie, Uncle Boetie. I want to come to Eldorado. I have decided to take your advice.'

'Why now?'

'My Volksie is gone. They took it. Nothing is safe here. I want to come and live in Eldorado if . . .'

Before Velie could continue, McCabel interrupted, 'It's no use, Velie. The disease has spread all over. We also have comrades here. They want solidarity with the people of Soweto. They say they are returning to their roots. They have wiped off the numbers from the houses. They say unless we are one the struggle against the settlers is forever lost.'

'Stay where you are. Injury to one oppressed is injury to all, they say. We all have to change. Just like the police say, they cannot keep up with all the cases. Gangs of hooligans, encouraged and armed by the police themselves, are on the rampage and nobody really cares. All the police and army are really concerned about is tracking down the so-called terrorists. It comes from the police themselves. They say they are tired, overworked. People are no longer joining the police force. The few who are still there also want to go on strike. They want to run away and they don't know how to do it . . . Are you still there Velie?'

Without another word, Velie dropped the receiver and sank on to the sofa next to him. He sighed and whispered to himself, 'It's no use. Real protection will come from the people themselves. From now on, I'm with the people.'

Critical Focus Questions

1. Both Jack Hodgins and Matt Cohen present narrators who can be seen as arriving at a sense of identity by the end of the story. Are there similarities in their struggles to come to terms with their own identities? To what extent do their conclusions about the nature of identity differ?

2. Cultural theorist Homi Bhabha observes that, in *The Satanic Verses*, Salman Rushdie has reminded us that "the truest eye may now belong to the migrant's double vision." Without necessarily being "migrants," many of these authors can be seen to possess "double vision." Consider the nature and advantages of this vision in the work of Michelle Cliff, Adrienne Rich, Derek Walcott and Miriam Tlali. What are the difficulties created by such a split?

3. To what extent is identity presented as something chosen or constructed in the selections in this section? In which selections is it seen as something that is implicit or given that must be discovered or accepted?

4. This chapter includes both fiction and non-fiction prose as well as one poem. What are the advantages of each medium [form]? Is there something inherently appropriate in the approach chosen by each author to express his/her ideas? What are the effects of each medium on you as a reader?

5. Examine a short story by Chinua Achebe ("Girls at War" and "Civil Peace" are widely anthologized) in the light of his description of the function of the writer as teacher. How can his fiction be seen as an instrument for education? Does its didactic function interfere with its status as "pure" art?

6. Consider other fictional works in this chapter in terms of Achebe's argument. To what extent are they educational in Achebe's sense? Should serious fiction always teach?

7. Both Adrienne Rich and Matt Cohen write about the process of coming to terms with their Jewishness. Compare and contrast the experiences they describe. Do you think the fact that Rich is a woman makes her experience more difficult? Rich's piece is written as an essay, while Cohen's is a short story. What differences (in terms of the selections' effects on the reader) do their differences in style and points of view make?

[p a r t   t w o]

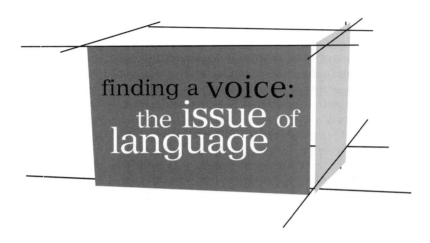

finding a **voice:**
the **issue** of
language

Los built the stubborn structure of the Language, acting against
Albion's melancholy, who might else have been a Dumb despair.

—William Blake, *Jerusalem*

Our appreciation of the suggestive, magical power of language was
reinforced by the games we played with words . . . musically arranged
words.

Culture embodies those moral, ethical and aesthetic values, the set of
spiritual eyeglasses, through which [people] come to view themselves and
their place in the universe. Values are the basis of a people's identity, their
sense of particularity as members of the human race. All this is carried by
language. Language as culture is the collective memory bank of a people's
experience in history.

— Ngugi wa Thiong'o, "The Language of African Literature"

anguage is the single most important tool human beings possess for the expression of who they are. In Blake's mythic poem *Jerusalem*, Los symbolizes the faculty of imagination which creates language to enable humanity to express and thus explore and affirm the significance of its experience. A poet who harnesses the power of language to articulate the experience of a people is performing precisely this function, giving voice to a history and culture that would otherwise be unheard and thus unrecognized.

Myths, legends and folk tales from a wide variety of cultures bear witness to the power of language. By knowing the right words to say or the real name of someone or something, the hero is able to triumph over powerful forces arrayed against him or her. In the West, this belief that language confers power can be traced back to the Genesis and Midrashic (folk tale) traditions that connect Adam's naming of the beasts to his power over them.

Because language is so powerful, because the particular language of a people carries their culture, history and their values, language has been at the centre of the struggle for cultural (and hence political and economic) control. As the editors of *The Post-Colonial Studies Reader* point out, "the colonial process itself begins in language" and language "remains the most potent instrument of cultural control"(283). By imposing their languages on the inhabitants of the countries they sought to colonize, the colonial powers (England, France, Spain, Germany, the Netherlands, Portugal) substituted their world view, values and sense of history for those of the native population. This process occurred in India and throughout much of Africa. It also happened in the Caribbean where African slaves lost their languages almost entirely, and in North America where some native languages have disappeared and others are threatened with what native author Basil Johnston calls "extinction." Within Britain itself, English has achieved dominance through the ruthless suppression of Irish, Welsh and Scottish Gaelic.

People, both as individuals and as groups, have responded variously to the domination of alien languages. Kenyan author Ngugi wa Thiong'o is one of many in both India and Africa who have rejected the use of English and work instead in their native languages. Refusing to use what Adrienne Rich in a feminist context calls an "oppressor's language," they believe that only through the use of their own languages can they perpetuate and express their true cultural identity. Others, like Chinua Achebe, have chosen to use English as the medium in which they work but not "English" English. Instead they have chosen to draw on the form of English that has developed within their own culture. Achebe believes that "the English language will be able to carry the weight of my African experience. But it will have to be a new English, still in full communion with its ancestral home but altered to suit new African surroundings" (qtd. in Ashcroft et al. 286). In India also, English, although initially imposed, has been transmogrified by its new environment, forced to carry the weight of different experience, and, argues Salman Rushdie, has emerged finally as a variant as vigorous and as richly appropriate to its context as American, Australian, Canadian or Caribbean English.

Another response has been to transform the imposed language, creating a dialect or Creole from a variety of linguistic roots. This is very much a phenomenon of the Caribbean where variants of English have developed in combination with African and Indian languages and the European languages, Spanish and French. Once considered "bad English," such languages have gained recognition as powerful mediums for the communication of the culture and experience of the people who developed and speak them. Creolised English has increasingly appeared in the work of highly respected Caribbean authors from Samuel Selvon, a pioneer of its literary use in his novel *The Lonely Londoners*, to Louise Bennett and Derek Walcott.

Whatever else it is, the issue of language is always political and always highly controversial—for feminists who have identified much that is patriarchal or sexist in conventional English constructions, and for Quebec nationalists who see French as the lifeblood of their nation and have deployed "language police" to ensure its preservation. The passion people bring to discussions about language is a measure of its immense power to structure our thoughts and arouse our emotions.

Works Cited

Ashcroft, Bill, Gareth Griffiths, and Helen Tiffin, eds. *The Post-Colonial Studies Reader*. London: Routledge, 1995. 283–4.

Blake, William. *The Complete Poetry and Prose of William Blake*. Ed. David Erdman. Berkeley: University of California Press, 1982.

Ostriker, Alicia Suskin. *Stealing the Language: The Emergence of Women's Poetry in America*. Boston: Beacon Press, 1986

Rushdie, Salman, ed. *The Vintage Book of Indian Writing 1947–1997*. London: Random House, 1997.

Ngugi wa Thiong'o. "The Language of African Literature." *Decolonising the Mind: The Politics of Language in African Literature*. London: James Currey, 1981. 285-290.

Marlene Nourbese-Philip

For isn't it odd that the only language I have in which to speak of this crime is the language of the criminal who committed the crime? And what can that really mean? For the language of the criminal can contain only the goodness of the criminal's deed . . .

—Jamaica Kincaid, *A Small Place*

In *She Tries Her Tongue. Her Silence Softly Breaks,* the volume of poetry from which "Discourse on the Logic of Language" is taken, Marlene Nourbese-Philip attempts to subvert English—"the language of the criminal"—and force it to become a vehicle for the expression of both "the crime" and of an authentic sense of history and self. Near the beginning of the book, Philip asserts that "for the African in the New World learning the English language was simultaneous with learning of her non-being." The language contains and perpetuates the racist, misogynist beliefs of its speakers, and yet, because slaves were forbidden to speak their own languages, the language of the colonizers (English, French, Spanish . . .) became the "mother tongue" or first language of their descendants. By employing both Standard English and West Indian demotic or popular English, and by tracing the historical roots of Caribbean English—the African as well as the European roots—Philip creates a sort of "cultural hybrid," a language that, as Sabine Milz points out, can express the linguistic, "cultural, and imaginative clashes and intersections that shape . . . identities" (2).

Like Dionne Brand with whom she shares a commitment to a range of issues, Philip is a deeply political writer. She is a founding member of Vision 21, a coalition of artists and writers (including Brand) who have been outspoken in their condemnation of racism and sexism in the Canadian arts. Born in Tobago, she completed a degree in economics at the

University of the West Indies in Trinidad before immigrating to Canada in 1968. She graduated from the University of Western Ontario with a law degree in 1973 and practised immigration and family law from 1975 to 1982 when she quit her practice in order to write full-time.

Philip is the author of two essay collections: *Frontiers: Essays and Writings on Racism and Culture* (1992) and *A Genealogy of Resistance and Other Essays* (1997); a novel: *Looking for Livingstone: An Odyssey of Silence* (1991), an allegorical quest-narrative which critically evaluates European assumptions about the silence of indigenous peoples; and a novel for young adults, *Harriet's Daughter* (1988), which was a finalist for three awards. In 1989 she won the prestigious Casa de las Americas prize for poetry for *She Tries Her Tongue*, and in 1990 she received a Guggenheim Fellowship which was followed by a 1995 Toronto Arts Award. In spite of this evidence of her success as a writer, she has often had a difficult time finding a publisher. It took five years for her to get *Harriet's Daughter* published and *She Tries Her Tongue* was turned down 55 times before receiving the prize for poetry in manuscript form. Philip attributes her difficulties in finding a publisher to systemic racism in the Canadian publishing industry. However, throughout periods of frustration and disappointment, she has never weakened in her determination to be heard.

Works Cited

Milz, Sabine. "Resistance in the Hybrid Space of Embodied Language and Body Memory: A Comparative Study of Marlene Nourbese-Philip's *She Tries Her Tongue. Her Silence Softly Breaks* and Emine Sevgi Ozdamar's 'Mutterzunge.'" **www.gradnet.de/pomo2.archives/pomo99.papers/Milz99.htm**

Other Sources and Weblinks

Kirchhoff, H.J. "The Obsession That Has Chosen Me Is Language." 4 Jan. 1990. **www.ChaptersGlobe.com**

Nourbese-Philip, Marlene. "The Disappearing Debate: Racism and Censorship." *Language in Her Eye: Writing and Gender.* Ed. Libby Scheier, Sarah Sheard, and Eleanor Wachtel. Toronto: Coach House Press, 1990. 209–219.

_____. The Scream in High Park. **scream.interlog.com,/94/philip.html**

_____. *She Tries Her Tongue. Her Silence Softly Breaks.* Charlottetown: Ragweed Press, 1989.

Williamson, Janice. "Writing a memory of losing that place." *Sounding Differences: Conversations with Seventeen Canadian Women Writers.* Toronto: University of Toronto Press, 1993. 226–244.

Discourse on the Logic of Language

WHEN IT WAS BORN, THE MOTHER HELD HER NEWBORN CHILD CLOSE: SHE BEGAN THEN TO LICK IT ALL OVER. THE CHILD WHIMPERED A LITTLE, BUT AS THE MOTHER'S TONGUE MOVED FASTER AND STRONGER OVER ITS BODY, IT GREW SILENT—THE MOTHER TURNING IT THIS WAY AND THAT UNDER HER TONGUE, UNTIL SHE HAD TONGUED IT CLEAN OF THE CREAMY WHITE SUBSTANCE COVERING ITS BODY.

English
is my mother tongue.
A mother tongue is not
not a foreign lan lan lang
language
l/anguish
anguish
—a foreign anguish.

English is
my father tongue.
A father tongue is
a foreign language,
therefore English is
a foreign language
not a mother tongue.

What is my mother
tongue
my mammy tongue
my mummy tongue
my momsy tongue
my modder tongue
my ma tongue?

I have no mother
tongue
no mother to tongue
no tongue to mother
to mother
tongue
me
I must therefore be tongue
dumb
dumb-tongued
dub-tongued
damn dumb
tongue

EDICT I

*Every owner of slaves
shall, wherever possible,
ensure that his slaves
belong to as many ethno-
linguistic groups as
possible. If they can-
not speak to each other,
they cannot then foment
rebellion and revolution.*

Those parts of the brain chiefly responsible for speech are named after two learned nineteenth century doctors,
the eponymous Doctors Wernicke and Broca respectively.

Dr. Broca believed the size of the brain determined intelligence; he devoted much of his time to 'proving' that white males of the Caucasian race had larger brains than, and were therefore superior to, women, Blacks and other peoples of colour.

Understanding and recognition of the spoken word takes place in Wernicke's area—the left temporal lobe, situated next to the auditory cortex; from there relevant information passes to Broca's area—situated in the left frontal cortex—which then forms the response and passes it on to the motor cortex. The motor cortex controls the muscles of speech.

but I have
a dumb tongue
tongue dumb
father tongue
and english is
my mother tongue
is
my father tongue
is a foreign lan lan lang
language
l/anguish
  anguish
a foreign anguish
is english—
another tongue
my mother
    mammy
    mummy
    moder
    mater
    macer
    moder
tongue
mothertongue
tongue mother
tongue me
mothertongue me
mother me
touch me
with the tongue of your
lan lan lang
language
l/anguish
  anguish
english
is a foreign anguish

EDICT II

Every slave caught speak-
ing his native language
shall be severely pun-
ished. Where necessary,
removal of the tongue is
recommended. The offending
organ, when removed,
should be hung on high
in a central place,
so that all may see and
tremble.

THE MOTHER THEN PUT HER FINGERS INTO HER CHILD'S MOUTH—GENTLY FORCING IT OPEN; SHE TOUCHES HER TONGUE TO THE CHILD'S TONGUE, AND HOLDING THE TINY MOUTH OPEN, SHE BLOWS INTO IT—HARD. SHE WAS BLOWING WORDS—HER WORDS, HER MOTHER'S WORDS, THOSE OF HER MOTHER'S MOTHER, AND ALL THEIR MOTHERS BEFORE—INTO HER DAUGHTER'S MOUTH.

A tapering, blunt-tipped, muscular, soft and fleshy organ describes
(a) the penis.
(b) the tongue.
(c) neither of the above.
(d) both of the above.

In man the tongue is
(a) the principal organ of taste.
(b) the principal organ of articulate speech.
(c) the principal organ of oppression and exploitation.
(d) all of the above.

The tongue
(a) is an interwoven bundle of striated muscle running in three planes.
(b) is fixed to the jawbone.
(c) has an outer covering of a mucous membrane covered with papillae.
(d) contains ten thousand taste buds, none of which is sensitive to the taste of foreign words.

Air is forced out of the lungs up the throat to the larynx where it causes the vocal cords to vibrate and create sound. The metamorphosis from sound to intelligible word requires
(a) the lip, tongue and jaw all working together.
(b) a mother tongue.
(c) the overseer's whip.
(d) all of the above or none.

Clark Blaise

I'm a kind of tropical tree with an awful lot of shallow roots and I can easily be blown over. On the other hand, I can survive a lot of changes. I adapt very easily to just about anything around me.

—Clark Blaise, quoted in *Canadian Fiction Magazine*

In many ways, Clark Blaise epitomizes the outsider, a "resident alien" to use the phrase which forms the title of the 1986 collection of short stories from which "North" is taken. Born in 1940 in the United States (in Fargo, North Dakota), to an English-Canadian mother from Manitoba and a French-Canadian father from Quebec, Blaise had an itinerant childhood. The dust jacket of his first book, *A North American Education* (1973), proclaims his attendance at no less than "twenty-five schools" during his early years. "That fact alone," suggests Barry Cameron, "might account for the predominance of alienation and dislocation as psychological and metamorphic motifs in his fiction" (2).

His father's job as a travelling furniture salesman led the family from North Dakota to Alabama and then to central Florida, the location for many of Blaise's early stories (some of which appear in the recently released *Southern Stories: The Selected Stories*). Blaise spent 1950 and 1951 in Winnipeg, his mother's hometown, and then lived in various places in the American Midwest until finally moving to Pittsburgh, Pennsylvania, where he attended high school. He received his university education at Harvard, where he was a student in the creative writing course taught by Pulitzer Prize–winning author Bernard Malamud, and at the University of Iowa, where he participated in the University of Iowa Writers' Workshop, graduating with a Masters of Fine Arts. Also while at Iowa, he met and married fellow author Bharati Mukherjee, with whom he wrote *Days and Nights in Calcutta* (1977) and *The Sorrow and the Terror: The Haunting Legacy of the Air India Disaster* (1987).

Blaise began his teaching career at the University of Wisconsin but he felt drawn back to Canada. In 1966 he moved to Montreal and began teaching at McGill University. He became a Canadian citizen in 1973. He has since returned to the United States and currently lives in San Francisco, teaching at the University of California, Berkeley. Nonetheless, his relationship to Canada has been significant for him. He writes in *Resident Alien*:

> Canada was always the large, locked attic of my sensibility, something I would never know, but was obliged to invent; it cultivated a part of me that America never touched. The significant blob of otherness in my life has always been Canada . . . (171–72)

> Of all the distinctions I have invented in my life and come to believe in with the force of myth, the difference between Canada and the United States—so frail in reality, so inconsequential in the consciousness of America or the world or even most Canadians—is still my last, my most important illusion. (171)

"Everywhere I see dualities," he states at the beginning of the book. And, in addition to the duality of Canada and the United States, there is the Canadian duality of English and French, a duality reproduced in the dynamic of Blaise's family.

Barry Cameron calls "the continental range of Blaise's personal history, its culturally disparate quality," . . . "the framework or 'shell' . . . of his fiction" (4) within which he constructs plots that are often quite unrelated to actual events of his life. In an interview with Geoff Hancock in 1980, Blaise pointed to the autobiographical nature of his fiction: "I've only written of three characters really and that's my mother, my father and myself. I'm utterly dependent upon the family conflicts as the source of my fiction." He describes the father character, that is the character of his father as Blaise presents him in his fiction, as sexually charming, "with confidence, with a fearlessness before the law . . . a kind of lawlessness . . . continually pushing out against definitions," while the "mother-figures are always the ones who are pulling within definitions." They are "acutely aware of restrictions and anticipating rebuffs." This, he asserts "is my landscape, my moral landscape" (58–60). We can discern this moral landscape and its associated dualities operating in "North."

Works Cited

Blaise, Clark. *Resident Alien*. Markham, Ontario. Penguin, 1986.
Cameron, Barry. *Clark Blaise and His Works*. Toronto: ECW Press, 1984.
Hancock, Geoff. "An Interview with Clark Blaise." *Canadian Fiction Magazine*. Nos. 34–35. 1980: 46–64.

Other Sources and Weblinks

The Clark Blaise Papers
**www.ucalgary.ca/UofC/departments/UP/0-919813/
0-919813-79-8.html**

Hancock, Geoff. "Interview." *Books in Canada*. March 1979: 30–31.
"Southern Stories." *New York Times*.
www.sentex.net/~pg1/southern.html

Special Collections
www.ucalgary.ca/library/SpecColl/blaise.hem

North

In the beginning, my mother would meet me at the *"Garçons°"* side of Papineau School. She might have been the tallest woman in the east end of Montreal in the early fifties. I was walking with my friend Mick. I was thirteen, and he was older but smaller. From the neck up he looked twenty. He was in my cousin Dollard's class. He had discovered me on the first day of school, standing by the iron gate looking puzzled. "Take the garkons," he had advised, under his breath. *Garkons* was an early word in my private vocabulary. In the beginning, I had to trust strangers' pronunciations, or worse, my own.

"You're not one of them, are you, eh?" I liked that; *them*—it sounded science-fictiony. How could he tell? Getting no answer, he went on, "My old lady, she ups and marries this Frog. What's your story?"

My story? Same old story, too preposterous. Until the week before, I'd been Phil Porter, content but lonely, riding the airwaves of Pittsburgh, attaching rabbit-ears to our apartmenthouse chimney, pulling in seven channels from adjacent states. All I said to Mick that first day was, "My name's Carrier, but I'm not French."

"Me too. Bloody Fortin. All the Fortins in my family are English and all the Sweeneys are French. Funny, eh? Where you from—the States? Vermont?"

Pittsburgh rang no bells for Mick Fortin. He only knew the cities that sent us tourists—Burlington, Plattsburgh, and half of Harlem, plus the cozy loop of the old NHL. "Do you have a job yet?" he asked me, and I feared for a minute that a job was required in this new world of the French eighth grade, like my pens and tie and white shirt for school. Mick was too

Garçons: boys

ignorant, too solicitous, too eager with his confessions to be trusted. He promised me a job in the spring, down along St Catherine Street, passing out peep-show leaflets to the Yanks. "You've heard of Lili St Cyr, eh?" I hadn't, but nodded. "All you gotta do is say, 'C'mon'n see her! Lili St Cyr's younger and sexier sister!' All the girls down there call themselves St Cyr something, Mimi or Fifi. The Yanks, they eat it up." In the beginning, I welcomed my mother's intervention.

We'd left Pittsburgh in the middle of the night. My father had assaulted a man at work. He'd found him seated at his desk, feet on an opened drawer, packing up my father's pictures and souvenirs. A younger man, brought in from the outside. He got his first three words in—"You're out, Porter"—and then my father grabbed his ankles and spilled him backwards out of the chair. Then he picked him off the floor and shoved him only once, and the new manager found himself bursting through fresh dry-wall and skidding to a halt by the water cooler. And my father caught the first elevator to Canada, convinced that no one knew his secret name and true identity. Some time in the middle of that night, somewhere in the middle of upstate New York, my father Reg Porter reverted to Réjean Carrier, and I was allowed to retain my name of Phil, but Porter was taken from me forever. "You weren't born in Cincinnati like we always said," my mother explained. "I'm sorry, but we had to tell you that. You were born in Montreal."

We moved into the apartment of his older brother, Théophile. I bumped Dollard from his room, and my parents took the living-room sofa. Théophile's six daughters were married, or in the Church. In a pantry-sized bedroom off the kitchen lived Aunt Louise who'd married an American in Woonsocket and seen all three of her sons go down with the *Dorchester* in 1942. She didn't speak, she only lit candles, and the smell of wax permeated the apartment. My mother would have the sheets and pillows stored away each morning by seven o'clock, and I don't think they went out during the day. I don't know what they and my aunt Béatrice, who spoke no English, did all day.

The first big fight had been over my schooling. School had been in session nearly a month when we arrived on Théophile's doorstep. I hadn't known a word of French, though I began collecting words from Dollard that first day. From him, everything began with "*maudit*°. . ." and ended with ". . . *de Christ sanglant*." In a week I knew some nouns, and adjectives; no verbs, no sentences. French neutralized my mother's education; she was like a silent actress. I learned to read her eyes, her lips, and to listen to her breathing, and her feelings came through like captions. She would nod her head and say, "wee-wee," which made the simplest French words come out like baby-talk. She was one of those western Canadians of profound good will and solid background, educated and sophisticated and acutely alert to

maudit: cursed, damnable
de Christ sanglant: the blood of Christ; a curse

conditions in every part of the world, who could not utter a syllable of French without a painful contortion of head, neck, eyes and lips. She was convinced that the French language was a deliberate debauchery of logic, and that people who persisted in speaking it did so to cloak the particulars of a nefarious design, behind which could be detected the gnarled, bejewelled claws of the Papacy. She was, of course, too well-bred to breathe a word of this suspicion to anyone but me. All evening, then, as she stood next to Béatrice at the sink, peeling, washing, baking and frying our food, it was Béatrice's steady stream of incomprehensible opinions and my mother's head-jerking wee-wees, the smell of wax and Dollard's obscene mutterings that initiated me into a world that would be, for all I knew, mine forever.

My mother had wanted to send me to an English school, although the nearest one was at the end of two trolley rides. I was silent about it. English would obviously be easier, but not necessarily preferable. I wanted to belong, and no one I knew in Montreal spoke English, except my mother. Canadian schools, my mother said, were light-years ahead of American, and English was the only language for an intelligent boy who didn't want to become a priest. French school was so fundamentally *wrong*, it was alluring to contemplate. For the first time in my life no one could possibly expect anything from me. Théophile settled it. He was a member of the St-Jean Baptiste Society. No one living under his roof would ever study English, let alone go to school in it. Anyway, it wasn't safe. There was no way to get to an English school that didn't cut through the middle of the Jewish ghetto, where French boys were routinely butchered. He had this on good authority, though they didn't dare print it in the communist press. Dozens of French boys had disappeared—altar boys—they only used the purest blood. My mother retired to the bathroom. My father chimed in, "They'd kill him on this street, for sure. They'd kill any kid on this street if he went to an English school."

Tricks of the mind. Even in my memories of those three strange years, nuns and classmates seem to be speaking to me in English—a clear violation of the natural universe—and I seem to be writing papers and speaking up in class, always in English. This is clearly not so, for there's a band of three years in my life when I discovered nature where even now I'm still learning the English names. Fish, trees, flowers, weeds, foods, drinks can all send me to the dictionary. And the discovery of myself as a sexual creature—slightly different from the discovery of sex itself—that too is a function of French.

For the first time in my life I felt that school was a punishment. Nuns were wardens, the cracking of the cane was arbitrary and malicious. We were prisoners serving time for a crime whose nature would presently be revealed. I assumed my guilt; it was my ignorance of the charge, not my innocence, that made the confusion so painful.

I was caned in the second week. The impossible had happened *to me*. I was made to mumble an act of contrition. I wasn't even Catholic. *"Pourquoi ça?°"* I kept demanding as the cane kept whizzing down, day after day for a week. Even harder, for my question suggested arrogance. There would be no explanation. He was a Brother of the Order of Mary, who otherwise smiled at me when he passed me in the halls. In the second week, Soeur Timothée let it out: my cousin Dollard had been cutting classes and acting unrepentant to the brothers. *"Hôtage!"* she hissed at me, taking over the caning. *"Tu sais hôtage?°"* I learned quickly enough. Finally my mother noticed the backs of my hands, the welts, and bruises. She raged, with only my father and me to understand her.

"Discipline!" he exclaimed. "That's what they give, and he has to learn to take it!" I hadn't told them about Dollard. I hadn't even told Dollard about the punishment I was taking on his behalf, but I hoped word would drift back to him before my fingers fell off. My father was defending them, in his way. Compared to *his* years with the brothers, when he'd been given to them at the age of five for eventual priesthood, my life had been one of silken pillows. If my hands hadn't been as soft as a girl's there wouldn't even be bruises. "Look at Dollard's hands—they're like hockey gloves," he shouted. My father wasn't defending the church—he hated it from the depths of his bowels—but he revered its implacable authority. Whatever they did to you, you should be grateful; it made you tough enough in later life to keep telling them to go to hell.

"Discipline!" my mother raged. "You fools. You bloody fools—is that what discipline is to you? Treating children like animals? Beating them into submission? It's medieval, it's madness. You're crazy, can't you see? You're twisted, and I won't have you twisting your son the same way." She grabbed my hands and clutched my fists to her chest. "Discipline isn't just learning how to take pain. Discipline doesn't mean you have to be stupid. God, if the bloody Church told you tomorrow the earth was flat, you'd start telling yourselves you knew it was flat all along, right? Wouldn't you? Wouldn't you?"

I felt guilty, terribly guilty, bringing on such an argument. There was injustice here, on every side. My father—that unemployed, wrecked shell of a man—was standing in for Théophile and Dollard, whose stupidities were unassailable, and for the brothers at school whose cruelties, given the system, were unremarkable and fairly even-handed. My father hadn't been inside a church in forty years, not since he'd fled the barbarities of a harsher time and place and taken those memories, that rage, into the streets of Montreal and beyond. But against my mother, his words and logic were pathetic.

Pourquoi ça?: Why? What's this?
Tu sais hôtage?: You know what hostage means?

Now his voice was weary. "Okay," he admitted. His fists were heavy in front of his face; he kept balling them up and flinging them open. "You don't know how they think. How they work . . . . It's . . . . " and he shrugged his shoulders, empty of words. I wanted to complete it for him; I understood more about it than he ever would. What the brothers were doing to me to get to Dollard would have worked in any family in Papineau School—we were the freaks. I was suffering a complicated shame. Then my father came up with a new inspiration. "You think the Sistine Chapel was painted without discipline?" There was a series of pictures taped to the dining-room wallpaper, cut from the pages of *Life* magazine, celebrating Vatican art. The Sistine Chapel won many arguments in the Hochelaga district of Montreal in the early fifties.

In memory, Pittsburgh came bursting through like a freak radio signal. In my junior-high classes, the sexes had mingled, the girls had steamed and giggled in a heavy-breasted, painted-up pool of pubescent sexuality. They wore whatever they could get away with. They stuffed lewd and graphic promises through the ventilation slats of our lockers and raced for the girls' rooms between classes to smoke like little hellions. They were utterly available, begging to be touched.

But in Papineau we entered and left by the *"Garçons"* and *"Filles"* sides of the building, as though joint entombment for eight hours a day was concession enough to sordid physiology; the nuns and brothers even positioned themselves like Holy Crossing Guards two and three blocks away, to prolong the segregation. Coeducation was a sad fact of life, but withering disapproval could safeguard our innocence at least till high school. The girls wore black jumpers and no make-up, and their hair was cut uniformly straight and short. Not a pony-tail, not a bleach job in the lot. I'd been too young in Pittsburgh to act on my impulses, to inhale those lusty vapours rising from the breeding pens of an American junior high school. Now, I felt, I could. Just turn me loose, anywhere in America. I burned in hell, remembering it.

And then, miraculously, the nuns gave me a girl. At four o'clock after another gruelling day of faint comprehension, Soeur Timothée told me to stay after class—not for discipline—but to meet my own, private, ninth-grade tutor, Thérèse Aulérie. Tutor and general *ange gardien* in everything from penmanship (we were on the continental system, with crossed sevens, ones like giant carat marks, whenever I require assurance that indeed these things happened to me I have it still, in my handwriting) to the foundations of all advanced knowledge: Latin, French and the Catholic religion. Thérèse was Papineau's outstanding student in Classics, French, Apologetics and even Natural Science.

Ninth-grade girls back in Pittsburgh simply had more going for them than Thérèse Aulérie, despite her brilliance. There was first of all the question of make-up, that bright impasto of sexual longing, so innovatively applied by American teenagers. They had Hollywood and television to guide them, not to mention the Terry Moore sweaters, stretched over the mountain-building process we runty seventh and eighth graders could measure by the week, if not the hour (just as I scrutinized my chin for each new black whisker; cherished each new fissure in my cracking vocal chords and checked every inch of my body for other rampant endocrinal signposts worth flaunting).

In Papineau, everything was hidden. Girls in jumpers, no make-up, no hair-styles; they took their cues from Soeur Timothée. But Thérèse Aulérie was a slight improvement. She had the palest skin and the greenest eyes I had ever seen (it was the first time I'd been forced to focus on such adult, literary features as fine skin and expressive eyes), and lips that were natural and pink to a sheen of edibility. She wore clear nail polish—a vanity, she later confessed—and the only other exposed acreage of flesh, her cheeks, were delicately flushed, and dimpled. Her voice was low and throaty, a woman' s voice coming from the face of Margaret O'Brien. She looked so *nearly* familiar it seemed impossible that she didn't speak a word of English and even regarded hearing it as a low-grade, unclassifiable sin.

We began with Apologetics. We had a small handbook of Nuns and Monks and Teaching Orders, and my first job was to learn how to identify the various orders by their special dress, their expertise, their place and date of founding. I'd thought of them as exotic wildlife anyway: tracking them with an imprimatured bestiary seemed a natural way of pinning them down. I started rattling off their dates and countries of origin with an ease that astonished her, leaving Thérèse to fill in the substantive issues—for her at least: were they known best for their piety or their charity? Their compassion or courage? Their humility or brilliance? Most of our brothers were Marists, with a Sacred Heart in the chapel. The nuns were mainly our local Greys and Ursulines, but a sharp eye could spot a Blessed Virgin on special assignment. This part was easy, like learning the makes and models of new cars. Thérèse, once she dropped the ninth-grade condescension, was full of unofficial data about every order. *Les laides, les bêtes, les gueules, les graisses.* Soeur Timothée, I learned, was called Soeur La Morse. "What's a *morse*?" I asked, and Thérèse tapped imaginary tusks and made deep seal-like grunts. "Walrus!" I laughed, and she repeated, in a voice suddenly high and girlish, "wal-russ." In fact, Thérèse Aulérie, for all her grades and piety and possible calling as a Sister of Charity, was a sharp little cookie who began confiding to me of her visits to the States, a Chinese restaurant she'd been taken to in Manchester, New Hampshire, the week-ends at Old Orchard Beach and the television she'd stared at for a solid, slothful week-end in a Burlington motel. She'd even gone to New York City when she was six, and she still had all the postcards. In her America, everyone spoke French, except the people on television.

"Did you really go to school in America?" she asked in French. My French wasn't good enough to answer more than an authentic, Dollardish "ouai." No way to describe its wonders.

"Comme Hartchie?" she asked. *"Et Véronique?"*

It took me a few seconds to catch on. *"Et Juggie° aussi,"* I laughed.

"Ah, Juggie," she nodded gravely. *"Juggie j'aime beaucoup."*

We sighed; I for the multiplicity of stories I couldn't build upon, the impossibility of representing myself in a language I didn't know, or to a girl who didn't know mine.

"Et ton nom, était-il toujours Carrier là-bas?"

It didn't seem strange to her that people changed names when they crossed the border. In America, I tried to explain, we'd sailed under a flag of translation. *"Porter,"* she tried, in her curious, high-pitched English. *"Non, c'est laid, ce nom-là. Carrier, c'est un bon nom canadien."*

I answered, with sad conviction sealing the linguistic gaps, "Anyway, names *ne fait rien."*

She drew her desk closer. *"Épeles mon nom de famille. Divines.* Go ahead. Try!"

"A-U—" I began. And she giggled, shaking her head.

"Mon vrai *nom. Commences avec 'o,'* like dis, eh?" I loved it when she tried her English. It came out like Dollard's, but without the threat. *"C'est le vrai français, mon nom, de la France, pas d'ici."* She wrote, "O'L—"

"O'Leery?' I spelled.

"O'Leary,' she corrected. *"Ça c'est le nom de mon grandpère."* She turned the paper as though admiring a work of art. "Nice," she said.

I felt I'd been handed a powerful interpretive tool, but I didn't yet know how to wield it. Here I was, a Carrier who spoke no French, and she was an O'Leary who read "Archie" comic books but knew no English, and we were together in a darkening classroom in Montreal under a cross, flanked by the photos of the Cardinal of Montreal and the Holy Father. We were linked beyond simple assignments. My guardian angel, according to Sister Walrus, who would lead me from ignorance to power, just as the sisters and brothers would lead me from hellfire to righteousness.

Thérèse closed her book after the quiz on habits and orders and asked me, slowly and with grand gestures, can girls (she pointed to herself) in the ninth grade in America really wear lipstick (she ran her pinkie over her lips) and dress the way they want? She formed a gentle, wavy outline with her hands, passing over an imaginary female form just outside her square-cut jumper with all the lewdness (I fantasized) of a sailor describing his last night's conquest. Can they really go out on dates? She clawed my wrist at the word *"rendez-vous."* Those new words burned themselves in my brain: *maquillage . . . se habiller comme l'on veut . . . rendez-vous.* Do they all have cars? How late can they stay out? She was suddenly like a little girl, and somewhere in the late fall gloom, and then under the yellow globes of a four-thirty northern autumn night, I started imagining a Thérèse O'Leary in make-up, and I noticed how her jumper flared out modestly in front and filled out gently in the rear, and how a nice wide belt would have pinched

Hartchie . . . Veronique . . . Juggie: Archie, Veronica, Jughead, teenage characters in an American comic book series

it together, just right. And how her voice, that deep French purr, would have driven American boys wild.

It must have been in those weeks in our daily hours after school and in our walks away from school for two low, mean, icy, glorious unsupervised blocks to her trolley stop, that the current in our little relationship shifted direction. By the end of our first month, her English improved to the level of fairly detailed conversation. I rummaged through my mother's suitcase and found a proper belt. Once one Saturday I passed her with her parents at Dupuis Frères department store, and she was in a sweater and skirt, wearing lipstick and pearl earrings.

I came to think of my five hours a week with Thérèse as my parole from solitary. I came to understand my mother's use of the word "drab" to describe the interiors and the streets, the minds and souls and conversations of east-end Montreal. One big icy puddle of frozen gutter water, devoid of joy, colour, laughter, pleasure, intellect or art. School and home and church and the narrow east-end streets that connect them are the same colour even now in my memory, linked in a language that I didn't understand except through its rhythms. Recitations in class took on a dirge-like quality, like the repeated Hail Marys on Sunday radio. Eventually even I, who knew neither Latin nor French nor the lists of martyrs to the Iroquois, could stand and repeat the proper syllables. The name of our school, Papineau, figured in Quebec history as a great patriot who had tried to rid the province of English and American influences, and his name was repeated on the street outside and on panel trucks: and signboards of plumbers and plasterers and in the *épicerie* where Aunt Béatrice did her shopping. It seemed slightly blasphemous, like Latin ballplayers carrying the name of Jesus. The same few names popped up everywhere, with six Tremblays in my class and over half of us clustered alphabetically at "La—" and nearly all of us ending in "—ier." Our names were as predictable as Armenians,' as unmistakable as Chinese, and mine was one of the commonest. We were common, and we learned to feel comfortable only in the presence of other *bons noms canadiens*." "Ignorance!" my mother had cried one night, fleeing the dinner table. She had bought red table napkins, something to brighten the winter gloom, and my uncle had slammed his to the floor, saying it would *"causer l'acide."*

And so, my mother began meeting me after school, a block from where I parted from Thérèse. Sometimes we would ride the trolley downtown and go into Eaton's or Ogilvy's—places that felt off-limits to the rest of the family. And there I would glow in the mystical power of speaking English, a power that wasn't furtive or dirty, as it felt in the apartment. The power of not having to scratch for words and not biting back the urge to comment, or even attack.

On the furniture floor of Eaton's she said, "I worked here, you know. I was even the head of this whole department." We walked through the model home, the half dozen bedrooms and dining-rooms featuring different styles of decoration. "Your father was one of the salesmen. Until I saw him, I never even bothered learning their names. I knew he was wrong for me. Knew from the beginning." No one recognized her now, though it had been only thirteen years. She'd gone to the States, been lost to history. "I was a very different woman in those days. I want you to understand that. It wasn't easy, back then, in this city. Women couldn't even vote. And they don't accept women here, not English women, not Protestant women. They'll never do that." I could read her eyes and breath; I wanted to avoid the tears that I knew were coming. "I deserve it all, don't I? Sleeping on a floor in Hochelaga. No wonder they don't want to remember me—I must look a sight." She trailed her fingers in the dust of the dining-room tables and nightstands, then took me up to the cafeteria on the top floor. We would have our tea and scones, sometimes served with a little lemon curd. She perked up, over tea. "I don't want you to despise them. They are what they are. Deep down, they're good people. They've taken us in when we could have ended up . . . I don't want to think how we could have ended up, and they've shared what they have. But I *do* resent them, I can't help it. I resent their tight little ways, not with money—darling, do you understand what I'm saying? Their fist-like little souls, always ready to fight you or slink away like a beaten dog—does that make sense? I don't want you growing up like them."

It was always harder, going back to Hochelaga after scones and lemon curd and a few hours of uninterrupted English. The urge to speak our language seemed to die when the trolley crossed St Lawrence. In a few weeks I would reach a linguistic equilibrium, and I probably could have been happy enough—given endless lemon curd or access to Thérèse O'Leary—existing like a child in either world. But I was being forced, subtly at first, every day, to make moral decisions. French or English were the terms, but they were merely covers for personalities inside and out that I wanted to keep hidden.

One Friday in early December my mother held me back from school. Quietly, she motioned me to put on my coat. We took the trolley downtown not quite to Eaton's, then walked up to Sherbrooke past the clean grey limestone and green copper roofs of McGill University, that Gibraltar of Englishness. "Some day you'll go here," she said. "I don't care what it takes or if you graduate from French school or American schools—they'll have to let you in." I welcomed her authority. We stood on Milton Street just outside the iron railings; I wanted to reach inside. I could understand the shouts of the students, their quiet conversations as young couples passed us on the sidewalk. "Who are those men in black robes?" I asked, "Judges?"

"Professors," she said. "This is the greatest university in the world." She so rarely allowed herself the luxury of an uncontested assertion—"too American" was her feeling about any claim to undisputed superiority—that I knew I'd been handed an indisputable fact. I trusted my mother more than any nun, even more than any Jesuit. "Come," she said, and we turned down

Prince Arthur, through a maze of small half-streets that curled between Pine and St Urbain. We stopped in front of a tall apartment block of dull cherry brick, where long icicles hung over the door. "I want you to meet an important person in my life," she said. "And in yours, I hope."

"Who?" And I swear, had she asked me, *Who do you think?* I would have answered, *My father. My real father.* There was something monumental inside, the clarity behind all the confusions. Her gloved finger ran down the row of buzzers. At "Perleman, E." she stopped.

We were buzzed inside: My mother's hands were shaking. "Ella is a brilliant woman. A professor at McGill." In the tiny elevator she whispered, "I used to live right here, in this building. When I came back from England and got that job at Eaton's."

"With her?"

"I called her last week. I haven't seen her in thirteen years. She sounded—" and her voice was stumbling now, "grand. She's a grand girl."

"You used to get letters from her, I remembered. Back in Pittsburgh I saved the high-denomination Canadian stamps that came to us on those thick envelopes from Montreal.

"She's my dearest friend. The times we had! Oh, Lord, the times . . ."

Ella was standing by the elevator, a gnome-like woman of my mother's age, wrapped in a stiff green skirt and a man's sweater that smothered her body like a duffel bag. My mother had to stoop to hug her, and she was already losing control, while Ella merely patted her back and shoulders and murmured "There, there, Hennie," in what seemed to be a lilting accent. Her dark brown eyes were wide and sad, and her skin was a fine, translucent pink. Her hair was entirely grey and nearly as short as mine. She looked, I thought, like Albert Einstein. She pulled us down the hall to her opened apartment door. I could easily see over her head into a living-room dingy with smoke and oppressive with apartment heat. It must have been eighty-five degrees inside, and I started clawing desperately at my scarf and *tuque*, as she picked up a lavender shawl and draped it over her shoulders.

"Dolly," she called out, and a gaunt woman, slightly younger, shuffled out from the bedroom. "This is Henny, whom I've spoken so much about. And her boy, Philip." I nodded, regretting the day of school I was missing. "This is Dolly. Dolly works in the accounts office at McGill. So." Dolly took that as a sign to go to the kitchen and prepare some tea.

If McGill was the world's finest university and Ella one of its professors, I reasoned that she must be the smartest woman in the world. That went a long way to forgiving her appearance and her strange habits. She picked up a pipe from the nearest coffee table, and as she sucked on it, drawing in the flame, I could swear it *was* Einstein peering at me over the flame and bowl of the pipe. My mother was bearing up. She too was watching me, and I was behaving myself; nothing strange about a woman smoking a pipe. It was impossible to think of Ella ever crying, ever getting too personal and sentimental, and for that I was grateful.

"So. You must forgive two old women who haven't seen each other . . ." Ella and my mother were seated across from me on the sofa, and Ella was patting my mother's hand. "I must say you look well, Hennie, everything considered. Some of us got old rather quickly."

"You look just the same, Ella." My mother was staring down at her lap, at Ella's hand.

"Well, nothing ever happens in Montreal, so who can tell? The city hasn't changed one bit. The things we fought for have gradually come to pass—we can vote now, Hennie—isn't that grand? But the workers are still oppressed and the church still runs things and the police behave like Tartars and the corruption is still a public joke and our candidates still lose their deposits every election. Remember our election parties?" My mother smiled, and Ella let out a sharp bark of a laugh. "We'd all come back here to this apartment"—she was looking at me again—"the finest candidates who ever ran for public office in this country, and we'd sit around sipping sherry waiting for a call. And outside the police were waiting. If we'd actually won we'd have gone directly to jail. Oh, Lord, such innocent hopes! I may as well be just off the boat for all that's changed in twenty years!"

"Ella came from Austria, dear," my mother explained. "She studied with Freud."

Ella was quick to jump in. "No, no, dear. Never studied. *Was analysed* by one of his pupils. Which means only I *was discussed* over *kaffee* and *küchen*. The Perleman Complex," she giggled. "No, I'm afraid I was too normal. I never made it into Freudian literature. You have heard perhaps of Freud, Philip?"

"Is it like a Freudian slip?"

"If you are not referring to a ladies' undergarment, yes, there is such a thing as a Freudian slip. You of course understand what this is—this Freudian slip as you call it?"

My mother was nodding fiercely, urging me on. What was it, a test? "Usually when you're talking and something dirty slips out accidentally. Or something embarrassing, like those radio bloopers. There's a nun in school I keep being afraid I'm going to call a *morse*, because that's her nickname."

"People always think Freud has to be dirty. Ah, well."

"You never told me about this nun, darling."

"What exactly is a *morse*, Philip?"

"You know, that big seal-like thing, with tusks."

"You mean a walrus, dear?" My mother's face looked stricken with pain, and she turned to Ella. "He's . . . you see?"

"Now, now. Mothers *worry*, don't they, Philip? It's perfectly all right to learn a second language. I've done it, many have done it."

"You were forced to," said my mother. "It's not like having your mother tongue taken from you. They won't let him speak English. I'm the only person he can speak English with."

Dolly came in from the kitchen, bearing a teapot on a silver tray, four fine china cups and a plate of biscuits around a jar of lemon curd. She lifted a lavender shawl off the teapot and Ella asked me, "Do you know what this is called, Philip?"

"A cover?"

"A cosy. A tea-cosy. Very strange word, I always thought."

"I like lemon curd," I said, emphasizing those last two words. "I don't see why it's called lemon curd. It's more like lemon pudding. I mean, milk gets curds. Curds and whey. Maybe because it's sour, but then why don't we have rhubarb curd and apple curd? Or do we? In French—" but I stopped myself.

"Dear," said my mother, "I'm sorry."

"English is not an especially logical language, Philip. As you have discovered. But tell me—are you enjoying yourself in. Montreal? At school?"

"It's all right."

"Your mother tells me it's sometimes . . . a little primitive."

"They *beat* you, darling."

"They apologized. That's a big thing, getting them to apologize. La Morse herself, showed remorse." They didn't appreciate my rhyme. "It wasn't easy at the beginning even understanding things. Basic words, basic anything."

"What do you study?"

"It seems all he studies is Catholicism," said my mother.

The truth was, Apologetics was the easiest subject since it required no thought, just memorization. It was also the quickest way to get good grades. The math was easier than Pittsburgh math, once I learned the number system. In Latin, though the text was in French, I was starting from the same place as other students. Given an even chance, I would always excel. "That's not true," I said. The truth, I realized, was unspeakable. The truth was, I *liked* Apologetics. I spooned deeply in the curd pot and smeared it over a biscuit.

"So. A difference of perception, maybe?"

'My mother took this as a rebuke. Her head sank. I wanted to console her, but instead helped Dolly drag over a dining-room chair.

Ella looked at my mother; she looked at Dolly; I helped myself to more lemon curd. Finally Ella asked, in a softer voice, "Do they make you go to Mass? Do they try to convert you?'"

"I don't think so. I mean, everyone's Catholic, so they just assume I am too. I mean with a name like Carrier—" But I could see that, too, hurt my mother. "I mumble the prayers, but I don't go to Mass."

"You can go, dear. I don't want you to feel . . . different."

"I don't feel different," I said.

"Would you like to go to an English school?"

"I can't. My uncle—"

"Never mind about your uncle. Would you *like* to go to a good English school? The *best* English school? A private school?"

"I don't know."

"Philip, your mother and I and Dolly have discussed a plan. If you say yes, your mother will discuss it with your father. Dolly and I, we have no children. Probably there's a limit to the amount of charitable contributions I can make. You can live with us, and we will send you. I know professors, I know musicians, writers, artists. We go out every night, or we have people here who are the leaders not just of this city, not just this country—"

"—the *world*, darling. Ella is known all over the world."

"That's not the point. The point is, we want to share this—what should I call it? Power? Connection? Good fortune? You could stay here in your own room and go home on the week-ends, of course. You would be prepared for McGill. I. don't know what else there is to say."

"Say you will think about it, dear."

"I don't think my mother really wants me to leave," I said.

"She is the one who brought it up. She is deeply worried, what is happening to you."

"Nothing is happening to me."

"She wants what is best. French schools in this city are, well, substandard."

Inwardly, I panicked. There seemed to be no way of saving myself from everyone's good intentions.

"Before it's *too* late, darling. Before you lose everything you've got. They'll take it from you, believe me," and her voice suddenly cracked and her head fell to Ella's lap and I could hear the words torn from her chest. "Like . . . they've . . . taken . . . it . . . from . . . me!"

Ella took little note of the distraction; she placed her hand in my mother's hair and said to me, coldly and evenly, "Guess, please, Philip, how many products of classic French Canadian education we have on the McGill faculty. Go ahead."

I knew that any answer would be humiliating. "Obviously," she said, "you've guessed correctly. How many French Canadian *students* do you think I have?" She waited. "Let me tell you a little parable about the power of education. On this continent at the present time there are approximately six million French Canadians—am I right?"

"Yes," I admitted. It depended on how you counted our lost brothers and sisters in the West, New England and Louisiana. I'd just been reading about them, grieving for them, in my history class. My palms were sweating, my neck hairs rising.

"And there are approximately five million Jews on this continent," she said. She smiled briefly. "End of parable. Do you understand what I am saying about education? Do they teach you *that* in French school? Do you know how the minds of those people have been *wasted*? How they continue to be wasted? Have they taught you anything about Freud?"

"No," I whispered.

"Einstein?"

"Back in Pittsburgh."

"Karl Marx°?"

I felt a terrible pressure in my chest. It was the name that seemed to be hovering in the air all afternoon. All that talk of *the workers* and *the people* and the candidates who never got elected. There had been a cartoon circulated in school on the eve of the latest election: Karl Marx in a Santa suit, with "Parti Libéral" stencilled on his sack of toys.

"No!" I retorted.

"They're doing a splendid job of educating you, aren't they? You should be spending your time learning about science, politics, history, literature—"

"—and how to get electrocuted for being Russian spies?" I demanded.

My mother raised her head, and Ella stared back at me, hard, for several seconds. "Ella, I'm sorry—" my mother began, but Ella raised her hand, and my mother was silent. Dolly carried the tray back to the kitchen.

"I can't say I'm surprised," said Ella.

"I'm going back to school," I said. My mother reached out for me, imploring me to wait, we would all go to Murray's for lunch, but I thanked her, and the other women, for the lemon curd and tea, and wished them a pleasant lunch and a good afternoon.

There's a special light that strikes Montreal in April; a light so strong, so angled, that it bores through windows and the glass panels of apartment doors with the intensity of a projection beam. It acts like a magnifying lens, picking out cobwebs and dust motes, adding dimensions to the grain of wood, nubbiness to the sleekest fabric, seams and crannies to the tightest skin. The sidewalks resemble tidal basins with their residues of sand, and the snow is shrunk to black tongues of gritty ice, seeking shade. The walk home from school took a little longer, as I crushed little ice bridges over the swirling melt, and stood on rims of rounded ice till they snapped with a hollow thud and I could kick the chunks away. The days were longer, and even my tutorials with Thérèse ended in plenty of daylight. My grades were better than average, and the nuns' comments were even flattering. Nevertheless, Thérèse and I agreed that the tutoring should continue. Her English was far from perfect.

I think my mother found the courage, some time that winter, to keep calling Ella and to make their lunches a regular event. I was going downtown on my own, now that the weather had improved. Mick had come through with a job on St Catherine Street, just as he'd promised. I took over an old stand of his just up from the train station, handing out mimeographed leaflets of naked girls behind strings of balloons, naked girls with one leg up in a bathtub, naked girls doing just about anything, plus the offer of a free drink or free admission. It was cold work and a little seedy; Mick, as a trusted long-time employee, had been promoted to inside work with the props, nearer the girls. My job next year, if I proved reliable.

Karl Marx: 1818–83; German social philosopher, the most significant theorist of modern communism and socialism

"Where's this place at, kid?" and it was a pleasure to direct the tourists in their language, to hear them mutter to their buddies just off the train, "Smart kid, you hear him?" and "Ask him if he has a sister." I learned to put on a touch of a Dollardish accent; to guarantee full credit for my linguistic accomplishment, and sometimes a little tip. I earned a quarter for every two hundred leaflets I passed, and a nickel for every one redeemed at the Club Lido.

Dollard had dropped out of school and gotten a job at Steinberg's, loading and delivering. Two of Théophile's sons-in-law got big jobs in the States, dry-walling for a motel chain, and suddenly our little apartment was filled with new appliances. Béatrice stored an automatic washing machine on the back gallery so that the hot soapy water could gush over the cars below. We got a television set, the first anyone had seen, even though Canadian television was barely launched, rudimentary. That didn't stop me from buying the wires and rigging some rabbit-ears and tying them to our chimney in an attempt to coax something, anything, from the air. Burlington, Plattsburgh—those towns that provided night-time English radio in my room—where were you when it really counted? Even KDKA in Pittsburgh came in, most nights.

There was talk of our moving out. My mother's old teaching licence was approved by the Protestant school board, but she didn't dare mention it in Théophile's house. Béatrice crossed herself whenever the word "Jew" entered the conversation, as it frequently did these days with Dollard's new employment; she might have thrown herself over the gallery at the mention of Protestants. My father looked for work, but he had to lie about previous employment—or find someone to lie for him. The future would always be insecure. I would hold up my hand against the glass of the front door, and April light passed through it like X-rays. The tangle over where to live and where to send me would flare again in the summer, and the fall could be another disaster. I studied my skeleton on the door while the grunts and curses and cleaning sounds passed in the air around me.

Everyone had a few hours to themselves on Sunday afternoon, after the Mass and big meal. We dressed for the meal, and even Dollard managed some pleasantness for the few hours it took. I kept him supplied with free drink passes at the Club Lido. Thanks to Mick, I even got in a few hours' work backstage, drew close to undressed women, heard and understood all their complaints. I told my mother those nights I was at the Forum, standing for hockey.

Those warming Sunday afternoons Thérèse and I would meet at the trolley stop nearest her apartment, and if the weather was nice we'd walk to Parc LaFontaine. We had a bet: she'd read two English books for every French book I read. It wasn't fair; she'd discovered Nancy Drew and the Hardy Boys while I slogged through Claudel and St-Denys-Garneau. She was doing well, she had wonderful discipline. And on Sundays she wore her church-going, dinner-eating dress and earrings, and she was a marvellous sight. Once, a priest walked by; she stiffened, but he smiled down at us and chuckled, *"Ah, jeune Montréal!"* She made me ashamed of the money I earned working the train station; I spent all of it I could on her.

By May we could walk all the way downtown if we wanted. May in Montreal is like April in Paris; the light is more forgiving, the haze of green is everywhere and the schoolwork, despite nuns' warnings, starts to relent. I remember a Sunday in May as though it is borne to me now on the laser beams of April light, imprinted and never to be forgotten. Walking down St Catherine Street with Thérèse O'Leary. We went to Murray's, and she'd taken my hand as we walked out. I'd ordered and paid in English, and she'd been terribly impressed. She'd promised me she'd do it, but had gotten too embarrassed at the last moment. We were walking behind a group of old ladies in white gloves and wide-brimmed hats, the tea-drinking ladies of Westmount, and Thérèse had been frightened of them, afraid of what they might be saying about her. Just gossip, I said, mindless things, and I translated some of it, to reassure her. She shook her head and acted ashamed. *"Sh'peux pas°!"* she declared, pounding the side of her head with her fists, *"Idiote!,"* then giggled. *"Mais tu peus, non?* You hunnerstan' every word, non? Smart guy!" She took my hand in both of hers and swung my arm like the clapper of the biggest bell in the world.

"Sh'peux pas!": phonetically in French, "I can't!"—"sh" represents a soft "je" and it's usually said quickly, hence the apostrophe

George Elliott Clarke

"All art is a cry for identity," writes George Elliott Clarke in the introduction to his two-volume anthology, *Fire on the Water: An Anthology of Black Nova Scotia Writing*. A widely acclaimed poet, Clarke is also a scholar and political activist with a strong interest in the history and culture of the Black Nova Scotian community in which he grew up. He was born in Windsor, Nova Scotia, a seventh-generation Canadian of African and Mi'kmaq descent, and spent his youth in North End Halifax where he participated in the creation of the Black Youth Organization of Nova Scotia (now disbanded) and organized the Weymouth Falls Justice Committee to protest racism in the provincial justice system.

Clarke has a Ph.D. from Queens University and in his work as a scholar he has focussed on exploring what he refers to as "Africadian" culture. The term is one of his own coinage "minted from 'Africa' and 'Acadia' (the old name for Nova Scotia and New Brunswick), to denote the Black populations of the Maritimes." Africadians are, he explains, "the descendants of the Black Loyalists and the Black Refugees who came to Nova Scotia in 1783 and 1815 as well as those of more recent immigrants"(10). Pointing to the connection of Africadian literature with orature (spoken literature), Clarke explains that his anthology, *Fire on the Water*, is intended to rescue from obscurity a literature that began with a tradition of song and religious oratory and remains "biblical in imagery and rhetoric." Africadian literature is, he writes, "obsessed with history, identity, and liberty . . . [and] committed to revolution and revelation (27)."

It is to this tradition that Clarke's own poetry belongs. Lyrical and passionate in its defence of his "too-often neglected . . . too often vilified community," his poetry is strongly marked by his Black Baptist background in its rhythms and allusions. In what he notes as characteristic of Africadian writers, he makes use of both Black English and Standard English and he has emphasized the importance of rescuing and honouring

Black English "not in ignorance or avoidance of Standard English, but to develop the skilled use of its innate music"(26).

Clarke's first poetry collection, *Saltwater Spirituals and Deeper Blues* (1983), was a finalist for the Bliss Carman Award. In 1991, he won the Archibald Lampman Award for Poetry for *Whylah Falls*, a long poem in which he explores a fictional community through the voices of its various inhabitants. He has also been awarded a Bellagio Center Residency by the Rockefeller Foundation (1998) and the Portia White Prize (named after the Black Nova Scotian classical singer) for cultural and artistic excellence, by the Nova Scotia Arts Council (1998). The year was an important one for Clarke. It also saw the publication of his verse play and opera libretto, *Beatrice Chauncy*, which deals with the slave experience in Nova Scotia. It received its first performance, with music by James Rolfe, in Toronto in June 1998. Clarke has also written the screenplay for a feature film, *One Heart Broken* (1999), which was nominated for a Gemini award, and a second verse play, *Whylah Falls: The Play* (1999). He currently teaches English at the University of Toronto and is working on a novel.

In *Fire on the Water*, Clarke writes that, "since identity is located not just in the self but in the community, Africadian writers are concerned with the public presentation and performance of their works." Performance becomes the "means of uniting the writer and the community in a ritual reclamation and declamation of being." Because art is communal, it is important to Clarke that the language of art "replicate, in varying degrees, Black speech" (25). Language thus becomes both a means of connecting the writer with the community and an expression of the identity of that community.

Works Cited

Clarke, George Elliott. *Fire on the Water*. Vol. 1. Lawrencetown Beach, Nova Scotia: Pottersfield Press, 1991.

———. *Beatrice Chauncy*. Victoria: Polestar Book Publishers, 1999.

Elias, Christine. "Laughing Out Loud." *English Studies at Toronto*. Vol. 7. December 2000.

Kamboureli, Smaro, ed. *Making a Difference: Canadian Multicultural Literature*. Toronto: Oxford University Press, 1996. 491.

Other Sources and Websites

George Elliott Clarke
www.chebucto.ns.ca/culture/WFNS/writers/gclarke.html

Writers in Electronic Residence: George Elliott Clarke
www.edu.yorku.ca/~WIER/clarke.html

Blank Sonnet

The air smells of rhubarb, occasional
Roses, or first birth of blossoms, a fresh,
Undulant hurt, so body snaps and curls
Like flower. I step through snow as thin as script,
Watch white stars spin dizzy as drunks, and yearn
To sleep beneath a patchwork quilt of rum.
I want the slow, sure collapse of language
Washed out by alcohol. Lovely Shelley°,
I have no use for measured, cadenced verse
If you won't read. Icarus°-like, I'll fall
Against this page of snow, tumble blackly
Across vision to drown in the white sea
That closes every poem—the white reverse
That cancels the blackness of each image.

Shelley, Percy Bysshe: (1792–1822) British Romantic poet

Icarus: According to a Greek myth, Icarus flew too close to the sun, using wings made by his father, Daedalus. The heat of the sun melted the wax holding the wings together, causing Icarus to fall to his death. The story can be seen as a parable about the danger of attempting to overstep the bounds of our natural limitations.

Eva Hoffman

The extremes of immigration and of living in a second language are a kind of exacerbation of the experience of being alienated from oneself, and of having language de-familiarised.

What I wanted to talk about was not just language but the conjunction of language and identity . . .

—Eva Hoffman, interviewed by Mary Zournazi

*e*va Hoffman was born in Cracow, Poland, but moved to Canada with her parents when she was fourteen years old. The experience of losing her home, her language and, as a result, her sense of self, lies at the heart of her first book, *Lost in Translation: Life in a New Language*, from which the following selection comes. She told interviewer Harry Kreisler that during the period when she first came to Canada, before she was able to speak English, she was "in effect, without language":

And I understood that to be without language is to live in a very dim world, a very dim external world and a very dim interior world. Language is not only something that we use instrumentally, but it is something that truly shapes us, and that truly shapes our perceptions of the world. (2)

Language is the means whereby we "articulate the world" but it is also, for Hoffman, the vehicle for defining the self. Through learning to write in English, she tells Kreisler, she "started constructing [her]self," a new *English* self, different from the self who had existed in Polish because shaped by the possibilities and restrictions of a different language.

Hoffman went on from her painful struggle to learn English to graduate with a Ph.D. from Harvard and become a professor of literature and creative writing and, from 1979 to 1990, an editor and writer at *The New York Times*. In three highly successful books and numerous articles, she has continued to explore the difficulties inherent in confrontations between different cultures and the complex experience of migration.

Hoffman's family is Jewish and she believes that the horrifying experience of the Holocaust was one of the factors determining their emigration from Poland. Her most recent book, *Shtetl: the Life and Death of a Small Town and the World of Polish Jews* (1997), examines the complicated and often painful relationship between Christians and Jews in Poland over a period of six hundred years and charts the development of the rich and vibrant culture of Poland's Jewish community. Reviewer Donna Seaman observes that the book is "written with tremendous clarity of mind and language" and "emphasizes all that Poland's tragedies can (and should) teach us about ethnic and religious prejudice."

In a sense, Hoffman's clarity is at least partially attributable to the painful experience of migration. As she told Mary Zournazi:

> The paradox and benefit of living in different historical times and cultural realities is that it gives you a kind of historical scope, a long view . . . Otherwise, you don't have this distance, you cannot see yourself internally and you become your own blind spot . . . If you have only your very private and inward identity then, in a sense, you cannot know yourself sufficiently, and it seems to me that you cannot know others; there has to be some movement of empathy, a kind of leaping out of yourself. (4)

Works Cited and Weblinks

"Between Memory and History: A Writer's Voice." Conversation with Eva Hoffman, by Harry Kreisler.
globetrotter.berkeley.edu/people/Hoffman/hoffman-con2.html

Seaman, Donna. Review of *Shtetl: The Life and Death of a Small Town and the World of Polish Jews*.
www.ala.org/booklist/v94/adult/se2/27hoffma.html

Zournazi, Mary. "Foreign Dialogues—Memories, Translations, Conversations."
abc.net.au/rn/arts/radioeye/transcripts/stories/s57848.htm

Life in a New Language

By the time we've reached Vancouver, there are very few people left on the train. My mother has dressed my sister and me in our best outfits—identical navy blue dresses with sailor collars and gray coats handmade of good gabardine. My parents' faces reflect anticipation and anxiety. "Get off the train on the right foot," my mother tells us. "For luck in the new life."

I look out of the train window with a heavy heart. Where have I been brought to? As the train approaches the station, I see what is indeed a bit of nowhere. It's a drizzly day, and the platform is nearly empty. Everything is the colour of slate. From this bleakness, two figures approach us—a nondescript middle-aged man and woman—and after making sure that we are the right people, the arrivals from the other side of the world, they hug us; but I don't feel much warmth in their half-embarrassed embrace. "You should kneel down and kiss the ground," the man tells my parents. "You're lucky to be here." My parents' faces fill with a kind of naïve hope. Perhaps everything will be well after all. They need signs, portents, at this hour.

Then we all get into an enormous car—yes, this is America—and drive into the city that is to be our home.

The Rosenbergs' house is a matter of utter bafflement to me. This one-storey structure surrounded by a large garden surely doesn't belong in a city—but neither can it be imagined in the country. The garden itself is of such pruned and trimmed neatness that I'm half afraid to walk in it. Its lawn is improbably smooth and velvety (Ah, the time and worry spent on the shaving of these lawns! But I will only learn of that later), and the rows of marigolds, the circles of geraniums seem almost artificial in their perfect symmetries, in their subordination to orderliness.

Still, I much prefer sitting out here in the sun to being inside. The house is larger than any apartment I have seen in Poland, with enormous "picture" windows, a separate room for every member of the family and soft pastel-coloured rugs covering all the floors. These are all features that, I know, are intended to signify good taste and wealth—but there's an incongruity between the message I'm supposed to get and my secret perceptions of these surroundings. To me, these interiors seem oddly flat, devoid of imagination, ingenuous. The spaces are plain, low-ceilinged, obvious; there are no curves, niches, odd angles, nooks, or crannies—nothing that gathers a house into itself, giving it a sense of privacy, or of depth—of interiority. There's no solid wood here, no accretion either of age or dust. There is only the open serenity of the simple spaces, open right on to the street. (No peering out the window here, to catch glimpses of exchanges on the street; the picture windows are designed to give everyone full view of everyone else, to declare there's no mystery, nothing to hide. Not true, of course, but that's the statement.) There is also the disingenuousness of the furniture, all of it whiteish with gold trimming. The whole thing is too revealing of an aspiration to good taste, but the unintended effect is thin and insubstantial—as if it was planned and put up just yesterday, and could just as well be dismantled tomorrow. The only rooms that really impress me are the bathroom and the kitchen—both of them so shiny, polished, and full of unfamiliar, fabulously functional appliances that they remind me of interiors which we occasionally glimpsed in French or American movies, and which, in our bedraggled Poland, we couldn't distinguish from fantasy. "Do you think people really live like this?" we would ask after one of these films, neglecting all the drama of the plot for the interest of these incidental features. Here is something worth describing to my friends in Cracow, down to such mind-boggling details as a shaggy rug in the bathroom and toilet paper that comes in different colours.

For the few days we stay at the Rosenbergs', we are relegated to the basement, where there's an extra apartment usually rented out to lodgers. My father looks up to Mr. Rosenberg with the respect, even a touch of awe due to someone who is a certified millionaire. Mr. Rosenberg is a big man in the small Duddy Kravitz community of Polish Jews, most of whom have made good in junk peddling and real estate—but none as good as he. Mr. Rosenberg, who is now almost seventy, had the combined chutzpah and good luck to ride on Vancouver's real-estate boom—and now he's the richest of them all. This hardly makes him the most popular, but it automatically makes him the wisest. People from the community come to him for business advice, which he dispenses, in Yiddish, as if it were precious currency given away for free only through his grandiose generosity.

In the uncompromising vehemence of adolescence and injured pride, I begin to see Mr. Rosenberg not as our benefactor but as a Dickensian figure of personal tyranny, and my feeling toward him quickly rises to something that can only be called hate. He had made stinginess into principle; I feel it as a nonhuman hardness, a conversion of flesh and feeling into stone. His face never lights up with humour or affection or wit. But then, he takes himself very seriously; to him too his wealth is the proof of his righteousness. In accordance with his principles, he demands money for our train tickets from Montreal as soon as we arrive. I never forgive him. We've brought gifts we thought handsome, but in addition, my father gives him all the dollars he accumulated in Poland—something that would start us off in Canada, we thought, but is now all gone. We'll have to scratch out our living somehow, starting from zero: my father begins to pinch the flesh of his arms nervously.

Mrs. Rosenberg, a worn-faced nearly inarticulate, diffident woman, would probably show us more generosity were she not so intimidated by her husband. As it is, she and her daughter, Diane, feed us white bread with sliced cheese and bologna for lunch, and laugh at our incredulity at the mushy textures, the plastic wrapping, the presliced convenience of the various items. Privately, we comment that this is not real food: it has no taste, it smells of plastic. The two women also give us clothing they can no longer use. I can't imagine a state of affairs in which one would want to discard the delicate, transparent bathrobes and the Angora sweaters they pass on to us, but luscious though these items seem—beyond anything I ever hoped to own—the show of gratitude required from me on receiving them sours the pleasure of new ownership. "Say thank you," my mother prompts me in preparation for receiving a batch of clothing. "People like to be appreciated." I coo and murmur ingratiatingly; I'm beginning to master the trick of saying thank you with just the right turn of the head, just the right balance between modesty and obsequiousness. In the next few years, this is a skill I'll have to use often. But in my heart I feel no real gratitude at being the recipient of so much mercy.

On about the third night at the Rosenbergs' house, I have a nightmare in which I'm drowning in the ocean while my mother and father swim farther and farther away from me. I know, in this dream, what it is to be cast adrift in incomprehensible space; I know what it is to lose one's mooring. I wake up in the middle of a prolonged scream. The fear is stronger than anything I've ever known. My parents wake up and hush me up quickly; they don't want the Rosenbergs to hear this disturbing sound. I try to calm myself and go back to sleep, but I feel as though I've stepped through a door into a dark place. Psychoanalysts talk about "mutative insights," through which the patient gains an entirely new perspective and discards some part of a cherished neurosis. The primal scream of my birth into the New World is a mutative insight of a negative kind—and I know that I can never lose the knowledge it brings me. The black, bituminous terror of the dream solders itself to the chemical base of my being—and from then on, fragments of the fear lodge themselves in my consciousness, thorns and pinpricks of anxiety, loose electricity floating in a psyche that has been forcibly pried from its structures. Eventually, I become accustomed to it; I know that it comes, and that it also goes; but when it hits with full force, in its pure form, I call it the Big Fear.

After about a week of lodging us in his house, Mr. Rosenberg decides that he has done enough for us, and, using some acquired American wisdom, explains that it isn't good for us to be dependent on his charity; there is of course no question of kindness. There is no question, either, of Mrs. Rosenberg intervening on our behalf, as she might like to do. We have no place to go, no way to pay for a meal. And so we begin.

"Shut up, shuddup," the children around us are shouting, and it's the first word in English that I understand from its dramatic context. My sister and I stand in the schoolyard clutching each other, while kids all around us are running about, pummelling each other, and screaming like whirling dervishes. Both the boys and the girls look sharp and aggressive to me—the girls all have bright lipstick on, their hair sticks up and out like witches' fury, and their skirts are held up and out by stiff, wiry crinolines. I can't imagine wanting to talk their harsh-sounding language.

We've been brought to this school by Mr. Rosenberg, who, two days after our arrival, tells us he'll take us to classes that are provided by the government to teach English to newcomers. This morning, in the rinky-dink wooden barracks where the classes are held, we've acquired new names. All it takes is a brief conference between Mr. Rosenberg and the teacher, a kindly looking woman who tries to give us reassuring glances, but who has seen too many people come and go to get sentimental about a name. Mine—"Ewa"—is easy to change into its near equivalent in English,

"Eva." My sister's name—"Alina"—poses more of a problem, but after a moment's thought, Mr. Rosenberg and the teacher decide that "Elaine" is close enough. My sister and I hang our heads wordlessly under this careless baptism. The teacher then introduces us to the class, mispronouncing our last name—"Wydra"—in a way we've never heard before. We make our way to a bench at the back of the room; nothing much has happened, except a small, seismic mental shift. The twist on our names takes them a tiny distance from us—but it's a gap into which the infinite hobgoblin of abstraction enters. Our Polish names didn't refer to us; they were as surely us as our eyes or hands. These new appellations, which we ourselves can't pronounce, are not us. They are identification tags, disembodied signs pointing to objects that happen to be my sister and myself. We walk to our seats into a roomful of unknown faces, with names that make us strangers to ourselves.

When the school day is over the teacher hands us a file card on which she has written, "I'm a newcomer. I'm lost. I live at 1785 Granville Street. Will you kindly show me how to get there? Thank you." We wander the streets for several hours, zigzagging back and forth through seemingly identical suburban avenues, showing this deaf-mute sign to the few people we see, until we eventually recognize the Rosenbergs' house. We're greeted by our quietly hysterical mother and Mrs. Rosenberg, who, in a ritual she has probably learned from television, puts out two glasses of milk on her red Formica counter. The milk, homogenized, and too cold from the fridge, bears little resemblance to the liquid we used to drink called by the same name.

Every day I learn new words, new expressions. I pick them up from school exercises, from conversations, from the books I take out of Vancouver's well-lit, cheerful public library. There are some turns of phrase to which I develop strange allergies. "You're welcome," for example, strikes me as a gaucherie°, and I can hardly bring myself to say it—I suppose because it implies that there's something to be thanked for, which in Polish would be impolite. The very places where language is at its most conventional, where it should be most taken for granted, are the places where I feel the prick of artifice.

Then there are words to which I take an equally irrational liking, for their sound, or just because I'm pleased to have deduced their meaning. Mainly they're words I learn from books, like "enigmatic" or "insolent"—words that have only a literary value, that exist only as signs on the page.

But mostly, the problem is that the signifier has become severed from the signified. The words I learn now don't stand for things in the same unquestioned way they did in my native tongue. "River" in Polish was a vital sound, energized with the essence of riverhood, of my rivers, of my being immersed in rivers. "River" in English is cold—a word without an

gaucherie: social awkwardness

aura. It has no accumulated associations for me, and it does not give off the radiating haze of connotation. It does not evoke.

The process, alas, works in reverse as well. When I see a river now, it is not shaped, assimilated by the word that accommodates it to the psyche—a word that makes a body of water a river rather than an uncontained element. The river before me remains a thing, absolutely other, absolutely unbending to the grasp of my mind.

When my friend Penny tells me that she's envious, or happy, or disappointed, I try laboriously to translate not from English to Polish but from the word back to its source, to the feeling from which it springs. Already, in that moment of strain, spontaneity of response is lost. And anyway, the translation doesn't work. I don't know how Penny feels when she talks about envy. The word hangs in a Platonic° stratosphere, a vague prototype of all envy, so large, so all-encompassing that it might crush me— as might disappointment or happiness.

I am becoming a living avatar of structuralist° wisdom; I cannot help knowing that words are just themselves. But it's a terrible knowledge, without any of the consolations that wisdom usually brings. It does not mean that I'm free to play with words at my wont; anyway, words in their naked state are surely among the least satisfactory play objects. No, this radical disjoining between word and thing is a desiccating alchemy, draining the world not only of significance but of its colours, striations, nuances—its very existence. It is the loss of a living connection.

The worst losses come at night. As I lie down in a strange bed in a strange house—my mother is a sort of housekeeper here, to the aging Jewish man who has taken us in in return for her services—I wait for that spontaneous flow of inner language which used to be my nighttime talk with myself, my way of informing the ego where the id had been. Nothing comes. Polish, in a short time, has atrophied, shrivelled from sheer uselessness. Its words don't apply to my new experiences; they're not coeval with any of the objects, or faces, or the very air I breathe in the daytime. In English, words have not penetrated to those layers of my psyche from which a private conversation could proceed. This interval before sleep used to be the time when my mind became both receptive and alert, when images and words rose up to consciousness, reiterating what had happened during the day, adding the day's experiences to those already stored there, spinning out the thread of my personal story.

Now, this picture-and-word show is gone; the thread has been snapped. I have no interior language, and without it, interior images—

Platonic: reference to the Greek philosopher Plato, who taught that everything that existed in this world had its original in the world of ideas. For example, each individual experience of envy is a manifestation of the idea of envy.

structuralism: the theory that locates the meaning of things (in this case, words) only in their relationships: words have no intrinsic meaning; they are only symbols which only make sense in the context of the language as a whole

those images through which we assimilate the external world, through which we take it in, love it, make it our own—become blurred too. My mother and I met a Canadian family who live down the block today. They were working in their garden and engaged us in a conversation of the "Nice weather we're having, isn't it?" variety, which culminated in their inviting us into their house. They sat stiffly on their couch, smiled in the long pauses between the conversation, and seemed at a loss for what to ask. Now my mind gropes for some description of them, but nothing fits. They're a different species from anyone I've met in Poland, and Polish words slip off of them without sticking. English words don't hook on to anything. I try, deliberately, to come up with a few. Are these people pleasant or dull? Kindly or silly? The words float in an uncertain space. They come up from a part of my brain in which labels may be manufactured but which has no connection to my instincts, quick reactions, knowledge. Even the simplest adjectives sow confusion in my mind; English kindliness has a whole system of morality behind it, a system that makes "kindness" an entirely positive virtue. Polish kindness has the tiniest element of irony. Besides, I'm beginning to feel the tug of prohibition, in English, against uncharitable words. In Polish, you can call someone an idiot without particularly harsh feelings and with the zest of a strong judgment. Yes, in Polish these people might tend toward "silly" and "dull"—but I force myself toward "kindly" and "pleasant." The cultural unconscious is beginning to exercise its subliminal influence.

The verbal blur covers these people's faces, their gestures with a sort of fog. I can't translate them into my mind's eye. The small event, instead of being added to the mosaic of consciousness and memory, falls through some black hole, and I fall with it. What has happened to me in this new world? I don't know. I don't see what I've seen, don't comprehend what's in front of me. I'm not filled with language anymore, and I have only a memory of fullness to anguish me with the knowledge that, in this dark and empty state, I don't really exist.

For my birthday, Penny gives me a diary, complete with a little lock and key to keep what I write from the eyes of all intruders. It is that little lock—the visible symbol of the privacy in which the diary is meant to exist—that creates my dilemma. If I am indeed to write something entirely for myself, in what language do I write? Several times, I open the diary and close it again. I can't decide. Writing in Polish at this point would be a little like resorting to Latin or ancient Greek—an eccentric thing to do in a diary, in which you're supposed to set down your most immediate experiences and unpremeditated thoughts in the most unmediated language. Polish is becoming a dead language, the language of the untranslatable past. But writing for nobody's eyes in English? That's like doing a school exercise, or performing in front of yourself, a slightly perverse act of self-voyeurism.

Because I have to choose something, I finally choose English. If I'm to write about the present, I have to write in the language of the present, even if it's not the language of the self. As a result, the diary becomes surely one of the more impersonal exercises of that sort produced by an adolescent girl. These are no sentimental effusions of rejected love, eruptions of familial anger, or consoling broodings about death. English is not the language of such emotions. Instead, I set down my reflections on the ugliness of wrestling; on the elegance of Mozart, and how Dostoyevsky° puts me in mind of El Greco.° I write down Thoughts. I Write.

There is a certain pathos to this naïve snobbery, for the diary is an earnest attempt to create a part of my persona that I imagine I would have grown into in Polish. In the solitude of this most private act, I write, in my public language, in order to update what might have been my other self. The diary is about me and not about me at all. But on one level, it allows me to make the first jump. I learn English through writing and, in turn, writing gives me a written self. Refracted through the double distance of English and writing, this self—my English self—becomes oddly objective; more than anything, it perceives. It exists more easily in the abstract sphere of thoughts and observations than in the world. For a while, this impersonal self, this cultural negative capability°, becomes the truest thing about me. When I write, I have a real existence that is proper to the activity of writing—an existence that takes place midway between me and the sphere of artifice, art, pure language. This language is beginning to invent another me. However, I discover something odd. It seems that when I write (or, for that matter, think) in English, I am unable to use the word "I." I do not go as far as the schizophrenic "she"—but I am driven, as by a compulsion, to the double, the Siamese-twin "you."

Dostoyevsky: great Russian novelist of the nineteenth century

El Greco: 1541–1614. Greek painter—who lived in Spain

negative capability: a term originally used by English poet John Keats to refer to Shakespeare's ability to avoid the expression of his own personality in his art, thus making it "universal"

Michael Ignatieff

ichael Ignatieff describes himself as someone "whose father was born in Russia, whose mother was born in England, whose education was in America, and whose working life has been spent in Canada, Great Britain, and France," and concludes, "if anyone has a claim to being a cosmopolitan, it must be me." On his father's side, he is the grandson of White Russians (landed aristocrats who fled Russia during the 1917 Bolshevik revolution). Ignatieff himself was born in Toronto, where he attended the University of Toronto, subsequently completing a Ph.D. in history at Harvard University. He has been senior research fellow at King's College, Cambridge, and has occupied academic posts in France, the United States and Canada.

Ignatieff's writing spans a wide range. *The Russian Album* (1987), a history of his family's migration from Russia and their struggle to build a new life in Europe and finally in Canada, won the Royal Society of Literature Award. It followed *The Needs of Strangers* (1984), which deals with social ethics, examining the nature and responsibilities of democratic communities. The trilogy of *Blood and Belonging* (1993) from which our selection is taken, *The Warrior's Honour* (1998) and *The Virtual War: Kosovo and Beyond* (1999) explores the nature of nationalism and the morality of violent conflict in the modern world. Ignatieff is also the author of two novels, one of which, *Scar Tissue*, was shortlisted for the Booker Prize. In 1998 he published a biography of liberal philosopher Isaiah Berlin.

In *Blood and Belonging*, Ignatieff records the death of his optimistic view that, with the falling of the Berlin Wall in 1989 and the dissolution of the monolithic Union of the Soviet Socialist Republics, a new age of freedom and enlightenment was dawning. "We assumed that the world was moving irrevocably beyond nationalism, beyond tribalism, beyond the provincial confines of the identities inscribed in our passports . . . [but] we were whistling in the dark" (5). Nationalism has experienced a rebirth in an especially virulent form in Serbia and Croatia, in Northern Ireland and in a variety of other places where there is a widespread belief that it is one's participation in a nation that provides the primary sense of identity and belonging:

> But belonging also means being recognized and being understood . . . To belong is to understand the tacit codes of the people you live with; it is to know that you will be understood without having to explain yourself. People, in short, 'speak your language.' This is why, incidentally, the protection and defence of a nation's language is such a deeply emotional nationalist cause, for it is language, more than land and history, that provides the essential form of belonging, which is to be understood. (10)

Ignatieff argues that "it is not obvious . . . why national identity should be a more important element of personal identity than any other"(6). He sees nationalism, and particularly ethnic nationalism, which argues for the organization of states on the principle of ethnicity, as a fundamentally dangerous system of beliefs. But he also cautions against disdainful dismissal of the nationalist agendas of many of the world's peoples. Arguing that "a cosmopolitan, post-nationalist spirit will always depend, in the end, on the capacity of nation-states to provide security and civility for their citizens," he asserts:

> In that sense alone, I am a civic nationalist, someone who believes in the necessity of nations and in the duty of citizens to defend the capacity of nations to provide the security and the rights we all need in order to live cosmopolitan lives. At the very least, cosmopolitan disdain and astonishment at the ferocity with which people will fight to win a nation-state of their own is misplaced. They are, after all, only fighting for a privilege cosmopolitans have long taken for granted. (14)

Works Cited

Ignatieff, Michael. *Blood and Belonging*. Toronto: Penguin, 1994.

Other Sources and Weblinks

Ignatieff, Michael. *The Needs of Strangers*. New York: Penguin, 1986.
——— "Varieties of experience."
   www.indexoncensorship.org/issue397/ignatieff.htm
Marcus, Steven. "Both Fox and Hedgehog." *The New York Times* on the Web. 29 Nov. 1998.
   www.thenewyorktimes/archives.html
Massey Lectures 2000: Michael Ignatieff
   www.masseylectures.cbc.ca/bio.html

Blood and Belonging

[excerpt]

. . . .

All of Quebec's anxiety about its modernization, its incorporation into the North American grain, has focused on preservation of language. *La survivance* is, above everything else, the survival of a language. The core demand of Quebec nationalist politics has been that Quebec become a unilingual nation. Nationalists fetishize language, yet the obsession that all signs, including STOP, should be in French is comprehensible if one is aware that signage is often the only sign that one is in Quebec, and not Minnesota or Vermont.

Nationalism has often been a revolt against modernity, a defense of the backwardness of economically beleaguered or declining classes and regions from the flames of individualism, capitalism, Judaism, and so on. Until the 1960s, Quebec nationalism often spoke in this tone. It does not do so now. This in itself is surprising. Given the speed with which modernization of the society has occurred since then, it might have been expected that Quebec nationalism would become a vocabulary of regret for what modernity has done to the distinctiveness of Quebec society. On the contrary. Nationalists invariably stress that theirs is the cause of modernity, of the reforming, secular state: attacking the power of the Church in education and moral life, advancing women's rights and sexual freedom, seeking to give Quebec a secure place at the very heart of the North American economy. In Quebec, being a nationalist means being a progressive, being modern, being a French North American.

The contrast between English Canadian and Quebecois attitudes to the United States is striking. In English Canada there has been an anguished debate for generations as to whether Canadian culture can preserve its distinctiveness amid the nightly electronic deluge of up to sixty cable TV stations in most Canadian homes.

At Videotron, Quebec's largest cable TV company, they beam all the American soaps into Quebec homes, but they know that the most popular shows—the ones that get up to 80 percent of the Quebec population staying home at night—are the ones written and acted in Quebec. As long as they can see what they want in their own language, Quebecois believe their culture will be secure.

Quebecois think of their language as a kind of invisible shield protecting their cultural integrity from the North American norm. The French language allows Quebecois a degree of cultural self-assurance toward the Americans that English Canadians can only envy. Yet the same Quebecois display none of the same self-assurance in relation to their own non-French-speaking minority. They incessantly fear that their declining birthrate and the rising tide of non-Francophone immigration will dilute the French presence in North America. They seek controls of immigration policy to maximize the selection of French-speaking immigrants. They legislate to restrict the rights of people to send their children to English-language schools. The language police are dispatched to happily bilingual towns in the Eastern Townships to photograph tiny English cardboard signs in corner stores. Storekeepers are prosecuted, much to the irritation of bilingual Anglophones and Francophones alike. There is a pettiness in language politics that belies the cultural self-confidence the Quebecois project about their capacity to survive and flourish.

At the Two Clowns Café

At the Two Clowns Café in old Montreal, on an arctic night, I meet a group of half a dozen nationalist Quebecois to talk about language. On my part, this encounter is charged with the same expectation I felt, age eight, climbing that cemetery hill. Now, as then, I am going to meet the Other. This is ridiculous, I know. After all, don't we have the same passports? Drink the same beers—Molson, Labatt? Aren't our memories full of the same heroes—Maurice Richard, Jean Béliveau, of the immortal Montréal Canadiens of the 1950s? Yet our political assumptions turn out to be so different that we might as well be living in different countries.

In the group at the Two Clowns is Nicole, exactly my age, an organizer for Quebec's teachers' union, the Centrale d'Education du Québec, or CEQ. Her union is independentist and so is she. Nicole and I discover that we share sports heroes, literary ones, too (Parisian writers), and an affection for the hard bright winter mornings after a snowfall. We also share a memory: the October crisis of 1970. For me, it was the moment when the Canadian government broke the back of radical nationalism in Quebec. The Prime Minister, Pierre Trudeau, ordered the arrest of more than five hundred Quebecois intellectuals and militants, following the kidnap and murder of a Quebec politician, Pierre Laporte. For Nicole, it was the moment she discovered she could no longer call herself a Canadian. For she was among those arrested, held without trial, and then just as suddenly released. "And why?" she says angrily, stubbing out her cigarette. "Not because I was making bombs in my basement. I wasn't. But because I had certain friends." This was a moment of fissure between us, a moment which mutual goodwill and an affection for the same things could not overcome. For me, Trudeau remains the champion of that ideal of federalism I have wanted to believe in all my life. For Nicole, he is the betrayer, the native son who would stop at nothing to smash the nationalism of his own people.

Besides Nicole, who dominated proceedings with her outspoken convictions and raucous laughter, there were some young post-graduates finishing up their doctorates in law and anthropology, together with a young, soft-spoken blond woman who was the chair of one of the oldest moderate nationalist societies in Quebec, the Société Saint Jean Baptiste, which among other things organizes the great parade through Montreal on Quebec's national day, June 24.

It was a typically Montreal conversation, switching between English and French with astonishing rapidity. Why, I asked, did Quebec have to be unilingual, if all of them were so fluently bilingual? Because, the president of the Saint Jean Baptiste Society said, "there are six million of us, and two hundred and fifty million of you in North America."

Besides, said a young female anthropology student, "the immigrants arrive here and they all want to learn English, and if they do, we will lose Montreal."

"Lose Montreal?"

"Yes! Lose Montreal. It will become an English-speaking island in a French nation, and that is intolerable."

"Intolerable," they all said.

"You all worry about survival. But you *have* survived, for God's sake. Why are you so worried?"

The woman from the Saint Jean Baptiste Society replied, "Yes, we have survived, but look at the cost. We would have been twelve million by now, but half of us left for the States."

"You want to stop them?"

"Of course not. But the point is, we are surrounded by a foreign civilization and we must protect ourselves."

I still couldn't understand it. The language is completely secure. The signage laws ban the public use of English. Quebec, alone among Canadian provinces, enjoys substantial jurisdiction over immigration and has secured the right to recruit French-speaking immigrants. The English public-school board is not allowed to accept pupils of French-speaking parentage (although private English schools are full of children of Quebecois who want their children to grow up bilingual).

"There," says one. "What other society allows a publicly funded school system in a language other than the majority?"

"Fine," I replied. "I'm not saying Quebecois are intolerant. You're not. I'm asking why do you feel so insecure? Why do you believe your language needs a state of your own to protect it?"

"We are not insecure," Nicole says, with exasperation. "We just want to be at home, with ourselves."

"Yes, frankly, we are tired of being a minority in Canada. We want to be a majority in our own place."

"Whoa," I cry. "That sounds ominous. What about the tyranny of the majority?"

"That's not tyranny, that's just democracy," says one bespectacled law student.

"Suppose you're right," I say. "Suppose you need a state to protect your language. Are you sure it's viable?"

"Of course. We are Quebec Inc.!"

"But what if you're wrong? *You* won't pay the price—you all have qualifications. You know who will pay? The pulp workers in Trois-Rivières. They're the ones who'll pay for a nationalist experiment that goes wrong."

"What a vicious statement!" Nicole exclaims, in mock fury. "Apologize. Apologize." She is laughing, but also half-serious.

"Answer the question."

"I work for a union, dear. Don't tell me about the workers. Don't divide us, either. They are as much for independence as we are."

And so it goes, as the beer empties accumulate at our table, and the bar gets noisier and noisier. Some of the group say nothing, as if holding something back, letting the pressure inside them build. In a hush between songs from the bar band, a young woman anthropology student says to me, very quietly, "Look, we just want a place where they treat us like adults. We just want to be treated like grownups, not like children." She is close to tears, and it dawns on me, in the silence that follows, that in her imagining of this community that we are supposed to share, she sees it as a family, where I, and my English kind, are the parents who never listen, and her Quebec is the young woman desperate to take her place in the world as an adult.

What can you say to such a deep myth? It is a feeling, and notoriously, feelings cannot be argued with. But they may be as productive of mischief as my childhood belief that there were Frenchies at the top of the cemetery cliff who would steal our bicycles if they could.

It is late at the Two Clowns and time to go. As I draw my winter coat around me in the frigid arctic air outside, one of the young men who had said nothing all evening comes up and whispers quietly, "It's strange how loud we talk, isn't it? As if we Quebecois were still trying to convince ourselves of something."

Two Conversations

Lise Bissonnette is my age, pert and businesslike, a newspaper editor, a columnist, a complicated and subtle supporter of sovereignty for Quebec. I talk to her in the new offices of her paper, *Le Devoir*, founded by the great nationalist hero of Edwardian Quebec, Henri Bourassa.

No, she said, she didn't want to be called a nationalist. "The narrow sense of a nation, you know, the ethnic meaning of the word 'nation'"—she made a gesture of distaste—"it's foreign to me." It is curious how few people anywhere, when seen to be nationalists from the outside, think of themselves as nationalists from the inside. The word, she says, suggests closing in on yourself, and for her, culture in Quebec should be open to the world.

I ask her whether being a nationalist, in the Quebec context, necessarily means a commitment to the sovereignty of an independent Quebec state. Through most of its history in Canada, Quebec nationalism has been about getting more from Canada, not about getting out of Canada. So I tell her the old joke—"What Quebec wants is a sovereign Quebec inside a united Canada"—and ask her whether it remains true. "Of course," she says. "Why not? Everywhere in the world, people want it both ways. There are risks to independence, so Quebecers may not love Canada, but they like it, and they want to keep the links, as a kind of reassurance." Even when they voted for Trudeau, she says, Quebecers were not necessarily voting for federalism and for Canada. They were voting for one of their own. "They were playing tribal politics." Trudeau himself would be surprised to hear this. His view of Quebec nationalism was that it is a language game played by the local elite to wrest maximum advantage from Ottawa and to ensure their domination of provincial politics. Ordinary voters, he insisted, see through the game, and when they voted for him, they voted for Canada.

But why, I persist, do you need a state if you already have exclusive jurisdiction in so many fields? Not true, she counters. Federalism in Canada "is getting to be more centralized by the day. The federal government is entering the field of education and manpower training and we must resist that." That is not how English-speaking Canada sees it. It has rejected proposals for the further decentralization of the federal system on the grounds that the country itself will not survive further provincial autonomy. Again, what is or is not true is not at issue. The crucial point is that our imagining of the same community barely intersects at all.

Why, I ask her, do Quebecois invest so little emotion in the idea of federalism, in the vision of two peoples living together within a single state? She leans forward on her desk and is briskly dismissive. "First of all, English Canadians have been saying that for a very short time. You didn't hear much about that in the sixties, when people were still fighting against the simple idea that French could be an official language in this country. In my view, the dream of the binational state is a Toronto cultural establishment way of seeing the country, and it is not shared by the majority of the people.

But, I persist, in a world being torn apart by ethnic nationalism, isn't there something to be said for a federalism that keeps ethnic groups living together in peace? She won't budge. That's an English Canadian idea, she says, politely but firmly. Canada has failed. It says it is a bilingual, bicultural state. But go to Halifax or Vancouver and you'll see it's not true. The only place that approaches the ideal is Montreal. Quebec, she seems to be saying, has turned out to be better at practicing the multi-ethnic, multi-cultural ideal than Canada itself.

She's not sure she'll ever see a Quebec with its own foreign embassies and its own seat at the United Nations. But she does believe that all the momentum of Quebec's history is leading it away from Canada.

. . . .

Tribe and Nation

One essential problem with the language of self-determination and nationhood is that it is contagious. Quebec has discovered a people within who also call themselves a nation.

About sixty-five kilometers away from the big red door that leads to LG-2 sits a trapper's cabin in the middle of a vast, flat expanse of snowy pine forest. A fire is going in the stove, and I am readying my snow gear for a day with Billy.

Billy is a Cree hunter, and these frozen forests are his kingdom. We are in the middle of the Cree nation, a huge territory of forest, river, marshland, and lake roughly the size of Germany. Billy's people, now numbering about eleven thousand, have been hunting and fishing in this land for five thousand years. Like many aboriginal peoples, they have taken up the European word "nation" to describe themselves, and while the word may not be native to their language, they definitely seem to be one. They have their own language and oral tradition, a way of life, based around cabins and traplines, and a knowledge of their environment so detailed it could be called a science.

Billy slings his carbine over his back, starts up his snowmobile, and gestures to me to get into the blood-smeared sled he has hitched up behind. Then we are off, hurtling through the forest trails, with fir branches snapping against my goggles and plumes of snow flying up behind. From time to time, Billy stops to examine caribou tracks in the snow, while I stamp my feet and rub my face to keep from freezing.

Suddenly the caribou break into the clearing in front of us, a pair of large males, the size of horses, with shaggy, cream-colored coats and ears bent in fear. They are close enough for Billy to get off a clear shot, but he pulls up instead, and we watch them bucking and plunging in the waist-high snow, struggling to make the safety of the tree cover. Within a few seconds they have vanished and the silence of the forest returns.

Billy worries that the caribou are deserting his country. His traps are empty, too, and the hooks don't bring in the fish they used to. His village was moved to higher ground, his traplines were bisected by power lines and firebreaks. The mercury levels in the new reservoirs are poisoning the fish. His land is changing before his eyes. His misfortune, and the misfortune of his tiny nation, is that they stand in the path of the LG project. Hydro-Québec dammed Billy's river, creating huge reservoirs and flooding his hunting grounds. The river is no longer his. It belongs to the with man from the south.

The word "belong" and the idea of property that goes with it are as alien to the Cree as the word "nation." Nationalism may be one form of Western romanticism about nature, but in the Western tradition, patriotism is related to property and implies unlimited dominion over nature. To Crees, this is an alien and offensive concept. Billy does not believe he owns the land; he believes he is part of it, one of the creatures who depend upon it, not only for his life but for his vision of the world. Western nationalism, when seen beneath Billy's frozen blue sky, sixteen hundred kilometers north of Montreal, is not a rhapsody to the land but a song of domination and capture. Nationalism celebrates the land of a nation the better to subdue it to human purposes. Billy's claim is to be its steward and servant.

The Cree have had money rained on them in compensation—hundreds of millions of dollars—for the taking of the land. They have trailer homes now, four-wheel drives, snowmobiles, and a guaranteed annual income from the government. Their village has a new community center, and there is a supermarket where you can buy fresh apples and tomatoes. There is a new hockey rink where the teenagers can play in the evenings. But nobody forgets what has been lost. Even the teenagers circle the ice wearing hockey shirts that say "Ex-hunters of Chisasibi."

The James Bay project is the powerhouse of a potential independent Quebec. Quebec calls it modernization, development, progress. Billy calls it an invasion. The rights of two nations are in conflict. One is very large, has multibillion-dollar resources to put into place. The other is very small. All it has on its side is an argument: if you claim self-determination for yourself, how can you deny it to us? For Billy and the Crees, the dams, the power stations, the Hydro lines, the reservoirs are a symbol, too—of their expropriation. The Cree are fighting back, and like aboriginal peoples all over the world, they are resorting to the language of nationhood and self-determination themselves. They are doing so because they shrewdly perceive that it is a language which hoists the Quebecois with their own petard. In documents filed with UN Commission on Human Rights in New York, Matthew Coon Come, grand chief of the Crees, spells out his people's claim.

> Self-determination is a right which belongs to peoples. It does not belong to states. It is a right of all peoples. It is universal and non-divisible, that is, either you have it or you do not. It is not a right that is given to peoples by someone else. Please understand, you may have to fight to exercise this right, but you do not negotiate for the right of self-determination because it is yours already.

This rhetoric alarms Quebec. Self-determination appears to mean something different from self-government. Quebec has been quick to concede the latter while denying the former. "The only limit to aboriginal autonomy will be the integrity of Quebec territory," a Quebec minister of native affairs said recently. He went on, "In this sense, there is no question of permitting the creation of ethnic ghettos where the laws of Quebec would no longer take precedence."

The Crees believe that self-determination is compatible with the territorial integrity of the state they live in. Self-determination need not be absolute; it need not imply formal statehood, flags, seats in the United Nations. In any event, the Crees are quick to point out, these are white men's inventions. Self-determination means an end to permanent dependence on government handouts and an end to being the passive spectators of the destruction of their lands. It implies something more than exclusive fishing and hunting rights over territory in the hydroelectric development; it implies more than the right to put up a checkpoint on the road into the main villages to limit the inflow of alcohol; it means something more than municipal self-government. Above all, it means stopping further hydroelectric development. The Quebec government has its eye on the Great Whale River system, to the north of La Grande; as well as on the Nottaway, Broadback, and Rupert river systems to the south. If both were completed, the entire Cree nation—its rivers, forests, and encampments—would be bound hand and foot, imprisoned within a tight network of power lines, roads, dams, and powerhouses. The Crees would become survivors on their own homeland.

And for what? The costs of development in the region are astronomically high—$12 to 15 billion. Already something like 40 percent of every consumer's electric bill is spent servicing Hydro-Québec's debt for existing projects. Cheap power, Quebec says, is the core of its competitive advantage in the North American economy, and its electricity rates are among the lowest in North America. But they are cheap only if the debt load of development in the north is kept out of the equation. If the new projects go ahead, the debt load will become crippling, and if energy-efficiency measures cause demand to drop, that load could become catastrophic. In other words, national development is pressing up against the very limits, not merely of the Crees' environment, but of the carrying capacity of the Quebec nation, too. The future demand for Quebec power is uncertain. The northeastern American states are not looking to sign new contracts for Quebec power; in several cases, the Crees have been able to persuade American regulatory authorities to cancel such deals.

If Quebec were to say enough is enough, some compromise between the nationalisms in conflict in the north of Quebec might be possible. Self-determination for the Crees does not mean statehood; it means cultural and economic survival, which in turn means being able to preserve a hunting, trapping, and fishing economy in the interstices of a major economic development. Aboriginal ways of life have demonstrated enormous flexibility: the gun, the snowmobile, the CB radio are all effortlessly absorbed into the traditional Cree hunter's way of life. But they need time to adjust, they need guarantees that further encroachments will not occur. There is no overwhelming economic argument for further construction.

If Quebec does not proceed with Great Whale, and with the destruction of the Cree nation, it will do so because the rhetoric of national pride will have prevailed over economic good sense. The trouble with nationalism, as applied to economics, is that it invests projects with a symbolic importance that makes governments blind to realities. If the James Bay project is what the Aswan Dam was for Egypt's Nasser, what Kwame Nkrumah's hydroelectric and aluminum-smelting projects were to post-independence Ghana, the message is one of warning. In these two examples, declarations of national independence took their societies to the edge of bankruptcy. It remains to be seen whether nationalist hubris will lead Quebec to overplay its hand. Quebec is neither Ghana nor Egypt. It is an advanced and developed society. But the risks are there. When economic development is vested in the imperatives of national pride, nemesis awaits.

Rights and Survival

Crees and Quebecois both argue their demand for national self-determination in terms of cultural survival. This link between survival and self-determination is central to nationalist claims everywhere, but it deserves skeptical examination.

The survival of Crees as individuals is not in doubt: their birthrate, per capita income, and level of education are all rising. Given these facts, they can certainly survive as individuals who think of themselves as Crees. Whether they can survive as a nation, that is, as a distinct people with a way of life rooted in the land, is less certain. You could take the view that it should be up to the next generation—the teenagers cruising the ice in their Ex-Hunters jerseys—to determine whether to remain true to the hunting and fishing economy that sustains the culture. If so, then it is not survival itself but the right to choose which way to survive that is at issue. The old ways of life must be preserved so that the freedom of choice of future generations can be preserved.

In order to preserve that choice, the Canadian federal government has begun turning local government, policing, and justice over to native peoples. Already, in many native communities of the north, justice is jointly administered by native elders and magistrates from the south. Canadian law remains paramount, but these communities enjoy a degree of self-administration that the Italian or Chinese peoples of southern Canada, for example, do not enjoy.

Meeting the claim of cultural survival, therefore, implies that native Canadians may come to have more rights of self-government than those enjoyed by the rest of the population. Provided that these rights do not infringe on the rights of other Canadians or amount to secession from the Canadian state—and they do not—federalism can thus accommodate some asymmetry in the rights individuals enjoy within a state.

But can federalism accommodate a situation where group rights accorded to one national people appear to encroach upon the individual rights of those who do not belong to that national group? This, at least for English Canadians, is the moral challenge represented by Quebec language legislation, which restricts signage in English and restricts access to English-language education.

Nationalists in Quebec maintain that entrenching the French language is the precondition for the very survival of Quebecois identity. They live on a continent of 300 million English speakers; their native birthrate is declining, and every day immigrants arrive whose first language is not French and whose first preference in learning a new language is English.

Here the standoff between Quebecois and English visions of political community is complete. Quebecois nationalists simply deny that basic freedoms *are* being curtailed by signage legislation, while the Anglophone community simply denies that Quebecois cultural survival is at stake

The same standoff can be observed in the Baltic republics. In Latvia, for example, the fact that ethnic Russians are in a majority in Riga, the capital, is held to justify a new citizenship law that makes the capacity to speak Latvian a condition of Latvian citizenship. Ethnic Russians born and brought up in Latvia lose their citizenship in the new republic unless they learn the rudiments of Latvian. As a minority, they lose the right to speak their language whenever and wherever they please for the sake of the cultural survival of the ethnic majority.

These are not just disagreements about rights; they are also disagreements about the very purpose of the state. Liberals tend to argue that states should not have purposes: any state that wishes to further some collective end will necessarily trample on the rights of those individuals who oppose that end. The federal policy of bilingualism, in this view, is a classic piece of liberal neutralism—protecting the rights of both linguistic groups, while privileging neither. To a Quebec nationalist, however, the state cannot afford to be neutral when the cultural survival of the nation is at stake. In the real world of modern nations, English—being the language of global commerce—will sweep other languages aside.

Many Canadian liberals—led by Pierre Trudeau—have argued that when a state protects collective rights, whether they be Quebecois or aboriginal, the result is inevitably to infringe on individual rights. The cardinal sin of nationalism, on this account, is that it invariably results in some form of majoritarian tyranny. In this regard, therefore, Trudeau has warned, Quebec may be an example of an ethnic state in the making. As long as it remains within Canada, its language policies can be constrained and in some cases overruled by reference to the Supreme Court and the Canadian Charter of Rights. Should Quebec become sovereign, individuals would lose this right of appeal, and the way would be open to majoritarian ethnic tyranny.

There is little doubt that the gut appeal of Quebec nationalism lies for most Quebecers in the vision of being a majority in their own society rather than a permanent, if powerful, minority, within a federal Canada. But most Quebecers insist that theirs is not an ethnic but a liberal nationalism, based on equal citizenship. What other society, I kept being told, funds a public-school system in a language other than that of the majority? What other society has such a full panoply of human-rights protection as that enshrined in the Quebec charter of rights?

What other nation, they also add, does not take steps to protect and develop the language of its cultural majority? All nations decree which languages will have official status: all nations run school systems in the language of the majority. The liberal ideal of a purely procedural state, one that takes no view as to what language or values should be taught in the state's public schools, is a fiction. In this view, in safeguarding its cultural heritage Quebec is simply behaving like any other nation-state. At which point, of course, English Canada cries in anguish, "But you're not a nation-state!"

Who Belongs to the Nation?

It is a cold February morning in Ayer's Cliff, a farming community about half an hour's drive from the Vermont border in southern Quebec. The fields of the McKinnon farm are white and bare, and the wind is drifting the snow up against the barn door. Inside, Angus and Peter McKinnon, two brothers in their twenties, are milking a hundred head of cattle, while their father, Dennis, looks on and reminisces. There used to be lots of English-speaking families around these parts, he says, and he rolls off their names—the Barclays, the Todds, the Buchanans—but now most of his neighbors are French. The farmers' association used to run its meetings in English, and the Ayer's Cliff town council, too. But that was in the old days, and now times have changed.

Dennis McKinnon was one of the farmers who figured which way the wind was blowing, and sent his two boys to primary school in French. Though they did their high-school and agronomy courses at McGill in English, his sons remain bilingual. "You have to be," says Angus. "All the business around here is done in French."

And so it is: at the town council, at the Quebec farmers' association meetings, at the feed store, at the machinery distributors, Angus speaks French. It is much more than a halting gesture at bilingualism. Angus is the real thing: a fluently Quebecois Anglophone. Two generations ago, such a person would not have existed among the farmers of this rolling countryside.

The two communities are cordial, and they work together, on the town council, in the farmers' organizations, but they keep to themselves socially. Angus McKinnon's mother plays the violin in the orchestra in Sherbrooke. She is from Belfast originally, but her French is good and she fits in well in a French-speaking orchestra. Yet she's never been invited home by any of the other players. When Angus goes out in his truck to a dance on a Friday night, he'll be driving a lot of kilometers to get to a dance of English-speaking farmers.

One hundred thousand Anglophones have left Quebec since the first independentist government was elected in 1976. But Angus is not going to take the road to Ontario. For one thing, Quebec agriculture is among the best-subsidized and best-administered of any province's in Canada, and certainly superior to anything south of the border, where there is little price maintenance and the dairy producers have to survive on tiny margins and bulk production. And then there are cultural reasons for staying. The McKinnons and families like them have been in these rolling valleys for two hundred years. They came up from New England because they didn't want to be part of the new republic, because they wanted to stay loyal to Britain and the Crown and British institutions, and because the land in these parts was good.

Not that the history in the Quebec school textbooks ever tells their story. In Quebec history, where Anglophones figure at all, they appear as the colonial elite, the Anglophones who lived in Westmount in Montreal and ran the railways and the department stores and the big businesses on Peel Street. There wasn't much room in the story for the small farmers of the Eastern Townships. They didn't quite fit the picture of the master class.

The McKinnons aren't resentful people. For one thing, they're doing too well. Besides, they can't recall any overt insults. The Quebecois slang for an Anglo is *tête-carrée*—blockhead—but in all their time in the bars and pool halls, shooting some racks with the French farmers around, they can't recall hearing that word.

But other things hurt, all the same. They feel that they are just as much part of Quebec as the French, but the history books, the politics, the language legislation all convey the message that they don't really belong.

"They had the language police down here last summer," Angus tells me when we are having lunch at a Greek grill in Coaticook, near his farm. The Parti Québécois (PQ)—the independentist party—hired some college students to go around the town taking pictures of English-only signs. Then they went back to Quebec City and reported the tradespeople for violating the language laws.

The interesting thing is, says Angus, waving a greeting to a French farmer and his wife who have come in for lunch across the room, "everyone was mad here. Not just the English. Everyone thought: we have a community here, what are outsiders coming in for and driving us apart?" He sips on his coffee. "I tell you, had we caught those students, we would have run them out of town."

It wasn't Angus McKinnon's rights that were being violated by the sneaky way the students slipped into town and took photos of the signs. Rights language doesn't really describe the problem. The problem is one of recognition. Are English-speaking Quebecers recognized by the majority as belonging to Quebec society or not?

The minority populations of Quebec, not just native Anglophones but immigrant communities as well, are intensely irritated by the phrase *"Québécois pur laine"* or *"Québécois de souche,"* used by some Quebecois to distinguish those who descend from the original French-speaking inhabitants and those, of English, Irish, or other extraction, who arrived later. In any event, the distinction is fraudulent. There are fervent Quebecois nationalists called O'Brien or O'Neil, for example. Centuries of intermarriage among English, French, and aboriginal Quebecers make nonsense of the idea that some Quebecois are more purely French than others. Some Francophone nationalists admit the distinction is fraudulent. When I talked to the head of the Saint Jean Baptiste Society, she confessed that while she could call herself a *Québécoise de souche* on her mother's side, her father was actually Spanish.

In every modern nation, the nationalist myth that nations have a self-contained, "pure" ethnic identity comes up against the recalcitrant desire of ordinary people to breed across ethnic lines. Faced with the contradiction between the myth of ethnic purity and the reality of ethnic intermixing, nationalists have to choose how to define membership in the nation. Does the Quebecois nation comprise all those who live there, or only those who were born French-speaking?

All nationalisms face such a choice. Is Croatia the nation of the Croatian people, or of all those—they may include Serbs—who chose to make Croatia their home? Is Germany the nation of the German people, or of the Turks, Yugoslavs, Portuguese, Spaniards, Romanians, and Poles who have chosen Germany as their home?

Recent declarations by Quebecois nationalist leaders have raised the suspicion that their definition of nationality is ethnic. Jacques Parizeau, the PQ leader, has said that Quebec independence can be achieved with or without the cooperation of the minority populations. This may be a statement of fact, but it appears to imply more than a little indifference to the opinions and rights of the minorities.

On balance, however, modern Quebec nationalists are at pains to differentiate their conception of the nation from the ethnic idea that they associate with the catastrophe of Yugoslavia. Thus, in its arguments for sovereignty, the Quebec teachers' union rejects the idea that Quebec is the "national state of the French Canadians." The Quebec state, they argue, should be the national state of everyone who chooses to live there, "regardless of their ethnic origins." A national state, they insist, need not be an ethnic state.

Even if it did become an ethnic state, Angus McKinnon muses, we will never go the way of Yugoslavia. Why? "Because there's the highway to Ontario," says Angus with a laugh. "We can always get on the highway and leave. The poor people in Yugoslavia can't leave, but we can. But I don't want to. This is the best place in the world."

. . . .

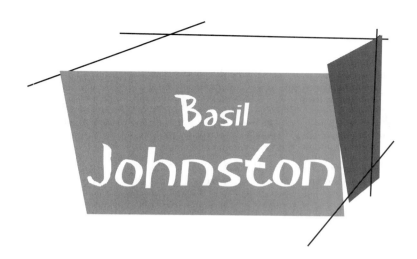

Basil Johnston

asil Johnston is a highly respected writer, educator and ethnologist. He was born in 1929 on the Parry Island Indian Reserve in Ontario and, like many native people of his generation, was educated at a residential school (in Spanish, Ontario). His experience of being taken away from his family and thrust into the context of white Canadian culture and language is recorded in his memoir, *Indian School Days* (1988). He subsequently attended Loyola College in Montreal, graduating cum laude in 1954, and the Ontario College of Education. He is now retired, but was a member of the ethnology department at the Royal Ontario Museum for more than twenty-five years.

In all of his various capacities Johnston has maintained a strong commitment to furthering an awareness of Ojibway history, language and culture. His work for the ROM has included recording Ojibway language and mythology. In nearly a dozen books he has presented traditional stories, myths and folklore, many of which derive from an oral tradition. His fiction is also deeply imbued with Ojibway traditions and beliefs. In several of his books, he has used both Ojibwa and English, an expression of his commitment to preserving his native language.

As an educator, Johnston has devoted most of his energy to the teaching of Aboriginal language and to increasing its use. He believes that "the language needs to be learned as it was spoken by traditional ancestors of the community" and that this goes well beyond merely absorbing grammatical rules and acquiring vocabulary. Learning the language "has to include the spirit and heart of the words . . . You need to know the meaning of words and their history" (McKinley 4) in order to grasp the significance of the language as a carrier of a particular culture. A reviewer of *Ojibway Heritage*, a book in which Johnston presents a collection of creation and origin myths, notes the power of names and specifically of native names in his criticism of Johnston's title. Pointing out the enormous geographical distribution of the Algonkian people, Keewaydinoquay Peschel remarks:

> No one noticed nor cared that all these people called themselves by the same name, the Anishinaubeg, lived in the same woodland and cultural style, practiced the same religion, and were capable of understanding each other linguistically. It was not politic to allow such a widely distributed people to feel that they were one. So I should like to see one word changed in the title of Mr. Johnston's book. It is the cultural heritage of the Anishinaubeg he has recorded. The time is overdue for the Anishinaubeg to reaffiliate if we are to preserve our common heritage. (Peschel 8)

In Peschel's view, to use the term "Anishinaubeg"—the traditional term by which the people refer to themselves and believed originally to have referred to the first people, the ancestors who came from the sky at the time of creation—is to invoke a sense of history and tradition that "Ojibway," which, according to some sources refers to the manner in which moccasins are made, does not. The point, that language always has political significance, is not lost on Johnston, who uses the term "Anishinaubae" throughout the selection that follows.

Native North American languages are unusual in that they do not belong to a single linguistic family as do the Indo-European languages (almost all European and some Asian languages). Each of the indigenous American languages is unique in a sense that other languages that belong to larger families are not. And, as Johnston points out, most are on the verge of extinction. Scholars have estimated that at the time of the first European contact, some 1,800 languages were spoken throughout the Western Hemisphere. By the mid-twentieth century, perhaps as many of two thirds of these languages had disappeared. When a language dies, the world loses a culture, a way of perceiving and understanding things that cannot be replaced. When a native Canadian language dies, Canada loses an important sense of its own history: the voice of the native experience of European colonization is silent and we are left only with the perspective of the white colonizers. And the descendants of the speakers of that language lose an important piece of their own sense of identity.

Works Cited

McKinley, Rob. *Aboriginal language—When it's gone, that's it. No more Indians.*
    www.ammsa.com/classroom/CLASS4language.html

Peschel, Keewaydinoquay. "Ojibway Heritage."
    richmond.edu/faculty/ASAIL/SAILns/33.html

Other Sources and Weblinks

Jenkinson, Dave. "The Star Man and Other Tales." *CM Magazine*. Vol. 4. No. 3. 3 Oct. 1997.
    www.umanitoba.ca/cm/vol4/no3/starman.html

"Native American Languages." *The Canadian Encyclopedia Plus* CD-ROM. Toronto: McClelland & Stewart, 1996.

One Generation from Extinction

Within the past few years Gregor Keeshig, Henry Johnston, Resime Akiwenzie, Norman McLeod, and Belva Pitwaniquot died. They all spoke their tribal language, Anishinaubae (Ojibwa). When these elders passed away, so did a portion of the tribal language come to an end as a tree disintegrates by degrees and in stages until it is no more; and, though infants were born to replenish the loss of life, not any one of them will learn the language of their grandfathers or grandmothers to keep it alive and to pass it on to their descendants. Thus language dies.

In some communities there are no more Gregor Keeshigs, Henry Johnstons, Resime Akiwenzies, Norman McLeods, Belva Pitwaniquots; those remaining have no more affinity to their ancestral language than they do to Swahili or Sanskrit; in other communities the languages may not survive beyond a generation. Some tribal languages are at the edge of extinction, not expected to survive for more than a few years. There remain but three aboriginal languages out of the original fifty-three found in Canada that may survive several more generations.

There is cause to lament but it is the native peoples who have the most cause to lament the passing of their languages. They lose not only the ability to express the simplest of daily sentiments and needs but they can no longer understand the ideas, concepts, insights, attitudes, rituals, ceremonies, institutions brought into being by their ancestors; and, having lost the power to understand, cannot sustain, enrich, or pass on their heritage. No longer will they think Indian or feel Indian. And though they may wear "Indian" jewellery and take part in pow-wows, they can never capture that kinship with and reverence for the sun and the moon, the sky and the water, or feel the lifebeat of Mother Earth or sense the change in her moods; no longer are the wolf, the bear and the caribou elder brothers but beasts, resources to be killed and sold. They will have lost their identity which no amount of reading can ever restore. Only language and literature can restore the "Indianness."

Now if Canadians of West European or other origin have less cause than "Indians" to lament the passing of tribal languages and cultures it is because they may not realize that there is more to tribal languages than "ugh" or "how" or "kimu sabi." At most and at best Euro-Canadians might have read or heard about Raven and Nanabush and Thunderbirds and other "tricksters"; some may have even studied "Culture Myths," "Hero Tales," "Transformation Tales," or "Nature Myths and Beast Fables," but these accounts were never regarded as bearing any more sense than "Little Red Riding Hood" or "The Three Little Pigs." Neither language nor literature were ever considered in their natural kinship, which is the only way in which language ought to be considered were its range, depth, force and beauty to be appreciated.

Perhaps our Canadian compatriots of West European origin have more cause to lament the passing of an Indian language than they realize or care to admit. Scholars mourn that there is no one who can speak the Huron° language and thus assist scholars in their pursuit of further knowledge about the tribe; scholars mourn that had the Beothuk language survived, so much more would be known about the Beothuk° peoples. In mourning the extinction of the language, scholars are implicitly declaring that the knowledge derived from a study of snowshoes, shards, arrowheads, old pipes, shrunken heads and old bones, hunting, fishing, transportation, food preparation, ornamentation and sometimes ritual is limited. And so it is; material culture can yield only so much.

Language is crucial. If scholars are to increase their knowledge and if they are to add depth and width to their studies, they must study a native language and literature. It is not enough to know linguistics or to know a few words or even some phrases or to have access to the Jesuit Relations, Chippewa *Exercises*, Ojibwa *Texts*, or a *Dictionary of the Otchipwe Language*. Without a knowledge of the language scholars can never take for granted the accuracy of an interpretation or translation of a passage, let alone a single word; nor can they presume that their articles, tracts, treatises, essays bear the kind of accuracy that scholarship and integrity demand. They would continue to labour under the impression that the word "manitou" means spirit and that it has no other meaning. Superstitious nonsense, according to the white man. They do not know that the word bears other meanings even more fundamental than "spirit," such as, and/or pertaining to the deities; of a substance, character, nature, essence, quiddity beyond comprehension and therefore beyond explanation, a mystery; supernatural; potency, potential. What a difference such knowledge might have made in the studies conducted by Ruth Landes or Thomas B. Leekley, and others of the Anishinaubae° tribe. Perhaps, instead of regarding "Indians" as super-stitious for positing "spirits" in trees or in other inanimate or insensate objects, they might have credited them with insight for having perceived a vital substance or essence that imparted life, form, growth, healing, and strength in all things, beings, and places. They might have understood that the expression "manitouwan" meant that an object possessed or was infused with an element or a feature that was beyond human ken; they might have understood that "w'manitouwih" meant that he or she was endowed with extraordinary talents, and that it did not mean that he or she was a spirit.

Huron: a confederacy of five Iroquoian-speaking Aboriginal tribes who occupied the area around Georgian Bay, Ontario, during the first half of the seventeenth century; the name was given to them by the French, with whom they traded furs

Beothuk: the now-extinct first peoples (Beothuk means "the people" or "true people") of Newfoundland

Anishinaubae (or Anishinabe): traditional name for the Chippewa or Ojibwa tribes indigenous to what is now north-central Minnesota and southern Manitoba

Language is essential. If scholars and writers are to know how "Indians" perceive and regard certain ideas they must study an "Indian" language. When an "Anishinaubae" says that someone is telling the truth, he says "w'daeb-awae." But the expression is not just a mere confirmation of a speaker's veracity. It is at the same time a philosophical proposition that, in saying, a speaker casts his words and his voice only as far as his vocabulary and his perception will enable him. In so doing the tribe was denying that there was absolute truth; that the best a speaker could achieve and a listener expect was the highest degree of accuracy. Somehow that one expression "w'daeb-awae" set the limits of a single statement as well as setting limits on all speech.

There was a special regard almost akin to reverence for speech and for the truth. Perhaps it was because words bear the tone of the speaker and may therefore be regarded as belonging to that person; perhaps it is because words have but a fleeting momentary existence in sound and are gone except in memory; perhaps it is because words have not ceased to exist but survive in echo and continue on in infinity; perhaps it is because words are medicine that can heal or injure; perhaps it is because words possess an element of the manitou that enabled them to conjure images and ideas out of nothing, and are the means by which the autissokanuk (muses) inspired men and women. It was not for nothing that the older generation did not solicit the autissokanuk to assist in the genesis of stories or in the composition of chants in seasons other than winter.

To instill respect for language the old counselled youth, "Don't talk too much" (Kegon zaum-doongaen), for they saw a kinship between language and truth. The expression is not without its facetious aspect but in its broader application it was intended to convey to youth other notions implicit in the expression "Don't talk too much," for the injunction also meant "Don't talk too often . . . Don't talk too long . . . Don't talk about those matters that you know nothing about." Were a person to restrict his discourse, and measure his speech, and govern his talk by what he knew, he would earn the trust and respect of his (her) listeners. Of that man or woman they would say "w'daeb-awae." Better still, people would want to hear the speaker again and by so doing bestow upon the speaker the opportunity to speak, for ultimately it is the people who confer the right of speech by their audience.

Language was a precious heritage; literature was no less precious. So precious did the tribe regard language and speech that it held those who abused language and speech and truth in contempt and ridicule and withheld from them their trust and confidence. To the tribe the man or woman who rambled on and on, or who let his tongue range over every subject or warp the truth was said to talk in circles in a manner no different from that of a mongrel who, not knowing the source of alarm, barks in circles (w'geewi-animoh). Ever since words and sounds were reduced to written symbols and have been stripped of their mystery and magic, the regard and reverence for them have diminished in tribal life.

As rich and full of meaning as may be individual words and expressions, they embody only a small portion of the entire stock and potential of tribal knowledge, wisdom, and intellectual attainment, the greater part is deposited in myths, legends, stories, and in the lyrics of chants that make up the tribe's literature. Therein will be found the essence and the substance of tribal ideas, concepts, insights, attitudes, values, beliefs, theories, notions, sentiments, and accounts of their institutions and rituals and ceremonies. Without language scholars, writers, and teachers will have no access to the depth and width of tribal knowledge and understanding, but must continue to labour as they have done these many years under the impression that "Indian" stories are nothing more than fairy tales or folklore, fit only for juvenile minds. For scholars and academics Nanabush, Raven, Glooscap, Weesaukeechauk and other mythological figures will ever remain "tricksters," culture heroes, deities whose misadventures were dreamed into being only for the amusement of children. Primitive and pagan and illiterate to boot, "Indians" could not possibly address or articulate abstract ideas or themes; neither their minds nor their languages could possibly express any idea more complex than taboos, superstitions and bodily needs.

But were ethnologists, anthropologists, linguists, teachers of native children and writers of native literature—yes, even archaeologists—to learn a native language, perhaps they might learn that Nanabush and Raven are not simply "tricksters" but the caricatured representations of human nature and character in their many facets; perhaps they might give thought to the meaning and sense to be found in Weessaukeetchauk [sic], The Bitter Soul. There is no other way except through language for scholars to learn or to validate their studies, their theories, their theses about the values, ideals or institutions or any other aspect of tribal life; there is no other way by which knowledge of native life can find increase. Not good enough is it to say in hushed tones after a reverential description of a totem pole or the lacing of a snowshoe, "My, weren't they clever."

Just consider the fate of "Indian" stories written by those who knew nothing of the language and never did hear any of the stories in their entirety or in their original version but derived everything that they knew of their subject from second, third and even fourth diluted sources. Is it any wonder then that the stories in *Indian Legends of Canada* by E. E. Clark or in *Manabozho* by T. B. Leekley are so bland and devoid of sense. Had the authors known the stories in their "Indian" sense and flavour, perhaps they might have infused their versions with more wit and substance. Had the authors known that the creation story as the Anishinaubae understood it to mean was intended to represent in the most dramatic way possible the process of individual development from the smallest portion of talent to be retrieved from the depths of one's being and then given growth by breath of life. Thus a man and a woman are to develop themselves, create their own worlds, and shape their being and give meaning to life. Had the authors known this meaning of the Creation Story, perhaps they might have written their accounts in terms more in keeping with the sense and thrust of the story. But not knowing the language nor having heard the story in its original text or state, the authors could not, despite their intentions, impart to their accounts the due weight and perspective the story deserved. The stories were demeaned.

With language dead and literature demeaned, "Indian" institutions are beyond understanding and restoration. Let us turn back the calendar two and a half centuries, to that period when the "Indian" languages were spoken in every home, when native literature inspired thought and when native "Indian" institutions governed native "Indian" life. It was then that a native institution caught the imagination of the newcomers to this continent. The men and women who founded a new nation to be known as the United States of America took as their model for their constitution and government the principles of government and administration embodied in The Great Tree of Peace of the Five Nations Confederacy°. The institution of The Great Tree of Peace was not then too primitive nor too alien for study or emulation to the founders of the United States. In more recent years even the architects of the United Nations regarded the "Indian" institution of The Great Tree of Peace not as a primitive organization beneath their dignity and intellect, but rather as an institution of merit. There exist still "Indian" institutions that may well serve and benefit this society and this nation, not as dramatically as did The Great Tree of Peace the United States of America, but bestow some good as yet undreamed or unimagined. Just how much good such institutions may confer upon this or some future generation will not be known unless the "Indian" languages survive.

And what is it that has undermined the vitality of some of the "Indian" languages and deprived this generation and this society the promise and the benefit of the wisdom and the knowledge embodied in tribal literature?

In the case of the Beothuk and their language, the means used were simple and direct: it was the blade, the bludgeon, and the bullet that were plied in the destruction of the Beothuk in their sleep, at their table, and in their quiet passage from home to place of work, until the tribe was no more. The speakers were annihilated; no more was the Beothuk language spoken; whatever their wisdom or whatever their institutions, the whole of the Beothuk heritage was destroyed.

In other instances, instead of bullets, bludgeons, and bayonets, other means were used to put an end to the speaking of an "Indian" language. A kick with a police riding boot administered by a 175-pound man upon the person of an eight-year-old boy for uttering the language of a savage left its pain for days and its bruise upon the spirit for life. A boy once kicked was not likely to risk a second or a third. A slap in the face or a punch to

Five Nations Confederacy: term that designates a union of five indigenous tribes (Seneca, Cayuga, Oneida, Onondaga, and Mohawk) inhabiting what is now the northern part of New York State, and whose population numbered between 10 000 and 15 000 at the time of European contact

the back of the head delivered even by a small man upon the person of a small boy left its sting and a humiliation not soon forgotten. And if a boot or a fist were not administered, then a lash or a yardstick was plied until the "Indian" language was beaten out. To boot and fist and lash was added ridicule. Both speaker and his language were assailed. "What's the use of that language? It isn't polite to speak another language in the presence of other people. Learn English! That's the only way you're going to get ahead. How can you learn two languages at the same time? No wonder kids can't learn anything else. It's a primitive language; hasn't the vocabulary to express abstract ideas, poor. Say 'ugh.' Say something in your language! . . . How can you get your tongue around those sounds?" On and on the comments were made, disparaging, until in too many the language was shamed into silence and disuse.

And how may the federal government assist in the restoration of the native languages to their former vigour and vitality and enable them to fulfil their promise?

The Government of Canada must finance the establishment of either provincial or regional language institutes to be affiliated with a museum or a university or a provincial native educational organization. The function of the "institute," to be headed by a native person who speaks, reads, and writes a native language, will be to foster research into language and to encourage the publication of lexicons, dictionaries, grammars, courses, guides, outlines, myths, stories, legends, genealogies, histories, religion, rituals, ceremonies, chants, prayers, and general articles; to tape stories, myths, legends, grammars, teaching guides and outlines and to build a collection of written and oral literature and to make same accessible to scholars, teachers and native institutions; and to duplicate and distribute written and oral literature to the native communities and learning institutions. The native languages deserve to be enshrined in this country's heritage as much as do snowshoes, shards, and arrowheads. Nay! More.

But unless the writings, the essays, stories, plays, the papers of scholars, academics, lexicographers, grammarians, etymologists, playwrights, poets, novelists, composers, philosophers are published and distributed, they can never nurture growth in language and literature. Taking into account the market represented by each tribe, no commercial publisher would risk publication of an "Indian" book. Hence, only the federal government has the means to sponsor publication of an "Indian text," either through a commercial publisher or through the Queen's Printer. The publication of an "Indian" book may not be a commercially profitable enterprise, but it would add to the nation's intellectual and literary heritage.

Critical Focus Questions

1. Basil Johnston's essay is concerned with the extinction of native languages while Eva Hoffman is describing the process of learning a new language. What concerns do they have in common? What parallels can you find in their attitudes toward language?

2. A number of the authors in this section view language as inextricably linked with identity. Focussing on two or three of these authors, explain how this is so for each of them. Do they mean different things when they discuss identity and language, or do you see their arguments as fundamentally similar?

3. At the beginning of this section there is a quote from Ngugi wa Thiong'o about the "magical power of language." Explain this quotation in the context of one or more of the selections.

4. A language can assume a symbolic significance in what Clark Blaise refers to as an individual's "moral landscape." Consider the ways in which language functions as symbol in the selections included here.

5. In Derek Walcott's poem "A Far Cry from Africa," which opens this book, the poet asks "how [to] choose between this Africa and the English tongue I love?" What is the nature of his dilemma? To what extent is it shared by other authors found throughout the text? How have some of them resolved it?

6. Using other selections to inform your understanding of the importance of language to a people's culture and identity, explain the phenomenon of Quebec nationalism discussed by Michael Ignatieff. Are there workable alternatives to the solutions proposed by the nationalists? What considerations would be involved in working out such alternatives?

7. In the excerpt from *Lost in Translation*, Eva Hoffman writes, "We want to be able to give voice accurately and fully to ourselves and our sense of the world." For Hoffman, this has meant achieving mastery of expression in English. What strategies have writers such as Marlene Nourbese-Philip used to accomplish the goal of "giving voice"? Would you expect a feminist writer such as Adrienne Rich to adopt an approach similar to that employed by Nourbese-Philip? Explain your view.

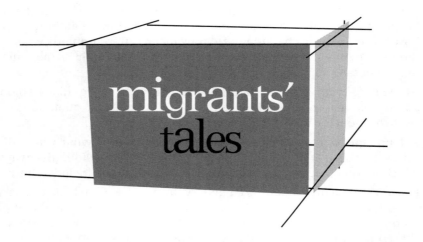

migrants' tales

In the 1990s the generic postcolonial writer is more likely to be a cultural traveller, or an 'extra-territorial,' than a national. Ex-colonial by birth, 'Third World' in cultural interest, cosmopolitan in almost every other way, he or she works within the precincts of the Western metropolis while at the same time retaining thematic and /or political connections with a national background.

—Elleke Boehmer, *Colonial and Postcolonial Literature*

After all, the geography of most Caribbean poets' lives suggests dual or multiple citizenship . . . We are multi-national; cosmopolitan—some of us multi-lingual in ways that encompass and extend beyond the standard-English national-language debate and have residences on earth that defy the makers of treaties and the laws of immigration.

—E.A. Markham, *Hinterland*

the title of this chapter comes from Salman Rushdie—perhaps the quintessential teller of migrants' tales—and what Homi Bhabha refers to as "the history of postcolonial migration, the narratives of cultural and political diaspora, the major social displacements of peasant and aboriginal communities, the poetics of exile, the grim prose of political and economic refugees" [pp. 1994–5]. Literature which takes migration, exile or cultural displacement as its theme is written about and from what Bhabha calls "culture's 'in-between'" (30), that is, the point of intersection of two or more cultures where a third "partial" culture emerges. Written primarily about European colonists, T.S. Eliot's *Notes Towards the Definition of Culture* nonetheless provides a perfect description of this "in-between" culture. Comparing modern migrations to religious schisms, Eliot observes:

> The people have taken with them only a part of the total culture . . . The culture which develops on the new soil must therefore be bafflingly alike and different from the parent culture: it will be complicated sometimes by whatever relations are established with some native race and further by immigration from other than the original source. In this way, peculiar types of culture-sympathy and culture-clash appear. (63–4, qtd. in Bhabha [30])

The culture of the immigrant, then, is not quite the culture of his/her homeland, nor is it the culture of the new country. Partaking of both, it can be seen to provide a perspective which is richer, and far less restrictive, than either.

Elleke Boehmer writes that the "melange which has resulted from immigration—the fragmented and mixed-up histories, the Khichri or goulash of languages" (235), has created a new culture and a new literature, a literature which draws on a multiplicity of cultures as well as on the experience of migration itself. For many writers this has been "an expansion of cultural and aesthetic experience," a "regenerative experience" (241).

But if the literary inspiration afforded by immigration has been welcome, the migrant experience itself is frequently fraught with loneliness, isolation and, sometimes, for those fleeing poor countries for the economic opportunities of the West, guilt. And the loss of home frequently entails a loss of self, a loss of identity. The many professionals who immigrate and can only find work in menial positions; those driven to emigrate by economic hardship who are forced to leave their children behind until they can establish themselves, or who, bringing their children, are faced with the difficulties of finding good, affordable daycare in a system they have not yet learned; those who are struggling, not only to communicate but also to express themselves in a new language, their incomplete grasp of which constantly reduces them to the simplest constructions: for these and so many others whose situations are equally problematic, emigration entails great loss as well as the potential for gain. If who we are depends to some extent on how others perceive us, who are we when surrounded by strangers who have no understanding of the culture and language that informs and gives meaning to our behaviour? Whatever its motivation, emigration is always an act of immense courage.

Works Cited

Bhabha, Homi. *The Location of Culture*. London and New York: Routledge, 1994.

_____. "Culture's in between." *Multicultural States*. Ed. David Bennett. London and New York: Routledge, 1998. 29–36.

Boehmer, Elleke. *Colonial and Postcolonial Literature*. New York: Oxford University Press, 1995.

Louise Bennett

I never compromise when it comes to the language, you know, I don't grovel, I say anything . . . I feel if I have something to say, I say it in the language that people have been saying it around me for years, for hundreds of years . . .

And this language is going on still; it is still the strongest thing that's happening around here . . .

—Louise Bennett, quoted in *New World Adams*

Louise Bennett has devoted herself to the struggle to win acceptance for Jamaican patois in "mainstream" culture and to the collection and study of Jamaican folklore. Born in Kingston, Jamaica, in 1919, she was educated at St. Simon's College and subsequently at the Royal Academy of Dramatic Art in England. Her extensive collections of folklore and Anancy (a Caribbean trickster figure) stories, together with her use of folklore and Jamaican dialect in her poetry have, according to D.C. Dance, "represented perhaps the single most significant contribution to the preservation and appreciation of Jamaican folk culture" (26).

As a performer and broadcaster, Bennett is better known as "Miss Lou." Her television and radio performances have reached thousands of Jamaicans (see "Clap Yuhself" below) and she has lectured, taught and performed in England and the United States. In addition to her many volumes of poetry and stories in dialect, she has made a number of long-playing records, including *The Honourable Miss Lou* (1980) and *Yes M'Dear* (1983).

Bennett's use of patois is an assertion of the value of Caribbean culture and identity. It also suggests that the Standard English of the colonizer is not an appropriate vehicle for describing the Jamaican experience and perspective. The sharp wit and profound sense of irony in the poem that follows are not simply conveyed by the use of dialect; they are inextricable from it—the poem couldn't mean what it does if it were written in Standard

English. One of the effects of the colonization of England by Jamaica will inevitably be (as was the case in England's colonization of Jamaica) the changing of the language.

Works Cited

Dance, Daryl Cumber. "Louise Bennett." *New World Adams*. Leeds: Peepal Tree, 1992. 26–29.
www.jamaicans.com/people/misslou.htm

Other Sources and Weblinks

"Clap Yuhself" Miss Lou.

Louise Bennett
www.balibeyond.com/~jaweb/lou-b-01.html

Markham, E.A., ed. *The Penguin Book of Caribbean Short Stories*. London: Penguin, 1996.

Colonisation in Reverse

Wat a joyful news, Miss Mattie,
I feel like me heart gwine burs'
Jamaica people colonizin
Englan in reverse.

By de hundred, by de t'ousan
From country and from town,
By de ship-load, by de plane-load
Jamaica is Englan boun.

Dem a-pour out o' Jamaica,
Everybody future plan
Is fe get a big-time job
An settle in de mother lan.

What a islan! What a people!
Man an woman, old an young
Jusa pack dem bag an baggage
An tun history upside dung!

Some people don't like travel,
But fe show dem loyalty
Dem all a-open up cheap-fare-
To-Englan agency.

An week by week dem shippin off
Dem countryman like fire,
Fe immigrate an populate
De seat o' de Empire.

Oonoo see de tunabout,
Jamaica live fe box bread
Outa English people mout'.

For wen dem catch a Englan,
An start play dem different role,
Some will settle down to work
An some will settle fe de dole.

Jane say de dole is not too bad
Because dey payin' she
Two pounds a week fe seek a job
Dat suit her dignity.

Me say Jane will never find work
At the rate how she dah-look,
For all day she stay pon Aunt Fan couch
An read love-story book.

Wat a devilment a Englan!
Dem face war an brave de worse,
But I'm wonderin' how dem gwine stan'
Colonizin' in reverse.

Anthony Akerman

born in Durban, South Africa, in 1949, Anthony Akerman read English and drama at Rhodes University in Grahamstown, but, appalled by the politics of apartheid South Africa, left the country immediately following his graduation in 1973. He trained as a director at the Bristol Old Vic Theatre School (in England) and subsequently settled in Amsterdam, where he worked as a director in Dutch theatre and began his career as a playwright, the work for which he is best known. He returned to South Africa in 1990 as the government began to relax its apartheid policy and the process of dismantling it entirely seemed underway. (The legal basis for apartheid was finally repealed in 1991–92, under then-president de Klerk). "The Exile" was written while Akerman was living in Amsterdam and first appeared in *Contrast* in Cape Town, South Africa, in December of 1987. In the short story, Akerman presents a theme that is central to much of his work: the terrible sense of loss and alienation of the exile.

South African reviewer Guy Willoughby has observed that "Anthony Akerman's career is symptomatic of the ruptures apartheid visited on us all"(1). In a series of three plays (gathered into a volume titled *Dark Outsider*), Akerman has explored the motivations for and experience of exile in ways that relate directly to his own experience. *A Man Out of the Country* (1989) has as its central character a man who seems to be utterly "psychically depleted by exile," and who is "trapped in Holland in a dying relationship with a Dutch woman who tries but cannot staunch his sense of loss." *Dark Outsider* (1995) deals with the life of South African poet Roy Campbell, another exile who is caught in an unsatisfying relationship with a woman and who, cut off from South Africa, is unable to connect himself with the source of his creativity. The last of the trilogy of plays, *Old Boys* (1996), explores the horrifying dynamics of a private boys' school, with "its autocratic hierarchies, its elitism, cruelty, hypocrisy," and what South

African critic Lesley Marx calls its "unnervingly close relationship to the fascist structures of government of the time"(15). Akerman's most recent play, *Comrades Arms* (2000), is a satiric farce about a returned political exile who, in a compromise with capitalism, has opened a bed and breakfast.

Responding to a question about the recurring theme of exile in his work, Akerman points out, "Most of my protagonists are first and foremost outsiders," rebels who are outside of mainstream culture even when they remain in their own country. Yet for Akerman, there is a particular sadness and isolation associated with physical exile. Remarking on how difficult a profession in the arts can be in the new South Africa with its financial problems and attendant cutbacks, he told Willoughby, "I love it here intensely, and don't want to leave ever again. I just know being an exile is a very, very alienating experience" (Willoughby 3).

Works Cited

Marx, Lesley. *Introduction to Dark Outsider*. Johannesberg: Witwatersrand University Press, 2000.
Willoughby, Guy. Getting Inside the Outsider. 6 Sept. 2000.
www.mg.co.za/mg/art/theatre/0009/000906-akerman.html

Other Sources and Weblinks

"Dark Outsider: Three Plays."
www.wits.ac.za/wits_university_press/Theatre_studies/dark_outsider.htm
Gray, Stephen, ed. *The Penguin Book of Contemporary South African Short Stories*. London: Penguin, 1993.

The Exile

We were giving the model a rest when the telephone rang. After thirty minutes under the lamps peering down into my Mamiya, I also needed to give my eyes and back a rest. I was in the studio kitchen making tea so Trudy, my stylist, answered. I normally don't take calls during a session with a model. I know it's a cliché, but in commercial photography time is money. Trudy came into the kitchen and told me that Sipho was on the line. He'd offered to call back if I was busy, but she said it sounded as if he had a problem. I remember feeling irritated. Immortalizing a fifteen-year-old model for the cover of a glossy magazine was giving me all the problems I could cope with that afternoon. I left Trudy to finish making the tea and took the call in the studio.

'I'm sorry to worry you,' said Sipho. 'It's just something I must tell you.' His voice was flat and toneless.

'What's the problem?' I asked. I looked up and saw the model watching me with her doe-like eyes. She smiled.

'Samson is dead,' said Sipho. 'Samson Kunene.'

'When?' I asked.

'Last night,' said Sipho. 'It happened last night. I had to go there and fix things up.'

'How did it happen?'

'He took his own life,' said Sipho. 'It was a suicide.'

I don't know exactly what I felt. Mostly disbelief I suppose, if that's a feeling. I was trying to make adjustments; adjusting to a new idea, the idea that I'd never again pass him in a street or see him in a café. I didn't know Samson Kunene all that well. I try to avoid South African exiles. I left the country eight years ago. When I say I left it, I mean I left it behind me. Amsterdam is my home now. My life is here; my woman and my job. Next year I'll have a Dutch passport and that's that. I didn't ask to be born in South Africa and I had no intention of dying there as a soldier on the border.

'Is everything all right?' asked Trudy.

'Oh yes,' I said and I smiled. I had to snap out of it. I wanted the model to look seductive and sophisticated, not serious or sad. I threw the mental switch and went back to work. The pictures were good and the magazine commissioned me to do another cover.

Saskia had left for Breda before I got home. She's an actress and in the Dutch theatre they tour everything. She was in a play by some East German writer. I had a steak and a glass of wine and sat down to write a proposal for a potential client. If I landed this job it would pay for our summer holiday in Greece. I made two abortive attempts to get started, but I didn't have an idea in my head. I turned on the television. As usual there was nothing worth watching. I was reading *Ragtime*° (I always get around to best-sellers ten years after they've been published) so I poured another glass of wine and sat down for a read. As I turned the page I realized I couldn't remember a word I had read. I had been thinking about Samson Kunene.

I suppose I'd spoken to him only about a dozen times during the last eight years. Sipho had introduced me to him. Sipho is one of the few South Africans I keep in touch with. Like me, he doesn't inhabit the South African exile ghetto; he's married to a Dutch woman and has a young daughter. The last time I'd spoken to Samson was at Sipho's birthday party. He was drunk and pedantic at the time. To humour him I told him I had been born in Thekwini, the Zulu° name for Durban. He spent at least half an hour

Ragtime: the novel by American author E.L. Doctorow about a 1906 murder trial in New York

Zulu: a Bantu language spoken by people in the Natal region of South Africa; an important literary language

explaining the etymological permutations the word *itheku* (meaning a bay or a harbour) had undergone before it emerged as *ethek-wini*. In presenting his case he digressed on Zulu linguistics and folklore. I wasn't sure if he was making it up. He had a round, gentle face and a sparse beard. There wasn't a wrinkle to suggest a life lived or a troubled spirit: just one unexplained scar, no doubt from a knife on a township Friday night. His hands were delicate and his voice was soft and persuasive. Only his eyes betrayed a restlessness. While he was talking to me they strayed around the room. Apparently he made a scene at the party after I left. Sipho didn't tell me exactly what happened, but I know he avoided Samson after that. Sipho is slow to anger, but when he's angry you'd better take cover. In that regard he's still very much a Zulu.

Whenever someone dies you are reminded of your own mortality. That someone has ceased to exist, the banal realization that it's possible, makes you consider the enormity of the fact that it can, it will happen to you. Samson Kunene didn't exist any longer. How long before his memory would fade away? There is no adequate way of responding to a suicide either. It's an unequivocal challenge. It asks: 'What have you got to live for that's so important?' It's also an accusation; 'we', those who knew him, had failed him. I was having an attack of bad conscience. I had in fact seen him the week before. I was on my way home from work when he came walking towards me along Nes. It's a narrow street and he was staggering from the hoarding on one side to the wall on the other. He was dead drunk and oblivious of everyone in the street. He didn't see me and I didn't go up to him. I remember thinking it would take him more than an hour in his condition to explain the etymological permutations of *itheku* to me. If he tagged on home with me, which was bound to happen if he recognized me, I would have to devote the next day to saving my relationship. Saskia's interest in the anguish of South African exiles has always seemed purely academic and she doesn't respond well to unexpected visitors. In this country hospitality is regulated, measured out carefully by appointments recorded in the diaries of both parties. I believe that doing in Rome as the Romans do is a workable survival policy and have conformed in this and in other forms of social behaviour. When I walked past Samson holding up a wall in Nes I was being practical. As I picked up the phone I knew I was feeling guilty. Sipho was at home babysitting his daughter.

'Yes, I'd like you to come around,' he said.

Sipho and I sat in his living room and stared into our glasses in silence. He had just finished recounting the events of the previous night; Samson lying dead in his bed, his wife in a state of shock, his three-year-old son asleep and unaware that he no longer had a daddy, the police, the ambulance men. He told everything slowly, evenly, with an intonation that suggested mild surprise. I told him about the last time I had seen Samson, about the guilt I felt for passing by on the other side of the street.

'I think you're not the only one,' he said. 'We weren't close, but I knew him. I feel sort of responsible, you know, because I didn't see things were so bad. Not that I could have stopped this, but maybe we could have talked about things. Sometimes things are not as bad as you think they are. I think I let him down. His drinking problem was one of the things that made me stop seeing him. After he buggered up my party he came back the next day to apologize. He sat in that chair and said he was sorry. He just looked at the floor and said he was sorry and kept quiet for a long time. And I was hard, man. I just said, "Yes". I didn't talk to him. Eventually he got up and said he would see me around. And I just said that was okay. And I think this is why I feel guilty. When I think about what happened to him now, I think it was a petty thing. It was so small I could have dealt with it.'

Samson's death had humbled us. It had given him dignity. Samson, whom we had come to regard as a troublesome drunk, had forced us to take him seriously. He'd left us with a question we'd never be able to answer: why did he do it?

'I know his marriage was in trouble,' said Sipho. 'Anita was telling him he must go. She couldn't take the drinking any more. I know she's blaming herself now, but it's not her fault.'

'Why did he drink so much?' I asked.

'I don't know,' said Sipho. 'I know he missed South Africa a lot. I'd been there for a family visit and when I came back he came around and I told him how things are at home. He never missed a detail. He wanted to know everything: how I arrived, what I did, how his family was. He sat there listening to me and nodding. I had brought some magazines and newspapers with me. He said: Well, you know, I'm just going to read these, but I want to take my time. He'd read a bit and then put the newspaper down, like he was saving up some for later. You could see he was really trying to place himself in the stories, rereading them and telling you small details. This is not true, he'd say, because I know that shop was in this street and not in that one. He knew where everything was. It hurt him very much that he could never go back home.'

Could homesickness drive a person to suicide? I found that hard to believe. Everything was hard to believe. I still found it hard to believe that Samson had committed suicide. He didn't seem the type, but obviously my notions of suicidal types had to be revised.

'Why couldn't he go home?' I asked. 'Had he been in the movement?'

'I think he used to be a soldier,' said Sipho, 'but he got out. There had been problems and he was quite cynical. Not about the soldiers, but about the leadership. He never told me why. He used to tell me these things just passing through, you know, not really sitting down. I felt I shouldn't try and dig. I never asked him how did he leave South Africa, but according to the things he told me he must have had a rough life. He's been to quite a lot of countries: Botswana, Zambia, Tanzania. Kenya for some time and I think Ethiopia. He's also lived in East Europe and then he came to Italy for maybe two years, Belgium, Ireland for one year, and then he tried to settle down here with the right papers and everything. He spent a long time looking for a country.'

I was asleep before Saskia got back from Breda and I left for the studio before she was up. I remember her getting into bed. Her feet were cold. That night I dreamt I was back in South Africa for the first time in years. (When I first left I used to have nightmares in which I was back there.) I remember a railway station with thousands of people. Then it became a hospital in Soweto. I was with Saskia. We were walking down long, echoing corridors and kept losing and finding each other. I only remembered this dream at lunchtime. The hospital in Soweto obviously meant I was thinking of Samson Kunene. I couldn't get him out of my mind. I kept seeing him lying in one of those fridges, being kept fresh for his funeral. It was affecting my concentration. Trudy asked me what the matter was and I told her. She asked me if I was going to the funeral. I hadn't thought about that. When I did, I decided it was a good idea. Perhaps I was mourning and the only thing to do was to go along with it. The funeral was bound to be the day after next and then everything would be literally dead and buried.

'It's only next week Monday,' said Sipho.

'Why only then,' I asked. 'It must cost a fortune to keep him so long.'

'Samson, he knew lots of people.' said Sipho. 'They must make arrangements to come here from all over: England, Belgium, Sweden and Germany. Also they are hoping someone from the family in South Africa, maybe his brother, can come to the burial.'

'So his parents know?'

'Anita phoned his mother.'

'Does she know how he died?'

'She didn't ask how he had died,' said Sipho. 'She just didn't ask, Anita was crying and the mother started consoling her. Here is this woman who has lost a son she hasn't seen for years and she can't even come to the burial. I know she has a bigger pain and still she was consoling Anita with quotations from the Bible.'

'I still can't really believe it,' I said.

'It's like an unfinished conversation,' said Sipho. 'There are things I would like to say to him now. It's so heavy.'

'I want to come to the funeral.'

'On Thursday evening there's a sort of memorial gathering for the people who've come from other countries. Maybe you can come to that.'

When I hung up I phoned Saskia and told her what had happened. I was surprised, pleasantly surprised, when she said she'd like to go with me to the memorial gathering. She sounded serious and moved and yet she'd only met Samson once. Perhaps it came more easily to her, the appropriate tone and expression, because she was an actress. She was free on Thursday evening.

The memorial gathering was held in a run-down building, which had been appropriated by some refugee group. I think they were South Americans.

About fifty people were there and, apart from Samson's wife and someone from the Anti-Apartheid Movement, we were the only whites present. I felt a bit conspicuous and reflected cynically that apartheid perpetuated itself among the exiles by a process of natural selection. Sipho caught my eye and indicated two empty seats near him. I was glad of that. He sort of legitimized my presence. I felt like a white interloper invading their black grief. I felt all that South African shit I'd left behind me. But maybe I was projecting that into the situation. I could hardly expect people to smile at me on an occasion like that.

'Who's that?' I asked, indicating a slight man who looked as though he was about to address us.

'That's Teboho,' said Sipho. 'He is sort of Master of Ceremonies.'

Teboho spoke softly as he welcomed us. He told us that while we were here the Kunene family was gathered in Soweto to remember their son and brother. He said that anyone who wanted to tell us something about Samson Kunene could speak. A speaker took the floor and told us where and how he had met Samson. He told us how Samson had been a brother to him when he first came to Europe. He was followed by a series of speakers.

None of the speakers was nervous. They were not being judged on their performance. They were there to share their sorrow with us and to remember Samson. Songs were sung between the speeches; doleful hymns in Sotho and Zulu. A shudder moved up through my body and I had to close my mouth to stop it escaping. There was something so familiar in the Zulu hymns; something I knew and yet didn't know. I fought back my tears. No one else was crying and I didn't want to draw attention to myself. I glanced at Saskia. She was serious and calm.

A woman was speaking. I heard her saying that Samson was not a traditionalist, but a lover of tradition and culture. She said that he had been brought up in the rural areas and, as a child, had tended his father's cattle. She said he understood and appreciated the rural traditions and culture. She told us how she had gone to his house when his son was born. Her household had been to see his household in the appropriate way. Then 'Nkosi Sikelel' iAfrika' was sung. I hadn't experienced such a sadness since I was a child. It was an empty, almost hopeless feeling. I held the back of the chair in front of me as swell after swell of inarticulate emotion heaved inside me. I wished they would finish singing. I saw Saskia out of the corner of my eye. She knew the tune and was trying to pick up the words as she went along. I saw a few fists clenched in sad and seemingly dutiful defiance.

When it was over Teboho closed the gathering. He said he hoped that by the year 2000 Samson's bones could be taken back to South Africa to be buried near those of his forefathers. He said that was the only way to ensure that the continuity in the line of the Kunenes would not be broken.

'Are you all right, love?' asked Saskia reaching out her hand to touch my face.

'I'm all right,' I said.

'It reminds me of funerals in Brabant. When I was a little girl I went to funerals there with my mother. They were also very emotional.'

We were in a pizzeria. The pizza was heavy, but the chianti was good. At the time I felt Saskia's comparison was misplaced. I know it was unreasonable, but for a moment I felt contempt for her. Had she not understood what was happening that evening?

'What are you thinking?' she asked.

'Nothing,' I said, 'and everything, of course.'

'You're very far away.'

'This whole bloody business has upset me. This evening has made it even worse.'

'I saw you were crying.'

'I wasn't crying, I'm not sentimental. Why should I cry about Samson? I hardly knew him.'

'You were crying for South Africa,' she said.

I let out a short, dismissive laugh. I seldom cry and when I do it's not for abstractions like 'my country'.

'It's nothing to be ashamed of,' she added. 'You should be more honest with your feelings. You're still trying to say goodbye. Perhaps you should go back there and do it properly.'

'If you come with me,' I said. I knew I was on safe ground because a team of wild horses couldn't drag Saskia down to South Africa.

'How could I do that?' she asked. I watched the expression on her face change. It became a sadly caring expression. 'I felt the longing and pain of all those people this evening. If they can't go back to their home, what gives me the right to go there just to satisfy a mild curiosity?'

When she said that, I became strangely proud of her. When I was younger I used to feel proud when I walked down the street holding hands with the prettiest girl in town. Every wolf whistle used to be a feather in my cap. Now I felt proud to walk down the street holding hands with a woman who could outshine the others in moral rectitude.

'You understand that, love?'

'Yes. It looks like you've just taken a decision for me.'

'As usual,' said Saskia. She smiled.

The days leading up to the funeral marked an unaccountable improvement in my sex life. Perhaps the word 'improvement' gives the impression that it was bad before, but it wasn't. What I mean is that Saskia was all over me. It may have been the mood I was in. I was depressed, I suppose, and a bit withdrawn. I've given up trying to understand what provokes an erotic response in women. It's probably more morbid than they'd ever admit. I'd wake up in the middle of the night and realize that she was making love to me. (Something I was well advised not to try on her.) It takes the merest suggestion of pelvic pressure to flatter the male ego and I have learnt to make hay while the sun shines. But Saskia's lovemaking felt curiously calculated, more compliant than passionate. I felt very close to her, but I was aware of her drawing me towards her. During our lovemaking she wanted me to repeat that I loved her, that I loved her, that I loved her.

Then on Sunday evening she announced that she couldn't go to the funeral. She had to meet a director° in the American Hotel on Monday afternoon. He had offered her a part in an Ibsen play and she wanted him to explain his production concept to her. We'd always said that work came first.

As I came out of the studio and started walking towards the taxi rank all the sirens and hooters in the city set up a baleful wail. They are tested at midday on the first Monday of every month. I've lived here for eight years and I still don't know what I'm supposed to do if they go off at any other time. If it meant that Russian missiles were on their way, I remember thinking, I was probably doing the right thing then: going to a cemetery. That was the first time I'd laughed in a few days.

The taxi dropped me outside Sipho's flat. He'd said I could drive along with him. I went into a nearby florist and bought the most expensive bunch of flowers I could find. As I paid the shop assistant I imagined Samson looking down from the spirit world and saying: 'Are you trying to buy me off?' The shop assistant pushed a little white card across the counter towards me. I took out my Mont Blanc and wrote: Hamba kahle°, Samson Kunene. I was surprised at what I had written and suddenly felt self-consciously emotional. I left the florist as fast as I could and rang Sipho's bell. I must have looked like the rejected lover in a romantic comedy standing on the pavement with that ostentatious bunch of flowers.

'Are you going to take a last look?' I asked as we got out of the car at the funeral parlour.

'No,' said Sipho. 'I don't think I can face it again.'

We crowded into a small room and waited with the coffin. We stood in a silence that was broken by an occasional shuffle or sob. People averted their eyes, not wanting to be drawn into greeting each other. Due to an error in stage management there was a fifteen-minute delay. Teboho asked if we would like to sing softly. The hymns started again and this time the women cried quietly. I placed my flowers on the coffin and looked at Samson. Behind the pane of glass he looked alive, asleep. I was trying to project a thought to him. I don't remember what it was. Perhaps it was just: we know each other.

More people were waiting when we arrived at the cemetery. The service was simple and almost amateurish. Some of Samson's favourite music was piped in from an off-stage taperecorder; Paul Robeson, Dollar Brand, Little Lemmy playing a kwela° on two penny-whistles. When I heard the penny-whistles, I began to cry.

"**Hamba kahle**": Zulu words meaning "farewell, my friend"

kwela: name of both a hip-swinging dance and penny-whistle music from the 1950s; comes from a call to get into the swing of things

We followed the coffin to the grave. It was a cold April day and the weather changed from sun to rain to wet snow. An old man was led forward by Teboho to speak to us. He had travelled from America to attend the funeral.

'Samson's family,' he said, 'is holding a service in Soweto at this selfsame moment. His brother collected the money for a ticket, but he was not able to get a passport in time. The government said it would take three weeks.' I knew that if I'd been lying in that coffin my parents would have been there. They would have been given passports in a day, in an hour. This spite, this perversity filled me with anger and shame.

'I have known Samson since he was a small boy,' said the old man. 'I have come here for the family. In August I will be going home to South Africa. I will go to the Kunene family and I will tell them what I have seen. I can say that everything happened properly and that their son and brother was not buried like a refugee.'

Teboho stepped into the middle of a wide circle around the grave and started singing 'Nkosi Sikelel' iAfrika', but his voice broke and he fell to his knees with his hands covering his face. Two people helped Teboho to his feet and a woman's voice picked up the anthem, held it high above us like a standard. While the professionals in tails and top hats lowered the coffin into the grave, the April wind scattered the phrases: Lord Bless Africa / Let its Horn of Hope be Raised / Come Spirit / Come Spirit. We all picked up a handful of earth and dropped it on to the coffin. Teboho regained his composure and announced that he would perform the washing of hands.

'African custom says we must do this at the house of the widow,' he said, 'but because we are in exile we have put a fire-bucket and a towel outside the place where we are invited to drink coffee.'

'Maybe I'll believe he's dead now,' said Sipho.

'Do you think they'll take his bones back before the year 2000?'

'I don't know. Did you feel the earth, how cold it was? When I felt it in my hand I just thought I wouldn't like to be buried here.'

'Neither would I,' I said.

A woman of my mother's age came over to Sipho bearing a cup of coffee in front of her. Sipho introduced her to me as Mrs Dlamini. 'He was born in Durban,' Sipho added.

'You come from Thekwini!' Mrs Dlamini exclaimed and she smiled at me. I nodded and smiled at her. Then I remarked that it was a sad day for all of us.

'But Samson Kunene's spirit is with us, said Mrs Dlamini. 'And his death has united us. Look at all the people who came. You see he is the one who has brought us together. Through Samson I have also met you.'

Hanif Kureishi

Britain doesn't yet have a vision of itself as a mixed place. The feeling is
that blacks and Asians were invited to Britain to work, but maybe they'll
somehow go back again. Britain still hasn't re-cast itself as a multi-racial,
multi-cultural society.

—Hanif Kureishi, quoted in *The New York Times*

h anif Kureishi first achieved prominence as the writer of the
screenplay for the film *My Beautiful Laundrette*. Written in 1985, it
focusses on the story of a young Pakistani immigrant who opens a
laundromat with his gay, white lover. It was enthusiastically reviewed both
in Britain (where Kureishi lives) and in North America by critics who were
delighted by the freshness and lack of cliché in his portrayal of immigrants.
Reviewer Ian Jack applauded *Laundrette* as a film "about immigrants which
shows them neither as victims nor tradition-bound aliens. They're
comprehensible, modern people with an eye to the main chance, no better
or worse than the rest of us" (Emory 1). A number of Pakistani organizations were less than pleased however, worrying that the presentation of
individual characters (as homosexuals and drug dealers) would be viewed
as representative of the Pakistani community. Kureishi himself has refused
the responsibility of representing the South Asian community to British
and American audiences, but he has consistently explored the problems
with racism that it faces.

Although born in Britain (in Bromley) in 1954, Kureishi is the product
of a mixed marriage between an English mother and an immigrant
Pakistani father and he grew up with direct experience of the racial and
cultural conflicts he presents in his work. As the only Asian in his school,
he was a target for racist attacks from skinheads and followers of Enoch
Powell's National Front in the late 1960s. "I tried to deny my Pakistani self,"
he writes in *The Rainbow Sign*, an autobiographical essay he published

together with the script for *My Beautiful Laundrette*, but ultimately finds he is unable to do so. Nor is he able to abandon Britain, which he once described as "an intolerant, racist, homophobic, narrow-minded, authoritarian rat hole." "It is strange to go away to the land of your ancestors," he remarks, "to find out how much you have in common with people there, yet at the same time to realize how British you are" (Gorra 2). Like so many other postcolonial writers, he writes from a position between cultures—able to see both from the outside, but suffering from the fact that he is never able to be an insider.

My Beautiful Laundrette won the Best Screenplay award from the New York Film Critics Circle. A second screenplay followed, *Sammy and Rosie Get Laid*. In 1990, his first novel, the semi-autobiographical *The Buddha of Suburbia*, won the Whitbread Book of the Year Award for a first novel. *London Kills Me*, a film that Kureishi both wrote and directed, was released in 1991. A second novel, *The Black Album* (1995), and a collection of short stories, *Love in a Blue Time* (1997), continue his exploration of the impact of racism and the difficulty and complexity of finding a way of belonging.

Works Cited and Weblinks

Collins, Glenn. "Screen Writer Turns to the Novel to Tell of Race and Class in London."
   www.nyt.com/books/97/11/09/home/kureishi-race.html
Gorra, Michael. He Could Never Be Like Everyone Else.
   www.nyt.com/books/97/11/09/home/kureishi-laundrette.html
Hanif Kureishi
   www.emory.edu/ENGLISH/Bahri/Kureishi.html
Kureishi, Hanif. *My Beautiful Laundrette and the Rainbow Sign*. London: Faber, 1986.

We're Not Jews

Azhar's mother led him to the front of the lower deck, sat him down with his satchel, hurried back to retrieve her shopping, and took her place beside him. As the bus pulled away Azhar spotted Big Billy and his son Little Billy racing alongside, yelling and waving at the driver. Azhar closed his eyes and hoped it was moving too rapidly for them to get on. But they not only flung themselves onto the platform, they charged up the almost empty vehicle hooting and panting as if they were on a fairground ride. They settled directly across the aisle from where they could stare at Azhar and his mother.

At this his mother made to rise. So did Big Billy. Little Billy sprang up. They would follow her and Azhar. With a sigh she sank back down. The conductor came, holding the arm of his ticket machine. He knew the Billys, and had a laugh with them. He let them ride for nothing.

Mother's grey perfumed glove took some pennies from her purse. She handed them to Azhar who held them up as she had shown him.

'One and a half to the Three Kings,' he said.

'Please,' whispered Mother, making a sign of exasperation.

'Please,' he repeated.

The conductor passed over the tickets and went away.

'Hold onto them tightly,' said Mother. 'In case the inspector gets on.'

Big Billy said, 'Look, he's a big boy.'

'Big boy,' echoed Little Billy.

'So grown up he has to run to teacher,' said Big Billy.

'Cry baby!' trumpeted Little Billy.

Mother was looking straight ahead, through the window. Her voice was almost normal, but subdued. 'Pity we didn't have time to get to the library. Still, there's tomorrow. Are you still the best reader in the class?' She nudged him. 'Are you?'

'S'pose so,' he mumbled.

Every evening after school Mother took him to the tiny library nearby where he exchanged the previous day's books. Tonight, though, there hadn't been time. She didn't want Father asking why they were late. She wouldn't want him to know they had been in to complain.

Big Billy had been called to the headmistress's stuffy room and been sharply informed—so she told Mother—that she took a 'dim view'. Mother was glad. She had objected to Little Billy bullying her boy. Azhar had had Little Billy sitting behind him in class. For weeks Little Billy had called him names and clipped him round the head with his ruler. Now some of the other boys, mates of Little Billy, had also started to pick on Azhar.

'I eat nuts!'

Big Billy was hooting like an orang-utan, jumping up and down and scratching himself under the arms—one of the things Little Billy had been castigated for. But it didn't restrain his father. His face looked horrible.

Big Billy lived a few doors away from them. Mother had known him and his family since she was a child. They had shared the same air-raid shelter during the war. Big Billy had been a Ted° and still wore a drape coat and his hair in a sculpted quiff. He had black bitten-down fingernails and a smear of grease across his forehead. He was known as Motorbike Bill because he repeatedly built and rebuilt his Triumph. 'Triumph of the Bill,' Father liked to murmur as they passed. Sometimes numerous lumps of metal stood on rags around the skeleton of the bike, and in the late evening Big Bill revved up the machine while his record player balanced on the

Ted: or Teddy boy, young man affecting the style of dress believed characteristic of the reign of Edward VII of England (1901–10)

windowsill repeatedly blared out a 45 called 'Rave On'. Then everyone knew Big Billy was preparing for the annual bank holiday run to the coast. Mother and the other neighbours were forced to shut their windows to exclude the noise and fumes.

Mother had begun to notice not only Azhar's dejection but also his exhausted and dishevelled appearance on his return from school. He looked as if he'd been flung into a hedge and rolled in a puddle—which he had. Unburdening with difficulty, he confessed the abuse the boys gave him, Little Billy in particular.

At first Mother appeared amused by such pranks. She was surprised that Azhar took it so hard. He should ignore the childish remarks: a lot of children were cruel. Yet he couldn't make out what it was with him that made people say such things, or why, after so many contented hours at home with his mother, such violence had entered his world.

Mother had taken Azhar's hand and instructed him to reply, 'Little Billy, you're common—common as muck!'

Azhar held onto the words and repeated them continuously to himself. Next day, in a corner with his enemy's taunts going at him, he closed his eyes and hollered them out. 'Muck, muck, muck—common as muck you!'

Little Billy was as perplexed as Azhar by the epithet. Like magic it shut his mouth. But the next day Little Billy came back with the renewed might of names new to Azhar: sambo, wog, little coon. Azhar returned to his mother for more words but they had run out.

Big Billy was saying across the bus, 'Common! Why don't you say it out loud to me face, eh? Won't say it, eh?'

'Nah,' said Little Billy. 'Won't!'

'But we ain't as common as a slut who marries a darkie.'

'Darkie, darkie,' Little Billy repeated. 'Monkey, monkey!'

Mother's look didn't deviate. But, perhaps anxious that her shaking would upset Azhar, she pulled her hand from his and pointed at a shop.

'Look.'

'What?' said Azhar, distracted by Little Billy murmuring his name.

The instant Azhar turned his head, Big Billy called, 'Hey! Why don't you look at us, little lady?'

She twisted round and waved at the conductor standing on his platform. But a passenger got on and the conductor followed him upstairs. The few other passengers, sitting like statues, were unaware or unconcerned.

Mother turned back. Azhar had never seen her like this, ashen, with wet eyes, her body stiff as a tree. Azhar sensed what an effort she was making to keep still. When she wept at home she threw herself on the bed, shook convulsively and thumped the pillow. Now all that moved was a bulb of snot shivering on the end of her nose. She sniffed determinedly, before opening her bag and extracting the scented handkerchief with which she usually wiped Azhar's face, or, screwing up a corner, dislodged any stray eyelashes around his eye. She blew her nose vigorously but he heard a sob.

Now she knew what went on and how it felt. How he wished he'd said nothing and protected her, for Big Billy was using her name: 'Yvonne, Yvonne, hey, Yvonne, didn't I give you a good time that time?'

'Evie, a good time, right?' sang Little Billy.

Big Billy smirked. 'Thing is,' he said, holding his nose, 'there's a smell on this bus.'

'Pooh!'

'How many of them are there living in that flat, all squashed together like, and stinkin' the road out, eatin' curry and rice!'

There was no doubt that their flat was jammed. Grandpop, a retired doctor, slept in one bedroom, Azhar, his sister and parents in another, and two uncles in the living room. All day big pans of Indian food simmered in the kitchen so people could eat when they wanted. The kitchen wallpaper bubbled and cracked and hung down like ancient scrolls. But Mother always denied that they were 'like that'. She refused to allow the word 'immigrant' to be used about Father, since in her eyes it applied only to illiterate tiny men with downcast eyes and mismatched clothes.

Mother's lips were moving but her throat must have been dry: no words came, until she managed to say, 'We're not Jews.'

There was a silence. This gave Big Billy an opportunity. 'What you say?' He cupped his ear and his long dark sideburn. With his other hand he cuffed Little Billy, who had begun hissing. 'Speak up. Hey, tart, we can't hear you?'

Mother repeated the remark but could make her voice no louder.

Azhar wasn't sure what she meant. In his confusion he recalled a recent conversation about South Africa, where his best friend's family had just emigrated—and there had been such talk—they too couldn't choose Cape Town. Painfully she replied that there the people with white skins were cruel to the black and brown people who were considered inferior and were forbidden to go where the whites went. The coloureds had separate entrances and were prohibited from sitting with the whites.

This peculiar fact of living history, vertiginously irrational and not taught in his school, struck his head like a hammer and echoed through his dreams night after night. How could such a thing be possible? What did it mean? How then should he act?

'Nah,' said Big Billy. 'You no Yid, Yvonne. You us. But worse. Goin' with the Paki.'

All the while Little Billy was hissing and twisting his head in imitation of a spastic.

Azhar had heard his father say that there had been 'gassing' not long ago. Neighbour had slaughtered neighbour, and such evil hadn't died. Father would poke his finger at his wife, son and baby daughter, and state, 'We're in the front line!'

These conversations were often a prelude to his announcing that they were going 'home' to Pakistan. There they wouldn't have these problems. At this point Azhar's mother would become uneasy. How could she go 'home' when she was at home already? Hot weather made her swelter; spicy food upset her stomach; being surrounded by people who didn't speak English made her feel lonely. As it was, Azhar's grandfather and uncle chattered away in Urdu, and when Uncle Asif's wife had been in the country, she had, without prompting, walked several paces behind them in the street. Not wanting to side with either camp, Mother had had to position herself, with Azhar, somewhere in the middle of this curious procession as it made its way to the shops.

Not that the idea of 'home' didn't trouble Father. He himself had never been there. His family had lived in China and India; but since he'd left, the remainder of his family had moved, along with hundreds of thousands of others, to Pakistan. How could he know if the new country would suit him, or if he could succeed there? While Mother wailed, he would smack his hand against his forehead and cry, 'Oh God, I am trying to think in all directions at the same time!'

He had taken to parading about the flat in Wellington boots with a net curtain over his head, swinging his portable typewriter and saying he expected to be called to Vietnam as a war correspondent, and was preparing for jungle combat.

It made them laugh. For two years Father had been working as a packer in a factory that manufactured shoe polish. It was hard physical labour, which drained and infuriated him. He loved books and wanted to write them. He got up at five every morning; at night he wrote for as long as he could keep his eyes open. Even as they ate he scribbled over the backs of envelopes, rejection slips and factory stationery, trying to sell articles to magazines and newspapers. At the same time he was studying for a correspondence course on 'How To Be A Published Author'. The sound of his frenetic typing drummed into their heads like gunfire. They were forbidden to complain. Father was determined to make money from the articles on sport, politics and literature which he posted off most days, each accompanied by a letter that began, 'Dear Sir, Please find enclosed . . .'

But Father didn't have a sure grasp of the English language which was his, but not entirely, being 'Bombay variety, mish and mash'. Their neighbour, a retired schoolteacher, was kind enough to correct Father's spelling and grammar, suggesting that he sometimes used 'the right words in the wrong place, and vice versa'. His pieces were regularly returned in the self-addressed stamped envelope that the *Writers' and Artists' Yearbook* advised. Lately, when they plopped through the letter box, Father didn't open them, but tore them up, stamped on the pieces and swore in Urdu, cursing the English who, he was convinced, were barring him. Or were they? Mother once suggested he was doing something wrong and should study something more profitable. But this didn't get a good response.

In the morning now Mother sent Azhar out to intercept the postman and collect the returned manuscripts. The envelopes and parcels were concealed around the garden like an alcoholic's bottles, behind the dustbins, in the bike shed, even under buckets, where, mouldering in secret, they sustained hope and kept away disaster.

At every stop Azhar hoped someone might get on who would discourage or arrest the Billys. But no one did, and as they moved forward the bus emptied. Little Billy took to jumping up and twanging the bell, at which the conductor only laughed.

Then Azhar saw that Little Billy had taken a marble from his pocket, and, standing with his arm back, was preparing to fling it. When Big Billy noticed this even his eyes widened. He reached for Billy's wrist. But the marble was released: it cracked into the window between Azhar and his mother's head, chipping the glass.

She was screaming, 'Stop it, stop it! Won't anyone help! We'll be murdered!'

The noise she made came from hell or eternity. Little Billy blanched and shifted closer to his father; they went quiet.

Azhar got out of his seat to fight them but the conductor blocked his way.

Their familiar stop was ahead. Before the bus braked Mother was up, clutching her bags; she gave Azhar two carriers to hold, and nudged him towards the platform. As he went past he wasn't going to look at the Billys, but he did give them the eye, straight on, stare to stare, so he could see them and not be so afraid. They could hate him but he would know them. But if he couldn't fight them, what could he do with his anger?

They stumbled off and didn't need to check if the crêpe-soled Billys were behind, for they were already calling out, though not as loud as before.

As they approached the top of their street the retired teacher who assisted Father came out of his house, wearing a three-piece suit and trilby hat and leading his Scottie. He looked over his garden, picked up a scrap of paper which had blown over the fence, and sniffed the evening air. Azhar wanted to laugh: he resembled a phantom; in a deranged world the normal appeared the most bizarre. Mother immediately pulled Azhar towards his gate.

Their neighbour raised his hat and said in a friendly way, 'How's it all going?'

At first Azhar didn't understand what his mother was talking about. But it was Father she was referring to. 'They send them back, his writings, every day, and he gets so angry . . . so angry . . . Can't you help him?'

'I do help him, where I can,' he replied.

'Make him stop, then!'

She choked into her handkerchief and shook her head when he asked what the matter was.

The Billys hesitated a moment and then passed on silently. Azhar watched them go. It was all right, for now. But tomorrow Azhar would be for it, and the next day, and the next. No mother could prevent it.

'He's a good little chap,' the teacher was saying, of Father.

'But will he get anywhere?'

'Perhaps,' he said. 'Perhaps. But he may be a touch—' Azhar stood on tiptoe to listen. 'Over hopeful. Over hopeful.'

'Yes,' she said, biting her lip.

'Tell him to read more Gibbon and Macaulay°,' he said. 'That should set him straight.'

'Right.'

'Are you feeling better?'

'Yes, yes,' Mother insisted.

He said, concerned, 'Let me walk you back.'

'That's all right, thank you.'

Instead of going home, mother and son went in the opposite direction. They passed a bomb site and left the road for a narrow path. When they could no longer feel anything firm beneath their feet, they crossed a nearby rutted muddy playing field in the dark. The strong wind, buffeting them sideways, nearly had them tangled in the slimy nets of a soccer goal. He had no idea she knew this place.

At last they halted outside a dismal shed, the public toilet, rife with spiders and insects, where he and his friends often played. He looked up but couldn't see her face. She pushed the door and stepped across the wet floor. When he hesitated she tugged him into the stall with her. She wasn't going to let him go now. He dug into the wall with his penknife and practised holding his breath until she finished, and wiped herself on the scratchy paper. Then she sat there with her eyes closed, as if she were saying a prayer. His teeth were clicking; ghosts whispered in his ears; outside there were footsteps; dead fingers seemed to be clutching at him.

For a long time she examined herself in the mirror, powdering her face, replacing her lipstick and combing her hair. There were no human voices, only rain on the metal roof, which dripped through onto their heads.

'Mum,' he cried.

'Don't you whine!'

He wanted his tea. He couldn't wait to get away. Her eyes were scorching his face in the yellow light. He knew she wanted to tell him not to mention any of this. Recognising at last that it wasn't necessary, she suddenly dragged him by his arm, as if it had been his fault they were held up, and hurried him home without another word.

The flat was lighted and warm. Father, having worked the early shift, was home. Mother went into the kitchen and Azhar helped her unpack the shopping. She was trying to be normal, but the very effort betrayed her, and she didn't kiss Father as she usually did.

Now, beside Grandpop and Uncle Asif, Father was listening to the cricket commentary on the big radio, which had an illuminated panel printed with the names of cities they could never pick up: Brussels, Stockholm,

Gibbon and Macaulay: eighteenth- and nineteenth-century British historians, respectively; both noted stylists

Hilversum, Berlin, Budapest. Father's typewriter, with its curled paper tongue, sat on the table surrounded by empty beer bottles.

'Come, boy.'

Azhar ran to his father who poured some beer into a glass for him, mixing it with lemonade.

The men were smoking pipes, peering into the ashy bowls, tapping them on the table, poking them with pipe cleaners, and relighting them. They were talking loudly in Urdu or Punjabi, using some English words but gesticulating and slapping one another in a way English people never did. Then one of them would suddenly leap up, clapping his hands and shouting, 'Yes—out—out!'

Azhar was accustomed to being with his family while grasping only fragments of what they said. He endeavoured to decipher the gist of it, laughing, as he always did, when the men laughed, and silently moving his lips without knowing what the words meant, whirling, all the while, in incomprehension.

Earl Lovelace

What he really want was for people to see in him a beauty that wasn't his alone, was theirs, ours, to let us know that we in this wilderness country was people too, with drums and songs and warriors.

—Earl Lovelace, *The Wine of Astonishment*

*e*arl Lovelace was born in Toco, Trinidad, in 1935 and grew up in Tobago. He worked as a forest ranger for two years and then began to write. After the publication of his first novel, *While Gods Are Falling* (1965), he left the West Indies for the United States, where he studied at Howard University (1966–7) and Johns Hopkins University (1974). He moved back to Trinidad, but he has spent extended periods of time in the United States as a writer-in-residence and as a visiting professor.

While Gods Are Falling won the BP Independence Literary Award, making possible Lovelace's study in the United States. It was followed by *The Schoolmaster* (1968), *The Dragon Can't Dance* (1979) and *The Wine of Astonishment* (1982). The publication of the latter two novels established his international reputation, prompting a West African magazine to describe him as being "in the front rank of Caribbean writers." A collection of plays, *Jestina's Calypso,* was published in 1984 and the short story collection, *A Brief Conversation,* from which the following selection is taken, appeared in 1988. In 1997, after a gap of nearly a decade, Lovelace published his fifth novel, *Salt,* for which he won the Commonwealth Writers' Prize.

New York Times reviewer Julius Lester described *The Wine of Astonishment* as "a poetic wonder." Written entirely in Trinidadian dialect, the novel explores one of the central themes in Lovelace's writing: the choice between traditional culture and identity and the economic temptations of modern society represented by Britain and America. The quotation above refers to a character who incarnates the traditional culture which derives from Africa, a culture which, in the presence of the American Army during the Second World War, falls victim to the desire for progress and economic opportunity.

Lovelace takes up this theme again in *Salt*, in which Bango, the narrator's uncle, who represents traditional Trinidadian values, is set in opposition to Alford George—also a Trinidadian, but who has adopted European values and is seen by others as "weakened by reading and the treason of his dreams" (qtd. in Ferguson 2). At issue is the idea of cultural integrity, of being true to one's own history and culture rather than being taken in by the seductions and apparent ease of the modern, affluent culture which is foreign and, ultimately, false.

Works Cited

Ferguson, William. "Island Magic." *The New York Times*. 20 Apr. 1997.
www.nyt.com/books

Lester, Julius. "Bee and Bolo vs. The Modern World." *The New York Times*. 6 Jan. 1985.
www.nyt.com/books

Other Sources and Weblinks

Dance, Daryl Cumber. "Earl Lovelace." *New World Adams*. Leeds: Peepal Tree, 1992. Earl Lovelace.
users.rcn.com/alana.interport/lovelace2.html

Lichtenstein, David P. A Brief Biography of Earl Lovelace.
landow.stg.brown.edu/post/caribbean/lovelace/bio.html

Joebell and America

One

Joebell find that he seeing too much hell in Trinidad so he make up his mind to leave and go away. The place he find he should go is America, where everybody have a motor car and you could ski on snow and where it have seventy-five channels of colour television that never sign off and you could sit down and watch for days, all the boxing and wrestling and basketball, right there as it happening. Money is the one problem that keeping him in Cunaripo; but that year as Christmas was coming, luck hit Joebell in the gamble, and for three days straight he win out the wappie°. After he give two good pardners a stake and hand his mother a raise and buy a watch for his girl, he still have nineteen hundred and seventy-five Trinidad and

wappie: a card game, played for money

Tobago dollars that is his own. That was the time. If Joebell don't go to America now, he will never go again.

But, a couple years earlier, Joebell make prison for a wounding, and before that they had him up for resisting arrest and using obscene language. Joebell have a record; and for him to get a passport he must first get a letter from the police to say that he is of good character. All the bribe Joebell try to bribe, he can't get this letter from the police. He prepare to pay a thousand dollars for the letter; but the police pardner who he had working on the matter keep telling him to come back and come back and come back. But another pardner tell him that with the same thousand dollars he could get a whole new American passport, with new name and everything. The only thing a little ticklish is Joebell will have to talk Yankee.

Joebell smile, because if is one gift he have it is to talk languages, not Spanish and French and Italian and such, but he could talk English and American and Grenadian and Jamaican; and of all of them the one he love best is American. If that is the only problem, well, Joebell in America already.

But it have another problem. The fellar who fixing up the passport business for him tell him straight, if he try to go direct from Trinidad to America with the US passport, he could get arrest at the Trinidad airport, so the pardner advise that the best thing to do is for Joebell to try to get in through Puerto Rico where they have all those Spanish people and where the immigration don't be so fussy. Matter fix. Joebell write another pardner who he went to school with and who in the States seven years, and tell him he coming over, to look out for him, he will ring him from Puerto Rico.

Up in Independence Recreation Club where we gamble, since Joebell win this big money, he is a hero. All the fellars is suddenly his friend, everybody calling out, 'Joebell! Joebell!' some asking his opinion and some giving him advice on how to gamble his money. But Joebell not in no hurry. He know just as how you could win fast playing wappie, so you could lose fast too; and, although he want to stay in the wappie room and hear how we talk up his gambling ability, he decide that the safer thing to do is to go and play poker where if he have to lose he could lose more slow and where if he lucky he could win a good raise too. Joebell don't really have to be in the gambling club at all. His money is his own; but Joebell have himself down as a hero, and to win and run away is not classy. Joebell have himself down as classy.

Fellars' eyes open big big that night when they see Joebell heading for the poker room, because in there it have Japan and Fisherman from Mayaro and Captain and Papoye and a fellar named Morgan who every Thursday does come up from Tunapuna with a paper bag full with money and a knife in his shoe. Every man in there could real play poker.

In wappie, luck is the master; but in poker skill is what make luck work for you. When day break that Friday morning, Joebell stagger out the poker room with his whole body wash down with perspiration, out five hundred of his good dollars. Friday night he come back with the money he had give his girl to keep. By eleven he was down three. Fellars get silent and all of us vex to see how many he wait so long to get he giving away so easy. But, Joebell was really to go America in truth. In the middle of the poker, he leave the game to pee. On his way back, he walk into the wappie room. If you see Joebell: the whole front of his shirt open and wiping sweat from all behind his head. 'Heat!' somebody laugh and say. On the table that time is two card: Jack and Trey. Albon and Ram was winning everybody. The both of them like Trey. They gobbling up all bets. Was a Friday night. Waterworks get pay, County Council get pay. It had men from Forestry. It had fellars from the Housing Project. Money high high on the table. Joebell favourite card is Jack.

Ram was a loser the night Joebell win big; now, Ram on top.

'Who against Trey?' Ram say. He don't look at Joebell, but everybody know is Joebell he talking to. Out of all Joebell money, one thousand gone to pay for the false passport, and, already in the poker he lose eight. Joebell have himself down as a hero. A hero can't turn away. Everybody waiting to see. They talking, but, they waiting to see what Joebell will do. Joebell wipe his face, then wipe his chest, then he wring out the perspiration from the handkerchief, fold the kerchief and put it round his neck, and bam, just like that, like how you see in pictures when the star boy, quiet all the time, begin to make his move, Joebell crawl right up the wappie table, fellars clearing the way for him, and, everything, he empty out everything he had in his two pocket, and, lazy lazy, like he really is that star boy, he say, 'Jack for this money!'

Ram was waiting, 'Count it, Casa,' Ram say.

When they count the money was two-hundred and thirteen dollars and some change. Joebell throw the change for a broken hustler, Ram match him. Bam! Bam! Bam! In three card, Jack play.

'Double!' Joebell say. 'For all,' which mean that Joebell betting that another Jack play before any Trey.

Ram put some, and Albon put the rest, they sure is robbery.

Whap! Whap! Whap! Jack play. 'Devine!' Joebell say. That night Joebell leave the club with fifteen hundred dollars. Fellars calling him The Gambler of Natchez.

When we see Joebell next, his beard shave off, his head cut in a GI trim, and he walking with a fast kinda shuffle, his body leaned forward and his hands in his pockets and he talking Yankee: 'How ya doin, Main! Hi-ya, Baby!' And then we don't see Joebell in Cunaripo.

'Joebell gone away,' his mother, Miss Myrtle say, 'Praise God!'

If they have to give a medal for patience in Cunaripo, Miss Myrtle believe that the medal is hers just from the trials and tribulations she undergo with Joebell. Since he leave school his best friend is Trouble and wherever Trouble is, right there is Joebell.

'I shoulda mind my child myself,' she complain. 'His grandmother spoil him too much, make him feel he is too much of a star, make him believe that the world too easy.'

'The world don't owe you anything, boy,' she tell him. 'Try to be decent, son,' she say. Is like a stick break in Joebell two ears, he don't hear a word she have to say. She talk to him. She ask his uncle Floyd to talk to him. She go by the priest in Mount St Benedict to say a novena for him. She say the ninety-first psalm for him. She go by a *obeah* woman in Moruga to see what really happening to him. The *obeah* woman tell her to bring him quick so she could give him a bath and a guard to keep off the evil spirit that somebody have lighting on him. Joebell fly up in one big vexation with his mother for enticing him to go to the *obeah* woman: 'Ma, what stupidness you trying to get me in? You know I don't believe in the negromancy business. What blight you want to fall on me now? That is why it so hard for me to win in gamble, you crossing up my luck.'

But Miss Myrtle pray and she pray and at last, praise God, the answer come, not as how she did want it—you can't get everything the way you want it—but, praise God, Joebell gone away. And to those that close to her, she whisper, 'America!' for that is the destination Joebell give her.

But Joebell aint reach America yet. His girl Alicia, who working at Last Chance snackette on the Cunaripo road is the only one he tell that Puerto Rico is the place he trying to get to. Since she take up with Joebell, her mother quarrelling with her every day, 'How a nice girl like you could get in with such a vagabond fellar? You don't have eyes in your head to see that the boy is only trouble?' They talk to her, they tell her how he stab a man in the gambling club and went to jail. They tell her how he have this ugly beard on his face and this ugly look in his face. They tell her how he don't work nowhere regular, 'Child, why you bringing this cross into your life?' they ask her. They get her Uncle Matthew to talk to her. They carry her to Mount St Benedict for the priest to say a novena for her. They give her the ninety-first psalm to say. They carry her to Moruga to a *obeah* woman who bathe her in a tub with bush, and smoke incense all over her to untangle her mind from Joebell.

But there is a style about Joebell that she like. Is a dream in him that she see. And a sad craziness that make her sad too but in a happy kinda way. The first time she see him in the snackette, she watch him and don't say nothing but, she think, Hey! who he think he is? He come in the snackette with this foolish grin on his face and this strolling walk and this kinda commanding way about him and sit down at the table with his legs wide open, taking up a big space as if he spending a hundred dollars, and all he ask for is a coconut roll and a juice. And then he call her again, this time he want a napkin and a toothpick. Napkins and toothpicks is for people who eating food; but she give them to him. And still he sit down there with some blight, some trouble hanging over him, looking for somebody to quarrel with or for something to get him vex so he could parade. She just do her work, and not a word she tell him. And just like that, just so by himself he cool down and start talking to her though they didn't introduce.

obeah: a form of magic, practised in West Africa and the Caribbean

Everything he talk about is big: big mountains and big cars and race horses and heavyweight boxing champions and people in America—everything big. And she look at him from behind the counter and she see his sad craziness and she hear him talk about all this bigness far away, that make her feel too that she would like to go somewhere and be somebody, and just like that, without any words, or touching it begin.

Sometimes he'd come in the snackette, walking big and singing, and those times he'd be so broke all he could afford to call for'd be a glass of cold water. He wanted to be a calypsonian, he say; but he didn't have no great tune and his compositions wasn't so great either and everything he sing had a kinda sadness about it, no matter how he sing it. Before they start talking direct to one another he'd sing, closing his eyes and hunching his shoulders, and people in the snackette'd think he was just making joke; but, she know the song was for her and she'd feel pretty sad and think about places far away. He used to sing in a country and western style, this song: his own composition:

> Gonna take ma baby
> Away on a trip
> Gonna take ma baby
> Yip yip yip
> We gonna travel far
> To New Orleans
> Me and ma baby
> Be digging the scene

If somebody came in and had to be served, he'd stop singing while she served them, then he'd start up again. And just so, without saying anything or touching or anything, she was his girl.

She never tell him about the trouble she was getting at home because of him. In fact she hardly talk at all. She'd just sit there behind the counter and listen to him. He had another calypso that he thought would be a hit.

> Look at Mahatma Gandhi
> Look at Hitler and Mussolini
> Look at Uriah Butler
> Look at Kwame Nkrumah
> Great as they was
> Everyone of them had to stand the pressure

He used to take up the paper that was on one side of the counter and sit down and read it. 'Derby day,' he would say. 'Look at the horses running,' and he would read out the horses' names. Or it would be boxing, and he would say Muhammed boxing today, or Sugar. He talked about these people as if they were personal friends of his. One day he brought her five pounds of deer wrapped in a big brown paper bag. She was sure he pay a lot of money for it. 'Put this in the fridge until you going home.' Chenette, mangoes, oranges, sapodillas, he was always bringing things for her. When her mother ask her where she was getting these things, she tell her that the owner of the place give them to her. For her birthday Joebell bring her a big box wrapped in fancy paper and went away, so proud and shy, he couldn't stand to see her open it, and when she open it it was a vase with a whole bunch of flowers made from coloured feathers and a big birthday card with an inscription: From guess who?

'Now, who give you this? The owner?' her mother asked.

She had to make up another story.

When he was broke she would slip him a dollar or two of her own money and if he win in the gamble he would give her some of the money to keep for him, but she didn't keep it long, he mostly always came back for it next day. And they didn't have to say anything to understand each other. He would just watch her and she would know from his face if he was broke and want a dollar or if he just drop in to see her, and he could tell from her face if she want him to stay away altogether that day or if he should make a turn and come again or what. He didn't get to go no place with her, cause in the night when the snackette close her big brother would be waiting to take her home.

'Thank God!' her mother say when she hear Joebell gone away. 'Thank you, Master Jesus, for helping to deliver this child from the clutches of that vagabond.' She was so happy she hold a thanksgiving feast, buy sweet drinks and make cake and invite all the neighbour's little children; and she was surprise that Alicia was smiling. But Alicia was thinking, Lord, just please let him get to America, they will see who is vagabond. Lord just let him get through that immigration they will see happiness when he send for me.

The fellars go round by the snackette where Alicia working and they ask for Joebell.

'Joebell gone away,' she tell them.

'Gone away and leave a nice girl like you? If was me I would never leave you.'

And she just smile that smile that make her look like she crying and she mumble something that don't mean nothing, but if you listen good is, 'Well, is not you.'

'Why you don't let me take you to the dance in the Centre Saturday? Joey Lewis playing. Why you don't come and forget that crazy fellar?'

But Alicia smile no, all the time thinking, wait until he send for me, you will see who crazy. And she sell the cake and the coconut roll and sweet drink and mauby that they ask for and take their money and give them their change and move off with that soft, bright, drowsy sadness that stir fellars, that make them sit down and drink their sweet drink and eat their coconut roll and look at her face with the spread of her nose and the lips stretch across her mouth in a full round soft curve and her far away eyes and think how lucky Joebell is.

When Joebell get the passport he look at the picture in it and he say, 'Wait! This fellar aint look like me. A blind man could see this is not me.'

'I know you woulda say that,' the pardner with the passport say, 'You could see you don't know nothing about the American immigration. Listen, in America, every black face is the same to white people. They don't see no difference. And this fellar here is the same height as you, roughly the same age. That is what you have to think about, those little details, not how his face looking.' That was his pardner talking.

'You saying this is me, this fellar here is me?' Joebell ask again. 'You want them to lock me up or what, man? This is what I pay a thousand dollars for? A lock up?'

'Look, you have no worry. I went America one time on a passport where the fellar had a beard and I was shave clean and they aint question me. If you was white you mighta have a problem, but black, man, you easy.'

And in truth when he think of it, Joebell could see the point, cause he aint sure he could tell the difference between two Chinese.

'But, wait!' Joebell say, 'Suppose I meet up a black immigration?'

'Ah!' the fellar say, 'You thinking. Anyhow, it aint have that many, but, if you see one stay far from him.'

So Joebell, with his passport in his pocket, get a fellar who running contraband to carry him to Venezuela where his brother was living. He decide to spend a couple days by his brother and from there take a plane to Puerto Rico, in transit to America.

His brother had a job as a motor car mechanic.

'Why you don't stay here?' his brother tell him, 'It have work here you could get. And TV does be on whole day.'

'The TV in Spanish,' Joebell tell him.

'You could learn Spanish.'

'By the time I finish learn Spanish I is a old man,' Joebell say, '*Caramba! Caramba! Habla! Habla!* No. And besides I done pay my thousand dollars. I have my American passport. I is an American citizen. And,' he whisper, softening just at the thought of her, 'I have a girl who coming to meet me in America.'

Joebell leave Venezuela in a brown suit that he get from his brother, a strong-looking pair of brown leather boots that he buy, with buckles instead of laces, a cowboy hat on his head and an old camera from his brother over his shoulder and in his mouth is a cigar, and now he is James Armstrong Brady of the one hundred and twenty-fifth infantry regiment from Alabama, Vietnam Veteran, twenty-six years old. And when he reach the airport in Puerto Rico he walk with a swagger and he puff his cigar like he already home in the United States of America. And not for one moment it don't strike Joebell that he doing any wrong.

No. Joebell believe the whole world is a hustle. He believe everybody running some game, putting on some show and the only thing that separate people is that some have power and others don't have none, that who in in and who out out, and that is exactly what Joebell kick against, because

Joebell have himself down as a hero too and he not prepare to sit down timid timid as if he stupid and see a set of bluffers take over the world, and he stay wasting away in Cunaripo; and that is Joebell's trouble. That is what people call his craziness, is that that mark him out. That is the 'light' that the *obeah*° woman in Moruga see burning on him, is that that frighten his mother and charm Alicia and make her mother want to pry her loose from him. Is that that fellars see when they see him throw down his last hundred dollars on a single card, as if he know it going to play. The thing is that Joebell really don't be betting on the card, Joebell does be betting on himself. He don't be trying to guess about which card is the right one, he is trying to find that power in himself that will make him call correct. And that power is what Joebell searching for as he queue up in the line leading to the immigration entering Puerto Rico. Is that power that he calling up in himself as he stand there, because if he can feel that power, if that power come inside him, then, nothing could stop him. And now this was it.

'Mr Brady?' The immigration man look up from Joebell passport and say, same time turning the leaves of the passport. And he glance at Joebell and he look at the picture. And he take up another book and look in it, and look again at Joebell; and maybe it is that power Joebell reaching for, that thing inside him, his craziness that look like arrogance, that put a kinda sneer on his face that make the immigration fellar take another look.

'Vietnam Veteran? Mr Brady, where you coming from?'

'Venezuela.'

The fellar ask a few more questions. He is asking Joebell more questions than he ask anybody.

'Whatsamatta? Watsa problem?' Joebell ask, 'Man, I ain't never seen such incompetency as you got here. This is boring. Hey, I've got a plane to catch. I aint got all day.'

All in the airport people looking at Joebell 'cause Joebell not talking easy, and he biting his cigar so that his words coming to the immigration through his teeth. Why Joebell get on so is because Joebell believe that one of the main marks of a real American is that he don't stand no nonsense. Any time you get a real American in an aggravating situation, the first thing he do is let his voice be heard in objection: in other words, he does get on. In fact that is one of the things Joebell admire most about Americans: they like to get on. They don't care who hear them, they going to open their mouth and talk for their rights. So that is why Joebell get on so about incompetency and missing his plane and so on. Most fellars who didn't know what it was to be a real American woulda take it cool. Joebell know what he doing.

'Sir, please step into the first room on your right and take a seat until your name is called.' Now is the immigration talking, and the fellar firm and he not frighten, 'cause he is American too. I don't know if Joebell didn't realise that before he get on. That is the kind of miscalculation Joebell does make sometimes in gambling and in life.

'Maan, just you remember I gotta plane to catch,' and Joebell step off, with that slow, tall insolence like Jack Palance getting off his horse in *Shane*, but he take off his hat and go and sit down where the fellar tell him to sit down.

It had seven other people in the room but Joebell go and sit down alone by himself because with all the talk he talking big, Joebell just playing for time, just trying to put them off; and now he start figuring serious how he going to get through this one. And he feeling for that power, that craziness that sometimes take him over when he in a wappie game, when every bet he call he call right; and he telling himself they can't trap him with any question because he grow up in America right there in Trinidad. In his grandmother days was the British; but he know from Al Jolson to James Brown. He know Tallahashie bridge and Rocktow mountain. He know Doris Day and Frank Sinatra. He know America. And Joebell settle himself down not bothering to remember anything, just calling up his power. And then he see this tall black fellar over six foot five enter the room. At a glance Joebell could tell he's a crook, and next thing he know is this fellar coming to sit down side of him.

Two

I sit down there by myself alone and I know they watching me. Everybody else in the room white. This black fellar come in the room, with beads of perspiration running down his face and his eyes wild and he looking round like he escape. As soon as I see him I say 'Oh God!' because I know with all the empty seats all about the place is me he coming to. He don't know my troubles. He believe I want friends. I want to tell him 'Listen, man, I love you. I really dig my people, but now is not the time to come and talk to me. Go and be friendly by those other people, they could afford to be friends with you.' But I can't tell him that 'cause I don't want to offend him and I have to watch how I talking in case in my situation I slip from American to Trinidadian. He shake my hand in the Black Power sign. And we sit down there side by side, two crooks, he and me, unless he's a spy they send to spy on me.

I letting him do all the talking, I just nodding and saying yeah, yeah.

He's an American who just come out of jail in Puerto Rico for dope or something. He was in Vietnam too. He talking, but I really aint listening to him, I thinking how my plane going. I thinking about Alicia and how sad her face will get when she don't get the letter that I suppose to send for her to come to America. I thinking about my mother and about the fellars up in Independence Recreation Club and around the wappie table when the betting slow, how they will talk about me, 'Natchez,' who win in the wappie and go to America—nobody ever do that before—and I thinking how nice it will be for me and Alicia after we spend some time in America to go back home to Trinidad for a holiday and stay in the Hilton and hire a big car and go to see her mother. I think about the Spanish I woulda have to learn if I did stay in Venezuela.

At last they call me inside another room. This time I go cool. It have two fellars in this room, a big tough one with a stone face and a jaw like a steel trap, and a small brisk one with eyes like a squirrel. The small one is smoking a cigarette. The tough one is the one asking questions. The small one just sit down there with his squirrel eyes watching me, and smoking his cigarette.

'What's your name?'

And I watching his jaw how they clamping down on the words. 'Ma name is James Armstrong Brady.'

'Age?'

And he go through a whole long set of questions.

'You're a Vietnam Veteran, you say? Where did you train?'

And I smile 'cause I see enough war pictures to know, 'Nor' Carolina,' I say.

'Went to school there?'

I tell him where I went to school. He ask questions until I dizzy.

The both of them know I lying, and maybe they coulda just throw me in jail just so without no big interrogation; but, America. That is why I love America. They love a challenge. Something in my style is a challenge to them, and they just don't want to lock me up because they have the power, they want to trap me plain for even me to see. So now is me, Joebell, and these two Yankees. And I waiting, 'cause I grow up on John Wayne and Gary Cooper and Audie Murphy and James Stewart and Jeff Chandler. I know the Dodgers and Phillies, the Redskins and the Dallas Cowboys, Green Bay Packers and the Vikings. I know Walt Frazier and Doctor J, and Bill Russell and Wilt Chamberlain. Really, in truth, I know America so much, I feel American. Is just that I aint born there.

As fast as the squirrel-eye one finish smoke one cigarette, he light another one. He aint saying nothing, only listening. At last he put out his cigarette, he say, 'Recite the alphabet.'

'Say what?'

'The alphabet. Recite it.'

And just so I know I get catch. The question too easy. Too easy like a calm blue sea. And, pardner, I look at that sea and I think about Alicia and the warm soft curving sadness of her lips and her eyes full with crying, make me feel to cry for me and Alicia and Trinidad and America and I know like when you make a bet you see a certain card play that it will be a miracle if the card you bet on play. I lose, I know. But I is still a hero. I can't bluff forever. I have myself down as classy. And, really, I wasn't frighten for nothing, not for nothing, wasn't afraid of jail or of poverty or of Puerto Rico or America and I wasn't vex with the fellar who sell me the passport for the thousand dollars, nor with Iron Jaw and Squirrel Eyes. In fact, I kinda respect them. 'A . . . B . . . C . . .' And Squirrel Eyes take out another cigarette and don't light it, just keep knocking it against the pack, Tock! Tock! Tock! K . . . L . . . M . . . And I Feel I love Alicia . . . V . . . W . . . and I hear Paul Robeson sing 'Old Man River' and I see Sammy Davis Junior dance Mr

Bojangle's dance and I hear Nina Simone humming humming 'Suzanne,' and I love Alicia; and I hear Harry Belafonte's rasping call, 'Daay-o, Daaay-o! Daylight come and me want to go home,' and Aretha Franklyn screaming screaming, '. . . Y . . . Zed°.'

'Bastard!' the squirrel eyes cry out, 'Got you!'

And straightaway from another door two police weighed down with all their keys and their handcuffs and their pistols and their night stick and torch light enter and clink their handcuffs on my hands. They catch me. God! And now, how to go? I think about getting on like an American, but I never see an American lose. I think about making a performance like the British, steady, stiff upper lip like Alec Guinness in *The Bridge over the River Kwai*, but with my hat and my boots and my piece of cigar, that didn't match, so I say I might as well take my losses like a West Indian, like a Trinidadian. I decide to sing. It was the classiest thing that ever pass through Puerto Rico airport, me with these handcuffs on, walking between these two police and singing,

> Gonna take ma baby
> Away on a trip
> Gonna take ma baby
> Yip yip yip
> We gonna travel far
> To New Orleans
> Me and ma Baby
> Be digging the scene

Zed: Americans pronounce this letter from the English alphabet as "Zee"

E.A. Markham

e dward Archibald Markham was born in 1939 in the former British colony of Montserrat, one of the Leeward Islands in the West Indies. In 1956 he moved to Britain, where he read philosophy and English (at the University of Wales in Lampeter) and taught in London. His subsequent work has included a wide range of endeavours. He has directed the Caribbean Theatre Workshop (1970–71), worked in a French building cooperative (1972–74), and acted as a media coordinator in Papua New Guinea (1983–85). He is the author of several volumes of poetry, including *Lambchops in Papua New Guinea* (1985), *Towards the End of a Century* (1989), and *Letter from Ulster* (1993), and three collections of short stories: *Something Unusual* (1986), *Ten Stories* (1994), and *Taking the Drawing-room through Customs* (1996). In addition, Markham has edited a variety of literary magazines and several anthologies, including *Hinterland: Caribbean Poetry from the West Indies and Britain* (1989) and *The Penguin Book of Caribbean Short Stories* (1996). Recently, he has been writer-in-residence at the University of Ulster in Northern Ireland. He is currently the coordinator of the Creative Writing Programme at Sheffield Hallam University.

In his introduction to the Penguin anthology, Markham observes that Caribbean literature is "still discovering rather than preserving its character" (xv) and points to the difficulty of "defining a national literature when its practitioners seem permanently encamped on all five continents" (xiii). The difficulty of identifying a specifically Caribbean literary character when fully as many West Indians are believed to live abroad as live "at home" is compounded by the fact that the Caribbean itself contains a highly diverse population, which includes Amerindians, Africans, Hindus, Muslims, Chinese and Europeans. Each group has contributed its own folk tales and histories, its own literary and religious traditions, to the culture from which West Indian writers draw.

One "bridge" that Markham sees connecting West Indian writers of various backgrounds is language—the Creoles that have evolved from a variety of linguistic resources which, while varying from island to island, still retain a recognizably Caribbean quality. The other connection is thematic. "'Exile' writing," he argues, has been "a persistent feature of Caribbean literature," and it is in the short story that "the loneliness of exile" has received its greatest emphasis (xiv). Certainly in the story that follows, Markham has created a powerful evocation of the isolation and loneliness of the exile.

Works Cited

Markham, E.A., ed. *The Penguin Book of Caribbean Short Stories*. London: Penguin, 1996.

Other Sources

Markham, E.A. "A Little Bit of Our Past." *'Return' in Post-Colonial Writing: A Cultural Labyrinth*. Ed. Vera Mihailovich-Dickman. Amsterdam: Rodophi, 1994. 39–40.

Higuamota's Montserratian Lover

I was beginning to be disturbed by my dreams, but fortunately I don't believe in dreams; so I'm not even going to try to recall these latest ones, as that would just give them credibility, give body to something already disappearing like tuffs of cloud when the sun is up: I don't want to be accused of dignifying what are, in fact, the consequences of indigestion. Nevertheless, something lingers, and dampens your spirit a little.

So I was a bit low when I rang my sister just to have a chat, nothing special. I was in Manchester doing Summer School, and really, wouldn't be going down to London for at least six weeks: how were things in London?

The same, except they had a visitor, Higges from St. Caesare, Higuamota: remember Higges who had bound some of our books that time and . . . ? She was here on some sort of Course; and she was asking about me.

'Is she still wearing the black dress?' I asked, and was immediately ashamed, feeling a bit cheap. But my sister didn't pick up on that; and we talked about this and that, about nothing; about growing old in this country with nothing much to show for it; about Life.

And that night I dreamt about Higuamota.

The general feeling, as I remember, was that Higges was either lucky or unlucky (which is an odd way to think of someone; you might think some people lucky or unlucky, but that wasn't the *first* thing that came to mind when their name was mentioned). Anyway, the feeling was that, on balance, Higges, despite her smart profession, was more unlucky than lucky. She was unlucky in her father, the Professeur; but that's another story. She was unlucky in her sister, Dulcima°, a delicate girl, everybody now claims, who had been forced to change her image because of her experiences in America, a country where she had to grow muscles and do a job which made nonsense of her name, Dulcima—a name that suggested if anything, the delicacy of early music, that sort of thing. And Higges herself didn't come out of this naming business too well, as "Higuamota" was a bit of a mouthful, something culled from her father's obscure reading, and wilfully imposed on the infant. (As we say, she was unlucky in her father.)

We called her Higges. Others in the village, people around Coderington who knew the family, called her Marta or Martha. Those who drank or gambled with the father called her Higges, but when they weren't drinking or gambling with the father they called her Marta or Martha. Just the fact of having two names—three, really, because she was called Higuamota on occasion—undermined her a bit, made her seem if not fuzzy at least shifting, somehow less solid than her bulk, not fully protected against jokes. (Though her profession earned her respect: she was one of the few to break into the family business of *Reliure°*, trained by M. Outran himself. Outran's was one of the most prestigious establishments in St. Caesare, and if local people didn't care about book-binding, they were nevertheless impressed by the kudos attached to someone who was part of the firm.)

Higges was big in stature, big as her sister was, well, trim. And although bigness in itself wasn't funny (and there were many who were bigger than she) this worked against her too, in an obscure way, because of the fate of Dulcima in America. Dulcima, although she still put New York, New York on her letters, had ended up in Chicago, Al Capone's city, working in a slaughterhouse, proof that women were equal to men in misery. This news was received at home, as you'd expect, with mixed feelings. When you went abroad, you represented the island, the islands; and there were some from Barville and Look Out—even Look Out—and many from Montserrat who were abroad representing us in the Professions, in Show Business, and the like. So it was an odd thing to have to contemplate a good-looking, "frail" woman from your village in far-off Chicago heaving slabs of beef on her shoulder, and herself so embarrassed about it that she felt she had to keep putting New York, New York on her letters. And having that musical name didn't help. Local wags rubbed it in by referring to her as Our Monica (Harmonica?) Or Accordion. Even weird things like Pianoforte and . . . But Dulcima, too, is another story.

Dulcima: from dulcimer, a stringed, musical instrument; prototype of a piano
Reliure: French word meaning bookbinding

Higuamota was here in England on a short course in book-binding, and this disappointed me slightly, because she had been trained by old Outran who really did have the best reputation for restoring books in the region; and we were always led to believe that restoring books in the tropics was a different "science" from book-binding in a cold country. Whenever there were hurricanes and floods in the neighbouring islands, crates and crates of sodden and disfigured books would eventually arrive at Barville, *c/o P. Outran & Sons, Reliure, Mons, St. Caesare*. With the weather getting worse, if anything, Outran's was said to be the fastest-growing industry in town, not excluding the construction of villas for the expatriates. Add to that the deterioration of books and papers in a hot climate—no one kept their libraries and archives at controlled temperatures—*reliure* was not only a prestigious but a gainful thing to be involved in. But it was still a slight of sorts, another blow to our collective pride to learn that even after Outran had passed on his skills, one of his "graduates" still needed a six-week course in England in *reliure*: a two-year Course you could deal with, that would suggest a different branch of the art, but six weeks seemed insulting. (I learnt later that Higuamota now worked for a rival establishment to Outran's, a Government-backed one, so maybe there were other factors at play there.) Anyway, I took note of her various telephone numbers and promised to get in touch.

Of course, there was another reason why I was a bit apprehensive about the resurfacing of Higuamota, apart from the retraining; it had to do with what she represented; about the sort of challenge she seemed to throw down to us, men from the islands: it was something that made us feel inadequate, or disloyal; more than a bit guilty that we had tended to turn our amorous attentions elsewhere, secure now with partners who no longer looked like friends we had grown up with. Or maybe this was a later concern.

I'm giving, perhaps, the wrong impression. Things were altogether more positive. Higges was lucky, too. The best bit of luck, according to her father, was that she was born at five o'clock in the morning. More precisely, on the morning of October 12th, 1942. The Professeur worked out, in some triumph, that 1942 was a *figure* anagram of 1492; that October 12th was October 12th, this, and the fact that his daughter was born at five o'clock in the morning meant that in a real sense she had arrived several hours *before* Columbus landed on these islands, which he did later that same morning, October 12th, 1492. Higuamota was, quite simply, pre-Columbian, and should have a name befitting her status. That, the Professeur claimed, was her luck, and always made sure that she and others were reminded of it with anecdotes from the history. On Higuamota's birthday the Professeur would recall, for the guests, the life that had been disturbed by the Italian desperado and his unruly Spaniards, enlightening the company about Tainoan° agriculture, about the people's dances and songs and ball games,

Tainoan: a pre-Columbian civilization in Central America

their red body-paint and their lack of small-pox. His only reservation, his only small point of criticism, was the habit of deforming the foreheads of their young. Not a practice he would revive; but then, every culture had its eccentricities.

It was on one of these ritual occasions that Higuamota's Montserratian suitor announced himself and risked ridicule by coming fully rigged out as one Cristobal Colon, the old Admiral himself, with his brother Bartolome in tow with the beads. Well, the rest is, if not quite history, more than myth. And everyone on the island has an opinion about that particular carnival.

Though that's not to explain Higuamota's black dress.

The Black Dress

Some demystify the black dress, like Carrington. Carrington was a fellow from Montserrat, a writer, who had lived abroad for years, and whose pronouncements on these things, perversely, carried weight. Carrington felt that the black dress should be seen not as a failure of love but something belonging entirely to another story, and irrelevant to this one. The romance between Higuamota and the Admiral, he insisted, was the best thing that had happened to St. Caesare; for the courtship had been passionate and full of metaphysical conceit, and it scotched the idea that only a Frenchman with fever in his blood was capable of negotiating our sort of love-thicket. It gave emotional hinterland, he said, to being in love in St. Caesare, despite the island's small size. Do not be side-tracked by Higuamota's black dress, he said: if you wanted more on the significance of that dress, that was all dealt with in an earlier monograph*. (Carrington, who had long been dabbling in literary archeology, assumed that interest in his listeners.)

Higuamota's own view of this aspect of her life isn't known, as she tended to treat confidants with what one might call the arms length principle; but she did this with considerable grace, which made it uncertain whether you'd been taken into her confidence—though, on reflection, you knew you hadn't been. Of the black dress she would say that some thought it was her only dress, others thought she had *only* black dresses, she didn't mind, it suited her. She told me this: once, in another country she visited a friend at university. He had just passed his exams and was packing to go down, to leave town, to go home. They went to the off-licence to buy some wine, to celebrate; and the man behind the counter, recognizing her friend who was a regular customer, invited him, invited them to a wine-tasting in the shop at the end of the week. That somewhat depressed her friend, the student, because it was just another example of things taking off just as you were about to abandon them: his presence in the town had at last been acknowledged after three years, just as he was leaving, etc. This, to her friend, seemed suspiciously like his life falling into a pattern. She remembered wearing a black dress to the wine-tasting, and telling the story

*Class Structure in Tanlan Economy by Austin Farrell (Monographs on Social Anthropology, 49, Athlone Press, 1983).

of the dress, and rescuing her friend from one of those moods that men fall into. She was playful with me.

But she told this story to some: her sister, Dulcima, who worked in the garment trade in New York, New York, one day found stacks of dresses in a warehouse, dresses her size, all black, and as the firm was going bust, Dulcima packed them up and sent them off to her sister, enough dresses to last her the rest of her life.

Geraldine's Story of the Montserratian Lover

You couldn't listen to people, that's why you had to listen to Geraldine; but first you had to gain her trust, which I think I did on the last visit, the one before the volcano; but then you never know.

The problem now is with this ridiculous, dreaming nonsense which has me here, awake. I'm thinking of the Montserratian who is alive and well and not molesting the woman he lives with, or her children. As far as we know.

So why am I in a sweat, here in the middle of the night, getting up to make myself a cup of tea—a hard day in the Language Lab ahead of me? Fortunately, there's no one about to notice. I run several theories through my head. I run several books through my head; conversations, and the ones that get replayed are the ones with Geraldine, who revealed enough to be interesting but concealed enough to be discreet. It was even said that Geraldine was our true Queen of France because she knew how to keep her head. At her famous dice table in Coderington people queued up to spill their secrets.

Geraldine had worked hard to gain her position of trust, of respect. She'd been twice married, so some called her greedy at having two bites of the cherry, sort of thing, while others went hungry. But there were saner heads about who pointed out that Geraldine's first husband was a young French boy rebelling against his family, and it wasn't obvious that he would have rebelled with just anyone—not to the point of marriage—had Geraldine said No to him. So there was a sort of acceptance that Geraldine by that marriage hadn't really held back others who were waiting in line. And the marriage didn't last, anyway, so there you are. The shame of that cancelled out any advantage that might have accrued. Though there was a son, and that was a bonus of sorts. Marriage Number Two took place so discreetly that it might not even have taken place: this was with a man from up the islands, an older man, so here again she was distancing herself from the competition, without being ostentatious or unfair. By now everyone on the island felt able to confide in Geraldine—as I had, though not at her dice table. And she reciprocated: she told me, of course, the story of Higges and her Montserratian lover.

He was an educated man of good family who had spent some time in England and returned, not in disgrace, but somewhat disappointed at his achievements there after years and years that had seemed to promise more. And he used to come and sit on Higuamota's porch and parade his knowledge of books she had for binding, and he would talk History with the Professeur, Higuamota's father—all that stuff about Cortez and the Incas and the tragedy of lesser civilizations overwhelming the greater by superior force of arms.

Though the Montserratian wasn't a big drinker, not by the standards of the Professeur, he drank enough not to disappoint the old man. But his moderation in this area pleased the mother, as she reckoned one drunkard in the family to be enough. The fellow was clever and adjusted his tastes to suit both parents, starting with alcohol and switching smartly to something soft. This was when they were all three together on the porch or in the drawing-room; what he was like when he was alone with Higuamota no one but the couple knew. Higges' subsequent claims that all was sweetness and light, and that it was her mother and father together who spoilt her chances of romance, wasn't something you liked to comment on. Certainly Geraldine, who knew the story, wasn't prepared to enlighten her guests further.

Talk that it was bad feeling between mother and daughter on this subject that drove the mother to her final illness (failing to recover from surgery abroad) was the usual St. Caesare malice. But the feeling that now the mother was gone, the daughter was determined to take it out on the old man, seemed reasonable enough. (That's why he protected himself by growing steadily more eccentric.)

Back to the man from Montserrat, the lover. He had two things about him that were the source of the problem (the Columbus entry at the birthday party being a bit of a red herring). He farted a lot and he had bad dreams. Of course, there may have been other things wrong with him, in that his eyesight was failing and he was slightly hard of hearing, and he was short of stature; but he had survived many years in England with these disabilities, and nevertheless bounced back to become a lover; so these clearly weren't as fatal as farting a lot and having bad dreams.

Obviously, he didn't fart a lot in the company of the parents, he did that when he was alone. But he admitted to Higuamota that the strain of farting alone and bad-dreaming alone were OK for now, but as new habits came upon him he would really have to ease up on himself and start sharing some of the old ones with a partner—the farting and bad-dreaming, for instance. Higges settled for the bad-dreaming, and that's where she made her mistake.

The parents, of course, misunderstood the arrangement, even the mother, who failed to interpret what Higges was doing. Farting, if not all honey and seabreeze, was no big deal, her mother said, because no man came to you perfect in this life; and farting, as handicaps went, was milder than most. What she couldn't accommodate were the bad dreams.

That was because the Montserratian's dreams were about murder, the murder of a wife or partner; and the last time a member of the family had such dreams, it had ended in tragedy.

Higuamota and her father joined forces now in defence of the lover, citing his unbalanced diet, the indigestion of previous relationships, even the truism that men from these parts were naturally afraid of women and took revenge by murdering them in their dreams, and reverted to being timid and pathetic in their waking life. But to the mother murder was murder and she wasn't going to invite it into her family.

The man was obsessive—it was that which in other areas, had made them call him the Lover. He had, on various occasions, offered to make Higges mistress of the rivers of the world, to rechristen them in their own private language. He was the non-painter who set up his easel among her father's dogs and her mother's chickens and made the subject in her black dress feel like Paris of the Twenties, etc. They turned lower Barville into the centre of night life, dining out in style, summoning the *sommelier*° for yet another chilled bottle of something not everybody could pronounce. Later, at home, she would hear the bells of Saint Germain des Pres chiming through his dream-commentaries.

But this obsession, this talk of murder, terrified the older woman—who was obviously still alive when all this was happening. The Montserratian never disguised the fact, of the dream taking place in this house, that house—in England, in France, at home—that he was not just a murderer but a serial killer; worse! He was fascinated that if these murders took place while he was awake, and the results were laid out side by side you would need more land for it than St. Caesare had available to accommodate them. So he was proud, in a way, of outgrowing the island. Some men merely dreamt of harems; that was boring.

In one of the last dreams before the break-up with Marta, the lover had been in the house, a big house, in France this time. For several days and nights he remained there awaiting the consequences of his act—though, this being a dream, the house shifted location a bit, from one country to another; and it wasn't always murder that he was dealing with then, but adultery, another woman appearing on the scene, sort of thing. But it was mainly murder . . . .

So, in this dream in the big house in France he is waiting. Someone comes in on some sort of pretext. He sees them off. Then someone else comes to take away a pile of fresh ashes in the garden, from one of the terraces; someone with a wheelbarrow, at night; and the Montserratian doesn't object, and, as he looks on from an upstairs window, he is trying to remember if the pile of ashes contains any evidence that might convict him. He's perfectly lucid, he just can't remember whether there's any evidence left in the ashes. And then, finally, the police arrive—a very frail girl and a square, Orson Wells-type man—neither of them in uniform. The girl approaches him from above, coming down little curved, concrete steps, and the man, of course, comes in from the other side; classic. Yet, their body-language suggests that they trust the suspect not to act violently or stupidly. And the suspect respects them for that. And as he starts talking to the square man, taking his time, the square man becomes less square, and

sommelier: wine steward

takes on normal human shape. And the suspect is clear in his mind that what he is saying is being secretly recorded; and he knows that it has a logic that will convict him (it's like a confession with extenuating circumstances); but there is no violence on any side . . . And the dream recurs differently, in another house, on another night.

More of the same; though, as the father pointed out, there was no actual violence. And when, other things being considered, he could no longer sustain this argument, he recalled the lover's old Columbus party-piece, and conceded that the man was unreliable.

Geraldine said there was something else to consider, something to do with Higuamota's invocation of certain Signs and Illustrations from ancient books she was charged to restore; but all of that was said to her in confidence, she couldn't pass it on.

The recurrent dreams didn't surprise me; eventually, I mentioned them, casually, to someone in the book trade; and she said that, y'know, these things happen.

Rohinton Mistry

n an *Atlantic Monthly* article, Jamie James has observed that "[s]ome of the finest English-language fiction of our time is being written in Canada." One of the writers he identifies in support of this contention is Rohinton Mistry, whose novel *Such a Long Journey* James describes as being unlike a first novel: "Elegantly plotted, inhabited by a large cast of vivid characters, written in luxuriant prose, it reads like the work of a master at the top of his form rather than that of a young writer finding himself" (James 3).

Born in Bombay, India, Mistry grew up in that city's Parsi community. The Parsis are followers of a monotheistic faith that predates Christianity and is named after its prophet—Zoroaster. Zoroastrianism sees human history as the record of the struggle between Ormuzd, god of light and righteousness, and Ahriman, god of darkness and evil. Originally an Iranian religion, Zoroastrianism was suppressed throughout the Middle East with the advent of Islam and many of its followers fled to India (where they are called Parsis) to escape persecution. Because of their religious difference and the fact that they enjoyed a positive relationship with the British colonizers, the Parsi community in India is sometimes viewed with suspicion by the Hindu majority and this, coupled with their attraction to Western culture, has led to a second migration—typically to England, the United States or Canada.

Mistry's collection of short stories, *Tales from Firozsha Baag* (the name of the apartment block where the stories' characters live), deals with this community, its religious beliefs, its values and sense of its own difference (often of superiority), and the tendency of its youth to leave India and establish a life in the West. Mistry has suggested that his own immigration to Canada was the product, at least in part, of cultural expectations:

After finishing college in Bombay or elsewhere in India, one had to go abroad for higher studies. If possible, one had to find a job after finishing a Masters or a Ph.D. in the States or in England, find a job and settle in the country. That's how success is defined by Indians. So that is why I say that coming to Canada was in some ways decided for me. (Qtd. in Takhar 1.)

After earning a B.A. in mathematics and economics at the University of Bombay, Mistry moved to Toronto, where he worked as an accounting clerk while taking literature and philosophy courses part-time at the University of Toronto. He began writing stories in 1982 when his wife drew his attention to the Hart House Literary Contest. He was awarded the Hart House prize for two successive years and continued writing short stories that were published in 1987 as *Tales from Firozsha Baag*. His first novel, *Such a Long Journey*, appeared in 1991 and won several awards including the Governor General's Award and the Commonwealth Writers' Prize for Best Book. A second novel, *A Fine Balance* (1995), was received with equal enthusiasm. It was awarded the Giller Prize, the Royal Society of Literature's Winifred Holtby Prize and the 1996 Los Angeles Times Award for fiction and was shortlisted for Britain's coveted Booker Prize.

Although Mistry is himself an immigrant and has dealt with the immigrant experience in some of his stories, he has resisted the notion that "when a person arrives here from a different culture, if that person is a writer, he must have some profound observations about the meeting of the cultures. And he must write about racism " (Novak 259). Unwilling to be seen as "an expert on racism," Mistry suggests that in fact many of the themes identified with immigrant writers are universal. In an interview, he remarked, "I don't think this looking forward and yearning backward is restricted to an immigrant. It's a universal phenomenon . . . except that here, the two worlds are so far apart geographically that it seems to take on more significance" (Novak 257–8).

In another of the stories from *Firozsha Baag*, "Swimming Lessons," the father and mother discuss the stories written by their son who has immigrated to Canada. Noting that "all his stories are about Bombay," the mother concludes that her son must be painfully homesick. The father insists "all writers worked in the same way, they used their memories and experiences and made stories out of them, changing some things, adding some, imagining some, all writers were very good at remembering details of their lives " (240).

Works Cited

James, Jamie. "The Toronto Circle." *The Atlantic* online.
  www.theatlantic.com/issues/2000/04/james.htm

Mistry, Rohinton. "Swimming Lessons." *Tales from Firozsha Baag*. Markham: Penguin, 1987. 227–247.

Novak, Dagmar. "Interview." *Other Solitudes*. Toronto: Oxford University Press, 1990. 255–262.

Takhar, Jennifer. "Rohinton Mistry, 'Writer from Elsewhere'."
  landow.stg.brown.edu/post/canada/literature/mistry/mistyov.html

Other Sources and Weblinks

Kakutani, Michiko. "Tales from a Bombay Apartment Complex." *The New York Times*. Section C. 3 Feb. 1989. (Available on *New York Times* Web site)
  www.nytimes.com

"Rohinton Mistry."
  www.emory.edu/English/Bahri/Mistry

Lend Me Your Light

. . . your lights are all lit—then where do you go with your lamp? My house is all dark and lonesome,—lend me your light.

—Rabindranath Tagore°
Gitanjali

We both left Bombay the same year. Jamshed first, for New York, then I, for Toronto. As immigrants in North America, sharing this common experience should have salvaged something from our acquaintanceship. It went back such a long way, to our school days at St Xavier's.

To sustain an acquaintance does not take very much. A friendship, that's another thing. Strange, then, that it has ended so completely, that he has erased himself out of our lives, mine and Percy's; now I cannot imagine him even as a mere bit player who fills out the action or swells a procession.

Jamshed was my brother's friend. The three of us went to the same school. Jamshed and my brother, Percy, both four years older than I, were in the same class, and spent their time together. They had to part company during lunch, though, because Jamshed did not eat where Percy and I did, in the school's drillhall-cum-lunchroom.

Rabindranath Tagore: revered Indian author of both fiction (poetry, plays, novels and short fiction) and philosophical/religious works. He was awarded the Nobel Prize for Literature in 1913.

The tiffin carriers would stagger into the school compound with their long, narrow rickety crates balanced on their heads, each with fifty tiffin boxes, delivering lunches from homes in all corners of the city. When the boxes were unpacked, the drillhall would be filled with a smell that is hard to forget, thick as swill, while the individual aromas of four hundred steaming lunches started to mingle. The smell must have soaked into the very walls and ceiling, there to age and rancidify. No matter what the hour of the day, that hot and dank grotto of a drillhall smelled stale and sickly, the way a vomit-splashed room does even after it is cleaned up.

Jamshed did not eat in this crammed and cavernous interior. Not for him the air redolent of nauseous odours. His food arrived precisely at one o'clock in the chauffeur-driven, air-conditioned family car, and was eaten in the leather upholstered luxury of the back seat, amidst his collection of hyphenated lavishness.

In the snug dining-room where chauffeur doubled as waiter, Jamshed lunched through his school-days, safe from the vicissitudes of climate The monsoon might drench the tiffin carriers to the bone and turn cold the boxes of four hundred waiting schoolboys, but it could not touch Jamshed or his lunch. The tiffin carriers might arrive glistening and stinking of sweat in the hot season, with scorching hot tiffin boxes, hotter than they'd left the kitchens of Bombay, but Jamshed's lunch remained unaffected.

During the years of high school, my brother, Percy, began spending many weekend afternoons at his friend's house at Malabar Hill. Formerly, these were the afternoons when we used to join Pesi *paadmaroo* and the others for our most riotous times in the compound, the afternoons that the adults of Firozsha Baag would await with dread, not knowing what new terrors Pesi had devised to unleash upon the innocent and the unsus-pecting.

But Percy dropped all this for Jamshed's company. And when he returned from his visits, Mummy would commence the questioning: What did they eat? Was Jamshed's mother home? What did the two do all afternoon? Did they go out anywhere? And so on.

Percy did not confide in me much in those days. Our lives intersected during the lunch routine only, which counted for very little. For a short while we had played cricket together with the boys of Firozsha Baag. Then he lost interest in that too. He refused to come when Daddy would take the whole gang to the Marine Dri *maidaan* on Sunday mornings. And soon, like all younger brothers, I was seen mainly as a nuisance.

But my curiosity about Percy and Jamshed was satisfied by Mummy's interrogations. I knew that the afternoons were usually spent making model airplanes and listening to music. The airplanes were simple gliders in the early years; the records, mostly Mantovani and from Broadway shows. Later came more complex models with gasoline engines and remote control, and classical music from Bach to Poulenc.

The model-airplane kits were gifts from Jamshed's itinerant aunties and uncles, purchased during business trips to England or the U.S. Everyone except my brother and I seemed to have uncles and aunties smitten by wanderlust, and Jamshed's supply line from the western world guaranteed for him a steady diet of foreign clothes, shoes, and records.

One Saturday, Percy reported during question period that Jamshed had received the original soundtrack of *My Fair Lady*. This was sensational news. The LP was not available in Bombay, and a few privately imported or "smuggled" copies, brought in by people like Jamshed's relatives, were selling in the black market for two hundred rupees. I had seen the records displayed side by side with foreign perfumes, chocolates, and cheeses at the pavement stalls of smugglers along Flora Fountain.

Sometimes, these stalls were smashed up during police raids. I liked to imagine that one day a raid would occur as I was passing, and in the mélee and chaos of the clash, *My Fair Lady* would fly through the air and land at my feet, unnoticed by anyone. Of course, there wasn't much I could have done with it following the miracle, because our old gramophone played only 78 rpms.

After strenuous negotiations in which Mummy, Percy, and I exhausted ourselves, Percy agreed to ask his friend if I could listen to the album. Arrangements were made. And the following Saturday we set off for Jamshed's house. From Firozsha Baag, the direction of Malabar Hill was opposite to the one we took to go to school every morning, and I was not familiar with the roads the bus travelled. The building had a marble lobby, and the lift zoomed us up smoothly to the tenth floor before I had time to draw breath. I was about to tell Percy that we needed one like this in Firozsha Baag, but the door opened, Jamshed welcomed us graciously, then wasted no time in putting the record on the turntable. After all, that was what I had come for.

The afternoon dragged by after the sound-track finished. Bored, I watched them work on an airplane. The box said it was a Sopwith Camel. The name was familiar from the Biggles books Percy used to bring home. I picked up the lid and read dully that the aircraft had been designed by the British industrialist and aeronautical engineer, Thomas Octave Murdoch Sopwith, born 1888, and had been used during the First World War. Then followed a list of the parts.

Later, we had lunch, and they talked. I was merely the kid brother; and nobody expected me to do much else but listen. They talked of school and the school library, of all the books that the library badly needed; and of the *ghatis* who were flooding the school of late.

In the particular version of reality we inherited, ghatis were always flooding places, they never just went there. *Ghatis* were flooding the banks, desecrating the sanctity of institutions, and taking up all the coveted jobs. *Ghatis* were even flooding the colleges and universities, a thing unheard of. Wherever you turned, the bloody *ghatis* were flooding the place.

With much shame I remember this word *ghatis*. A suppurating sore of a word, oozing the stench of bigotry. It consigned a whole race to the mute roles of coolies and menials, forever unredeemable.

During one of our rare vacations to Matheran, as a child, I watched with detachment while a straining coolie loaded the family's baggage on his person. The big metal trunk was placed flat on his head, with the leather suitcase over it. The enormous hold-all was slung on his left arm, which he raised to steady the load on his head, and the remaining suitcase went in the right hand. It was all accomplished with much the same approach and consideration used in loading a can or barrow—the main thing was balance, to avoid tipping over. This skeletal man then tottered off towards the train that would transport us to the little hill station. There, similar skeletal beings would be waiting with rickshaws. Automobiles were prohibited in Matheran, to preserve the pastoral purity of the place and the livelihood of the rickshawallas.

Many years later I found myself at the same hill station, a member of my college hikers' club, labouring up its slopes with a knapsack. Automobiles were still not permitted in Matheran, and every time a rickshaw sped by in a flurry of legs and wheels, we'd yell at the occupant ensconced within: "Capitalist pig! You bastard! Stop riding on your brother's back!" The bewildered passenger would lean forward for a moment, not quite understanding, then fall back into the cushioned comfort of the rickshaw.

But this kind of smug socialism did not come till much later. First we had to reckon with school, school uniforms, brown paper covers for textbooks and exercise books, and the mad morning rush for the school bus. I remember how Percy used to rage and shout at our scrawny *ghaton* if the pathetic creature ever got in his way as she swept and mopped the floors. Mummy would proudly observe "He has a temper just like Grandpa's." She would also discreetly admonish Percy, since this was in the days when it was becoming quite difficult to find a new *ghaton,* especially if the first one quit due to abuse from the scion of the family and established her reasons for quitting among her colleagues.

I was never sure why some people called them *ghatons* and others, *gungas.* I supposed the latter was intended to placate—the collective conferment of the name of India's sacred river° balanced the occasions of harshness and ill-treatment. But the good old days, when you could scream at a *ghaton* that you would kick her and hurl her down the steps, and expect her to show up for work next morning, had definitely passed.

After high school, Percy and Jamshed went to different colleges. If they met at all, it would be at concerts of the Bombay Chamber Orchestra. Along with a college friend, Navjeet, and some others, my brother organized a charitable agency that collected and distributed funds to destitute farmers in a small Maharashtrian village. The idea was to get as many of these wretched souls as possible out of the clutches of the village money-lenders.

sacred river: the Ganges or Ganga; the most sacred river in India, known to Hindus as a goddess and mother. The water of the river is believed to have purifying and life-giving powers.

Jamshed showed a very superficial interest in what little he knew about Percy's activities. Each time they met, he would start with how he was trying his best to get out of the country. "Absolutely no future in this stupid place," he said. "Bloody corruption everywhere. And you can't buy any of the things you want, don't even get to see a decent English movie. First chance I get, I'm going abroad. Preferably the U.S."

After a while, Percy stopped talking about his small village, and they only discussed the concert program or the soloist's performance that evening. Then their meetings at concerts ceased altogether because Percy now spent very little time in Bombay.

Jamshed did manage to leave. One day, he came to say goodbye. But Percy was away working in the small village: his charitable agency had taken on the task full time. Jamshed spoke to those of us who were home, and we all agreed that he was doing the right thing. There just weren't any prospects in this country; nothing could stop its downhill race towards despair and ruin.

My parents announced that I, too, was trying to emigrate, but to Canada, not the U.S. "We will miss him if he gets to go," they told Jamshed, "but for the sake of his own future, he must. There is a lot of opportunity in Toronto. We've seen advertisements in newspapers from England, where Canadian Immigration is encouraging people to go to Canada. Of course, they won't advertise in a country like India—who would want these bloody *ghatis* to come charging into their fine land?—but the office in New Delhi is holding interviews and selecting highly qualified applicants." In the clichés of our speech was reflected the cliché which the idea of emigration had turned into for so many. According to my parents, I would have no difficulty being approved, what with my education, and my westernized background, and my fluency in the English language.

And they were right. A few months later things were ready for my departure to Toronto.

Then the neighbours began to arrive. Over the course of the last seven days, they came to confer their blessings and good wishes upon me. First was Bulsara Bookworm's mother, her hair in a bun as usual and covered with the *mathoobanoo*.° She said, "I know you and Jehangir were never very good friends, but that does not matter at a time like this. He says best of luck." She put her arm over my shoulder in lieu of a hug and said, "Don't forget your parents and all they did for you, maintain your good name at all times."

And Tehmina, too, using the occasion to let bygones be bygones with Mummy and Daddy, arrived sucking cloves and shuffling in slippers and duster-coat. Her cataracts were still a problem, refusing to ripen, she said.

Then one morning Nariman Hansotia stopped me in the compound. He was on his way to the Cawasji Framji Memorial Library, and I to the airline office for a final confirmation of my seat.

mathoobanoo: a scarf

"Well, well," he said, "so you were serious when you used to tell everyone that you would go abroad. Who would have thought of it! Who would have imagined that Silloo Boyce's little Kersi would one day go to Canada. Knee high I had seen you, running around in the compound with your brother, trying to do everything he did. Well, lead a good life, do nothing to bring shame to you or the Parsi community. And don't just land there and say, where are the girls? like this other chap had done. Did I ever tell you that story?"

And Nariman launched into an anecdote: "A sex-crazy young fellow was going to California. For weeks he used to tell his friends about how the women there went around on the beaches with hardly any clothes on, and how easy it was to find women who would go with you for a little bit of this and that, and what a wonderful time he was going to have as soon as he got there. Well, when he landed at Los Angeles, he tried to joke with the immigration officer and asked him, 'Where are the girls?' What do you think happened then?"

"What, Nariman Uncle?"

"He was deported on the very next plane, of course. Never did find out where the girls were."

Good old Nariman Uncle. He would never stop telling his tales. We finally parted, and as he pulled out of the compound in his old Mercedes-Benz, someone called my name from the ground floor of A Block. It was Rustomji-the-curmudgeon, skulking in the shadows and waiting for Nariman to leave. He shook my hand and gruffly wished me well.

But as I slept on my last night in Bombay a searing pain in my eyes woke me up. It was one o'clock. I bathed my eyes and tried to get back to sleep. Half-jokingly I saw myself as someone out of a Greek tragedy, guilty of the sin of hubris for seeking emigration out of the land of my birth, and paying the price in burnt-out eyes: I, Tiresias°, blind and throbbing between two lives, the one in Bombay and the one to come in Toronto . . .

In the morning. Dr Sidhwa arrived and said it was conjunctivitis, nothing very serious. But I would need some drops every four hours and protective dark glasses till the infection was gone No charge, he said, because he was going to drop by anyway to say goodbye and good luck.

Just before noon came Najamai. She must have been saving herself for an auspicious *chogeryoori*.° She sympathized about my eyes before bringing forth her portable celebration kit: a small silver *thaali*° holding a garland, and a tiny cup for the vermilion. They were miniatures of her regular apparatus which was too heavy to lug around. She put the garland round my neck, made a large, bright red *teelo*° on my forehead and hugged

---

Tiresias: a blind prophet in Greek mythology

chogeryoori: a special day or occasion

thaali: a flat pan or metal platter with a low rim that can be used for serving meals

teelo: (or teeko or bindi or tilak) a vermillion circle on the forehead signifying marital status

me several times: "Lots and lots of years you must live, see lots of life, study lots, earn lots, make us all very proud of you."

Then Najamai succumbed to reminiscing: "Remember when you used to come upstairs with the meat? Such a good boy, always helping your mother. And remember how you used to kill rats, with your bat, even for me? I always used to think, how brave for such a small boy to kill rats with a bat. And one day you even ran after Francis with it! Oh, I'll never forget that!"

She left, and Daddy found me a pair of dark glasses, And thus was spent my last day in Bombay; the city of all my days till then. The last glimpses of my bed, my broken cricket bat, the cracks in the plaster, the chest of drawers I shared with Percy till he went away to the small village, came through dark glasses; the neighbourhood I grew up in, with the chemist's store ("Open Twenty-Four Hours"), the Irani restaurant, the sugar-cane juice vendor, the fruit-and-vegetable stall in Tar Gully, all of these I surveyed through dark glasses; the huddle of relatives at the airport, by the final barrier through which only ticket holders can pass, I waved to and saw one last time through dark glasses.

Tense with excitement I walked across the tarmac. The slight chill I felt was due to the gusting night winds, I convinced myself.

Then, eyes red with conjunctivitis, pocket bulging with the ridiculously large bottle of eye-drops, and mind confused by a thousand half-formed thoughts and doubts, I boarded the aircraft sitting white and roaring upon the concrete. I tried to imagine Mummy and Daddy on the visitors' gallery, watching me being swallowed up into its belly, I imagined them consoling each other and fighting back the tears (as they had promised me they would) while I vanished into the night.

After almost a year in Toronto I received a letter from Jamshed. From New York—a very neat missive, with an elegant little label showing his name and address. He wrote that he'd been to Bombay the previous month because in every single letter his mother had been pestering him to visit: "While there, I went to Firozsha Baag and saw your folks. Glad to hear you left India. But what about Percy? Can't understand what keeps him in that dismal place. He refuses to accept reality. All his efforts to help the farmers will be in vain. Nothing ever improves, just too much corruption. It's all part of the *ghati* mentality. I offered to help him immigrate if he ever changes his mind. I've got a lot of contacts now, in New York. But it's up to him to make up his mind," and on and on.

Finally: "Bombay is horrible. Seems dirtier than ever, and the whole trip just made me sick. I had my fill of it in two weeks and was happy to leave." He ended with a cordial invitation to New York.

What I read was only the kind of stuff I would have expected in a letter from Jamshed. That was the way we all used to talk in Bombay. Still, it irritated me. It was puzzling that he could express so much disdain and discontentment even when he was no longer living under those conditions.

Was it himself he was angry with, for not being able to come to terms with matters as Percy had? Was it because of the powerlessness that all of us experience who, mistaking weakness for strength, walk away from one thing or another?

I started a most punctilious reply to his letter. Very properly I thanked him for visiting my parents and his concern for Percy. Equally properly, I reciprocated his invitation to New York with one to Toronto. But I did not want to leave it at that. It sounded as if I was agreeing with him about Percy and his work, and about India.

So instead, I described the segment of Toronto's Gerrard Street known as Little India. I promised that when he visited, we would go to all the little restaurants there and gorge ourselves with *bhelpuri, panipuri, batata-wada, kulfi,* as authentic as any in Bombay; then we could browse through the shops selling imported spices and Hindi records, and maybe even see a Hindi movie at the Naaz Cinema. I often went to Little India, I wrote; he would be certain to have a great time.

The truth is, I have been there just once. And on that occasion I fled the place in a very short time, feeling extremely ill at ease and ashamed, wondering why all this did not make me feel homesick or at least a little nostalgic. But Jamshed did not have to know any of it. My letter must have told him that whatever he suffered from, I did not share it. For a long time afterwards I did not hear from him.

My days were always full. I attended evening classes at the University of Toronto, desultorily gathering philosophy credits, and worked during the day. I became a member of the Zoroastrian Society of Ontario. Hoping to meet people from Bombay, I also went to the Parsi New Year celebrations and dinner.

The event was held at a community centre rented for the occasion. As the evening progressed it took on, at an alarming rate, the semblance of a wedding party at Bombay's Cama Garden, with its attendant sights and sounds and smells, as we Parsis talked at the top of our voices, embraced heartily; drank heartily, and ate heartily. It was Cama Garden refurbished and modernized, Cama Garden without the cluster of beggars waiting by the entrance gate for the feast to end so they could come in and claim the dustbins.

My membership in the Society led to dinner invitations at Parsi homes. Many of the guests at these gatherings were not the type who would be regulars at Little India, but who might go there with the air of tourists, equipped with a supply of ohs and aahs for ejaculation at suitable moments, pretending to discover what they had always lived with.

These were people who knew all about the different airlines that flew to Bombay. These were the virtuosi of transatlantic travel. If someone inquired of the most recent traveller, "How was your trip to India?" another would be ready with "What airline?" The evening would then become a convention of travel agents expounding on the salient features of their preferred carriers.

After a few such copiously educational evenings, 1 knew what the odds were of my luggage getting lost if I travelled airline A. The best food was served on airline B. Departures were always delayed with airline C (the company had a *ghati* sense of time and punctuality, they said). The washrooms were filthy and blocked up on airline D (no fault of airline D, they explained, it was the low class of public that travelled on it).

Of Bombay itself the conversation was restricted to the shopping they'd done. They brought back tales of villainous shopkeepers who tried to cheat them because they sensed that here was the affluence of foreign exchange: "Very cunning, they all are. God knows how, but they are able to smell your dollars before you even open your wallet. Then they try to fool you in the way they fool all the other tourists. 1 used to tell them"—this, in broken Hindi—"'go, go, what you thinking, I someone new in Mumbai? I living here thirty years, yes thirty, before going phoren.' Then they would bargain sensibly."

Others told of the way they had made a shrewd deal with shopkeepers who did not know the true value of brass and copper artifacts and knick-knacks, what did bloody *ghatis* know about such things anyway. These collectors of bric-a-brac, self-appointed connoisseurs of art and antiques, must have acquired their fancies along with their immigration visas.

But their number was small. And though they were as earnest about their hobbies as the others were, they never quite succeeded in holding the gathering transfixed the way the airline clique managed to. Art was not as popular as airlines were at these evenings.

Six months after Jamshed's trip to Bombay, I received a letter from my brother Percy. Among other things, he wrote about his commitment in the small village:

> Our work with the farmers started successfully. They got interest-free loans in the form of seed and fertilizer, which we purchased wholesale, and for the first time in years they did not have to borrow from those bloodthirsty money-lenders.
>
> Ever since we got there the money-lenders hated us. They tried to persuade us to leave, saying that what we were doing was wrong because it was upsetting the delicate balance of village life and destroying tradition. We in turn pointed out things like exploitation, usury, inhumanity, and other abominations whose time was now up. We may have sounded like bold knights-errant, but they turned to threats and said it would soon become so unhealthy for us that we would leave quickly enough.
>
> One day when we were out visiting a loan applicant, a farmer brought news that a gang of thugs wielding sticks and cudgels was waiting at the hut—our office and residence. So we stayed the night with the loan applicant and, in the morning, escorted by a band of villagers who insisted on coming along, started for our hut. But all we found were smouldering embers. It had been razed to the ground during the night, and no one had dared interfere.

Now we're back in Bombay, and Navjeet and I are working on a plan for our return. We've spoken to several reporters, and the work is getting much publicity. We're also collecting fresh donations, so that when we go back we won't fail for lack of funds.

Having read this far, I put down the letter for a moment. There you were, my brother, waging battles against corruption and evil, while I was watching sitcoms on my rented Granada TV. Or attending dinner parties at Parsi homes to listen to chit-chat about airlines and trinkets. And it was no use wishing that we had talked more to each other about our hopes and visions and dreams. I thought of our school-days, trying to locate the point when the gulf had appeared between us. Did it grow bit by bit or suddenly happen one morning? I cannot remember, but it did throw everything into silence and secrecy.

The rest of the letter concerned Jamshed's visit to Bombay six months ago:

I wish he'd stayed away, if not from Bombay then at least from me. At best, the time I spent with him was a waste. I expected that we would look at things differently, but was not prepared for the crassly materialistic boor that he's turned into. To think he was my "best friend" in school.

No doubt he believes the highlight of his visit came when he took some of us to dinner at the Rendezvous—nothing but the most expensive, of course. It was a spectacle to surpass anything he'd done so far. He reminded us to eat and drink all we wanted without minding the prices and enjoy ourselves as much as we could, because we wouldn't get such a chance again, at least, not until his next visit.

When the soup came he scolded the waiter that it was cold and sent it back. The rest of us sat silent and embarrassed. He looked at us nonchalantly, explaining that this was the only way to handle incompetence; Indians were too meek and docile, and should learn to stand up for their rights the way people do in the States.

We were supposed to be impressed by his performance, for we were in an expensive restaurant where only foreign tourists eat on the strength of their U.S. dollars. And here was one of our own, not intimidated within the walls of the five-star Taj Mahal Hotel. In our school-days we could only stand outside and watch the foreigners come and go, wondering what opulent secrets lay inside, what comforts these fair-skinned superior beings enjoyed. Here was one of our own showing us how to handle it all without feeling a trace of inferiority, and now we were ashamed of him.

We spent the evening watching Jamshed in disbelief, in silence, which he probably thought was due to the awesome splendour of our surroundings.

I was determined not to see him again, not even when he came to say goodbye on the day of his departure, and I don't intend to meet him when he visits Bombay the next time . . .

As I finished reading, I felt that my brother had been as irritated by Jamshed's presence as I had been by Jamshed's letter six months ago. But I did not write this to Percy. After all, I was planning to be in Bombay in four or five months. We could talk then. In just four months I would complete two years in Canada—long enough a separation, I supposed with a naive pomposity, to have developed a lucidity of thought which I would carry back with me and bring to bear on all of India's problems.

Soon it was time to go shopping for gifts. I packed chocolates, cheeses, jams, jellies, puddings, cake mixes, panty hose, stainless steel razor blades—all the items I used to see displayed in the stalls of the smugglers along Flora Fountain, always priced out of reach. I felt like one of those soldiers who, in wartime, accumulates strange things to use as currency for barter. What was I hoping to barter them for? Attention? Gratitude? Balm to soothe guilt or some other malady of the conscience? I wonder now. And I wonder more that I did not wonder then about it.

The suitcase I had come with proved insufficient. And although I bought a new one, an extra leather strap around each seemed wise, for they were both swelled to threatening dimensions.

Then, arms still sore from the typhoid and cholera inoculations, luggage bursting at the seams with a portable grocery store, and mind suffused with groundless optimism, I boarded the plane.

The aircraft was losing height in preparation for landing. The hard afternoon sun revealed the city I was coming back to after two years. When the plane had taken off two years ago, it had been in the dark of night, and all I saw from the sky through shaded and infected eyes were the airport lights of Santa Cruz. But now it was daytime, and I was not wearing dark glasses. I could see the parched land: brown, weary, and unhappy

A few hours earlier the aircraft had made its scheduled landing in London, and the view from the air had been lush, everywhere green and hopeful. It enraged me as I contrasted it with what I was now seeing. Gone was the clearness with which I'd promised myself I would look at things. All that was left was a childish and helpless reaction. "It's not fair!" I wanted to stamp my foot and shout. "it's just not fair!"

Construction work was under way at the airport. The van transporting passengers from the aircraft to the terminal building passed improvised dwellings of corrugated metal, cardboard, packing crates, plastic sheets, even newspaper.

The van was reduced to a crawl in the construction zone A few naked children emerged from the corrugated metal and cardboard and ran to keep up with us, screaming for money. When they came dangerously close to the van, the driver screamed back. On board was a group of four businessmen, and three of them tossed some change out the window. They sounded Australian. The fourth was the seasoned traveller, and the others hung on every word he said. He warned them, "If you try that when you're on the street, you'll create something like a bloody feeding frenzy of sharks." The children fell far behind when the construction zone ended and the van picked up speed.

Bombay seemed dirtier than ever. I remembered what Jamshed had written in his letter, and how it had annoyed me, but now I couldn't help thinking he was right. Hostility and tension seemed to be perpetually present in buses, shops, trains. It was disconserting to discover I'd become unused to it. Now I knew what soldiers must experience in the trenches after a respite far behind the lines.

As if enacting a scene for my benefit with all the subtlety of a sixteenth-century morality play, a crowd clawed its way into a local train. All the players were there: Fate and Reality, and the latter's offspring, the New Reality, and also Poverty and Hunger, Virtue and Vice, Apathy and Corruption.

The drama began when the train, Reality, rolled into the station. It was overcrowded because everyone wanted to get on it: Virtue, Vice, Apathy, Corruption, all of them. Someone, probably Poverty, dropped his plastic lunch bag amidst the stampede, nudged on by Fate. Then Reality rolled out of the station with a gnashing and clanking of its metal, leaving in its wake the New Reality. And someone else, probably Hunger, matter-of-factly picked up Poverty's mangled lunch, dusted off a *chapati* which had slipped out of the trampled bag, and went his way. In all of this, was there a lesson for me? To trim my expectations and reactions to things, trim them down to the proper proportions?

I wasn't sure, but when I missed my bus an old instinctive impulse returned: to dash after it, to leap and join the crowd already hanging from the door rail. In the old days I would have been off and running. I used to pride my agility at this manoeuvre. After all, during rush hour it was the only way to catch a bus, or you'd be left at the bus-stop with the old and the feeble.

But while the first flush of confidence flowed through me, the bus had moved well into the stream of traffic. My momentary hesitation gave the game away. With the old and feeble was my place, as long as I was a tourist here, and not committed to life in the combat zone.

In Firozsha Baag things were still roughly the same, but Mrs Mody had died, and no one knew what Pesi was doing now. In fact, ever since he had been sent away to boarding-school some years ago, Pesi's doings were not spoken of at all. My friend Viraf of A Block, whom I had been unable to say goodbye to two years ago because he was away in Kharagpur studying at the Indian Institute of Technology, was absent for my hello as well. He did not return to Bombay because he had found a job in nearby Calcutta.

Tehmina had at last rid herself of the cataracts. She was suddenly very spry, very sure of herself in all she did. Along with her cataracts she had also jettisoned her old slippers and duster-coat. Her new ensemble consisted of a long, flowing floral-patterned kaftan and a smart pair of *chappals* with little heels that rang out her presence on the stairs and in the hallway.

But Najamai had aged considerably. She kept asking me why I had not yet been to see her daughters even though she had given me their addresses: Vera was somewhere in Alberta, and Dolly in British Columbia.

My brother, Percy, wrote from the small village that he wanted to meet me, but: "I cannot come to Bombay right now because I've received a letter from Jamshed. He's flying in from New York, and has written about reunions and great times for all the old crowd. That's out of the question as far as I'm concerned. I'm not going to see him again."

I wrote back saying I understood.

Our parents were disappointed. They had been so happy that the whole family would be together again for a while. And now this. They could not understand why Percy did not like Jamshed any more, and I'm sure at the back of their minds they thought their son envied his friend because of the fine success he'd made of himself in America. But who was I to explain things, and would they understand even if tried? They truly believed that Jamshed was the smart young fellow, and Percy the idealist who forgot that charity begins at home.

This trip was not turning out to be anything I'd hoped it would. Jamshed was coming and Percy wasn't, our parents were disappointed with Percy, I was disappointed with them, and in a week I would be flying out of Bombay, confused and miserable. I could feel it already.

Without any destination in mind I left the house and took the first empty bus to come along. It went to Flora Fountain. The offices were now closing for the day. The dirty, yellow-grey buildings would soon spill out typists and clerks and peons into a swelling stream surging towards bus-stops and train stations.

Roadside stalls were open for business. This would be their busy hour. They were lined up along the edge of the pavement, displaying their merchandise. Here a profusion of towels and napkins from shocking pink to peacock green; there, the clatter and gleam of pots and pans; further down, a refreshment stall selling sizzling *samosas* and ice-cold sherbet.

The pavement across the road was the domain of the smugglers with their stalls of foreign goods. But they did not interest me, I stayed where I was. One man was peddling an assortment of toys. He demonstrated them all in turn, calling out, "Baba play and baby play! Daddy play and Mummy play!" Another, with fiendish vigour, was throwing glass bowls to the ground, yelling: "Un-ber-rakable! Un-ber-rakable!"

Sunlight began to fade as I listened to the hawkers singing their tunes. Kerosene lamps were lit in some of the stalls, punctuating at random the rows on both sides of the street.

Serenely I stood and watched. The disappointment which had overcome me earlier began to ebb. All was fine and warm within this moment after sunset when the lanterns were lit, and I began to feel a part of the crowds which were now flowing down Flora Fountain. I walked with them.

Suddenly, a hand on my shoulder made me turn around. It was Jamshed. "Bet you weren't expecting to see me in Bombay."

"Actually, I was. Percy wrote you were coming." Then I wished I hadn't volunteered this bit of information.

But there was no need to worry about awkward questions regarding Percy. For Jamshed, in fine fettle, had other thoughts he was anxious to share.

"So what are you doing here? Come shopping?" he asked jokingly, indicating the little stalls with a disdainful sweep of his hand. "Terrible, isn't it, the way these buggers think they own the streets—don't even leave you enough room to walk. The police should drive them off, break up their bloody stalls, really."

He paused. I wondered if I should say something. Something that Percy would love to hear me say. Like: these people were only trying to earn a meagre living by exercising, amidst a paucity of options, this one; at least they were not begging or stealing. But I didn't have a chance.

"God, what a racket! Impossible to take even a quiet little walk in this place. I tell you, I'll be happy when it's time to catch my plane back to New York."

It was hopeless. It was his letter all over again, the one he'd written the year before from New York. He had then temporarily disturbed the order I was trying to bring into my new life in Toronto, and I'd struck back with a letter of my own. But this time I just wanted to get away from him as quickly as possible. Before he made the peace of mind I was reaching out for dissipate, become forever unattainable,

Suddenly, I understood why Percy did not want to meet him again—he, too, sensed and feared Jamshed's soul-sapping presence.

Around us, all the pavement stalls were immersed in a rich dusk. Each one was now lit by a flickering kerosene lantern. What could I say to Jamshed? What would it take, I wondered, to light the lantern in his soul?

He was waiting for me to speak. I asked, perfunctorily, how much longer he would be in Bombay.

"Another week. Seven whole days, and they'll go so slowly. But I'll be dropping in at Firozsha Baag in a couple of days, tell Percy." We walked to my bus-stop. A beggar tugged at his sleeve and he mechanically reached in his pocket for change. Then we said good-night.

On the bus I thought about what to say if he asked me, two days later, why I hadn't mentioned that Percy was not coming.

As it turned out, I did not have to say anything.

Late next evening, Percy came home unexpectedly. I rushed to greet him, but his face revealed that he was not returning in this manner to give us a pleasant surprise. Something was dreadfully wrong. His colour was ashen. He was frightened and shaken, and straggled to retain his composure. He tried to smile as he shook my hand limply, but could not muster the effort to return my hug.

"What's the matter?" said Mother. "You don't look well."

Silently, Percy sat down and began to remove his shoes and socks. After a while he looked up and said, "They killed Navjeet."

No one spoke for the next few minutes. Percy sat with his socks dangling from his hands, looking sad, tired, defeated.

Then Mummy rose and said she would make tea. Over tea, he told us what had happened. Slowly, reluctantly at first, then faster, in a rush, to get the remembering and telling over with as soon as possible. "The money-lenders were ready to make trouble for us again. We didn't think they'd do anything as serious as the last time. The press was following our progress and had reported the arson in many newspapers. Yesterday we were out at the wholesaler's. Ordering seed for next year. But Navjeet had stayed behind. He was working on the accounts. When we returned he was lying unconscious. On the floor. His face and head were bleeding badly. We carried him to the makeshift clinic in the village—there is no hospital. The doctor said there was severe internal damage—massive head injuries—a few hours later he was dead."

There was silence again. Perhaps when we were together later, sharing our old room again, Percy would talk to me. But he lay on his bed in the darkness, wide awake, staring silently at the ceiling, tracing its old familiar cracks as I was, by the hints of streetlights straying through the worn curtains. Was there nothing to say? There had to be something I could do to help.

Strangely enough, it was Jamshed who provided this something the next day.

When he arrived in the evening, he presented Mummy with a box of chocolates and some cheese triangles. She asked him how he'd been enjoying his trip so far. He replied, true to form, "Oh Auntie, I'm tired of this place, really. The dust and heat and crowds—I've had enough of it." And Mummy nodded sympathetically.

Soon, the moment Percy had been dreading was at hand. Mummy asked him to narrate, for Jamshed's benefit, the events which had brought him home so suddenly. But Percy just shook his head, so she told the story herself.

When she finished, we shifted uneasily. What was next? But Jamshed could not contain himself. He heaved the sigh of the worldly-wise: "I told you from the beginning, all this was a waste of time and nothing would come of it, remember? Every time we met we would talk about it, and you used to make fun of me wanting to go abroad. But I still think the best thing for you is to move to the States. There is so much you could achieve there. There, if you are good at something, you are appreciated, and you get ahead. Not like here, where everything is controlled by uncle-auntie, and . . . ."

When Jamshed concluded his harangue, Percy calmly turned to Mummy and said in his quiet voice, "Could we have dinner right away? I have to meet my friends at eight o'clock. To decide our next move in the village."

Five days later I was back in Toronto. I unpacked my suitcases, which were quite flat on the return trip and had not required the extra leather straps. I put my things away and displayed in the apartment the little knick-knacks bought in handicraft places and the Cottage Industries store.

Gradually, I discovered I'd brought back with me my entire burden of riddles and puzzles, unsolved. The whole sorry package was there, not lightened at all. The epiphany would have to wait for another time, another trip.

I mused, I gave way to whimsy: I Tiresias, throbbing between two lives, humbled by the ambiguities and dichotomies confronting me . . .

I thought of Jamshed and his adamant refusal to enjoy his trips to India, his way of seeing the worst in everything. Was he, too, waiting for some epiphany and growing impatient because, without it, life in America was bewildering? Perhaps the contempt and disdain which he shed was only his way of lightening his own load.

That Christmas, I received a card from Jamshed. The Christmas seal, postage stamp, address label were all neatly and correctly in place upon the envelope, like everything else about his surface existence. I put it down without opening it, wondering if this innocuous outer shell concealed more of his confusion, disdain, arrogance.

Later, I walked out of the apartment and down the hallway, and dropped the envelope down the chute of the garbage incinerator.

Critical Focus Questions

1. Anthony Akerman calls his short story "The Exile." What is the difference between an exile and an immigrant? What associations does each word have? What do you think Rushdie is getting at with the term "migrant"? How do its connotations differ from those of immigrant? Do any of the other stories in this section qualify as "exiles' tales"?

2. The introduction to this chapter discusses the concept of "culture's 'in between'" as a dynamic space in which creativity and artistic innovation can occur, but the phrase could also be used to designate the uncomfortable experience of belonging neither to one's culture of origin nor to the culture of one's adopted home. Discuss the ways in which some of these stories present the emigrant/immigrant experience in this, more problematic fashion.

3. Several of the stories in this section explore stereotypical thinking either on the part of the central character or in those around him or her. Considering the stories by Blaise, Kureishi and Lovelace, identify some of the negative consequences of using stereotypes to try to understand the world.

4. Focussing on two or more of the stories (in this or other sections), discuss the nature of the loss experienced by immigrants to a new country. Given the difficulty of their experience, what impels people to emigrate from their homelands?

5. Describe the nature of the difficulty facing Joebell in Lovelace's "Joebell and America." What does he have in common with Mistry's Jamshed ("Lend Me Your Light")? How can Lovelace's ideas about the importance of cultural integrity be related to Mistry's story?

6. Discuss the implications of Kureishi's title, "We're Not Jews." What comment is the author making about English society? What other means does he use to make the same kind of statement?

7. At both the beginning and end of "Higuamota's Monserratian Lover," the narrator dismisses his dreams as unimportant, yet they are clearly disturbing him. What significance do they have for him? Compare/contrast his dreams with the dream-like experiences of the narrator in Okri's "Incidents at the Shrine." Is there any similarity in the ways in which the two authors use the concept of dreams? Explain your view.

race relations
and the stuggle
for justice

The profoundly racist and sexist heritage of the European Age has bequeathed to us a set of deeply ingrained perceptions about people of color, including, of course, the self-perceptions that people of color bring. It is not surprising that most intellectuals of color in the past exerted much of their energies and efforts to gain acceptance from and approval by 'white normative gazes.' The new cultural politics of difference advises critics and artists of color to put aside this mode of mental bondage, thereby freeing themselves to both interrogate the ways in which they are bound by certain conventions and to learn from and build on these very norms and models.

Cornel West, *Keeping Faith*

he title of this chapter is more than a little problematic. The trouble has to do with the first word. Race is defined by the authors of *Key Concepts in Post-Colonial Studies* as "a term for the classification of human beings into physically, biologically and genetically distinct groups." The concept assumes the existence of fixed categories, "natural types," into which human beings can be divided. These categories ("races") are based on physical characteristics which are genetically determined and assumed to indicate corresponding intellectual and moral characteristics. Thus, a belief in the concept of "race" involves the belief that the behaviour and capacities of individual human beings are biologically determined, that one group is unalterably different from another. Historically, this kind of thinking led very quickly to a hierarchical ordering of races with, from the perspective of the European colonizing powers, the white European at the top and Black Africans at the bottom. Race thinking supported and justified the colonizing and enslaving of other peoples—peoples who could be assumed to be intrinsically "other" and inferior to Europeans. Thus Ashcroft et al. argue that "'racism' [the belief that inherited physical characteristics provide a basis for distinguishing "superior" from "inferior" groups] is not so much a product of the concept of race as the very reason for its existence" (199).

In the last twenty years, the concept of race has gradually yielded to that of ethnicity as the focus of academic discussion about human difference. Ethnicity is a much more flexible concept and relates not to presumed biological differences, but rather to religious, cultural and linguistic factors which can be seen to play a role in shaping individual identity. In the context of these discussions, "race" has come to be perceived as "a cultural rather than a biological phenomenon, the product of historical processes not of genetically determined physical differences" (205).

Yet "race" (which seldom appears without the scare quotes in academic discourse) remains very much a part of popular thought, and hence of individual experience. Perhaps the most damaging aspect of racial thinking has been its impact on the ways in which members of various groups have come to perceive themselves. In the early fifties, Martiniquan psychiatrist Frantz Fanon, whose work on the psychology of racism has been tremendously influential in the field of postcolonial studies, pointed out that people belonging to what had been seen as "inferior races" displayed a tendency to internalize negative images of themselves presented over generations and thus "however lacking in objective reality racist ideas" were, they became in time a part of how colonized or enslaved peoples saw and defined themselves (205). Fanon's ideas have clearly played a role in what Charles Taylor calls "the politics of identity," discussed in the introduction to Part I.

Neither has the concept of ethnicity remained free of what is, essentially, racist thinking. In ordinary speech, for example, many North Americans still have a tendency to refer to anyone who possesses a different cultural background as an "ethnic," implying that one kind of ancestry or culture is somehow "normal" and anything else exotic, a deviation. "Ethnic purity" is a concept which has been in the news for the last few years, especially in the context of the violent struggle in the former Yugoslavia where the Serbs in particular have identified their efforts as part of a campaign of "ethnic cleansing." As we can see in several of the selections that follow, however, they have no monopoly on these pernicious ideas.

Racism, prejudice, discrimination, ethnic conflict—whatever the terms we use to discuss the phenomenon, and however mild or extreme its outcome, it seems always to begin with the process of "othering," of seeing some groups of people as so fundamentally "different" from whatever norm is understood to exist, that they are somehow less human, less entitled to respect and, sometimes, to freedom or life itself. Thus exploitation, enslavement, extermination (racial/ethnic cleansing) are seen as justified. In our contemporary struggle to acknowledge and respect each other's cultural differences, it is important that we avoid the trap of seeing those whose culture is other than ours as "the other."

Works Cited

Ashcroft, Bill, Gareth Griffiths, and Helen Tiffin, eds. "Ethnicity," "Fanon," "Race." *Key Concepts in Post-Colonial Studies*. London and New York: Routledge, 1998.

Fanon, Frantz. *The Wretched of the Earth*. Trans. Constance Farrington. New York: Grove, 1965; 1970.

_____. *Black Skin: White Masks*. Trans. Charles Lam Markmann. London: MacGibbon and Kee, 1968.

West, Cornel. *Keeping Faith: Philosophy and Race in America*. New York and London: Routledge, 1993.

Other Sources and Weblinks

A collection of articles on race from the *Atlantic* magazine:

www.theatlantic.com/politics/race/race.htm.collection

Information about "race" and "apartheid" in South Africa:

search.ananzi.co.za/index.html?ql=a

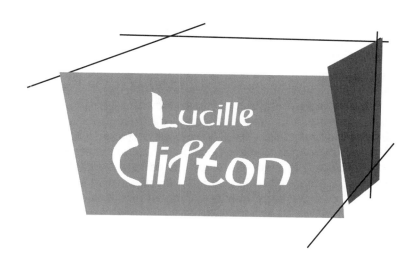

Lucille Clifton

orn in Depew, New York, in 1936, Lucille Sayles Clifton is a prolific and much honoured author of both fiction and poetry. The child of parents who were without formal education, she nonetheless grew up surrounded by books, particularly those written by African Americans. She entered Howard University in Washington, D.C., at sixteen and graduated as a drama major. While there she met Chloe Wofford (now Toni Morrison), who subsequently edited her work for Random House, and Fred Clifton, who became an educator and a writer and, in 1955, her husband.

Clifton's career as a successful poet began in 1969 when she won the YW-YMHA Poetry Center Discovery Award and, with it, the publication of her first volume of poetry, *Good Times*, applauded by *The New York Times* as one of the best books of the year. The author of some nine volumes of poetry and a memoir, *Generations* (1970), she has also written more than a dozen books of juvenile fiction. She has been twice nominated for the Pulitzer Prize and for the National Book Award (which she won for *Blessing the Boats: New and Selected Poems, 1988–2000*), and is the recipient of fellowships and honorary degrees from a number of universities and other institutions. She is also the winner of an Emmy Award from the American Academy of Television Arts and Sciences. She is currently Distinguished Professor of Humanities at St. Mary's College in Maryland.

Clifton's poetry has been described as minimalist, spare and often deceptively simple (Houston 3). She draws on a vocabulary of simple but powerfully evocative words to articulate her concerns with family relationships, African-American history, and the dark underside of the American dream. Her early poems, beginning with *Good Times*, celebrate the culture and heritage of Black Americans, and throughout her work she has challenged negative characterizations of women and people of colour as exploitative predators or powerless victims. She emphasizes the humanity and nobility of lives lived under the oppression of slavery or in the ghettoes of the inner city, consistently reflecting a belief in the human capacity for survival and even transcendence in a world scarred by racism and social injustice.

James Miller observes that Clifton "defines herself as a poet whose task is to keep historical memory alive" while refusing "to be trapped or defeated" by the pain or difficulty of that history (4). In *Generations: A Memoir*, she traces her ancestry from her great-great-grandmother, Caroline Sale Donald (1823–1910), who was abducted from Dahomey in West Africa and brought to New Orleans, Louisiana. Caroline's daughter, Lucille, became the first Black woman lynched in Virginia. Clifton uses the figures of these women to "conjure up images of survival and endurance on the one hand, and avenging spirits on the other" (Miller 4). By locating herself within a family history that stretches back to Africa and includes a tradition of strong women, Clifton integrates the past with the present and arms herself with a positive sense of her own heritage.

In "at the cemetery, walnut grove plantation," Clifton is also concerned with integrating the past and present. In an interview, she told Bill Moyers about her experience of taking the tour of the plantation. The guide talked about the family who had lived there and showed them the original house and furnishings but made no mention of slavery. When she saw the burying ground, Clifton felt sure some of the graves belonged to slaves and asked why they hadn't been mentioned. The guide hadn't been aware of the existence of slaves on the plantation but when they checked the inventory, they found that there had been ten slaves inventoried (as property) but there were probably more because "women were not considered valuable enough to inventory." In her poem, Clifton exposes the truth about the history of the plantation and who created it. She was moved, she told Moyers, by the fact that "half the children in the town were denied the knowledge that their ancestors had helped to build that plantation . . . We cannot ignore history. History doesn't go away. The past isn't back there, the past is here too." Perhaps, as she suggested to Moyers, "[a]ll that may be needed is that the injustice in the world be mentioned so that nobody can ever say, 'Nobody told me'" (Moyers 85).

Works Cited

Houston, Helen R. "Lucille Clifton." *The Oxford Companion to Women's Writing in the United States*. Oxford: Oxford University Press, 1995.

Miller, James. "Lucille Clifton." *The Heath Anthology of American Literature*. 3d ed. Vol. 2. Boston: Houghton Mifflin, 1998.

Moyers, Bill. *The Language of Life: A Festival of Poets*. Ed. James Haba. New York: Doubleday, 1995. 85–86. Some of this is available online at:

www.english.uiuc.edu/maps/poets/a_f/clifton/cemetery.htm

The two articles cited above, as well as Jane Cooper's and Jocelyn Moody's below, can be found at:

www.english.uiuc.edu/maps/poets/a_clifton/about.htm

Other Sources and Weblinks

Cooper, Jane Todd. "Lucille Clifton." *The Oxford Companion to Twentieth-Century Poetry in English*. Oxford: Oxford University Press, 1994.

"Lucille Clifton." Poetry Exhibits.

www.poets.org/poets/poets.cfm?prm1D=80

Moody, Jocelyn K. "Lucille Clifton." *The Oxford Companion to African American Literature*. Oxford: Oxford University Press, 1997.

at the cemetery, walnut grove plantation, south carolina, 1989

among the rocks
at walnut grove
your silence drumming
in my bones,
tell me your names.

nobody mentioned slaves
and yet the curious tools
shine with your fingerprints.
nobody mentioned slaves
but somebody did this work
who had no guide, no stone,
who moulders under rock.
tell me your names.
tell me your bashful names
and i will testify.

the inventory lists ten slaves
but only men were recognized.

among the rocks
at walnut grove
some of these honored dead
were dark
some of these dark
were slaves
some of these slaves
were women
some of them did this
honored work.
tell me your names
foremothers, brothers,
tell me your dishonored names.
here lies
here lies
here lies
here lies
hear

James Baldwin

Cultural critic Henry Louis Gates, Jr. calls James Baldwin one of "the holy male trinity of the black tradition" (1992:140; see "What's in a Name" in Part IV), which includes Richard Wright and Ralph Ellison. The author of both fiction and essays, Baldwin was a highly influential figure in the American civil rights movement of the early 1960s. (Gates observes that when Baldwin's *The Fire Next Time* appeared in 1963, "he was exalted as *the* voice of black America" [1997:8].) Reading Baldwin's *Notes of a Native Son* in 1965, against the backdrop of the race riots in Watts, California, Gates felt that he was hearing for the first time "a voice capturing the terrible exhilaration and anxiety of being a person of African descent in this country . . . The book performed for me the Adamic function of naming the complex racial dynamic of the American cultural imagination" (7).

James Baldwin was born in Harlem, the illegitimate son of Emma Birdis Jones. When he was three, his mother married preacher David Baldwin, who adopted James but seemed unable to conquer his feelings of revulsion at the latter's illegitimacy. Baldwin's childhood was made more difficult by the family's acute poverty and the squalor of their surroundings, and by the racism that permeated contemporary society. A precocious student, he was encouraged in his writing by his teachers but he was also drawn to the ministry and he worked as a Pentecostal preacher for three years. He turned away from the church at seventeen and eventually moved to Greenwich Village (a neighbourhood famous for attracting creative artists) to begin his career as a writer. But although he left the ministry, the rhythm and language of religious oratory and the Bible remain evident in his work.

Living in Greenwich Village, Baldwin supported himself with an assortment of day jobs while writing reviews, essays and short stories for periodicals at night. He was fortunate enough to become the protegé of novelist Richard Wright, who helped him to secure financial support. In

1948, struggling to write his first novel and appalled by American prejudice against blacks and homosexuals, Baldwin bought himself a one-way ticket to Paris, France, where he spent most of the remainder of his life.

While in "the early sixties, his authority seemed nearly unchallenged" (Gates 9), by the end of the decade Baldwin was increasingly under attack from a new generation of radical black militants who thought him too conciliatory. He was also under attack for his homosexuality. Eldridge Cleaver accused him of being engaged in "a despicable underground guerrilla war, waged on paper, against black masculinity," while "young militants referred to him, unsmilingly, as Martin Luther Queen" (12). Gates considers that a major reason for Baldwin's fall from grace was the complexity and sophistication of his vision. In refusing to adopt the simpler formulations of the contemporary Black Muslim movement which equated all whites with evil and advocated terrorism as a means to black liberation, Baldwin counselled against letting hatred control one's life and argued that the future of America lay in the integration of blacks and whites. "And if the word integration means anything," he wrote in *The Fire Next Time*, "this is what it means: that we, with love, shall force our brothers to see themselves as they are, to cease fleeing from reality and begin to change it" (21).

To the end of his life, in 1987, Baldwin continued to explore the pain and isolation of being black in America:

> [Y]es it does indeed mean something—something unspeakable—to be
> born, in a white country, an Anglo-teutonic, antisexual country, black. You
> very soon, without knowing it, give up all hope of communion." (45)

But his exploration always included a profound awareness of the individual's responsibility for rescuing his or her own life, together with an understanding of how steeply the odds were stacked against that rescue, an awareness of what he called "the evil within . . . and . . . the evil without" (1962:28). Recently, his reputation has undergone a renaissance. A new generation of readers values his writing for what Gates himself identified as "just those qualities of ambivalence and equivocality, just that sense of the contingency of identity, that made him useless to the ideologues of liberation and anathema to so many black nationalists" (20).

Works Cited

Baldwin, James. *The Fire Next Time*. New York: Dell, 1962.
Gates, Henry Louis, Jr. *Loose Canons*. New York and Oxford: Oxford University Press, 1992.
———. *Thirteen Ways of Looking at a Black Man*. New York: Random House, 1997.

Other Sources and Weblinks

"Baldwin, James." *Microsoft Encarta Online Encyclopedia 2000.*
   encarta.msn.com

Stevenson, John. "James Baldwin: An Appreciation." *The Boston Book Review.*
   www.bookwire.com/bbr/interviews/baldwin.html

Sonny's Blues

I read about it in the paper, in the subway, on my way to work. I read it, and I couldn't believe it, and I read it again. Then perhaps I just stared at it, at the newsprint spelling out his name, spelling out the story. I stared at it in the swinging lights of the subway car, and in the faces and bodies of the people, and in my own face, trapped in the darkness which roared outside.

It was not to be believed and I kept telling myself that, as I walked from the subway station to the high school. And at the same time I couldn't doubt it. I was scared, scared for Sonny. He became real to me again. A great block of ice got settled in my belly and kept melting there slowly all day long, while I taught my classes algebra. It was a special kind of ice. It kept melting, sending trickles of ice water all up and down my veins, but it never got less. Sometimes it hardened and seemed to expand until I felt my guts were going to come spilling out or that I was going to choke or scream. This would always be at a moment when I was remembering some specific thing Sonny had once said or done.

When he was about as old as the boys in my classes his face had been bright and open, there was a lot of copper in it, and he'd had wonderfully direct brown eyes, and great gentleness and privacy. I wondered what he looked like now. He had been picked up, the evening before, in a raid on an apartment downtown, for peddling and using heroin.

I couldn't believe it: but what I mean by that is that I couldn't find any room for it anywhere inside me. I had kept it outside me for a long time. I hadn't wanted to know. I had had suspicions, but I didn't name them, I kept putting them away. I told myself that Sonny was wild, but he wasn't crazy. And he'd always been a good boy, he hadn't ever turned hard or evil or disrespectful, the way kids can, so quick, so quick, especially in Harlem. I didn't want to believe that I'd ever see my brother going down, coming to nothing, all that light in his face gone out, in the condition I'd already seen so many others. Yet it had happened and here I was, talking about algebra to a lot of boys who might, every one of them for all I knew, be popping off needles every time they went to the head°. Maybe it did more for them than algebra could.

I was sure that the first time Sonny had ever had horse°, he couldn't have been much older than these boys were now. These boys, now, were living as we'd been living then, they were growing with a rush and their heads bumped abruptly against the low ceiling of their actual possibilities. They were filled with rage. All they really knew were two darknesses, the darkness of their lives, which was now closing in on them, and the darkness of the movies, which had blinded them to that other darkness, and in which they now, vindictively, dreamed, at once more together than they were at any other time, and more alone.

When the last bell rang, the last class ended, I let out my breath. It seemed I'd been holding it for all that time. My clothes were wet—I may have looked as though I'd been sitting in a steam bath, all dressed up, all afternoon. I sat alone in the classroom a long time. I listened to the boys outside, downstairs, shouting and cursing and laughing. Their laughter struck me for perhaps the first time. It was not the joyous laughter which— God knows why—one associates with children. It was mocking and insular, its intent was to denigrate. It was disenchanted, and in this, also, lay the authority of their curses. Perhaps I was listening to them because I was thinking about my brother and in them I heard my brother. And myself.

One boy was whistling a tune, at once very complicated and very simple, it seemed to be pouring out of him as though he were a bird, and it sounded very cool and moving through all that harsh, bright air, just holding its own through all those other sounds.

I stood up and walked over to the window and looked down into the courtyard. It was the beginning of the spring and the sap was rising in the boys. A teacher passed through them every now and again, quickly, as though he or she couldn't wait to get out of that courtyard, to get those boys out of their sight and off their minds. I started collecting my stuff. I thought I'd better get home and talk to Isabel.

The courtyard was almost deserted by the time I got downstairs. I saw this boy standing in the shadow of a doorway, looking just like Sonny. I almost called his name. Then I saw that it wasn't Sonny, but somebody we used to know, a boy from around our block. He'd been Sonny's friend. He'd never been mine, having been too young for me, and, anyway, I'd never liked him. And now, even though he was a grown-up man, he still hung around that block, still spent hours on the street corners, was always high and raggy. I used to run into him from time to time and he'd often work around to asking me for a quarter or fifty cents. He always had some real good excuse, too, and I always gave it to him. I don't know why.

But now, abruptly, I hated him. I couldn't stand the way he looked at me, partly like a dog, partly like a cunning child. I wanted to ask him what the hell he was doing in the school courtyard.

head: toilet
horse: heroin

He sort of shuffled over to me, and he said, "I see you got the papers. So you already know about it."

"You mean about Sonny? Yes, I already know about it. How come they didn't get you?"

He grinned. It made him repulsive and it also brought to mind what he'd looked like as a kid. "I wasn't there. I stay away from them people."

"Good for you." I offered him a cigarette and I watched him through the smoke. "You come all the way down here just to tell me about Sonny?"

"That's right." He was sort of shaking his head and his eyes looked strange, as though they were about to cross. The bright sun deadened his damp dark brown skin and it made his eyes look yellow and showed up the dirt in his kinked hair. He smelled funky°. I moved a little away from him and I said, "Well, thanks. But I already know about it and I got to get home."

"I'll walk you a little ways," he said. We started walking. There were a couple of kids still loitering in the courtyard and one of them said good-night to me and looked strangely at the boy beside me.

"What're you going to do?" he asked me. "I mean, about Sonny?"

"Look. I haven't seen Sonny for over a year. I'm not sure I'm going to do anything. Anyway, what the hell *can* I do?"

"That's right," he said quickly, "ain't nothing you can do. Can't much help old Sonny no more, I guess."

It was what I was thinking and so it seemed to me he had no right to say it.

"I'm surprised at Sonny, though," he went on—he had a funny way of talking, he looked straight ahead as though he were talking to "himself—"I thought Sonny was a smart boy, I thought he was too smart to get hung."

"I guess he thought so too," I said sharply, "and that's how he got hung. And now about you? You're pretty goddamn smart, I bet."

Then he looked directly at me, just for a minute. "I ain't smart," he said. "If I was smart, I'd have reached for a pistol a long time ago."

"Look. Don't tell *me* your sad story, if it was up to me, I'd give you one." Then I felt guilty—guilty, probably, for never having supposed that the poor bastard *had* a story of his own, much less a sad one, and I asked, quickly, "What's going to happen to him now?"

He didn't answer this. He was off by himself some place. "Funny thing," he said, and from his tone we might have been discussing the quickest way to get to Brooklyn, "when I saw the papers this morning, the first thing I asked myself was if I had anything to do with it. I felt sort of responsible."

I began to listen more carefully. The subway station was on the corner, just before us, and I stopped. He stopped, too. We were in front of a bar and he ducked slightly, peering in, but whoever he was looking for didn't seem to be there. The juke box was blasting away with something black and bouncy and I half watched the barmaid as she danced her way from the juke

funky: having an offensive odour

box to her place behind the bar. And I watched her face as she laughingly responded to something someone said to her, still keeping time to the music. When she smiled one saw the little girl, one sensed the doomed, still-struggling woman beneath the battered face of the semi-whore.

"I never *give* Sonny nothing," the boy said finally, "but a long time ago I come to school high and Sonny asked me how it felt." He paused, I couldn't bear to watch him, I watched the barmaid, and I listened to the music which seemed to be causing the pavement to shake. "I told him it felt great." The music stopped, the barmaid paused and watched the juke box until the music began again. "It did."

All this was carrying me some place I didn't want to go. I certainly didn't want to know how it felt. It filled everything, the people, the houses, the music, the dark, quicksilver barmaid, with menace; and this menace was their reality.

"What's going to happen to him now?" I asked again.

"They'll send him away some place and they'll try to cure him." He shook his head. "Maybe he'll even think he's kicked the habit. Then they'll let him loose"—he gestured, throwing his cigarette into the gutter. "That's all."

"What do you mean, that's *all?*"

But I knew what he meant.

"I *mean*, that's *all*." He turned his head and looked at me, pulling down the corners of his mouth. "Don't you know what I mean?" he asked, softly.

"How the hell *would* I know what you mean?" I almost whispered it, I don't know why.

"That's right," he said to the air, "how would *he* know what I mean?" He turned toward me again, patient and calm, and yet I somehow felt him shaking, shaking as though he were going to fall apart. I felt that ice in my guts again, the dread I'd felt all afternoon; and again I watched the barmaid, moving about the bar, washing glasses, and singing. "Listen. They'll let him out and then it'll just start all over again. That's what I mean."

"You mean—they'll let him out. And then he'll just start working his way back in again. You mean he'll never kick the habit. Is that what you mean?"

"That's right," he said, cheerfully. "*You* see what I mean."

"Tell me," I said at last, "why does he want to die? He must want to die, he's killing himself, why does he want to die?"

He looked at me in surprise. He licked his lips. "He don't want to die. He wants to live. Don't nobody want to die, ever."

Then I wanted to ask him—too many things. He could not have answered, or if he had, I could not have borne the answers. I started walking. "Well, I guess it's none of my business."

"It's going to be rough on old Sonny," he said. We reached the subway station. "This is your station?" he asked. I nodded. I took one step down. "Damn!" he said, suddenly. I looked up at him. He grinned again. "Damn it if I didn't leave all my money home. You ain't got a dollar on you, have you? Just for a couple of days is all."

All at once something inside gave and threatened to come pouring out of me. I didn't hate him any more. I felt that in another moment I'd start crying like a child.

"Sure," I said. "Don't sweat." I looked in my wallet and didn't have a dollar, I only had a five. "Here," I said. "That hold you?"

He didn't look at it—he didn't want to look at it. A terrible, closed look came over his face, as though he were keeping the number on the bill a secret from him and me. "Thanks," he said, and now he was dying to see me go. "Don't worry about Sonny. Maybe I'll write him or something."

"Sure," I said. "You do that. So long."

"Be seeing you," he said. I went on down the steps.

And I didn't write Sonny or send him anything for a long time. When I finally did, it was just after my little girl died, and he wrote me back a letter which made me feel like a bastard.

Here's what he said:

> Dear brother,
>
> You don't know how much I needed to hear from you. I wanted to write you many a time but I dug how much I must have hurt you and so I didn't write. But now I feel like a man who's been trying to climb up out of some deep, real deep and funky hole and just saw the sun up there, outside. I got to get outside.
>
> I can't tell you much about how I got here. I mean I don't know how to tell you. I guess I was afraid of something or I was trying to escape from something and you know I have never been very strong in the head (smile). I'm glad Mama and Daddy are dead and can't see what's happened to their son and I swear if I'd known what I was doing I would never have hurt you so, you and a lot of other fine people who were nice to me and who believed in me.
>
> I don't want you to think it had anything to do with me being a musician. It's more than that. Or maybe less than that. I can't get anything straight in my head down here and I try not to think about what's going to happen to me when I get outside again. Sometime I think I'm going to flip and never get outside and sometime I think I'll come straight back. I tell you one thing, though, I'd rather blow my brains out than go through this again. But that's what they all say, so they tell me. If I tell you when I'm coming to New York and if you could meet me, I sure would appreciate it. Give my love to Isabel and the kids and I was sure sorry to hear about little Gracie. I wish I could be like Mama and say the Lord's will be done, but I don't know it seems to me that trouble is the one thing that never does get stopped and I don't know what good it does to blame it on the Lord. But maybe it does some good if you believe it.
>
> Your brother,
>
> Sonny

Then I kept in constant touch with him and I sent him whatever I could and I went to meet him when he came back to New York. When I saw him many things I thought I had forgotten came flooding back to me. This was because I had begun, finally, to wonder about Sonny, about the life that Sonny lived inside. This life, whatever it was, had made him older and thinner and it had deepened the distant stillness in which he had always moved. He looked very unlike my baby brother. Yet, when he smiled, when we shook hands, the baby brother I'd never known looked out from the depths of his private life, like an animal waiting to be coaxed into the light.

"How you been keeping?" he asked me.

"All right. And you?"

"Just fine." He was smiling all over his face. "It's good to see you again."

"It's good to see you."

The seven years' difference in our ages lay between us like a chasm: I wondered if these years would ever operate between us as a bridge. I was remembering, and it made it hard to catch my breath, that I had been there when he was born; and I had heard the first words he had ever spoken. When he started to walk, he walked from our mother straight to me. I caught him just before he fell when he took the first steps he ever took in this world.

"How's Isabel?"

"Just fine. She's dying to see you."

"And the boys?"

"They're fine, too. They're anxious to see their uncle."

"Oh, come on. You know they don't remember me."

"Are you kidding? Of course they remember you."

He grinned again. We got into a taxi. We had a lot to say to each other, far too much to know how to begin.

As the taxi began to move, I asked, "You still want to go to India?"

He laughed. "You still remember that. Hell, no. This place is Indian enough for me."

"It used to belong to them," I said.

And he laughed again. "They damn sure knew what they were doing when they got rid of it."

Years ago, when he was around fourteen, he'd been all hipped on the idea of going to India. He read books about people sitting on rocks, naked, in all kinds of weather, but mostly bad, naturally, and walking barefoot through hot coals and arriving at wisdom. I used to say that it sounded to me as though they were getting away from wisdom as fast as they could. I think he sort of looked down on me for that.

"Do you mind," he asked, "if we have the driver drive alongside the park? On the west side—I haven't seen the city in so long."

"Of course not," I said. I was afraid that I might sound as though I were humoring him, but I hoped he wouldn't take it that way.

So we drove along, between the green of the park and the stony, lifeless elegance of hotels and apartment buildings, toward the vivid, killing streets of our childhood. These streets hadn't changed, though housing projects jutted up out of them now like rocks in the middle of a boiling sea. Most of the houses in which we had grown up had vanished, as had the stores from which we had stolen, the basements in which we had first tried sex, the rooftops from which we had hurled tin cans and bricks. But houses exactly like the houses of our past yet dominated the landscape, boys exactly like the boys we once had been found themselves smothering in these houses, came down into the streets for light and air and found themselves encircled by disaster. Some escaped the trap, most didn't. Those who got out always left something of themselves behind, as some animals amputate a leg and leave it in the trap. It might be said, perhaps, that I had escaped, after all, I was a school teacher; or that Sonny had, he hadn't lived in Harlem for years. Yet, as the cab moved uptown through streets which seemed, with a rush, to darken with dark people, and as I covertly studied Sonny's face, it came to me that what we both were seeking through our separate cab windows was that part of ourselves which had been left behind. It's always at the hour of trouble and confrontation that the missing member aches.

We hit 110th Street and started rolling up Lenox Avenue. And I'd known this avenue all my life, but it seemed to me again, as it had seemed on the day I'd first heard about Sonny's trouble, filled with a hidden menace which was its very breath of life.

"We almost there," said Sonny.

"Almost." We were both too nervous to say anything more.

We live in a housing project. It hasn't been up long. A few days after it was up it seemed uninhabitably new, now, of course, it's already rundown. It looks like a parody of the good, clean, faceless life—God knows the people who live in it do their best to make it a parody. The beat-looking grass lying around isn't enough to make their lives green, the hedges will never hold out the streets, and they know it. The big windows fool no one, they aren't big enough to make space out of no space. They don't bother with the windows, they watch the TV screen instead. The playground is most popular with the children who don't play at jacks, or skip rope, or roller skate, or swing, and they can be found in it after dark. We moved in partly because it's not too far from where I teach, and partly for the kids; but it's really just like the houses in which Sonny and I grew up. The same things happen, they'll have the same things to remember. The moment Sonny and I started into the house I had the feeling that I was simply bringing him back into the danger he had almost died trying to escape.

Sonny has never been talkative. So I don't know why I was sure he'd be dying to talk to me when supper was over the first night. Everything went fine, the oldest boy remembered him, and the youngest boy liked him, and Sonny had remembered to bring something for each of them; and Isabel, who is really much nicer than I am, more open and giving, had gone to a lot of trouble about dinner and was genuinely glad to see him. And she's always been able to tease Sonny in a way that I haven't. It was nice to see her face so vivid again and to hear her laugh and watch her make Sonny laugh. She wasn't, or, anyway, she didn't seem to be, at all uneasy or embarrassed. She chatted as though there were no subject which had to be avoided and she got Sonny past his first, faint stiffness. And thank God she was there, for I was filled with that icy dread again. Everything I did seemed awkward to me, and everything I said sounded freighted with hidden meaning. I was trying to remember everything I'd heard about dope addiction and I couldn't help watching Sonny for signs. I wasn't doing it out of malice. I was trying to find out something about my brother. I was dying to hear him tell me he was safe.

"Safe!" my father grunted, whenever Mama suggested trying to move to a neighborhood which might be safer for children. "Safe, hell! Ain't no place safe for kids, nor nobody."

He always went on like this, but he wasn't, ever, really as bad as he sounded, not even on weekends, when he got drunk. As a matter of fact, he was always on the lookout for "something a little better," but he died before he found it. He died suddenly, during a drunken weekend in the middle of the war, when Sonny was fifteen. He and Sonny hadn't ever got on too well. And this was partly because Sonny was the apple of his father's eye. It was because he loved Sonny so much and was frightened for him, that he was always fighting with him. It doesn't do any good to fight with Sonny. Sonny just moves back, inside himself, where he can't be reached. But the principal reason that they never hit it off is that they were so much alike. Daddy was big and rough and loud-talking, just the opposite of Sonny, but they both had—that same privacy.

Mama tried to tell me something about this, just after Daddy died. I was home on leave from the army.

This was the last time I ever saw my mother alive. Just the same, this picture gets all mixed up in my mind with pictures I had of her when she was younger. The way I always see her is the way she used to be on a Sunday afternoon, say, when the old folks were talking after the big Sunday dinner. I always see her wearing pale blue. She'd be sitting on the sofa. And my father would be sitting in the easy chair, not far from her. And the living room would be full of church folks and relatives. There they sit, in chairs all around the living room, and the night is creeping up outside, but nobody knows it yet. You can see the darkness growing against the windowpanes and you hear the street noises every now and again, or maybe the jangling beat of a tambourine from one of the churches close by, but it's real quiet in the room. For a moment nobody's talking, but every face looks darkening, like the sky outside. And my mother rocks a little from the waist, and my father's eyes are closed. Everyone is looking at something a child can't see. For a minute they've forgotten the children. Maybe a kid is lying on the rug, half asleep. Maybe somebody's got a kid in his lap and is absent-mindedly stroking the kid's head. Maybe there's a kid, quiet and big-eyed, curled up in a big chair in the corner. The silence, the darkness coming, and the darkness in the faces frighten the child obscurely. He hopes that the hand which strokes his forehead will never stop—will never die. He hopes that there will never come a time when the old folks won't be sitting around the living room, talking about where they've come from, and what they've seen, and what's happened to them and their kinfolk.

But something deep and watchful in the child knows that this is bound to end, is already ending. In a moment someone will get up and turn on the light. Then the old folks will remember the children and they won't talk any more that day. And when light fills the room, the child is filled with darkness. He knows that every time this happens he's moved just a little closer to that darkness outside. The darkness outside is what the old folks have been talking about. It's what they've come from. It's what they endure. The child knows that they won't talk any more because if he knows too much about what's happened to *them*, he'll know too much too soon, about what's going to happen to *him*.

The last time I talked to my mother, I remember I was restless. I wanted to get out and see Isabel. We weren't married then and we had a lot to straighten out between us.

There Mama sat, in black, by the window. She was humming an old church song, *Lord, you brought me from a long ways off*. Sonny was out somewhere. Mama kept watching the streets.

"I don't know," she said, "if I'll ever see you again, after you go off from here. But I hope you'll remember the things I tried to teach you."

"Don't talk like that," I said, and smiled. "You'll be here a long time yet."

She smiled, too, but she said nothing. She was quiet for a long time. And I said, "Mama, don't you worry about nothing. I'll be writing all the time, and you be getting the checks. . . ."

"I want to talk to you about your brother," she said, suddenly. "If anything happens to me he ain't going to have nobody to look out for him."

"Mama," I said, "ain't nothing going to happen to you *or* Sonny. Sonny's all right. He's a good boy and he's got good sense."

"It ain't a question of his being a good boy," Mama said, "nor of his having good sense. It ain't only the bad ones, nor yet the dumb ones that gets sucked under." She stopped, looking at me. "Your Daddy once had a brother," she said, and she smiled in a way that made me feel she was in pain. "You didn't never know that, did you?"

"No," I said, "I never knew that," and I watched her face.

"Oh, yes," she said, "your Daddy had a brother." She looked out of the window again. "I know you never saw your Daddy cry. But I did—many a time, through all these years."

I asked her, "What happened to his brother? How come nobody's ever talked about him?"

This was the first time I ever saw my mother look old.

"His brother got killed," she said, "when he was just a little younger than you are now. I knew him. He was a fine boy. He was maybe a little full of the devil, but he didn't mean nobody no harm."

Then she stopped and the room was silent, exactly as it had sometimes been on those Sunday afternoons. Mama kept looking out into the streets.

"He used to have a job in the mill," she said, "and, like all young folks, he just liked to perform on Saturday nights. Saturday nights, him and your father would drift around to different places, go to dances and things like that, or just sit around with people they knew, and your father's brother would sing, he had a fine voice, and play along with himself on his guitar. Well, this particular Saturday night, him and your father was coming home from some place, and they were both a little drunk and there was a moon that night, it was bright like day. Your father's brother was feeling kind of good, and he was whistling to himself, and he had his guitar slung over his shoulder. They was coming down a hill and beneath them was a road that turned off from the highway. Well, your father's brother, being always kind of frisky, decided to run down this hill, and he did, with that guitar banging and clanging behind him, and he ran across the road, and he was making water behind a tree. And your father was sort of amused at him and he was still coming down the hill, kind of slow. Then he heard a car motor and that same minute his brother stepped from behind the tree, into the road, in the moonlight. And he started to cross the road. And your father started to run down the hill, he says he don't know why. This car was full of white men. They was all drunk, and when they seen your father's brother they let out a great whoop and holler and they aimed the car straight at him. They was having fun, they just wanted to scare him, the way they do sometimes, you know. But they was drunk. And I guess the boy, being drunk, too, and scared, kind of lost his head. By the time he jumped it was too late. Your father says he heard his brother scream when the car rolled over him, and he heard the wood of that guitar when it give, and he heard them strings go flying, and he heard them white men shouting, and the car kept on a-going and it ain't stopped till this day. And, time your father got down the hill, his brother weren't nothing but blood and pulp."

Tears were gleaming on my mother's face. There wasn't anything I could say.

"He never mentioned it," she said, "because I never let him mention it before you children. Your Daddy was like a crazy man that night and for many a night thereafter. He says he never in his life seen anything as dark as that road after the lights of that car had gone away. Weren't nothing, weren't nobody on that road, just your Daddy and his brother and that busted guitar. Oh, yes. Your Daddy never did really get right again. Till the day he died he weren't sure but that every white man he saw was the man that killed his brother."

She stopped and took out her handkerchief and dried her eyes and looked at me.

"I ain't telling you all this," she said, "to make you scared or bitter or to make you hate nobody. I'm telling you this because you got a brother. And the world ain't changed."

I guess I didn't want to believe this. I guess she saw this in my face. She turned away from me, toward the window again, searching those streets.

"But I praise my Redeemer," she said at last, "that He called your Daddy home before me. I ain't saying it to throw no flowers at myself, but, I declare, it keeps me from feeling too cast down to know I helped your father get safely through this world. Your father always acted like he was the roughest, strongest man on earth. And everybody took him to be like that. But if he hadn't had me there—to see his tears!"

She was crying again. Still, I couldn't move. I said, "Lord, Lord, Mama, I didn't know it was like that."

"Oh, honey," she said, "there's a lot that you don't know. But you are going to find out." She stood up from the window and came over to me. "You got to hold on to your brother," she said, "and don't let him fall, no matter what it looks like is happening to him and no matter how evil you gets with him. You going to be evil with him many a time. But don't you forget what I told you, you hear?"

"I won't forget," I said. "Don't you worry, I won't forget. I won't let nothing happen to Sonny."

My mother smiled as though she was amused at something she saw in my face. Then, "You may not be able to stop nothing from happening. But you got to let him know you's *there*."

Two days later I was married, and then I was gone. And I had a lot of things on my mind and I pretty well forgot my promise to Mama until I got shipped home on a special furlough for her funeral.

And, after the funeral, with just Sonny and me alone in the empty kitchen, I tried to find out something about him.

"What do you want to do?" I asked him.

"I'm going to be a musician," he said.

For he had graduated, in the time I had been away, from dancing to the juke box to finding out who was playing what, and what they were doing with it, and he had bought himself a set of drums.

"You mean, you want to be a drummer?" I somehow had the feeling that being a drummer might be all right for other people but not for my brother Sonny.

"I don't think," he said, looking at me very gravely, "that I'll ever be a good drummer. But I think I can play a piano."

I frowned. I'd never played the role of the oldest brother quite so seriously before, had scarcely ever, in fact, *asked* Sonny a damn thing. I sensed myself in the presence of something I didn't really know how to handle, didn't understand. So I made my frown a little deeper as I asked: "What kind of musician do you want to be?"

He grinned. "How many kinds do you think there are?"

"Be serious," I said.

He laughed, throwing his head back, and then looked at me. "I *am* serious."

"Well, then, for Christ's sake, stop kidding around and answer a serious question. I mean, do you want to be a concert pianist, you want to play classical music and all that, or—or what?" Long before I finished he was laughing again. "For Christ's *sake*, Sonny!"

He sobered, but with difficulty. "I'm sorry. But you sound so—*scared!*" and he was off again.

"Well, you may think it's funny now, baby, but it's not going to be so funny when you have to make your living at it, let me tell you *that*." I was furious because I knew he was laughing at me and I didn't know why.

"No," he said, very sober now, and afraid, perhaps, that he'd hurt me, "I don't want to be a classical pianist. That isn't what interests me. I mean"—he paused, looking hard at me, as though his eyes would help me to understand, and then gestured helplessly, as though perhaps his hand would help—"I mean, I'll have a lot of studying to do, and I'll have to study *everything*, but, I mean, I want to play *with*—jazz musicians." He stopped. "I want to play jazz," he said.

Well, the word had never before sounded as heavy, as real, as it sounded that afternoon in Sonny's mouth. I just looked at him and I was probably frowning a real frown by this time. I simply couldn't see why on earth he'd want to spend his time hanging around nightclubs, clowning around on bandstands, while people pushed each other around a dance floor. It seemed—beneath him, somehow. I had never thought about it before, had never been forced to, but I suppose I had always put jazz musicians in a class with what Daddy called "good-time people."

"Are you serious?"

"Hell, *yes*, I'm *serious*."

He looked more helpless than ever, and annoyed, and deeply hurt.

I suggested, helpfully: "You mean—like Louis Armstrong?"

His face closed as though I'd struck him. "No. I'm not talking about none of that old-time, down home crap."

"Well, look, Sonny, I'm sorry, don't get mad. I just don't altogether get it, that's all. Name somebody—you know, a jazz musician you admire."

"Bird."

"Who?"

"Bird! Charlie Parker°? Don't they teach you nothing in the goddamn army?"

I lit a cigarette. I was surprised and then a little amused to discover that I was trembling. "I've been out of touch," I said. "You'll have to be patient with me. Now. Who's this Parker character?"

"He's just one of the greatest jazz musicians alive," said Sonny, sullenly, his hands in his pockets, his back to me. "Maybe *the* greatest," he added, bitterly, "that's probably why you never heard of him."

Charlie "Bird" Parker (1920-55): with jazz musician "Dizzy" Gillespie, made the first bop or bebop recordings and became the leader of the bop movement in jazz. Parker's addiction to drugs was believed responsible for shortening his life.

"All right," I said, "I'm ignorant. I'm sorry. I'll go out and buy all the cat's records right away, all right?"

"It don't," said Sonny, with dignity, "make any difference to me. I don't care what you listen to. Don't do me no favors."

I was beginning to realize that I'd never seen him so upset before. With another part of my mind I was thinking that this would probably turn out to be one of those things kids go through and that I shouldn't make it seem important by pushing it too hard. Still, I didn't think it would do any harm to ask: "Doesn't all this take a lot of time? Can you make a living at it?"

He turned back to me and half leaned, half sat, on the kitchen table. "Everything takes time," he said, "and—well, yes, sure, I can make a living at it. But what I don't seem to be able to make you understand is that it's the only thing I want to do."

"Well, Sonny," I said gently, "you know people can't always do exactly what they *want* to do—"

"No, I don't know that," said Sonny, surprising me. "I think people *ought* to do what they want to do, what else are they alive for?"

"You getting to be a big boy," I said desperately, "it's time you started thinking about your future."

"I'm thinking about my future," said Sonny, grimly. "I think about it all the time."

I gave up. I decided, if he didn't change his mind, that we could always talk about it later. "In the meantime," I said, "you got to finish school." We had already decided that he'd have to move in with Isabel and her folks. I knew this wasn't the ideal arrangement because Isabel's folks are inclined to be dicty° and they hadn't especially wanted Isabel to marry me. But I didn't know what else to do. "And we have to get you fixed up at Isabel's."

There was a long silence. He moved from the kitchen table to the window. "That's a terrible idea. You know it yourself."

"Do you have a *better* idea?"

He just walked up and down the kitchen for a minute. He was as tall as I was. He had started to shave. I suddenly had the feeling that I didn't know him at all.

He stopped at the kitchen table and picked up my cigarettes. Looking at me with a kind of mocking, amused defiance, he put one between his lips. "You mind?"

"You smoking already?"

He lit the cigarette and nodded, watching me through the smoke. "I just wanted to see if I'd have the courage to smoke in front of you." He grinned and blew a great cloud of smoke to the ceiling. "It was easy." He looked at my face. "Come on, now. I bet you was smoking at my age, tell the truth."

I didn't say anything but the truth was on my face, and he laughed. But now there was something very strained in his laugh. "Sure. And I bet that ain't all you was doing."

dicty: dictatorial, bossy

He was frightening me a little. "Cut the crap," I said. "We already decided that you was going to go and live at Isabel's. Now what's got into you all of a sudden?"

"You decided it," he pointed out. "I didn't decide nothing." He stopped in front of me, leaning against the stove, arms loosely folded. "Look, brother. I don't want to stay in Harlem no more, I really don't." He was very earnest. He looked at me, then over toward the kitchen window. There was something in his eyes I'd never seen before, some thoughtfulness, some worry all his own. He rubbed the muscle of one arm. "It's time I was getting out of here."

"Where do you want to go, Sonny?"

"I want to join the army. Or the navy, I don't care. If I say I'm old enough, they'll believe me."

Then I got mad. It was because I was so scared. "You must be crazy. You goddamn fool, what the hell do you want to go and join the *army* for?"

"I just told you. To get out of Harlem."

"Sonny, you haven't even finished *school*. And if you really want to be a musician, how do you expect to study if you're in the *army*?"

He looked at me, trapped, and in anguish. "There's ways. I might be able to work out some kind of deal. Anyway, I'll have the G.I. Bill when I come out."

"*If* you come out." We stared at each other. "Sonny, please. Be reasonable. I know the setup is far from perfect. But we got to do the best we can."

"I ain't learning nothing in school," he said. "Even when I go." He turned away from me and opened the window and threw his cigarette out into the narrow alley. I watched his back. "At least, I ain't learning nothing you'd want me to learn." He slammed the window so hard I thought the glass would fly out, and turned back to me. "And I'm sick of the stink of these garbage cans!"

"Sonny," I said, "I know how you feel. But if you don't finish school now, you're going to be sorry later that you didn't." I grabbed him by the shoulders. "And you only got another year. It ain't so bad. And I'll come back and I swear I'll help you do *whatever* you want to do. Just try to put up with it till I come back. Will you please do that? For me?"

He didn't answer and he wouldn't look at me.

"Sonny. You hear me?"

He pulled away. "I hear you. But you never hear anything I say."

I didn't know what to say to that. He looked out of the window and then back at me. "OK," he said, and sighed. "I'll try."

Then I said, trying to cheer him up a little, "They got a piano at Isabel's. You can practice on it."

And as a matter of fact, it did cheer him up for a minute. "That's right," he said to himself. "I forgot that." His face relaxed a little. But the worry, the thoughtfulness, played on it still, the way shadows play on a face which is staring into the fire.

But I thought I'd never hear the end of that piano. At first, Isabel would write me, saying how nice it was that Sonny was so serious about his music and how, as soon as he came in from school, or wherever he had been when he was supposed to be at school, he went straight to that piano and stayed there until suppertime. And, after supper, he went back to that piano and stayed there until everybody went to bed. He was at the piano all day Saturday and all day Sunday, Then he bought a record player and started playing records. He'd play one record over and over again, all day long sometimes, and he'd improvise along with it on the piano. Or he'd play one section of the record, one chord, one change, one progression, then he'd do it on the piano. Then back to the record. Then back to the piano.

Well, I really don't know how they stood it. Isabel finally confessed that it wasn't like living with a person at all, it was like living with sound. And the sound didn't make any sense to her, didn't make any sense to any of them—naturally. They began, in a way, to be afflicted by this presence that was living in their home. It was as though Sonny were some sort of god, or *monster*. He moved in an atmosphere which wasn't like theirs at all. They fed him and he ate, he washed himself, he walked in and out of their door; he certainly wasn't nasty or unpleasant or rude, Sonny isn't any of those things; but it was as though he were all wrapped up in some cloud, some fire, some vision all his own; and there wasn't any way to reach him.

At the same time, he wasn't really a man yet, he was still a child, and they had to watch out for him in all kinds of ways. They certainly couldn't throw him out. Neither did they dare to make a great scene about that piano because even they dimly sensed, as I sensed, from so many thousands of miles away, that Sonny was at that piano playing for his life.

But he hadn't been going to school. One day a letter came from the school board and Isabel's mother got it—there had, apparently, been other letters but Sonny had torn them up. This day, when Sonny came in, Isabel's mother showed him the letter and asked where he'd been spending his time. And she finally got it out of him that he'd been down in Greenwich Village, with musicians and other characters, in a white girl's apartment. And this scared her and she started to scream at him and what came up, once she began—though she denies it to this day—was what sacrifices they were making to give Sonny a decent home and how little he appreciated it.

Sonny didn't play the piano that day. By evening, Isabel's mother had calmed down but then there was the old man to deal with, and Isabel herself. Isabel says she did her best to be calm but she broke down and started crying. She says she just watched Sonny's face. She could tell, by watching him, what was happening with him. And what was happening was that they penetrated his cloud, they had reached him. Even if their fingers had been a thousand times more gentle than human fingers ever are, he could hardly help feeling that they had stripped him naked and were spitting on that nakedness. For he also had to see that his presence, that music, which was life or death to him, had been torture for them and that they had endured it, not at all for his sake, but only for mine. And

Sonny couldn't take that. He can take it a little better today than he could then but he's still not very good at it and, frankly, I don't know anybody who is.

The silence of the next few days must have been louder than the sound of all the music ever played since time began. One morning, before she went to work, Isabel was in his room for something and she suddenly realized that all of his records were gone. And she knew for certain that he was gone. And he was. He went as far as the navy would carry him. He finally sent me a postcard from some place in Greece and that was the first I knew that Sonny was still alive. I didn't see him any more until we were both back in New York and the war had long been over.

He was a man by then, of course, but I wasn't willing to see it. He came by the house from time to time, but we fought almost every time we met. I didn't like the way he carried himself, loose and dreamlike all the time, and I didn't like his friends, and his music seemed to be merely an excuse for the life he led. It sounded just that weird and disordered.

Then we had a fight, a pretty awful fight, and I didn't see him for months. By and by I looked him up, where he was living, in a furnished room in the Village, and I tried to make it up. But there were lots of other people in the room and Sonny just lay on his bed, and he wouldn't come downstairs with me, and he treated these other people as though they were his family and I weren't. So I got mad and then he got mad, and then I told him that he might just as well be dead as live the way he was living. Then he stood up and he told me not to worry about him any more in life, that he *was* dead as far as I was concerned. Then he pushed me to the door and the other people looked on as though nothing were happening, and he slammed the door behind me. I stood in the hallway, staring at the door. I heard somebody laugh in the room and then the tears came to my eyes. I started down the steps, whistling to keep from crying. I kept whistling to myself, *You going to need me, baby, one of these cold, rainy days.*

I read about Sonny's trouble in the spring. Little Grace died in the fall. She was a beautiful little girl. But she only lived a little over two years. She died of polio and she suffered. She had a slight fever for a couple of days, but it didn't seem like anything and we just kept her in bed. And we would certainly have called the doctor, but the fever dropped, she seemed to be all right. So we thought it had just been a cold. Then, one day, she was up, playing, Isabel was in the kitchen fixing lunch for the two boys when they'd come in from school, and she heard Grace fall down in the living room. When you have a lot of children you don't always start running when one of them falls, unless they start screaming or something. And, this time, Gracie was quiet. Yet, Isabel says that when she heard that *thump* and then that silence, something happened to her to make her afraid. And she ran to the living room and there was little Grace on the floor, all twisted up, and the reason she hadn't screamed was that she couldn't get her breath. And when she did scream, it was the worst sound, Isabel says, that she'd ever heard in all her life, and she still hears it sometimes in her dreams. Isabel will sometimes wake me up with a low, moaning, strangled sound and I have to be quick to awaken her and hold her to me and where Isabel is weeping against me seems a mortal wound.

I think I may have written Sonny the very day that little Grace was buried. I was sitting in the living room in the dark, by myself, and I suddenly thought of Sonny. My trouble made his real.

One Saturday afternoon, when Sonny had been living with us, or anyway, been in our house, for nearly two weeks, I found myself wandering aimlessly about the living room, drinking from a can of beer, and trying to work up the courage to search Sonny's room. He was out, he was usually out whenever I was home, and Isabel had taken the children to see their grandparents. Suddenly I was standing still in front of the living room window, watching Seventh Avenue. The idea of searching Sonny's room made me still. I scarcely dared to admit to myself what I'd be searching for. I didn't know what I'd do if I found it. Or if I didn't.

On the sidewalk across from me, near the entrance to a barbecue joint, some people were holding an old-fashioned revival meeting. The barbecue cook, wearing a dirty white apron, his conked° hair reddish and metallic in the pale sun, and a cigarette between his lips, stood in the doorway, watching them. Kids and older people paused in their errands and stood there, along with some older men and a couple of very tough-looking women who watched everything that happened on the avenue, as though they owned it, or were maybe owned by it. Well, they were watching this, too. The revival was being carried on by three sisters in black, and a brother. All they had were their voices and their Bibles and a tambourine. The brother was testifying° and while he testified two of the sisters stood together, seeming to say, amen, and the third sister walked around with the tambourine outstretched and a couple of people dropped coins into it. Then the brother's testimony ended and the sister who had been taking up the collection dumped the coins into her palm and transferred them to the pocket of her long black robe. Then she raised both hands, striking the tambourine against the air, and then against one hand, and she started to sing. And the two other sisters and the brother joined in.

It was strange, suddenly, to watch, though I had been seeing these street meetings all my life. So, of course, had everybody else down there. Yet, they paused and watched and listened and I stood still at the window. *"'Tis the old ship of Zion,"* they sang, and the sister with the tambourine kept a steady, jangling beat, *"it has rescued many a thousand!"* Not a soul under the sound of their voices was hearing this song for the first time, not one of them had been rescued. Nor had they seen much in the way of rescue work being done around them. Neither did they especially believe in the holiness of the three sisters and the brother, they knew too much about

conked: straightened, plastered down with grease
testifying: bearing witness to his religious belief

them, knew where they lived, and how. The woman with the tambourine, whose voice dominated the air, whose face was bright with joy, was divided by very little from the woman who stood watching her, a cigarette between her heavy, chapped lips, her hair a cuckoo's nest, her face scarred and swollen from many beatings, and her black eyes glittering like coal. Perhaps they both knew this, which was why, when, as rarely, they addressed each other, they addressed each other as Sister. As the singing filled the air the watching, listening faces underwent a change, the eyes focusing on something within; the music seemed to soothe a poison out of them; and time seemed, nearly, to fall away from the sullen, belligerent, battered faces, as though they were fleeing back to their first condition, while dreaming of their last. The barbecue cook half shook his head and smiled, and dropped his cigarette and disappeared into his joint. A man fumbled in his pockets for change and stood holding it in his hand impatiently, as though he had just remembered a pressing appointment further up the avenue. He looked furious. Then I saw Sonny, standing on the edge of the crowd. He was carrying a wide, flat notebook with a green cover, and it made him look, from where I was standing, almost like a schoolboy. The coppery sun brought out the copper in his skin, he was very faintly smiling, standing very still. Then the singing stopped, the tambourine turned into a collection plate again. The furious man dropped in his coins and vanished, so did a couple of the women, and Sonny dropped some change in the plate, looking directly at the woman with a little smile. He started across the avenue, toward the house. He has a slow, loping walk, something like the way Harlem hipsters walk, only he's imposed on this his own half-beat. I had never really noticed it before.

I stayed at the window, both relieved and apprehensive. As Sonny disappeared from my sight, they began singing again. And they were still singing when his key turned in the lock.

"Hey," he said.

"Hey, yourself. You want some beer?"

"No. Well, maybe." But he came up to the window and stood beside me, looking out. "What a warm voice," he said.

They were singing *If I could only hear my mother pray again!*

"Yes," I said, "and she can sure beat that tambourine."

"But what a terrible song," he said, and laughed. He dropped his notebook on the sofa and disappeared into the kitchen. "Where's Isabel and the kids?"

"I think they went to see their grandparents. You hungry?"

"No." He came back into the living room with his can of beer. "You want to come some place with me tonight?"

I sensed, I don't know how, that I couldn't possibly say no. "Sure. Where?"

He sat down on the sofa and picked up his notebook and started leafing through it. "I'm going to sit in with some fellows in a joint in the Village."

"You mean, you're going to play, tonight?"

"That's right." He took a swallow of his beer and moved back to the window. He gave me a sidelong look. "If you can stand it."

"I'll try," I said.

He smiled to himself and we both watched as the meeting across the way broke up. The three sisters and the brother, heads bowed, were singing *God be with you till we meet again*. The faces around them were very quiet. Then the song ended. The small crowd dispersed. We watched the three women and the lone man walk slowly up the avenue.

"When she was singing before," said Sonny, abruptly, "her voice reminded me for a minute of what heroin feels like sometimes—when it's in your veins. It makes you feel sort of warm and cool at the same time. And distant. And—and sure." He sipped his beer, very deliberately not looking at me. I watched his face. "It makes you feel—in control. Sometimes you've got to have that feeling."

"Do you?" I sat down slowly in the easy chair.

"Sometimes." He went to the sofa and picked up his notebook again. "Some people do."

"In order," I asked, "to play?" And my voice was very ugly, full of contempt and anger.

"Well"—he looked at me with great, troubled eyes, as though, in fact, he hoped his eyes would tell me things he could never otherwise say—"they *think* so. And if they think so—!"

"And what do *you* think?" I asked.

He sat on the sofa and put his can of beer on the floor. "I don't know," he said, and I couldn't be sure if he were answering my question or pursuing his thoughts. His face didn't tell me. "It's not so much to *play*. It's to *stand* it, to be able to make it at all. On any level." He frowned and smiled: "In order to keep from shaking to pieces."

"But these friends of yours," I said, "they seem to shake themselves to pieces pretty goddamn fast."

"Maybe." He played with the notebook. And something told me that I should curb my tongue, that Sonny was doing his best to talk, that I should listen. "But of course you only know the ones that've gone to pieces. Some don't—or at least they haven't *yet* and that's just about all *any* of us can say." He paused. "And then there are some who just live, really, in hell, and they know it and they see what's happening and they go right on. I don't know." He sighed, dropped the notebook, folded his arms. "Some guys, you can tell from the way they play, they on something *all* the time. And you can see that, well, it makes something real for them. But of course," he picked his beer from the floor and sipped it and put the can down again, "they want to, too, you've got to see that. Even some of them that say they don't— *some*, not all."

"And what about you?' I asked—I couldn't help it. "What about you? Do *you* want to?"

He stood up and walked to the window and remained silent for a long time. Then he sighed. "Me," he said. Then: "While I was downstairs before, on my way here, listening to that woman sing, it struck me all of a sudden how much suffering she must have had to go through—to sing like that. It's *repulsive to* think you have to suffer that much."

I said: "But there's no way not to suffer—is there, Sonny?"

"I believe not," he said and smiled, "but that's never stopped anyone from trying." He looked at me. "Has it?" I realized, with this mocking look, that there stood between us, forever, beyond the power of time or forgiveness, the fact that I had held silence—so long!—when he had needed human speech to help him. He turned back to the window. "No, there's no way not to suffer. But you try all kinds of ways to keep from drowning in it, to keep on top of it, and to make it seem—well, like *you*. Like you did something, all right, and now you're suffering for it. You know?" I said nothing. "Well you know," he said, impatiently, "why *do* people suffer? Maybe it's better to do something to give it a reason, *any* reason."

"But we just agreed," I said, "that there's no way not to suffer. Isn't it better, then, just to—take it?"

"But nobody just takes it," Sonny cried, "that's what I'm telling you! *Everybody* tries not to. You're just hung up on the *way* some people try—it's not *your* way!"

The hair on my face began to itch, my face felt wet. "That's not true," I said, "that's not true. I don't give a damn what other people do, I don't even care how they suffer. I just care how *you* suffer." And he looked at me. "Please believe me," I said, "I don't want to see you—die—trying not to suffer."

"I won't," he said flatly, "die trying not to suffer. At least, not any faster than anybody else."

"But there's no need," I said, trying to laugh, "is there? in killing yourself."

I wanted to say more, but I couldn't. I wanted to talk about will power and how life could be—well, beautiful. I wanted to say that it was all within; but was it? or, rather, wasn't that exactly the trouble? And I wanted to promise that I would never fail him again. But it would all have sounded—empty words and lies.

So I made the promise to myself and prayed that I would keep it.

"It's terrible sometimes, inside," he said, "that's what's the trouble. You walk these streets, black and funky and cold, and there's not really a living ass to talk to, and there's nothing shaking, and there's no way of getting it out—that storm inside. You can't talk it and you can't make love with it, and when you finally try to get with it and play it, you realize *nobody's* listening. So *you've* got to listen. You got to find a way to listen."

And then he walked away from the window and sat on the sofa again, as though all the wind had suddenly been knocked out of him. "Sometimes you'll do *anything* to play, even cut your mother's throat." He laughed and looked at me. "Or your brother's." Then he sobered. "Or your own." Then: "Don't worry. I'm all right now and I think I'll *be* all right. But I can't forget—where I've been. I don't mean just the physical place I've been, I mean where I've *been*. And *what* I've been."

"What have you been, Sonny?" I asked.

He smiled—but sat sideways on the sofa, his elbow resting on the back, his fingers playing with his mouth and chin, not looking at me. "I've been something I didn't recognize, didn't know I could be. Didn't know anybody could be." He stopped, looking inward, looking helplessly young, looking old. "I'm not talking about it now because I feel *guilty* or anything like that—maybe it would be better if I did, I don't know. Anyway, I can't really talk about it. Not to you, not to anybody," and now he turned and faced me. "Sometimes, you know, and it was actually when I was most *out* of the world, I felt that I was in it, that I was *with* it, really, and I could play or I didn't really have to *play*, it just came out of me, it was there. And I don't know how I played, thinking about it now, but I know I did awful things, those times, sometimes, to people. Or it wasn't that I *did* anything to them—it was that they weren't real." He picked up the beer can; it was empty; he rolled it between his palms: "And other times—well, I needed a fix, I needed to find a place to lean, I needed to clear a space to *listen*—and I couldn't find it, and I—went crazy, I did terrible things to *me*, I was terrible *for* me." He began pressing the beer can between his hands. I watched the metal begin to give. It glittered, as he played with it like a knife, and I was afraid he would cut himself, but I said nothing. "Oh well. I can never tell you. I was all by myself at the bottom of something, stinking and sweating and crying and shaking, and I smelled it, you know? *my* stink, and I thought I'd die if I couldn't get away from it and yet, all the same, I knew that everything I was doing was just locking me in with it. And I didn't know," he paused, still flattening the beer can, "I didn't know, I still *don't* know, something kept telling me that maybe it was good to smell your own stink, but I didn't think that *that* was what I'd been trying to do—and—who can stand it?" and he abruptly dropped the ruined beer can, looking at me with a small, still smile, and then rose, walking to the window as though it were the lodestone rock. I watched his face, he watched the avenue. "I couldn't tell you when Mama died—but the reason I wanted to leave Harlem so bad was to get away from drugs. And then, when I ran away, that's what I was running from—really. When I came back, nothing had changed, *I* hadn't changed, I was just—older." And he stopped, drumming with his fingers on the windowpane. The sun had vanished, soon darkness would fall. I watched his face. "It can come again," he said, almost as though speaking to himself. Then he turned to me. "It can come again," he repeated. "I just want you to know that."

"All right," I said, at last. "So it can come again. All right."

He smiled, but the smile was sorrowful. "I had to try to tell you," he said.

"Yes," I said. "I understand that."

"You're my brother," he said, looking straight at me, and not smiling at all.

"Yes," I repeated, "yes. I understand that."

He turned back to the window, looking out. "All that hatred down there," he said, "all that hatred and misery, and love. It's a wonder it doesn't blow the avenue apart."

We went to the only nightclub on a short, dark street, downtown. We squeezed through the narrow, chattering, jampacked bar to the entrance of the big room, where the bandstand was. And we stood there for a moment, for the lights were very dim in this room and we couldn't see. Then, "Hello, boy," said the voice and an enormous black man, much older than Sonny or myself, erupted out of all that atmospheric lighting and put an arm around Sonny's shoulder. "I been sitting right here," he said, "waiting for you."

He had a big voice, too, and heads in the darkness turned toward us.

Sonny grinned and pulled a little away, and said, "Creole, this is my brother. I told you about him."

Creole shook my hand. "I'm glad to meet you, son," he said, and it was clear that he was glad to meet me *there*, for Sonny's sake. And he smiled, "You got a real musician in *your* family," and he took his arm from Sonny's shoulder and slapped him, lightly, affectionately, with the back of his hand.

"Well. Now I've heard it all," said a voice behind us. This was another musician, and a friend of Sonny's, a coal-black, cheerful-looking man, built close to the ground. He immediately began confiding to me, at the top of his lungs, the most terrible things about Sonny, his teeth gleaming like a lighthouse and his laugh coming up out of him like the beginning of an earthquake. And it turned out that everyone at the bar knew Sonny, or almost everyone; some were musicians, working there, or nearby, or not working, some were simply hangers-on, and some were there to hear Sonny play. I was introduced to all of them and they were all very polite to me. Yet, it was clear that, for them, I was only Sonny's brother. Here, I was in Sonny's world. Or, rather: his kingdom. Here, it was not even a question that his veins bore royal blood.

They were going to play soon and Creole installed me, by myself, at a table in a dark corner. Then I watched them, Creole, and the little black man, and Sonny, and the others, while they horsed around, standing just below the bandstand. The light from the bandstand spilled just a little short of them and, watching them laughing and gesturing and moving about, I had the feeling that they, nevertheless, were being most careful not to step into that circle of light too suddenly; that if they moved into the light too suddenly, without thinking, they would perish in flame. Then, while I watched, one of them, the small black man, moved into the light and crossed the bandstand and started fooling around with his drums. Then— being funny and being, also, extremely ceremonious—Creole took Sonny by the arm and led him to the piano. A woman's voice called Sonny's name and a few hands started clapping. And Sonny, also being funny and being ceremonious, and so touched, I think, that he could have cried, but neither hiding it nor showing it, riding it like a man, grinned, and put both hands to his heart and bowed from the waist.

Creole then went to the bass fiddle and a lean, very bright-skinned brown man jumped up on the bandstand and picked up his horn. So there they were, and the atmosphere on the bandstand and in the room began to change and tighten. Someone stepped up to the microphone and announced them. Then there were all kinds of murmurs. Some people at the bar shushed others. The waitress ran around, frantically getting in the last orders, guys and chicks got closer to each other, and the lights on the bandstand, on the quartet, turned to a kind of indigo. Then they all looked different there. Creole looked about him for the last time, as though he were making certain that all his chickens were in the coop, and then he—jumped and struck the fiddle. And there they were.

All I know about music is that not many people ever really hear it. And even then, on the rare occasions when something opens within, and the music enters, what we mainly hear, or hear corroborated, are personal, private, vanishing evocations. But the man who creates the music is hearing something else, is dealing with the roar rising from the void and imposing order on it as it hits the air. What is evoked in him, then, is of another order, more terrible because it has no words, and triumphant, too, for that same reason. And his triumph, when he triumphs, is ours. I just watched Sonny's face. His face was troubled, he was working hard, but he wasn't with it. And I had the feeling that, in a way, everyone on the bandstand was waiting for him, both waiting for him and pushing him along. But as I began to watch Creole, I realized that it was Creole who held them all back. He had them on a short rein. Up there, keeping the beat with his whole body, wailing on the fiddle, with his eyes half closed, he was listening to everything, but he was listening to Sonny. He was having a dialogue with Sonny. He wanted Sonny to leave the shoreline and strike out for the deep water. He was Sonny's witness that deep water and drowning were not the same thing—he had been there, and he knew. And he wanted Sonny to know. He was waiting for Sonny to do the things on the keys which would let Creole know that Sonny was in the water.

And, while Creole listened, Sonny moved, deep within, exactly like someone in torment. I had never before thought of how awful the relation-ship must be between the musician and his instrument. He has to fill it, this instrument, with the breath of life, his own. He has to make it do what he wants it to do. And a piano is just a piano. It's made out of so much wood and wires and little hammers and big ones, and ivory. While there's only so much you can do with it, the only way to find this out is to try; to try and make it do everything.

And Sonny hadn't been near a piano for over a year. And he wasn't on much better terms with his life, not the life that stretched before him now. He and the piano stammered, started one way, got scared, stopped; started another way, panicked, marked time, started again; then seemed to have found a direction, panicked again, got stuck. And the face I saw on Sonny I'd never seen before. Everything had been burned out of it, and, at the same time, things usually hidden were being burned in, by the fire and fury of the battle which was occurring in him up there.

Yet, watching Creole's face as they neared the end of the first set, I had the feeling that something had happened, something I hadn't heard. Then they finished, there was scattered applause, and then, without an instant's warning, Creole started into something else, it was almost sardonic, it was *Am I Blue*. And, as though he commanded, Sonny began to play. Something began to happen. And Creole let out the reins. The dry, low, black man said something awful on the drums, Creole answered, and the drums talked back. Then the horn insisted, sweet and high, slightly detached perhaps, and Creole listened, commenting now and then, dry, and driving, beautiful and calm and old. Then they all came together again, and Sonny was part of the family again. I could tell this from his face. He seemed to have found, right there beneath his fingers, a damn brand-new piano. It seemed that he couldn't get over it. Then, for a while, just being happy with Sonny, they seemed to be agreeing with him that brand-new pianos certainly were a gas.

Then Creole stepped forward to remind them that what they were playing was the blues. He hit something in all of them, he hit something in me, myself, and the music tightened and deepened, apprehension began to beat the air. Creole began to tell us what the blues were all about. They were not about anything very new. He and his boys up there were keeping it new, at the risk of ruin, destruction, madness, and death, in order to find new ways to make us listen. For, while the tale of how we suffer, and how we are delighted, and how we may triumph is never new, it always must be heard. There isn't any other tale to tell, it's the only light we've got in all this darkness.

And this tale, according to that face, that body, those strong hands on those strings, has another aspect in every country, and a new depth in every generation. Listen, Creole seemed to be saying, listen. Now these are Sonny's blues. He made the little black man on the drums know it, and the bright, brown man on the horn. Creole wasn't trying any longer to get Sonny in the water. He was wishing him Godspeed. Then he stepped back, very slowly, filling the air with the immense suggestion that Sonny speak for himself.

Then they all gathered around Sonny and Sonny played. Every now and again one of them seemed to say, amen. Sonny's fingers filled the air with life, his life. But that life contained so many others. And Sonny went all the way back, he really began with the spare, flat statement of the opening phrase of the song. Then he began to make it his. It was very beautiful because it wasn't hurried and it was no longer a lament. I seemed to hear with what burning he had made it his, and what burning we had yet to make it ours, how we could cease lamenting. Freedom lurked around us and I understood, at last, that he could help us to be free if we would listen, that he would never be free until we did. Yet, there was no battle in his face now, I heard what he had gone through, and would continue to go through until he came to rest in earth. He had made it his: that long line, of which we knew only Mama and Daddy. And he was giving it back, as everything must be given back, so that, passing through death, it can live forever. I saw my mother's face again, and felt, for the first time, how the stones of the road she had walked on must have bruised her feet. I saw the moonlit road where my father's brother died. And it brought something else back to me, and carried me past it, I saw my little girl again and felt Isabel's tears again, and I felt my own tears begin to rise. And I was yet aware that this was only a moment, that the world waited outside, as hungry as a tiger, and that trouble stretched above us, longer than the sky.

Then it was over. Creole and Sonny let out their breath, both soaking wet, and grinning. There was a lot of applause and some of it was real. In the dark, the girl came by and I asked her to take drinks to the bandstand. There was a long pause, while they talked up there in the indigo light and after awhile I saw the girl put a Scotch and milk on top of the piano for Sonny. He didn't seem to notice it, but just before they started playing again, he sipped from it and looked toward me, and nodded. Then he put it back on top of the piano. For me, then, as they began to play again, it glowed and shook above my brother's head like the very cup of trembling.°

---

cup of trembling: Isaiah 51: 17 & 22: "Behold, I have taken out of thine hand the cup of trembling, even the dregs of the cup of my fury; thou shalt no more drink it again . . ."

Cyril Dabydeen

C yril Dabydeen was born in Bebice, Guyana, in 1945. By the time he immigrated to Canada in 1970, he had already made a name for himself as a poet, winning the Sandback Parker Gold Medal in 1964 and the A.J. Seymour Prize in 1967. In Canada he completed a B.A. in English at Lakehead University and an M.A. at Queens in 1974. He has worked as a race relations professional for the federal government as well as for groups and municipalities, and as a teacher at Algonquin College and the University of Ottawa, where he currently teaches postcolonial literary theory. He is the editor of one of the first Canadian anthologies of Black and Caribbean writing, *A Shapely Fire: Changing the Literary Landscape* (1987), and of *Another Way to Dance: An Anthology of Canadian Asian Poets* (1989). A widely anthologized author himself, Dabydeen has produced eight volumes of poetry (his most recent, *Stoning the Wind,* appeared in 1994), two novels (or novellas—neither exceeds 150 pages), and three collections of short stories: *Still Close to the Island* (1980), *To Monkey Jungle* (1988), and *Jogging in Havana* (1992). In Canada, he has been awarded the Louise Plumb Poetry Prize (1978), the Okanagan Fiction Prize, and the Canadian Author and Bookman Award (1982). From 1984 to 1987, Dabydeen was Ottawa's poet laureate.

In his fiction, as in his work in race relations, Dabydeen is concerned with the experience of the outsider, the immigrant to a new country whose culture is suspect, the member of a minority group who is rejected by and alienated from the dominant culture. His evident commitment to Canada does not blind him to the difficulty of the "other" who is not easily accepted by the society he or she is seeking to enter. In his second novel, *Dark Swirl* (1989), Dabydeen uses the mythic figure of the massacouraman, a Guyanese water monster, as a perceptual test which connects the outsider (the Western scientist who has come to Guyana to collect wildlife specimens) with the people of the village. Although initially seen by the villagers as very much the "other," the scientist becomes increasingly less strange with the passage of time. He remains, however, an isolated figure:

> The stranger was no longer a stranger in mood or spirit. His skin, at first mottled, was now healthily dark. His hard-edged pragmatism had given way to a mild openness. He no longer walked along the edge of the creek picking up objects. His odd behaviour was over, though some of the villagers still wondered if he was still mad . . . Others countered, 'He just like all ahwe now. He act like we, not so?' Yet a few always recalled the reason for his presence among them. They saw him as an outsider—he'd always be that. (90)

In observations quoted on the book's back cover, distinguished West Indian scholar and author Wilson Harris comments:

> Massacouraman is a formidable Guyanese folk legend whose roots in memory and tradition are obscure. *Dark Swirl* is one of the first novels I have read that seeks to plumb its pertinence to all factions, groups, races, insiders, outsiders. The novel seeks to evoke an inner region lying somewhere between the science of the stranger, or outsider, and the fantasies and visions of the insider, the village folk. Before they part company, they appear to see through interchangeable eyes into the mysteries of a nature in a state of long eclipse.

It is perhaps this "inner region" in which very different perspectives meet, where "insider" and "outsider" are no longer relevant categories, that Dabydeen is most concerned with finding.

Works Cited

Dabydeen, Cyril. *Dark Swirl*. Leeds: Peela, 1989.

Kamboureli, Smaro. *Making a Difference*. Toronto: Oxford University Press, 1996. 248.

McLeod, A.L. "The Fictions of Cyril Dabydeen." *Span: Journal of the South Pacific Association for Commonwealth Literature and Language Studies*, No. 36 (1993). **wwwmcc.murdoch.edu.au/ReadingRoom/litserv/SPAN/36/McLeod.html**

MULTICULTURALISM

I continue to sing of other loves,
Places . . . moments when I am furious;
When you are pale and I am strong—
As we come one to another.

The ethnics at our door
Malingering with heritage,
My solid breath—like stones breaking;
At a railway station making much ado about much,
This boulder and Rocky Mountain,

CPR heaving with a head tax°
As I am Chinese in a crowd,
Japanese at the camps,°
It is also World War II.
Panting, I am out of breath.

So I keep on talking
With blood coursing through my veins,
The heart's call for employment equity,
The rhapsody of police shootings in Toronto,
This gathering of the stars one by one, codifying them
And calling them planets, one country, really . . .

---

head tax: in an effort to discourage Chinese immigration to Canada, the federal government established a "head" or entry tax. By 1900, the tax was $100 but, as a result of pressure from British Columbian politicians, it was raised to $500 in 1903.

Japanese at the camps: Twelve weeks after the Japanese bombing of Pearl Harbor, the Canadian government invoked the War Measures Act to order the relocation of all Canadians of Japanese descent who lived within one hundred miles of the Pacific Coast. They were sent either to detention camps in the British Columbian interior or to sugar beet farms in Alberta or Manitoba. Their possessions were confiscated. After many years of political agitation from the Japanese-Canadian community, the federal government under Prime Minister Brian Mulroney issued a formal acknowledgement of the wrongful actions of the Canadian government and announced a compensation package in 1988.

Or galaxies of province after province,
A distinct society too:
Québec or Newfoundland; the Territories . . .
How far we make a map out of our solitudes
As we are still Europe, Asia,
Africa; and the Aborigine in me
Suggests love above all else—
The bear's configuration in the sky;
Other places, events; a turbanned RCMP,
These miracles—

My heritage and quest, heart throbbing;
Voices telling me how much I love you.
YOU LOVE ME; and we're always springing surprises,
Like vandalism at a Jewish cemetery
Or Nelson Mandela's° visit to Ottawa
As I raise a banner high on Parliament Hill
Crying 'Welcome!' we are, you are—
OH CANADA!

Nelson Mandela: South African leader, imprisoned for years for his opposition to the
apartheid policy of the South African government

Edwidge Danticat

born in 1969 in Port-au-Prince, Haiti, Edwidge Danticat spent her first twelve years in Haiti before joining her parents in New York, where they had immigrated several years earlier to establish a better life for themselves and their family. Lonely and ill at ease in her new country, she began to keep a journal and at nine, she wrote her first short story.

Widely viewed as one of the most important young American writers (*The New York Times, Granta* and *The New Yorker* have all identified her as a rising star), Danticat writes in English, her third language. Her first language is Haitian Creole, or "Kreyol," a mixture of French, Spanish, African and English, the cadences of which enrich her writing. She learned French in school and earned a bachelor's degree in French literature from Barnard College. Danticat's first novel, *Breath, Eyes, Memory* (1994), which tells the story of four generations of Haitian women struggling with poverty and powerlessness, was written as a thesis for her Master of Fine Arts degree at Brown University.

Krik? Krak!, the collection of stories from which the following selection is taken, was a finalist for the 1995 National Book Award. Its title is derived from the oral tradition of call and response in Haitian story-telling: the story-teller calls out "Krik?" to summon an interested audience, while the reply "Krak!" indicates a desire to hear the tale. In the stories, Danticat has said that she "wanted to raise the voice of a lot of people that I knew growing up . . . poor people who had extraordinary dreams but also very amazing obstacles" (qtd. in "Story Weaver's Web" 1).

Danticat's second novel, *The Farming of Bones* (1998), revisits the issue that lies at the heart of "Nineteen Thirty-Seven": the 1937 massacre of some 35,000 Haitian workers by the Dominican Republic under dictator Rafael Trujillo. Like most Haitians, a majority of the Spanish-speaking Dominicans are the descendants of African slaves but they are more often the product of mixed African and European ancestry and thus have lighter skin. Trujillo believed the dark-skinned Haitian migrants were undermining the economic and "racial" health of his country. "Nineteen Thirty-Seven" incorporates a popular legend about a group of women who developed wings and flew across the Massacre River to escape the Dominican soldiers. In both story and novel Danticat is concerned with perpetuating the memory, not only of the atrocity, but also of those who lost their lives, of those who struggled and perhaps triumphed over the savagery of their attackers.

In an article written in 1996 for *Caribbean Writer Online,* Danticat recalled a Haitian expression which translates as "We are ugly, but we are here," observing that it "makes a deeper claim for poor Haitian women than maintaining beauty, be it skin deep or otherwise. For most of us, what is worth celebrating is the fact that we are here, that we—against all the odds—exist."

> My grandmother believed that if a life is lost, then another one springs up replanted somewhere else, the next life even stronger than the last. She believed that no one really dies as long as someone remembers, someone who will acknowledge that this person had—in spite of everything—been here. We are part of an endless circle . . . . We have stumbled, but have not fallen. We are ill-favored, but we still endure. Every once in a while, we must scream this as far as the wind can carry our voices: We ugly, but we are here! And here to stay. ("We Are Ugly but We Are Here" 3–4)

Works Cited

Danticat, Edwidge. "We Are Ugly, but We Are Here." *Caribbean Writer Online* 10. 1996. 137–41.
www.uvi.edu/CaribbeanWriter/volume10/ugly

Helmers, Marguerite. "Story Weaver's Web: Edwidge Danticat's *Krik? Krak!.*"
www.english.uwash.edu/helmers/storyweaver.html

Other Sources and Weblinks

Atanasoski, Neda. "Edwidge Danticat."
www.voices.cla.umn.edu/authors/edwidgeDanticat.html

Cryer, Dan. "The Farming of Bones."
www.salon.com/books/sneaks/1998/08/31sneaks.html
wwwrandomhouse.com/features/danticat

Nurse, Donna Bailey. "Island Life, Island Death." *The Globe and Mail.* Books. 24 Oct. 1998: D12.

Wucker, Michele. "Edwidge Danticat: A Voice for the Voiceless." *Americas.* June 2000: 40–45.

Nineteen Thirty-Seven

My Madonna cried. A miniature teardrop traveled down her white porcelain face, like dew on the tip of early morning grass. When I saw the tear I thought, surely, that my mother had died.

I sat motionless observing the Madonna the whole day. It did not shed another tear. I remained in the rocking chair until it was nightfall, my bones aching from the thought of another trip to the prison in Port-au-Prince. But, of course, l had to go.

The roads to the city were covered with sharp pebbles only half buried in the thick dust. I chose to go barefoot, as my mother had always done on her visits to the Massacre River, the river separating Haiti from the Spanish-speaking country that she had never allowed me to name because I had been born on the night that El Generalissimo, Dios Trujillo, the honorable chief of state, had ordered the massacre of all Haitians living there.

The sun was just rising when I got to the capital. The first city person I saw was an old woman carrying a jar full of leeches. Her gaze was glued to the Madonna tucked under my arm.

'May I see it?' she asked.

I held out the small statue that had been owned by my family ever since it was given to my great-great-great-grandmother Défilé by a French man who had kept her as a slave.

The old woman's index finger trembled as it moved toward the Madonna's head. She closed her eyes at the moment of contact, her wrists shaking.

'Where are you from?' she asked. She had layers of 'respectable' wrinkles on her face, the kind my mother might also have one day, if she has a chance to survive.

'I am from Ville Rose,' I said, 'the city of painters and poets, the coffee city, with beaches where the sand is either black or white, but never mixed together, where the fields are endless and sometimes the cows are yellow like cornmeal.'

The woman put the jar of leeches under her arm to keep them out of the sun.

'You're here to see a prisoner?' she asked.

'Yes.'

'I know where you can buy some very good food for this person.'

She led me by the hand to a small alley where a girl was selling fried pork and plantains wrapped in brown paper. I bought some meat for my mother after asking the cook to fry it once more and then sprinkle it with spiced cabbage.

The yellow prison building was like a fort, as large and strong as in the days when it was used by the American marines who had built it. The Americans taught us how to build prisons. By the end of the 1915 occupation, the police in the city really knew how to hold human beings trapped in cages, even women like Manman who was accused of having wings of flame.

The prison yard was as quiet as a cave when a young Haitian guard escorted me there to wait. The smell of the fried pork mixed with that of urine and excrement was almost unbearable. I sat on a pile of bricks, trying to keep the Madonna from sliding through my fingers. I dug my buttocks farther into the bricks, hoping perhaps that my body might sink down to the ground and disappear before my mother emerged as a ghost to greet me.

The other prisoners had not yet woken up. All the better, for I did not want to see them, these bone-thin women with shorn heads, carrying clumps of their hair in their bare hands, as they sought the few rays of sunshine that they were allowed each day.

My mother had grown even thinner since the last time I had seen her. Her face looked like the gray of a late evening sky. These days, her skin barely clung to her bones, falling in layers, flaps, on her face and neck. The prison guards watched her more closely because they thought that the wrinkles resulted from her taking off her skin at night and then putting it back on in a hurry, before sunrise. This was why Manman's sentence had been extended to life. And when she died, her remains were to be burnt in the prison yard, to prevent her spirit from wandering into any young innocent bodies.

I held out the fried pork and plantains for her. She uncovered the food and took a peek before grimacing, as though the sight of the meat nauseated her. Still she took it and put it in a deep pocket in a very loose fitting white dress that she had made herself from the cloth that I had brought her on my last visit.

I said nothing. Ever since the morning of her arrest, I had not been able to say anything to her. It was as though I became mute the moment I stepped into the prison yard. Sometimes I wanted to speak, yet I was not able to open my mouth or raise my tongue. I wondered if she saw my struggle in my eyes.

She pointed at the Madonna in my hands, opening her arms to receive it. I quickly handed her the statue. She smiled. Her teeth were a dark red, as though caked with blood from the initial beating during her arrest. At times, she seemed happier to see the Madonna than she was to see me.

She rubbed the space under the Madonna's eyes, then tasted her fingertips, the way a person tests for salt in salt water.

'Has she cried?' Her voice was hoarse from lack of use. With every visit, it seemed to get worse and worse. I was afraid that one day, like me, she would not be able to say anything at all.

I nodded, raising my index finger to show that the Madonna had cried a single tear. She pressed the statue against her chest as if to reward the Madonna and then, suddenly, broke down and began sobbing herself.

I reached over and patted her back, the way one burps a baby. She continued to sob until a guard came and nudged her, poking the barrel of his rifle into her side. She raised her head, keeping the Madonna lodged against her chest as she forced a brave smile.

'They have not treated me badly,' she said. She smoothed her hands over her bald head, from her forehead to the back of her neck. The guards shaved her head every week. And before the women went to sleep, the guards made them throw tin cups of cold water at one another so that their bodies would not be able to muster up enough heat to grow those wings made of flames, fly away in the middle of the night, slip into the slumber of innocent children and steal their breath.

Manman pulled the meat and plantains out of her pocket and started eating a piece to fill the silence. Her normal ration of food in the prison was bread and water, which is why she was losing weight so rapidly.

'Sometimes the food you bring me, it lasts for months at a time,' she said. 'I chew it and swallow my saliva, then I put it away and then chew it again. It lasts a very long time this way.'

A few of the other women prisoners walked out into the yard, their chins nearly touching their chests, their shaved heads sunk low on bowed necks. Some had large boils on their heads. One, drawn by the fresh smell of fried pork, came to sit near us and began pulling the scabs from the bruises on her scalp, a line of blood dripping down her back.

All of these women were here for the same reason. They were said to have been seen at night rising from the ground like birds on fire. A loved one, a friend, or a neighbor had accused them of causing the death of a child. A few other people agreeing with these stories was all that was needed to have them arrested. And sometimes even killed.

I remembered so clearly the day Manman was arrested. We were new to the city and had been sleeping on a cot at a friend's house. The friend had a sick baby who was suffering with colic. Every once in a while, Manman would wake up to look after the child when the mother was so tired that she no longer heard her son's cries.

One morning when I woke up, Manman was gone. There was the sound of a crowd outside. When I rushed out I saw a group of people taking my mother away. Her face was bleeding from the pounding blows of rocks and sticks and the fists of strangers. She was being pulled along by two policemen, each tugging at one of her arms as she dragged her feet. The woman we had been staying with carried her dead son by the legs. The policemen made no efforts to stop the mob that was beating my mother.

'Lougarou, witch, criminal!' they shouted.

I dashed into the street, trying to free Manman from the crowd. I wasn't even able to get near her.

I followed her cries to the prison. Her face was swollen to three times the size that it had been. She had to drag herself across the clay floor on her belly when I saw her in the prison cell. She was like a snake, someone with no bones left in her body. I was there watching when they shaved her head for the first time. At first I thought they were doing it so that the open gashes on her scalp could heal. Later, when I saw all the other women in the yard, I realized that they wanted to make them look like crows, like men.

Now, Manman sat with the Madonna pressed against her chest, her eyes staring ahead, as though she was looking into the future. She had never talked very much about the future. She had always believed more in the past.

When I was five years old, we went on a pilgrimage to the Massacre River, which I had expected to be still crimson with blood, but which was as clear as any water that I had ever seen. Manman had taken my hand and pushed it into the river, no further than my wrist. When we dipped our hands, I thought that the dead would reach out and haul us in, but only our own faces stared back at us, one indistinguishable from the other.

With our hands in the water, Manman spoke to the sun. 'Here is my child, Josephine. We were saved from the tomb of this river when she was still in my womb. You spared us both, her and me, from this river where I lost my mother.'

My mother had escaped El Generalissimo's soldiers, leaving her own mother behind. From the Haitian side of the river, she could still see the soldiers chopping up *her* mother's body and throwing it into the river along with many others.

We went to the river many times as I was growing up. Every year my mother would invite a few more women who had also lost their mothers there.

Until we moved to the city, we went to the river every year on the first of November. The women would all dress in white. My mother would hold my hand tightly as we walked toward the water. We were all daughters of that river, which had taken our mothers from us. Our mothers were the ashes and we were the light. Our mothers were the embers and we were the sparks. Our mothers were the flames and we were the blaze. We came from the bottom of that river where the blood never stops flowing, where my mother's dive toward life—her swim among all those bodies slaughtered in flight—gave her those wings of flames. The river was the place where it had all begun.

'At least I gave birth to my daughter on the night that my mother was taken from me,' she would say. 'At least you came out at the right moment to take my mother's place.'

Now in the prison yard, my mother was trying to avoid the eyes of the guard peering down at her.

'One day I will tell you the secret of how the Madonna cries,' she said.

I reached over and touched the scabs on her fingers. She handed me back the Madonna.

I know how the Madonna cries. I have watched from hiding how my mother plans weeks in advance for it to happen. She would put a thin layer of wax and oil in the hollow space of the Madonna's eyes and when the wax melted, the oil would roll down the little face shedding a more perfect tear than either she and I could ever cry.

'You go. Let me watch you leave,' she said, sitting stiffly.

I kissed her on the cheek and tried to embrace her, but she quickly pushed me away.

'You will please visit me again soon,' she said.

I nodded my head yes.

'Let your flight be joyful,' she said, 'and mine too.'

I nodded and then ran out of the yard, fleeing before I could flood the front of my dress with my tears. There had been too much crying already.

Manman had a cough the next time I visited her. She sat in a corner of the yard, and as she trembled in the sun, she clung to the Madonna.

'The sun can no longer warm God's creatures,' she said. 'What has the world come to when the sun can no longer warm God's creatures?'

I wanted to wrap my body around hers, but I knew she would not let me.

'God only knows what I have got under my skin from being here. I may die of tuberculosis, or perhaps there are worms right now eating me inside.'

When I went again, I decided that I would talk. Even if the words made no sense, I would try to say something to her. But before I could even say hello she was crying. When I handed her the Madonna, she did not want to take it. The guard was looking directly at us. Manman still had a fever that made her body tremble. Her eyes had the look of delirium.

'Keep the Madonna when I am gone,' she said. 'When I am completely gone, maybe you will have someone to take my place. Maybe you will have a person. Maybe you will have some flesh to console you. But if you don't you will always have the Madonna.'

'Manman, did you fly?' I asked her.

She did not even blink at my implied accusation.

'Oh, now you talk,' she said, 'when I am nearly gone. Perhaps you don't remember. All the women who came with us to the river, they could go to the moon and back if that is what they wanted.'

A week later, almost to the same day, an old woman stopped by my house in Ville Rose on her way to Port-au-Prince. She came in the middle of the night, wearing the same white dress that the women usually wore on their trips to dip their hands in the river.

'Sister,' the old woman said from the doorway. 'I have come for you.'

'I don't know you,' I said.

'You *do* know me,' she said. 'My name is Jacqueline. I have been to the river with you.'

I had been by the river with many people. I remembered a Jacqueline who went on the trips with us, but I was not sure this was the same woman. If she were really from the river, she would know. She would know all the things that my mother had said to the sun as we sat with our hands dipped in the water, questioning each other, making up codes and disciplines by which we could always know who the other daughters of the river were.

'Who are you?' I asked her.

'I am a child of that place,' she answered. 'I come from that long trail of blood.'

'Where are you going?'

'I am walking into the dawn.'

'Who are you?'

'I am the first daughter of the first star.'

'Where do you drink when you're thirsty?'

'I drink the tears from the Madonna's eyes.'

'And if not there?'

'I drink the dew.'

'And if you can't find dew?'

'I drink from the rain before it falls.'

'If you can't drink there?'

'I drink from the turtle's hide.'

'How did you find your way to me?'

'By the light of the mermaid's comb.'

'Where does your mother come from?'

'Thunderbolts, lightning, and all things that soar.'

'Who are you?'

'I am the flame and the spark by which my mother lived.'

'Where do you come from?'

'I come from the puddle of that river.'

'Speak to me.'

'You hear my mother who speaks through me. She is the shadow that follows my shadow. The flame at the tip of my candle. The ripple in the stream where I wash my face. Yes. I will eat my tongue if ever I whisper that name, the name of that place across the river that took my mother from me.'

I knew then that she had been with us, for she knew all the answers to the questions I asked.

'I think you do know who I am; she said, staring deeply into the pupils of my eyes. 'I know who *you* are, You are Josephine. And your mother knew how to make the Madonna cry.'

I let Jacqueline into the house. I offered her a seat in the rocking chair, gave her a piece of hard bread and a cup of cold coffee.

'Sister, I do not want to be the one to tell you,' she said, 'but your mother is dead. If she is not dead now, then she will be when we get to Port-au-Prince. Her blood calls to me from the ground. Will you go with me to see her? Let us go to see her.'

We took a mule for most of the trip. Jacqueline was not strong enough to make the whole journey on foot. I brought the Madonna with me, and Jacqueline took a small bundle with some black rags in it.

When we got to the city, we went directly to the prison gates. Jacqueline whispered Manman's name to a guard and waited for a response.

'She will be ready for burning this afternoon,' the guard said.

My blood froze inside me. I lowered my head as the news sank in.

'Surely, it is not that much a surprise,' Jacqueline said, stroking my shoulder. She had become rejuvenated, as though strengthened by the correctness of her prediction.

'We only want to visit her cell,' Jacqueline said to the guard. 'We hope to take her personal things away.'

The guard seemed too tired to argue, or perhaps he saw in Jacqueline's face traces of some long-dead female relative whom he had not done enough to please while she was still alive.

He took us to the cell where my mother had spent the last year. Jacqueline entered first, and then I followed. The room felt damp, the clay breaking into small muddy chunks under our feet.

I inhaled deeply to keep my lungs from aching, Jacqueline said nothing as she carefully walked around the women who sat like statues in different corners of the cell. There were six of them. They kept their arms close to their bodies, like angels hiding their wings. In the middle of the cell was an arrangement of sand and pebbles in the shape of a cross for my mother. Each woman was either wearing or holding something that had belonged to her.

One of them clutched a pillow as she stared at the Madonna. The woman was wearing my mother's dress, the large white dress that had become like a tent on Manman.

I walked over to her and asked, 'What happened?'

'Beaten down in the middle of the yard,' she whispered.

'Like a dog,' said another woman.

'Her skin, it was too loose,' said the woman wearing my mother's dress. 'They said prison could not cure her.'

The woman reached inside my mother's dress pocket and pulled out a handful of chewed pork and handed it to me. I motioned her hand away.

'No no, I would rather not.'

She then gave me the pillow, my mother's pillow. It was open, half filled with my mother's hair. Each time they shaved her head, my mother had kept the hair for her pillow. I hugged the pillow against my chest, feeling some of the hair rising in clouds of dark dust into my nostrils.

Jacqueline took a long piece of black cloth out of her bundle and wrapped it around her belly.

'Sister,' she said, 'life is never lost, another one always comes up to replace the last. Will you come watch when they burn the body?'

'What would be the use?' I said.

'They will make these women watch, and we can keep them company.'

When Jacqueline took my hand, her fingers felt balmy and warm against the lifelines in my palm. For a brief second, I saw nothing but black. And then I saw the crystal glow of the river as we had seen it every year when my mother dipped my hand in it.

'I would go,' I said, 'if I knew the truth, whether a woman can fly.'

'Why did you not ever ask your mother,' Jacqueline said, 'if she knew how to fly?'

Then the story came back to me as my mother had often told it. On that day so long ago, in the year nineteen hundred and thirty-seven, in the Massacre River, my mother did fly. Weighted down by my body inside hers, she leaped from Dominican soil into the water, and out again on the Haitian side of the river. She glowed red when she came out, blood clinging to her skin, which at that moment looked as though it were in flames.

In the prison yard, I held the Madonna tightly against my chest, so close that I could smell my mother's scent on the statue. When Jacqueline and I stepped out into the yard to wait for the burning, I raised my head toward the sun thinking, One day I may just see my mother there.

'Let her flight be joyful,' I said to Jacqueline. 'And mine and yours too.'

Henry Louis Gates, Jr.

ike bell hooks, Henry Louis Gates, Jr. is one of what New Yorker writer Michael Berube calls the "new African-American intelligentsia" (73). Gates is the Director of the W.E.B. Du Bois Institute for Afro-American Research at Harvard University, where he is also the W.E.B. Du Bois Professor of Humanities and the Chair of Afro-American Studies. He is the author of a number of books of cultural and literary criticism including *Loose Canons: Notes on the Culture Wars* (1992), which deals with the role of education in creating a multicultural and pluralist society, and *The Signifying Monkey: A Theory of Afro-American Literary Criticism* (1998), which won the 1989 American Book Award. He co-authored (with Cornel West) *The Future of Race* (1996) and is the editor of several anthologies including *The Norton Anthology of African American Literature* (1986) and *The Oxford-Schomburg Library of Nineteenth Century Black Women Writers* (1991) and, with K.A. Appiah, the encyclopedia *Africana*, which covers the history of Africa and the African diaspora. He is also the author of *Wonders of the African World,* the book companion to the PBS series of the same title. Very much a *public* intellectual, with a commitment to communicating with those outside the academic world, Gates regularly writes cultural criticism for periodicals such as *The New Yorker, The Atlantic Monthly* and, occasionally, even *Sports Illustrated.* In 1997 he was included in *Time* magazine's list of the "25 Most Influential Americans."

In *The Signifying Monkey*, Gates explores the significance of the development of Black languages in the New World from African and European roots and particularly the relationship between the Black vernacular and Standard English. New York reviewer John Wideman writes: "It is not difficult to understand why Africans forcibly transported across an ocean would be suspicious of a language that gave them the status of chattel slaves and defined them as less than human." By subverting the language, by creating a vernacular which "turned the joke back upon those who would destroy them"(2), they were able to resist the process of total cultural destruction aimed at them. For Gates the development of Black vernacular is the foundation of Black culture and the Black literary heritage. In Wideman's view, Gates' book suggests "new ways of seeing," replacing racist assumptions (about the absence or inferiority of Black culture) with "multicultural awareness" (4), replacing stereotypes with fresh and informed perceptions. This is an endeavour which lies at the heart of much of Gates' work.

Thirteen Ways of Looking at a Black Man (1997) profiles eight prominent Black Americans in the context of twentieth-century American society and its attitudes toward race. "To be a black man in twentieth-century America is to be heir to a set of anxieties," he observes, "beginning with what it means to be a black man." In some sense, these remarkable men must inevitably be seen as representative: "The cultural script of being a black man . . . gives you a good idea of the issues history has presented him with. And so it is with the men in this book. In them, the contradictions and anxieties of the moment and milieu are writ large." Yet, Gates argues, "the notion of a unitary black man is . . . imaginary"(1997: xvii). Each of the individuals he has profiled has resisted the "burden of representation" of his race, his culture and its values, and each has ultimately failed to free himself from the burden of the perceptions of others. In his own treatment of these figures, Gates emphasizes the individuality of their responses and contributions, striving to present each in so far as possible as embedded in his social, political and historical context but also as a unique individual whose strengths and weaknesses, whose accomplishments, are his own. Here, as in The Signifying Monkey and "What's in a Name?" (1992), Gates is resisting attempts to limit perception of Black American culture, to ghettoize it in a "special" and separate compartment as something with no relevance to the broader American culture. As his title implies, Gates' work is about seeing; most of all, it is about seeing beyond racial stereotypes and prejudices.

Works Cited

Berube, Michael. "Public Academy." The New Yorker. 9 Jan. 1994: 73–80.

Gates, Henry Louis, Jr. The Signifying Monkey: A Theory of Afro-American Literary Criticism. New York: Oxford University Press, 1988.

———. Loose Canons: Notes on the Culture Wars. New York and Oxford: Oxford University Press, 1992.

———. Thirteen Ways of Looking at a Black Man. New York: Random House, 1997.

Wideman, John. "Playing, Not Joking, With Language." The New York Times. 14 Aug. 1988: 3.

Other Sources and Weblinks

"What's in a Name?" Some Meanings of Blackness

The question of color takes up much space in these pages, but the question of color, especially in this country, operates to hide the graver questions of the self.

—JAMES BALDWIN, *1961*

. . . blood, darky, Tar Baby, Kaffir, shine . . . moor, blackamoor, Jim Crow, spook . . . quadroon, meriney, red bone, high yellow . . . Mammy, porch monkey, home, homeboy, George . . . spear-chucker, schwarze, Leroy, Smokey . . . mouli, buck, Ethiopian, brother, sistah . . .

—TREY ELLIS, 1989

I had forgotten the incident completely, until I read Trey Ellis's essay, "Remember My Name," in a recent issue of the *Village Voice* (June 13, 1989). But there, in the middle of an extended italicized list of the bynames of "the race" ("the race" or "our people" being the terms my parents used in polite or reverential discourse, "jigaboo" or "nigger" more commonly used in anger, jest, or pure disgust) it was: "George." Now the events of that very brief exchange return to mind so vividly that I wonder why I had forgotten it.

My father and I were walking home at dusk from his second job. He "moonlighted" as a janitor in the evenings for the telephone company. Every day but Saturday, he would come home at 3:30 from his regular job at the paper mill, wash up, eat supper, then at 4:30 head downtown to his second job. He used to make jokes frequently about a union official who moonlighted. I never got the joke, but he and his friends thought it was hilarious. All I knew was that my family always ate well, that my brother and I had new clothes to wear, and that all of the white people in Piedmont, West Virginia, treated my parents with an odd mixture of resentment and respect that even we understood at the time had something directly to do with a small but certain measure of financial security.

He had left a little early that evening because I was with him and I had to be in bed early. I could not have been more than five or six, and we had stopped off at the Cut-Rate Drug Store (where no black person in town but my father could sit down to eat, and eat off real plates with real silverware) so that I could buy some caramel ice cream, two scoops in a wafer cone, please, which I was busy licking when Mr. Wilson walked by.

Mr. Wilson was a very quiet white man, whose stony, brooding, silent manner seemed designed to scare off any overtures of friendship, even from white people. He was Irish, as was one third of our village (another third being Italian), the more affluent among whom sent their children to "Catholic School" across the bridge in Maryland. He had white straight hair, like my Uncle Joe, whom he uncannily resembled, and he carried a black worn metal lunch pail, the kind that Riley carried on the television show. My father always spoke to him, and for reasons that we never did understand, he always spoke to my father.

"Hello, Mr. Wilson," I heard my father say.

"Hello, George."

I stopped licking my ice cream cone and asked my Dad in a loud voice why Mr. Wilson had called him "George."

"Doesn't he know your name, Daddy? Why don't you tell him your name? Your name isn't George."

For a moment I tried to think of who Mr. Wilson was mixing Pop up with. But we didn't have any Georges among the colored people in Piedmont; nor were there colored Georges living in the neighboring towns and working at the mill.

"Tell him your name, Daddy."

"He knows my name, boy," my father said after a long pause. "He calls all colored people George."

A long silence ensued. It was "one of those things," as my mom would put it. Even then, that early, I knew when I was in the presence of "one of those things," one of those things that provided a glimpse, through a rent curtain, at another world that we could not affect but that affected us. There would be a painful moment of silence, and you would wait for it to give way to a discussion of a black superstar such as Sugar Ray or Jackie Robinson.

"Nobody hits better in a clutch than Jackie Robinson."

"That's right. Nobody."

I never again looked Mr. Wilson in the eye.

But I loved the names that we gave ourselves when no white people were around. And I have to confess that I have never really cared too much about what we called ourselves publicly, except when my generation was fighting the elders for the legitimacy of the word *black* as our common, public name. "I'd rather they called me 'nigger,'" my Uncle Raymond would say again and again. "I can't *stand* the way they say the word *black*. And, by the way," he would conclude, his dark brown eyes flashing as he looked with utter disgust at my tentative Afro°, "when are you going to get that nappy shit *cut*?"

There was enough in our public name to make a whole generation of Negroes rail against our efforts to legitimize, to naturalize, the word *black*. Once we were black, I thought, we would be free, inside at least, and maybe from inside we would project a freedom outside of ourselves. "Free your mind," the slogan went, "and your behind will follow." Still, I value those all-too-rare, precious moments when someone "slips," in the warmth and comfort of intimacy, and says the dreaded words: "Was he colored?"

I knew that there was power in our name, enough power so that the prospect frightened my maternal uncles. To open the "Personal Statement" for my Yale admission application in 1968, I had settled upon the following: "My grandfather was colored, my father is Negro, and I am black." (If that doesn't grab them, I thought, then nothing will.) I wonder if my daughters, nine years hence, will adapt the line, identifying themselves as "I am an African-American." Perhaps they'll be Africans by then, or even feisty rapper-dappers. Perhaps, by that time, the most radical act of naming will be a return to "colored."

I began to learn about the meanings of blackness—or at least how to give voice to what I had experienced—when I went off to Yale. The class of 1973 was the first at Yale to include a "large" contingent of "Afro-Americans," the name we quickly and comfortably seized upon at New Haven. Like many of us in those years, I gravitated to courses in Afro-American studies, at least one per semester, despite the fact that I was pre-med, like almost all the other black kids at Yale—that is, until the ranks were devastated by organic chemistry. (Pre-law was the most common substitute.) The college campus, then, was a refuge from explicit racism, freeing us to read and write about our "racial" selves, to organize for recruitment of minority students and faculty, and to demand the constitutional rights of the Black Panther Party° for Self-Defense—an action that led, at New Haven at least, to a full-fledged strike in April of 1970, two weeks before Nixon and Kissinger invaded Cambodia. The campus was our sanctuary, where we could be as black as the ace of spades and nobody seemed to mind.

Today the white college campus is a rather different place. Black studies, where it has survived—and it has survived only at those campuses where *someone* believed enough in its academic integrity to insist upon a

Afro: full and rather rounded hairstyle worn by many Blacks in the sixties; the effect of letting nappy (naturally kinky) hair grow; often a political statement

Black Panther Party: American Black militant party founded in 1966 in California; initially presented violent revolution as the only means of achieving Black liberation

sound academic foundation—is entering its third decade. More black faculty members are tenured than ever before, despite the fact that only eight hundred or so Afro-Americans took the doctorate in 1989, and fully half of these were in education. Yet for all the gains that have been made, racial tensions on college campuses appear to be on the rise. The dream of the university as a haven of racial equity, as an ultimate realm beyond the veil, has not been realized. Racism on our college campuses has become a palpable, ugly thing.

Even I—despite a highly visible presence as a faculty member at Cornell—have found it necessary to cross the street, hum a tune, or smile when confronting a lone white woman in a campus building or on the Commons late at night. (Once a white coed even felt it necessary to spring from an elevator that I was about to enter, in the very building where my department is housed.) Nor can I help but feel some humiliation as I try to put a white person at ease in a dark place on campus at night, coming from nowhere, confronting that certain look of panic in his or her eyes, trying to think grand thoughts like Du Bois° but—for the life of me—looking to him or her like Wille Horton. Grinning, singing, scratching my head, I have felt like Steppin Fetchit with a Ph.D. So much for Yale; so much for Cambridge.

The meanings of blackness are vastly more complex, I suspect, than they ever have been before in our American past. But how to explain? I have often imagined encountering the ghost of the great Du Bois, riding on the shoulders of the Spirit of Blackness.

"Young man," he'd say, "what has happened in my absence? Have things changed?"

"Well, sir," I'd respond, "your alma mater, Fair Harvard, has a black studies department, a Du Bois Research Center, and even a Du Bois Professor of History. Your old friend Thurgood Marshall° sits like a minotaur as an associate justice on the Supreme Court. Martin Luther King's birthday is a *federal* holiday, and a black man you did not know won several Democratic presidential primaries last year. Black women novelists adorn the *New York Times* best-seller lists, and the number one television show in the country is a situation comedy concerning the lives and times of a refined Afro-American obstetrician and his lovely wife, who is a senior partner in a Wall Street law firm. Sammy Davis, Jr.'s second autobiography has been widely—"

"Young man, I have come a long way. Do not trifle with the Weary Traveler."

"I would not think of it, sir. I revere you, sir, why, I even—"

W.E.B. Du Bois (1868–1963): writer, intellectual and civil rights leader

Thurgood Marshall (1908–93): lawyer and associate justice of the U.S. Supreme Court; the first African American to sit on the court and a consistent opponent of racial and sexual discrimination

"How many of them had to die? How many of our own? Did Nkrumah°
and Azikiwe° send troops? Did a nuclear holocaust bring them to their
senses? When Shirley Graham and I set sail for Ghana, I pronounced all
hope for our patient people doomed."

"No, sir," I would respond. "The gates of segregation fell rather quickly
after 1965. A new middle class defined itself, a talented tenth, the cultured
few, who, somehow, slipped through the cracks."

"Then the preservation of the material base proved to be more
important then the primal xenophobia that we had posited?"

"That's about it, Doctor. But regular Negroes still catch hell. In fact, the
ranks of the black underclass have never been larger."

I imagine the great man would heave a sigh, as the Spirit of Blackness
galloped away.

From 1831, if not before, to 1965, an ideology of desegregation, of "civil
rights," prevailed among our thinkers. Abolitionists, Reconstructors,
neoabolitionists, all shared one common belief: If we could only use the
legislature and the judiciary to create and interpret the laws of desegregation
and access, all else would follow. As it turns out, it was vastly easier to
dismantle the petty forms of apartheid in this country (housing, marriage,
hotels, and restaurants) than anyone could have possibly believed it would
be, *without* affecting the larger patterns of inequality. In fact, the economic
structure has not changed one jot, in any fundamental sense, except that
black adult and teenage unemployment are much higher now than they have
been in my lifetime. Considering the out-of-wedlock birthrate, the high
school dropout rate, and the unemployment figures, the "two nations"
predicted by the Kerner Commission in 1968 may be upon us. And the
conscious manipulation of our public image, by writers, filmmakers, and
artists, which many of us *still* seem to think will bring freedom, has had very
little impact in palliating our structural social problems. What's the most
popular television program in South Africa? The "Cosby Show." Why not?

Ideology, paradoxically, was impoverished when we needed it most, during
the civil rights movement of the early 1960s. Unable to theorize what Cornel
West calls "the racial problematic," unwilling (with very few exceptions) to
theorize class, and scarcely able even to contemplate the theorizing of the
curious compound effect of class-cum-race, we have—since the day after the
signing of the Civil Rights Act of 1965—utterly lacked any instrumentality of
ideological analysis, beyond the attempts of the Black Power and Black
Aesthetic movements, to *invert* the signification of "blackness" itself.

Nkrumah, Kwame (1909–72): African political leader, prime minister (1957–60) and president
(1960–66) of Ghana; under his leadership the Gold Coast achieved independence from Britain
(1957) and became the Republic of Ghana

Azikiwe, Benjamin Nnamdi (1904–6): Nigerian political leader; president of Nigeria from
1963 to 1966; leading Igbo nationalist who worked for Biafran succession. (For more
information on Nigerian political history, see notes for Achebe, "The Novelist as Teacher.")

Recognizing that what had passed for "the human," or "the universal" was in fact white essentialism, we substituted one sort of essentialism° (that of "blackness") for another. That, we learned quickly enough, was just not enough. But it led the way to a gestural politics captivated by fetishes and feel-bad rhetoric. The ultimate sign of our sheer powerlessness is all of the attention that we have given, in the past few months, to declaring the birth of the African-American and pronouncing the Black Self dead. Don't we have anything better to do?

Now, I myself happen to like African-American, especially because I am, as a scholar, an Africanist as well as an African-Americanist. Certainly the cultural continuities among African, Caribbean, and black American cultures cannot be denied. (The irony is that we often thought of ourselves as "African" until late into the nineteenth century. The death of the African was declared by the Park school of sociology, in the first quarter of this century, which thought that the hyphenated ethnicity of the Negro American would prove to be ultimately liberating.) But so tame and unthreatening is a politics centered on onomastics° that even the *New York Times*, in a major editorial, declared its support of this movement:

> If Mr. Jackson is right and blacks now prefer to be called African-Americans, it is a sign not just of their maturity but of the nation's success. . . . Blacks may now feel comfortable enough in their standing as citizens to adopt the family surname: American. And their first name, African, conveys a pride in cultural heritage that all Americans cherish. The late James Baldwin once lamented, "Nobody knows my name." Now everyone does. (December 22, 1988)

To which one young black writer, Trey Ellis, responded recently: "When somebody tries to tell me what to call myself in all uses just because they come to some decision at a cocktail party to which I wasn't even invited, my mama raised me to tell them to kiss my ass" (*Village Voice*, June 13, 1989). As he says, sometimes African-American just won't do.

Ellis's amused rejoinder speaks of a very different set of concerns and made me think of James Baldwin's prediction of the coming of a new generation that would give voice to blackness:

> While the tale of how we suffer, and how we are delighted, and how we may triumph is never new, it always must be heard. There isn't any other to tell, it's the only light we've got in all this darkness. . . . And this tale, according to that face, that body, those strong hands on those strings, has another aspect in every country, and a new depth in every generation. *(The Price of the Ticket)*

essentialism: the belief that there is a collection of traits or characteristics intrinsic to and unique to each race (or gender) and that membership in a particular group can be identified on this basis

onomastics: having to do with naming

In this spirit, Ellis has declared the birth of a "New Black Aesthetic" movement, comprising artists and writers who are middle-class, self-confident, and secure with black culture, and not looking over their shoulders at white people, wondering whether or not the Mr. Wilsons of their world will call them George. Ellis sees creative artists such as Spike Lee, Wynton Marsalis, Anthony Davis, August Wilson, Warrington Hudlin, Joan Armatrading, and Lisa and Kelly Jones as representatives of a new generation who, commencing with the publication in 1978 of Toni Morrison's *Song of Solomon* (for Ellis, a founding gesture) "no longer need to deny or suppress any part of our complicated and sometimes contradictory cultural baggage to please either white people or black. The culturally mulatto *Cosby* girls are equally as black as a black teenage welfare mother" ("The New Black Aesthetic," *Before Columbus Review*, May 14, 1989). And Ellis is right: something quite new is afoot in African-American letters.

In a recent *New York Times Book Review* of Maxine Hong Kingston's new novel, Le Anne Schreiber remarks, "Wittman Ah Singh can't be Chinese even if he wants to be. . . . He is American, as American as Jack Kerouac or James Baldwin or Allen Ginsberg." I remember a time, not so very long ago, when almost no one would have thought of James Baldwin as typifying the "American." I think that even James Baldwin would have been surprised. Certainly since 1950, the meanings of blackness, as manifested in the literary tradition, have come full circle.

Consider the holy male trinity of the black tradition: Wright, Ellison, and Baldwin. For Richard Wright, "the color curtain"—as he titled a book on the Bandung Conference° in 1955 when the "Third World" was born—was something to be rent asunder by something he vaguely called the "Enlightenment." (It never occurred to Wright, apparently, that the sublime gains in intellection in the Enlightenment took place simultaneously with the slave trade in African human beings, which generated an unprecedented degree of wealth and an unprecedentedly large leisure and intellectual class.) Wright was hardly sentimental about black Africa and the Third World: he actually told the first Conference of Negro-African Writers and Artists in Paris in 1956 that colonialism had been "liberating, since it smashed old traditions and destroyed old gods, freeing Africans from the 'rot' of their past," their "irrational past" (James Baldwin, *Nobody Knows My Name*). Despite the audacity of this claim, however, Wright saw himself as chosen "in some way to inject into the American consciousness" a cognizance of "other people's mores or national habits" ("I Choose Exile," unpublished essay). Wright claimed that he was "split": "I'm black. I'm a man of the West. . . . I see and understand the non- or anti-Western point of view." But, Wright confessed, "when I look out upon the vast stretches of this earth inhabited by brown, black and yellow men . . . my reactions and

Bandung Conference: meeting of representatives of twenty-nine African and Asian nations held at Bandung, Indonesia, to promote economic and cultural cooperation

attitudes are those of the West" (*White Man, Listen!*). Wright never had clearer insight into himself, although his unrelentingly critical view of Third World cultures may make him a problematic figure among those of us bent upon decentering the canon.°

James Baldwin, who in *Nobody Knows My Name,* parodied Wright's 1956 speech, concluded that "this was, perhaps, a tactless way of phrasing a debatable idea." Blackness, for Baldwin, was a sign, a sign that signified through the salvation of the "gospel impulse," as Craig Werner character-izes it, seen in his refusal "to create demons, to simplify the other in a way that would inevitably force him to simplify himself. . . . The gospel impulse—its refusal to accept oppositional thought; its complex sense of presence; its belief in salvation—sounds in Baldwin's voice no matter what his particular vocabulary at a particular moment" (Craig Werner, "James Baldwin: Politics and the Gospel Impulse," *New Politics* [Winter 1989]). Blackness, if it would be anything, stood as the saving grace of both white *and* black America.

Ralph Ellison, ever the trickster, felt it incumbent upon him to show that blackness was a metaphor of the human condition, and yet to do so through a faithful adherence to its particularity. Nowhere is this idea rendered more brilliantly than in his sermon "The Blackness of Blackness," the tradition's classic critique of blackness as an essence:

"Brothers and sisters, my text this morning is the 'Blackness of Blackness.'"

And a congregation of voices answered: "That blackness is most black, brother, most black . . ."

In the beginning . . ."

"At the very start," they cried.

". . . there was blackness . . ."

"Preach it . . ."

"and the sun . . ."

"The sun, Lawd . . ."

". . . was bloody red . . ."

"Red . . ."

"Now black is . . . " the preacher shouted.

"Bloody . . ."

"I said black is . . ."

"Preach it, brother . . ."

". . . an' black ain't . . ."

"Red, Lawd, red: He said it's red!"

---

decentering the canon: expanding the conception of what is valuable and appropriate to a University curriculum to include more than simply the productions of white Europeans

"Amen, brother . . ."

"Black will git you . . ."

"Yes, it will . . ."

". . . an' black won't . . ."

"Naw, it won't!"

"It do . . ."

"It do, Lawd . . ."

". . . an' it don't."

"Hallelujah . . ."

"It'll put you, glory, glory, Oh my Lawd, in the WHALE'S BELLY."

"Preach it, dear brother . . ."

". . . an' make you tempt . . ."

"Good God a-mighty!"

"Old aunt Nelly!"

"Black will make you . . ."

"Black . . ."

". . . or black will un-make you."

"Ain't it the truth, Lawd?"

(Invisible Man)

Ellison parodies the idea that blackness can underwrite a metaphysics or even a negative theology, that it can exist outside and independent of its representation.

And it is out of this discursive melee that so much contemporary African-American literature has developed.

The range of representations of the meanings of blackness among the post-*Song of Solomon* (1978) era of black writing can be characterized—for the sake of convenience—by the works of C. Erie Lincoln *(The Avenue, Clayton City)*; Trey Ellis's manifesto, "The New Black Aesthetic"; and Toni Morrison's *Beloved*, in many ways the Ur-text° of the African-American experience.

Each of these writers epitomizes the points of a post-Black Aesthetic triangle, made up of the realistic representation of black vernacular culture: the attempt to preserve it for a younger generation (Lincoln), the critique through parody of the essentialism of the Black Aesthetic (Ellis), and the transcendence of the ultimate horror of the black past—slavery—through myth and the supernatural (Morrison).

Ur-text: fundamental, defining, a model for whatever follows

The first chapter of Erie Lincoln's first novel, *The Avenue, Clayton City* (1988), contains an extended recreation of the African-American ritual of signifying, which is also known as "talking that talk," "the dozens," "nasty talk," and so on. To render the dozens in such wonderful detail, of course, is a crucial manner of preserving it in the written cultural memory of African-Americans. This important impulse to preserve (by recording) the vernacular links Lincoln's work directly to that of Zora Neale Hurston°. Following the depiction of the ritual exchange, the narrator of the novel analyzes its import in the following way:

> But it was playing the dozens that perplexed and worried Dr. Tait the most of all when he first tuned in on what went on under the streetlight. Surely it required the grossest level of depravity to indulge in such willful vulgarity. He had thought at first that Guts Gallimore's appraisal of talking that talk as "nasty" was too generous to be useful. . . . But the truth of the matter was that in spite of his disgust, the twin insights of agony and intellection had eventually paid off, for suddenly not only the language but the logic of the whole streetlight ritual finally became clear to him. What he was observing from the safety and the anonymity of his cloistered front porch was nothing less than a teenage rite of passage. A very critical *black* rite of passage! How could he not have recognized it for so long? The public deprecation of black men and women was, of course, taken for granted in Clayton City, and everywhere else within the experience of the Flame Gang. But when those black men and women were one's fathers, mothers, and sisters, how could one approaching manhood accept that deprecation and live with it? To be a *man* implied responsibilities no colored man in Clayton City could meet, so the best way to deal with the contradiction was to deny it. Talkin' that talk—that is, disparaging one's loved ones within the in-group—was an obvious expression of self-hatred, but it also undercut the white man's style of black denigration by presupposing it, and to some degree narcotizing the black boys who were on the way to manhood from the pain of their impotence. After all, *they had said it first!* Playing the dozens, Tait reasoned, was an effort to prepare one to be able to "take it." Anyone who refused to play the dozens was unrealistic, for the dozens were a fact of life for every black man. They were implicit in the very structure of black-white relations, and if one didn't "play," he could "pat his foot" while the play went on, over and around him. No one could exempt himself from the cultural vulgarity of black debasement, no matter how offensive it might be.

Trey Ellis, whose first novel, *Platitudes*, is a satire on contemporary black cultural politics, is an heir of Ishmael Reed, the tradition's great satirist.

Zora Neale Hurston (1901–60): black novelist and anthropologist who interpreted African American folk tales in collections such as *Mules and Men* (1935) and *Tell My Horse* (1938)

Ellis describes the relation of what he calls "The New Black Aesthetic" (NBA) to the black nationalism of the sixties, engaged as it is in the necessary task of critique and revision:

> Yet ironically, a telltale sign of the work of the NBA is our parodying of the black nationalist movement: Eddie Murphy, 26, and his old *Saturday Night Live* character, prison poet Tyrone Green, with his hilariously awful angry black poem, "Cill [sic] My Landlord," ("See his dog Do he bite?"); fellow Black Packer Keenan Wayans' upcoming blaxploitation parody *I'ma Get You Sucka!*; playwright George Wolfe, and his parodies of both "A Raisin in the Sun" and "For Colored Girls . . . " in his hit play "The Colored Museum" ("Enter Walter-Lee-Beau-Willie-Jones . . . His brow is heavy from 300 years of oppression."); filmmaker Reginald Hudlin, 25, and his sacrilegious *Reggie's World of Soul* with its fake commercial for a back scratcher, spatula and toilet bowl brush all with black clenched fists for their handle ends; and Lisa Jones' character Clean Mama King who is available for both sit-ins and film walk-ons. There is now such a strong and vast body of great black work that the corny or mediocre doesn't need to be coddled. NBA artists aren't afraid to publicly flout the official, positivist black party line.

This generation, Ellis continues, cares less about what white people think than any other in the history of Africans in this country: "The New Black Aesthetic says you just have to *be* natural, you don't necessarily have to *wear* one."

Ellis dates the beginning of this cultural movement to the publication of *Song of Solomon* in 1978. Morrison's blend of magical realism and African-American mythology proved compelling: this brilliantly rendered book was an overnight bestseller. Her greatest artistic achievement, however, and most controversial, is her most recent novel, *Beloved*, which won the 1988 Pulitzer Prize for Fiction.

In *Beloved*, Morrison has found a language that gives voice to the unspeakable horror and terror of the black past, our enslavement in the New World. Indeed, the novel is an allegorical representation of this very unspeakability. It is one of the few treatments of slavery that escapes the pitfalls of *kitsch.°* Toni Morrison's genius is that she has found a language by which to thematize this very unspeakability of slavery:

> Everybody knew what she was called, but nobody knew her name. Disremembered and unaccounted for, she cannot be lost because no one is looking for her, and even if they were, how can they call her if they don't know her name? Although she has claim, she is not claimed. In the place where long grass opens, the girl who waited to be loved and cry shame erupts into her separate parts, to make it easy for the chewing laughter to swallow her all away.
>
> It was not a story to pass on.

kitsch: something trite, simplistically sentimental

They forgot her like a bad dream. After they made up their tales, shaped and decorated them, those that saw her that day on the porch quickly and deliberately forgot her. It took longer for those who had spoken to her, lived with her, fallen in love with her, to forget, until they realized they couldn't remember or repeat a single thing she said, and began to believe that, other than what they themselves were thinking, she hadn't said anything at all. So, in the end, they forgot her too. Remembering seemed unwise. They never knew where or why she crouched, or whose was the underwater face she needed like that. Where the memory of the smile under her chin might have been and was not, a latch latched and lichen attached its apple-green bloom to the metal. What made her think her fingernails could open locks the rain rained on?

It was not a story to pass on.

Only by stepping outside the limitations of realism and entering a realm of myth could Morrison, a century after its abolition, give a voice to the silence of enslavement.

For these writers, in their various ways, the challenge of the black creative intelligence is no longer to *posit* blackness, as it was in the Black Arts movement of the sixties, but to render it. Their goal seems to be to create a fiction *beyond* the color line, one that takes the blackness of the culture for granted, as a springboard to write about those human emotions that we share with everyone else, and that we have always shared with each other, when no white people are around. They seem intent, paradoxically, on escaping the very banality of blackness that we encountered in so much Black Arts poetry, by *assuming* it as legitimate grounds for the creation of art.

To declare that race is a trope°, however is not to deny its palpable force in the life of every African-American who tries to function every day in a still very racist America. In the face of Anthony Appiah's and my own critique of what we might think of as "black essentialism," Houston Baker demands that we remember what we might characterize as the "taxi fallacy."

Houston, Anthony, and I emerge from the splendid isolation of the Schomburg Library, and stand together on the corner of 135th Street and Malcolm X Boulevard attempting to hail a taxi to return to the Yale Club. With the taxis shooting by us as if we did not exist, Anthony and I cry out in perplexity, "But sir, it's only a trope."

If only that's *all* it was.

My father, who recently enjoyed his seventy-sixth birthday, and I attended a basketball game at Duke this past winter. It wasn't just any game; it was "the" game with North Carolina, the ultimate rivalry in American basketball competition. At a crucial juncture of the game, one of the overly avid Duke fans bellowing in our section of the auditorium called J. R. Reid, the Carolina center, "rubber lips."

trope: figure of speech, use of a word in a sense other than its literal one

"Did you hear what he said?" I asked my father, who wears *two* hearing aids.

"I heard it. Ignore it, boy."

"I can't, Pop," I replied. Then, loud-talking all the way, I informed the crowd, while ostensibly talking only to my father, that we'd come too far to put up with shit like this, that Martin Luther King didn't die in vain, and we won't tolerate this kind of racism again, etc., etc., etc. Then I stood up and told the guy not to say those words ever again.

You could have cut the silence in our section of that auditorium with a knife. After a long silence, my Dad leaned over and whispered to me, "Nigger, is you *crazy?* We am in de Souf." We both burst into laughter.

Even in the South, though, the intrusion of race into our lives usually takes more benign forms. One day my wife and my father came to lunch at the National Humanities Center in Research Triangle Park, North Carolina. The following day, the only black member of the staff cornered me and said that the kitchen staff had a bet, and that I was the only person who could resolve it. "Shoot," I said. "Okay," he said. "The bet is that your Daddy is Mediterranean—Greek or Eyetalian, and your wife is High Yellow." "No," I said, "it's the other way around: my dad is black; my wife is white."

"Oh, yeah," he said, after a long pause, looking at me through the eyes of the race when one of us is being "sadiddy," or telling some kind of racial lie. "You, know, *brother*," he said to me in a low but pointed whisper, "we black people got ways to *tell* these things, you know." Then he looked at me to see if I was ready to confess the truth. Indeterminacy had come home to greet me.

What, finally, is the meaning of blackness for my generation of African-American scholars? I think many of us are trying to work, rather self-consciously, within the tradition. It has taken white administrators far too long to realize that the recruitment of black faculty members is vastly easier at those institutions with the strongest black studies departments, or at least with the strongest representation of other black faculty. Why? I think the reason for this is that many of us wish to be a part of a community, of something "larger" than ourselves, escaping the splendid isolation of our studies. What can be lonelier than research, except perhaps the terror of the blank page (or computer screen)? Few of us—and I mean *very few*—wish to be the "only one" in town. I want my own children to grow up in the home of intellectuals, but with black middle-class values as common to them as the air they breathe. This I cannot achieve alone. I seek out, eagerly, the company of other African-American academics who have paid their dues; who understand the costs, and the pleasures, of achievement; who care about "the race"; and who are determined to leave a legacy of self-defense against racism in all of its pernicious forms.

Part of this effort to achieve a sense of community is understanding that our generation of scholars is just an extension of other generations, of "many thousands gone." We are no smarter than they; we are just a bit more fortunate, in some ways, the accident of birth enabling us to teach at "white" research institutions, when two generations before we would have been teaching at black schools, overworked and underfunded. Most of us define ourselves as extensions of the tradition of scholarship and academic excellence epitomized by figures such as J. Saunders Redding, John Hope Franklin, and St. Clair Drake, merely to list a few names. But how are we *different* from them?

A few months ago I heard Cornel West deliver a memorial lecture in honor of James Snead, a brilliant literary critic who died of cancer this past spring at the age of thirty-five. Snead graduated valedictorian of his class at Exeter, then summa cum laude at Yale. Fluent in German, he wrote his Scholar of the House "essay" on the uses of repetition in Thomas Mann and William Faulkner. (Actually, this "essay" amounted to some six hundred pages, and the appendices were written in German.) He was also a jazz pianist and composer and worked as an investment banker in West Germany, after he took the Ph.D. in English literature at the University of Cambridge. Snead was a remarkable man.

West, near the end of his memorial lecture, told his audience that he had been discussing Snead's life and times with St. Clair Drake, as Drake lay in bed in a hospital recovering from a mild stroke that he had experienced on a flight from San Francisco to Princeton, where Drake was to lecture. When West met the plane at the airport, he rushed Drake to the hospital, and sat with him through much of the weekend.

West told Drake how Snead was, yes, a solid race man, how he loved the tradition and wrote about it, but that his real goal was to redefine *American Studies* from the vantage point of African-American concepts and principles. For Snead, taking the black mountaintop was not enough; he wanted the entire mountain range. "There is much about Dr. Snead that I can understand," Drake told West. "But then again," he concluded, "there is something about his enterprise that is quite unlike ours." Our next move within the academy, our next gesture, is to redefine the whole, simultaneously institutionalizing African-American studies. The idea that African-American culture is exclusively a thing apart, separate from the whole, having no influence on the shape and shaping of American culture, is a racialist fiction. There can be no doubt that the successful attempts to "decenter" the canon stem in part from the impact that black studies programs have had upon traditional notions of the "teachable," upon what, properly, constitutes the universe of knowledge that the well-educated should know. For us, and for the students that we train, the complex meaning of blackness is a vision of America, a refracted image in the American looking-glass.

Snead's project, and Ellis's—the project of a new generation of writers and scholars—is about transcending the I-got-mine parochialism of a desperate era. It looks beyond that overworked master plot of victims and victimizers so carefully scripted in the cultural dominant, beyond the paranoid dream of cultural autarky°, and beyond the seductive ensolacements of nationalism. Their story—and it is a new story—is about elective affinities, unburdened by an ideology of descent; it speaks of blackness without blood. And this *is* a story to pass on.

autarky: state of being self-sufficient

The Aboriginal writer is a Janus-type figure, with one face turned to the past and the other to the future while existing in a postmodern, multicultural Australia.

—Mudrooroo, *Writing from the Fringe*

a t his birth in 1938, Mudrooroo Narrogin (who is usually referred to by the single name of Mudrooroo) was called Colin Johnson. He changed his name in 1988 to reflect his Aboriginal heritage, taking his last name from his place of birth, Narrogin, Western Australia. Mudrooroo means paperbark (a type of tree) in Bibbulmum, the southwestern Australian Aboriginal language of his mother. The image seemed appropriate to his work as a writer.

Describing his childhood, Mudrooroo says, "I've always been aware of my black heritage," and he has always been aware of racism: "You were always discriminated against if you lived in a country town; and if you're an Aboriginal then you're discriminated against since the time you were born. This discrimination becomes part of your psyche" (57). Taken away from his mother when he was eight or nine (he is unsure), Mudrooroo was raised in a Catholic orphanage. Later, as a young man, he travelled to Thailand and India where he lived as a Buddhist monk for seven years. He still considers himself a Buddhist and finds strong links between Buddhism and Aboriginal tradition.

Mudrooroo has published autobiography, criticism, fiction, poetry, plays and novels. *Wildcat Falling*, which appeared in 1965, was the first novel by an Australian/Aboriginal writer to receive publication. He has received the Jessie Litchfield Award (1965), the Patricia Weickhardt Award (1980), and the WA (West Australian) Literary Award for Poetry (1989).

Elleke Boehmer points out that while "Aboriginal or 'Koori' writers in Australia . . . identify with the vision and objectives of other postcolonial writing [in that they share] the quest for personal and racial/cultural identity, the belief that writing is an integral part of self-definition, [and] the emphasis on historical reconstruction," they also recognize that their own history, and hence identity, is bound up with that of white Australians (228). In Mudrooroo's novel *Dr. Wooreddy's Prescription for Enduring the Ending of the World*, which deals with the impact of European colonization on Tasmania, the protagonist advises: "Now we must become pliable and seek allies and accommodate with fate" (qtd. in Boehmer: 229). Wooreddy's great strength is his ability to accept what cannot be altered: the whites are here to stay. This acceptance doesn't negate the value of Aboriginal culture; it simply means that affirming the value of that culture does not entail a wholesale rejection of European culture. Thus Mudrooroo, like many indigenous writers, utilizes "white forms" such as the novel but inter-weaves them with Aboriginal language, myth and perspective, creating a hybrid form.

Mudrooroo himself comments that "[w]e shouldn't be so concerned with exposing the crimes of Europeans anymore, it just becomes tedious." Instead, he believes Aboriginal writers should return to their own rich cultural roots. What intrigues him most about Aboriginal thought is the concept of dreaming, which he calls "the field of creation" (Thompson 58). "The Dreaming" or "Dreamtime" refers to the traditional Aboriginal myth of creation in which the Ancestors were awakened from their long sleep and began to walk the land, singing all living creatures into existence. Rejecting the realism that dominates much of contemporary Australian fiction, Mudrooroo argues "Aboriginal reality is more akin to surrealism° in fact, because it's based on the Dreaming—the 'dreaming' we did when we had a really dynamic traditional culture" (59). In *Dr. Wooreddy* he uses Aboriginal myth and legend, a non-linear plot line and an Aboriginal perspective to upset the conventions of the Western novel, to create a work of fiction which is less realistic than surreal, more like myth than "reportage" which, he comments, "can be pretty bloody dreary" (Thompson 58).

Works Cited

Boehmer, Elleke. *Colonial and Postcolonial Literature*. Oxford and New York: Oxford University Press, 1995.

Thompson, Liz. *Aboriginal Voices: Contemporary Aboriginal Artists, Writers and Performers*. Brookvale, Australia: Simon & Schuster, 1990.

surrealism: a movement in art and literature influenced by Freudian psychoanalytic theory; focussed on the expression of the imagination as revealed in dreams, emphasizing freedom from the control of the conscious mind, freedom from reason and convention

Other Sources and Weblinks

Mudrooroo. *Writing from the Fringe: A Study of Modern Aboriginal Literature.* Melbourne: Hyland House, 1990.
"Mudrooroo." OzLit.
dargo.vicnet.net.au/ozlit/writers.cfm?id=1044

Dr. Wooreddy's Prescription for Enduring the Ending of the World
[excerpt]

Wooreddy stood on the shore staring across the narrow stretch of water. He saw the familiar dips and swells of his island and recognised the few thin lines of smoke as those belonging to his people—but at one point thick foggy masses of *num* smoke hung in the air like a bad omen. As he watched, fog streaked in from the sea to unite with the thick masses of smoke from the fires used to render down whale-blubber into oil. Things had indeed changed since the good doctor had been away. The island vanished from his view, and muttering a spell of protection, Wooreddy set about building a catamaran large enough to transport himself and his children.

Using the sharp *num* hatchet which had been his share of the loot from the hut°, he hacked away at the bottom of reeds. He cut and collected a large pile. After laying them out and separating them into three bundles, he bound them together with the thin grass-cord his wife was twisting together. He went to the trees above the beach and using his hatchet cut out long squares of bark which he trimmed to the length of the reed rolls. These he bound around the bundles. If the voyage had been longer, grease would have been smeared over the outer surface of the bark to make them watertight. Wooreddy placed the long three-metre roll in the middle of the two shorter ones, then tightened them together with the net his wife had roughly woven. Now the catamaran had a canoe-shape with the bow and stern higher than the middle. Wooreddy hesitated to push it into the water. He trusted his work, but he did not trust the sea with all its lurking demons or demon, depending on the viewpoint held. He evaded any urge to ponder on the mystery and set about the ritual to keep it or them at bay. After patting mud into a square-shaped fireplace on the high stern of the catamaran, he lit a small fire there while singing the appropriate spell. The earth and the square shape of the fireplace and of the netting held the

loot from the hut: prior to this passage in the novel, Wooreddy has participated in an Aboriginal raid on a white settler's hut

magic and not the fire. Wooreddy carefully finished the ritual and spell. Everything had been just right. A mistake, even a tiny one, might cause disaster. Gingerly, he pushed the craft into the surf until it floated. After putting the two boys aboard, he scrambled on. The catamaran settled a little, but still rode high fore and aft. His wife, Lunna, protected by her femaleness from the sea, pushed the craft into deeper water, then clinging onto the stern propelled it forward with kicks from her powerful legs.

Wooreddy's eyes clung to the shape of his approaching island. This kept his mind from the encircling water; it gave him solace, and then the earth, which had formed his body and given the hardness to his bones, did have the power to draw him back. This, in a sense, was what was happening now. He had not determined to return home, but forces had determined that he return home. One such force was that of the earth of his home. He dreaded what he would find there. Then he noticed that the catamaran, for apparently no reason, was making a wide detour around an open patch of water. His nervous eyes had glanced down for a second. Now they stayed on the water. Alarm thudded his heart. If he had been able he would have returned to the mainland at once. But then, what if he had returned to the mainland? Only the west coast remained free, and for how long? In the long run, to survive meant accepting that the ghosts were here to stay and learning to live amongst them, or at least next to them until—until the ending of the world! This was the only reason why Wooreddy wanted to live on—and in a friendless world! It was one of the reasons why he had left the relative peace and security of his wife's village.

He let the sight in the water enter into his mind. A bloody patch slowly spreading in circles of pinkish foam as a drizzle of rain fell from the grey sky. He shivered, feeling the presence of *Ria Warrawah*. The patch of blood turned a dull red, the colour of the ochre smeared in his hair. Just below the surface of the water, the dark body of a man drifted hazily like some evil sea creature. It quivered and turned dead eyes on him as Lunna's powerful kick sent the catamaran past and scooting towards what might be the safety of the shore.

At last they grounded. Wooreddy leapt out and raced to the shelter of the undergrowth. Behind him pelted his wife and children. Safely hidden, they stared back towards the beach. The waves marched in assault lines against the land. Wooreddy saw the smoke rising from the stern of the catamaran and remembered his vow always to protect fire. But he hesitated and caused its death. The waves had driven the catamaran broadside to the surf. Now they capsized it. *Ria Warrawah* killed the fire. Then he found that he had left his spear behind. It floated in the surf. He left it there. He still had his club, and a spear, these days, was too much like a broken arm. Calling to his wife and children, he walked along the remembered track leading off this side of the bay. They followed it up over a rise, through thick undergrowth, then around the edge of a small cove. There another sight struck them a blow. The island, Wooreddy's own earth, had been taken over by ghosts. His wife and children huddled in terror at his side, but the good Doctor Wooreddy donned his cloak of numbness and observed the scene with all the detachment of a scientist.

On the soft, wet beach-sand a naked brown-skinned woman was being assaulted by four ghosts. One held both of her arms over her head causing her breasts to jut into the low-lying clouds; two more each clung to a powerful leg, and the fourth thudded away in the vee. Wooreddy could see only the cropped head of the woman and not her face. The ghost stopped his thudding between her legs and fell limply on her body for a minute, then jerked away, knelt and got to his feet. The doctor noted with interest the whiteness of the ghost's penis. He had accepted the fact of their having a penis—after all they were known to attack women—but he had never thought it would be white. He filed this probably useless piece of information in his mind and watched on. The ghost hid his unnatural organ in his pants, then reached for the arms of the woman. The one holding them, possibly eager for his turn, released his grip and she had her arms free. She did nothing. Experimentally, the other two loosened their hold on her legs. She remained still. The three stood up and watched as the fourth jerked out his pale, bloodless penis, knelt, and lunged forward.

'Hey, Paddy, leave a bit for us,' one yelled. The sound drifted up to Wooreddy. He wondered about the grammatical structure and idiosyncrasies of their language as the rape continued.

'Arrh, Jack, got her all loosened up. Now she's just lying there enjoying every minute of it,' Paddy finally grunted up, spacing the words to the rhythm of his body.

Wooreddy wondered if the ghosts had honorifics and specific forms of address. Perhaps it was not even a real language?—but then each and every species of animal had a language, and so it must be! The kangaroos, possums and even snakes—and though it was not universally accepted, the trees and plants—all had a language. Even the clouds and wind conversed together. Some gifted men and women could listen and understand what they were talking about. It was even debated that such men and women could make them carry them to see a distant friend and after return them to their starting point. It could be true, for he knew that the whole earth murmured with the conversations of the myriad species of things and to understand what they were saying would be to understand all creation.

Paddy finished with a grunt and got off and up. Another took his place while Wooreddy wondered about the necessity of covering the body with skins rather than grease. It was the way of these *num* and could be compared with the strange custom of the North West Nation where women did not crop their hair. He thought about how different peoples held and shaped spears. Variations based on the series of actions of holding and sharpening which were individual to each person, and as they were individual to each person so were they to each nation and even community. Another *num* came and went—to be replaced by another.

The circle circled while the day flowed towards the evening. Wooreddy knew that he and his family had to leave soon if they were to make the camping place by nightfall. He was beginning to find the rape a little tedious. What was the use of knowing that the *num* were overgreedy for women just as they were overgreedy for everything? He could have deduced this from the record of their previous actions and they did appear fixed and immutable in their ways. At long last the rape ground to an end. The *num* without a final glance at the sprawling woman walked off to a boat Wooreddy had not noticed drawn up on the beach. They got in and began rowing across the bay like a spider walking on water.

A few minutes after they had left, the woman got to her feet. The doctor parted the mists of seven years to recognise the youngest daughter of Mangana grown into a woman of seventeen years. She looked a good strong female with the firm, squat body of a provider. Unsteadily she managed a few steps, then stood swaying on her feet. Slowly her face lifted and her dull eyes brightened as she saw Wooreddy standing in the undergrowth. She glared into his eyes, spat in his direction, then turned and dragged her hips down to the waves subsiding in the long rays of the sun setting in a swirl of clearing cloud. He watched as she squatted in the water and began cleaning herself. Then he turned to his wife, told her to follow him, and waddled away with Trugernanna's glare, that dull then bright gaze filled with spite and contempt, in his mind. It upset him and dispelled his numbness which, fortunately for Wooreddy (though he often didn't realise it) was not the impervious shield of his theorising, and could be easily penetrated. Why had she looked at him in such a way? After all it had been the *num* who had raped her. He would never do such a thing! He thought on as he waddled along in that peculiar gait which had earned him the name, Wooreddy—'duck'—and finally concluded that it was a waste of time to try to divine anything about females. What was important about Trugernanna, he recalled, was that she was a survivor. This was what made her important to him—though she did have the body of a good provider!

The track ended in a clearing at the side of a long sweeping bay. Here he found Mangana much the same as seven years ago. He sat alone, smiling into his fire. Wooreddy waited until the older man glanced up and beckoned to him to sit. He sat and waited. Mangana looked across and smiled, not a smile of greeting, but one of resignation. To the old man's despondency over the loss of his first wife had been added that caused by the loss of a second. Now he filled Wooreddy in with the details; using the rich language of an elder. It was part gesture, part expression, part pure feeling allied to a richness of words moulded together in a grammatic structure complex with the experience of the life lived. It was a new and full experience for Wooreddy. The white cloud sails bulged, fluttered like the wings of birds and collapsed in a torrent of rain; a baby boat crawled from the strangeness of its mother ship-island; tottered across the waves on unsteady legs; dragged its tiny body up onto the shore—and reached out insect arms to Mangana's mate. Charmed, she enticed herself to it; charmed, she wanted the insect arms around her and her own arms around the soft body; charmed, she let herself be enticed by the infant-boat to the terrible mothership. Many legs walked the child to it and Mangana's wife was taken along to where the sails fluttered like seagulls, and flew out to sea. The loss of the mate was conveyed by a terrible feeling of emptiness, of the lack felt by the absence of a good provider not filled by the presence of a single young daughter, fickle and strange with the times and often not to be found and not to be managed. Mangana took up the subject of his daughter. With a finger he painted in the soft ashes at the edge of the fire her symbol and her actions.

She spent too much time watching the *num* and being with the *num*. From them she received ghost food, two whites and a black: flour, sugar and tea. He himself had acquired a taste for these strange foods since he rarely hunted and relied on his daughter for provisions. He projected the death of a son at Wooreddy. They lived through it right to the final ashes. Mangana left mental pain to wander in physical pain. He relived the time he had been washed out to sea. His water-logged catamaran sagged beneath his weight and every wave washed over him. All around him the surge of the sea, the breathing of *Ria Warrawah*. A *num* boat came sailing along. Ghosts pulled him from the clutches of *Ria Warrawah*. This affected him even more than the other events as it involved a contradiction: why had the *num*, who allegedly came from *it*, saved him from *its* domain? Unable to formulate a theory to explain this, he now felt that he belonged, or at the least owed his very life, to the ghosts and thus existed only on their whim. They had claimed his soul and sooner rather than later would take it if he could not create a nexus to prevent them from doing so.

Mangana declared with more determination than he had so far shown: 'The *num* think they have me—but an initiated man is never had. He knows how to walk the coloured path to the sparkling path which leads to where the fires flicker in Great Ancestor's camp. There they are forbidden to come, and even now I am building up my fire there.'

Wooreddy nodded. He knew that the older a man grew the more he received and found. Sometimes the old ones had so much knowledge that they could make the very earth tremble. It was even rumoured that they could fly to the sky-land while still alive. Respectfully he kept his eyes lowered. Here was one of the last elders of the Bruny Island people famed for their spiritual knowledge.

'My daughter, she is yours when I go,' the old man said suddenly to him, smiling with a humour which showed that he knew a little too much about Trugernanna—and about Wooreddy!

Wooreddy lifted his head in surprise and lowered it in confusion. He tried to mask his thoughts from the old man. Thankfully Lunna returned with her basket filled with abalone and four crayfish which occupied all of Mangana's attention. His daughter might have the body of a good provider, but she failed to live up to it. Mangana slavered for the succulent crayfish. His eyes flickered from them to Wooreddy's motions in heaping up the coals of the fire. His eyes lingered on the dark-greenish body of a giant cray as Wooreddy gently and lovingly [at least so it seemed to Mangana) placed it on the coals. He watched as the dark shell began to turn a lightish ochre-red. He openly sighed as Wooreddy with two forked sticks lifted it off the fire, placed it on a piece of bark and put it in front of him. It was delicious, and the first bite freed his attention. He smiled as Wooreddy gave the next one to his wife, and the third to be divided between his children. The younger man felt the eyes on him and would have blushed if he could. On Bruny Island the custom was that first (or, in this case, secondly) the husband took what he wanted and left the remainder for his wife and children. He, without thinking, had done what he had done from the time he had been married and then a father. Ayah! Indeed he had been caught like the crayfish he was eating and put in the basket of this foreign woman without even realising it. He consoled himself with the thought that it must be the times.

Bruny Island had become a cemetery. When Wooreddy had left he had known that his community was dying. Now he found it all but gone. Only Mangana, he and a few females remained alive. The ownership of the island would pass to him, but this was meaningless. Bruny Island belonged to the ghosts. The land rang with their axes, marking it anew just as Great Ancestor had done in the distant past. He heard the crash of falling trees as he watched *num* boats towing to the shore one of the huge animals cursed by *Ria Warrawah*. Like all good animals, they had never got over their capture and often tried to return to the land. *Ria Warrawah* to prevent their escape had slashed off their legs, but this did not stop them from flinging themselves onto the beach. Huge and legless, they would lie helpless on the land, baking under the sun or wheezing under the clouds. They suffered, but never did they try to return to the hated ocean. These large animals, because they belonged to the land, could be eaten along with crayfish, penguins, seals and shellfish. The blubber provided the best oil for smearing the body and catamarans. After one came ashore and was eaten, the giant cradle of bones was flung back into the sea, not as an offering, but in contempt and defiance—to show *Ria Warrawah* that land animals would never belong to him.

Although Wooreddy went to the whaling station to get some of the flesh which the ghosts flung away, he took care that his woman did not go with him. Trugernanna and the other island women went there for both food and excitement They often spent days at the station and when they finally came back to the camp, they carried with them ghost food. Mangana liked this food and had even begun to smoke the strange herb, tobacco, which his daughter had shown him how to use. He wore over his body a large soft skin which had been given to Trugemanna. He wore this as a sign of surrender and urged Wooreddy to do the same. The *num* were provoked by a naked body so much so that they often killed it. *Num* skins protected a person and if one continued to go naked one courted death. With such a choice before him, Wooreddy took to wearing a blanket.

The ghosts had twisted and upturned everything, Wooreddy thought one day as he went a step further and accepted a *num* skin from a ghost he found with his wife. This did not upset him much as the woman had so increased her demands on him that he had found himself a typical Bruny Islander saddled with a foreign wife. He still consoled himself with the thought that it was the times, and the *num* skin did hide his manhood scars. Not so very long ago, Wooreddy had prided himself on showing the serried rows of arc-shaped scars which showed the degrees of initiation he had passed. Now they had lost all meaning, just as all else had lost meaning. Such alienation brought lassitude and the sudden panic fear that his soul was under attack. To counter this, he pushed his way into the depths of a thicket and made a circular clearing while muttering powerful protection spells. Then he built a small fire in the centre of the circle, heated a piece of shell in the smoke and opened a number of his scars with it. Blood drops fell towards the flames. Anxiously he watched each drop hiss into steam before touching any of the burning brands. This was good: his spells potent and protection assured. Lighting a firestick in order to preserve the strong life of this fire, he took it back and thrust it into the main campfire. His wife was still absent at the whaling station.

Lunna finally returned from the embraces of the *num*. She carried a bag in which twists of cloth held flour, tea and sugar. Already she had learnt to boil the dark leaves in a shell-like container which did not catch fire and to make 'damper' by mixing the white powder with water and spreading it on hot coals. Wooreddy found that he liked the tea especially when some of the white sand-like grains were added, but the damper stuck in his throat. He preferred seafood, when he could get it, for sometimes when he ordered his wife to go and get some she appeared not to hear. Her large dark eyes would cling to whatever she was doing and she would ignore him. Once when he asked her she continued eating a piece of damper and he took up his spear and felt the tip. It was blunt. He went to the shelter for a sharp piece of stone, then remembered the hatchet and got that instead.

After sharpening his spear, he waddled off to the hunt without a word to his wife. She watched his bottom wobbling off into the bush and smiled. It was one of the things that had attracted her to him. It added a touch of humour which helped to soften his stiff formality of manner. They had had a good relationship, but not as deep as it could have been. Perhaps it was because he belonged to a nation noted for their stiffness. She sighed and began thinking of the *num*.

Wooreddy, not thinking of his wife or his problems, began prowling towards a clearing which had been maintained for a long time and was still not overgrown. With his senses straining for the slightest movement or sound, he achieved a state of blissful concentration which smothered all disagreeable thought. In the clearing three large grey kangaroos hunched, nibbling at the tufts of grass. He crouched behind the trunk of a tree, thanking Great Ancestor that the wind blew in his face, though as a good hunter he had allowed for this. Wooreddy inched forward. One of the animals lifted a delicate face to peer his way. He stopped and after a few moments the animal bent its back to eat the grass. The stalking continued until Wooreddy judged himself close enough to risk a spear throw. Slowly he lifted his leg to take the shaft from between his big toe. Ever so slowly his arm rose as his leg descended at an angle to support his throw. With a lightning-fast stroke, which contrasted with his previous slowness, his spear flashed towards the prey. The force of the blow sent it sprawling onto its side. It leapt up and tried to bound away. It managed only a stagger. The long spear aborted its bound. The kangaroo recovered enough to hop away. Wooreddy trotted after the animal.

In the sudden joy at his success, he had forgotten his club, but no matter. He ran on in his curious duck-like gait which appeared clumsy but was effective. He quickly came upon the animal. It turned to face its pursuer with its back protected by the trunk of a thick tree. Wooreddy picked up a piece of wood as he circled the animal. At bay, it was dangerous. One sudden upward rip of a hind leg could disembowel him. If Only he had a companion such as Mangana! Alone, he devised a tactic and ran straight at the kangaroo. At the very last moment he bounded to the left. Animals were like human beings and usually favoured the right side—but not always. He breathed a sigh of relief as the animal brought up its right leg. A fatal move: before the animal could recover he had bashed the thick stick down upon its nose, then belted it on one side of the neck. Wooreddy flung the carcass across his shoulder and took it back to camp. He would feed his sons real food, and not that white junk their mother too often served up.

Njabulo Simakahle Ndebele

I believe we should produce works that will not only inspire us through the enchanting powers of art, but will also be embraced well beyond our borders as a joyful lesson too.

—Njabulo Ndebele,
"Turkish Tales and Some Thoughts on South African Fiction"

Words . . . are a gift from the Almighty, the Eternal Wisdom. He gave us all a little pinch of his mind and called on us to think. That is why it is folly to misuse words or not to know how to use them well.

Bless this water; fill it with your power; and may it bring rebirth . . . let those who drink it, break the chains of despair, and may they realise that the desert wastes are really not barren, but the vast sands that stretch into the horizon are the measure of the seed in us.

—Njabulo Ndebele,"The Prophetess."

ike Miriam Tlali (see "Metamorphosis"), Njabulo Simakahle Ndebele is a South African writer whose work has been profoundly affected by the experience of living under apartheid. A poet and award-winning short story writer (he won the 1983 NOMA award for *Fools and Other Stories*), Ndebele is also a scholar and university administrator who has played an important role in shaping the cultural policy of South Africa. "Since the publication of his review of Kemal's *Anatolian Tales* in *Staffrider* ("Turkish Tales," 1988), reviewer Kelwyn Sole said in 1995, "no one has held the attention of practitioners and commentators of South African culture quite to the extent of Njabulo Ndebele" (1). In a 1993 review of Ndebele's essays, "Rediscovery of the Ordinary. Essays on South African Literature and Culture" (1992), Peter Horn called him "one of the most potent thinkers in the arena of cultural politics in South Africa" (1).

Born in 1948, Ndebele grew up in Charterston, South Africa, and received his education in South Africa, England (at Cambridge) and in the United States. After a long absence, he returned to South Africa, and began teaching at the University of the Witwatersrand. He has held posts as the De Beers Chair of English at the University of Cape Town (where he is currently vice-chancellor), and as vice-chancellor and principal of the University of the North. He has also been scholar-in-residence at the Ford Foundation in New York. Ndebele is a recipient of honorary doctorates from Natal University, Chicago State University, Vrije Universiteit in the Netherlands and Soka University in Japan.

Ndebele began his writing career with poetry and is described by Piniel Viriri Shava as being an important poetic voice, particularly in the sixties, a period characterized by a particularly vicious wave of arrests, exiles and censorship. By the end of the decade, Ndebele had begun to write short fiction in which he continued his exploration of the themes presented in his poetry, in particular, as he observed in an interview for *Staffrider*, "the harsh injustices in this society and the ways in which this could be countered by means of the creative imagination."

It is the importance of the creative imagination that Ndebele has most clearly emphasized in his critical writings. In his review "Turkish Tales" he praises Turkish writer Yashar Kemal as "a writer who is rooted firmly in the timeless tradition of storytelling"(321), and deplores the tendency of some South African authors to focus so exclusively on "offering political insights" that their work has become morally simplistic and artistically shallow. Single-minded devotion to a political cause has given rise to a writing that "has been largely superficial . . . fiction that is built around the interaction of surface symbols of the South African reality . . . [which] can easily be characterised as ones of either good or evil, or, even more accurately, symbols of evil on the one hand, and symbols of the victims of evil on the other hand." Because such fiction does not present its readers with fully developed characters capable of making an emotional appeal, it reproduces the experience of "human anonymity" experienced under apartheid by its readership: "instead of clarifying the tragic human experience of oppression, such fiction becomes grounded in the very negation it seeks to transcend" (328–29). In contrast to such writing, Ndebele points to South African writers who "are storytellers, not just case makers. They give African readers the opportunity to experience themselves as makers of culture." He emphasizes the difference "between art that 'sells' ideas to the people, and that whose ideas are *embraced* by the people, because they have been made to understand them through the evocation of lived experience in all its complexities" (338). It is absolutely essential, he believes, that fiction not be reduced to the level of propaganda, that it present the interior life of individuals, not simply the external political realities. "Thus a reader, confronted with a dramatisation of process in character development, grows with the story." Equally, it is important that evil not be presented in simplistic terms, since this view is neither accurate, nor is it helpful: "We cannot wish away evil; but genuine art makes us understand it. Only then can we purposefully deal with it" (335–36).

Works Cited

Horn, Peter. "Rediscovery of the Ordinary. Essays on South African Literature and Culture," by Njabulo Ndebele." *Southern African Review of Books.* 26. July/Aug. 1993.
www.uni-ulm.de/~rturrell/antho2html/horn2.html

Ndebele, Njabulo Simakahle. "The Prophetess." *Staffrider.* Vol. 7. Nos. 3 & 4. Rprt. in *Ten Years of Staffrider: 1978–1988.* Johannesburg: Raven Press, 1988. 120–135.
———. "Turkish Tales and Some Thoughts on South African Fiction." *Staffrider* Vol. 7. Nos. 3 & 4, 1988. *Ten Years of Staffrider.* 318–340.

Shava, Piniel Viriri. *A People's Voice: Black South African Writing in the Twentieth Century.* London: Zed Books, 1989.

Sole, Kelwyn. "Reading the Nation." *Southern African Review of Books.* 39 & 40. Sept./Oct., Nov./Dec. 1995.
www/uni-ulm.de/~rturrell/antho3html/sole.htm

Other Sources and Weblinks

"Discussions with Professor Njabulo Ndebele." *Unitech Online.*
www.unitech.org.za/wcr2.asp

Oliphant, A.W. "Interview with Njabulo Ndebele." *Staffrider.* Vol. 7. Nos. 3 & 4, 1988. Rprt. in *Ten Years of Staffrider.* 341–350.

Death of a Son

At last we got the body. Wednesday. Just enough time for a Saturday funeral. We were exhausted. Empty. The funeral still ahead of us. We had to find the strength to grieve. There had been no time for grief, really. Only much bewilderment and confusion. Now grief. For isn't grief the awareness of loss?

That is why when we finally got the body, Buntu said: "Do you realize our son is dead?" I realized. Our awareness of the death of our first and only child had been displaced completely by the effort to get his body. Even the horrible events that caused the death: we did not think of them as such. Instead, the numbing drift of things took over our minds: the pleas, letters to be written, telephone calls to be made, telegrams to be dispatched, lawyers to consult, "influential" people to "get in touch with," undertakers to be contacted, so much walking and driving. That is what suddenly mattered: the irksome details that blur the goal (no matter how terrible it is), each detail becoming a door which, once unlocked, revealed yet another door. Without being aware of it, we were distracted by the smell of the skunk and not by what the skunk had done.

We realized something too, Buntu and I, that during the two-week effort to get our son's body, we had drifted apart. For the first time in our marriage, our presence to each other had become a matter of habit. He was there. He'll be there. And I'll be there. But when Buntu said: "Do you realize our son is dead?" he uttered a thought that suddenly brought us together again. It was as if the return of the body of our son was also our coming together. For it was only at that moment that we really began to grieve; as if our lungs had suddenly begun to take in air when just before, we were beginning to suffocate. Something with meaning began to emerge.

We realized. We realized that something else had been happening to us, adding to the terrible events. Yes, we had drifted apart. Yet, our estrangement, just at that moment when we should have been together, seemed disturbingly comforting to me. I was comforted in a manner I did not quite understand.

The problem was that I had known all along that we would have to buy the body anyway. I had known all along. Things would end that way. And when things turned out that way, Buntu could not look me in the eye. For he had said: "Over my dead body! Over my dead body!" as soon as we knew we would be required to pay the police or the government for the release of the body of our child.

"Over my dead body! Over my dead body!" Buntu kept on saying.

Finally, we bought the body. We have the receipt. The police insisted we take it. That way, they would be "protected." It's the law, they said.

I suppose we could have got the body earlier. At first I was confused, for one is supposed to take comfort in the heroism of one's man. Yet, inwardly, I could draw no comfort from his outburst. It seemed hasty. What sense was there to it when all I wanted was the body of my child? What would happen if, as events unfolded, it became clear that Buntu would not give up his life? What would happen? What would happen to him? To me?

For the greater part of two weeks, all of Buntu's efforts, together with friends, relatives, lawyers and the newspapers, were to secure the release of the child's body without the humiliation of having to pay for it. A "fundamental principle."

Why was it difficult for me to see the wisdom of the principle? The worst thing, I suppose, was worrying about what the police may have been doing to the body of my child. How they may have been busy prying it open "to determine the cause of death"?

Would I want to look at the body when we finally got it? To see further mutilations in addition to the "cause of death"? What kind of mother would not want to look at the body of her child? people will ask. Some will say: "It's grief." She is too grief-stricken.

"But still . . . ," they will say. And the elderly among them may say: "Young people are strange."

But how can they know? It was not that I would not want to see the body of my child, but that I was too afraid to confront the horrors of my own imagination. I was haunted by the thought of how useless it had been to have created something. What had been the point of it all? This body filling up with a child. The child steadily growing into something that could be seen and felt. Moving, as it always did, at that time of day when I was all alone at home waiting for it. What had been the point of it all?

How can they know that the mutilation to determine "the cause of death" ripped my own body? Can they think of a womb feeling hunted? Disgorged?

And the milk that I still carried. What about it? What had been the point of it all?

Even Buntu did not seem to sense that that principle, the "fundamental principle," was something too intangible for me at that moment, something that I desperately wanted should assume the form of my child's body. He still seemed far from ever knowing.

I remember one Saturday morning early in our courtship, as Buntu and I walked hand-in-hand through town, window-shopping. We cannot even be said to have been window-shopping, for we were aware of very little that was not ourselves. Everything in those windows was merely an excuse for words to pass between us.

We came across three girls sitting on the pavement, sharing a packet of fish and chips after they had just bought it from a nearby Portuguese café. Buntu said: "I want fish and chips too." I said: "So seeing is desire." I said: "My man is greedy!" We laughed. I still remember how he tightened his grip on my hand. The strength of it!

Just then, two white boys coming in the opposite direction suddenly rushed at the girls, and, without warning, one of them kicked the packet of fish and chips out of the hands of the girl who was holding it. The second boy kicked away the rest of what remained in the packet. The girl stood up, shaking her hand as if to throw off the pain in it. Then she pressed it under her armpit as if to squeeze the pain out of it. Meanwhile, the two boys went on their way laughing. The fish and chips lay scattered on the pavement and on the street like stranded boats on a river that had gone dry.

"Just let them do that to you!" said Buntu, tightening once more his grip on my hand as we passed on like sheep that had seen many of their own in the flock picked out for slaughter. We would note the event and wait for our turn. I remember I looked at Buntu, and saw his face was somewhat glum. There seemed no connection between that face and the words of reassurance just uttered. For a while, we went on quietly. It was then that I noticed his grip had grown somewhat limp. Somewhat reluctant. Having lost its self-assurance, it seemed to have been holding on because it had to, not because of a confident sense of possession.

It was not to be long before his words were tested. How could fate work this way, giving to words meanings and intentions they did not carry when they were uttered? I saw that day, how the language of love could so easily be trampled underfoot, or scattered like fish and chips on the pavement, and left stranded and abandoned like boats in a river that suddenly went dry. Never again was love to be confirmed with words. The world around us was too hostile for vows of love. At any moment, the vows could be subjected to the stress of proof. And love died. For words of love need not be tested.

On that day, Buntu and I began our silence. We talked and laughed, of course, but we stopped short of words that would demand proof of action. Buntu knew. He knew the vulnerability of words. And so he sought to obliterate words with acts that seemed to promise redemption.

On that day, as we continued with our walk in town, that Saturday morning, coming up towards us from the opposite direction, was a burly Boer° walking with his wife and two children. They approached Buntu and me with an ominously determined advance. Buntu attempted to pull me out of the way, but I never had a chance. The Boer shoved me out of the way, as if clearing a path for his family. I remember, I almost crashed into a nearby fashion display window. I remember, I glanced at the family walking away, the mother and the father each dragging a child. It was for one of those children that I had been cleared away. I remember, also, that as my tears came out, blurring the Boer family and everything else, I saw and felt deeply what was inside of me: a desire to be avenged.

But nothing happened. All I heard was Buntu say: "The dog!" At that very moment, I felt my own hurt vanish like a wisp of smoke. And as my hurt vanished, it was replaced, instead, by a tormenting desire to sacrifice myself for Buntu. Was it something about the powerlessness of the curse and the desperation with which it had been made? The filling of stunned silence with an utterance? Surely it ate into him, revealing how incapable he was of meeting the call of his words.

And so it was, that that afternoon, back in the township°, left to ourselves at Buntu's home, I gave in to him for the first time. Or should I say I offered myself to him? Perhaps from some vague sense of wanting to heal something in him? Anyway, we were never to talk about that event. Never. We buried it alive deep inside of me that afternoon. Would it ever be exhumed? All I vaguely felt and knew was that I had the keys to the vault. That was three years ago, a year before we married.

The cause of death? One evening I returned home from work, particularly tired after I had been covering more shootings by the police in the East Rand.° Then I had hurried back to the office in Johannesburg to piece together on my typewriter the violent scenes of the day, and then to file my report to meet the deadline. It was late when I returned home and when I got there, I found a crowd of people in the yard. They were those who could not get inside. I panicked. What had happened? I did not ask those who were outside, being desperate to get into the house. They gave way easily when they recognized me.

Boers: a Dutch word meaning "farmers"; (see note in Miriam Tlali, "Metamorphosis")

township: a segregated Black residential area

East Rand: area east of Johannesburg that was South Africa's manufacturing and mining centre during the 1970s. Now known as Eastern Gauteng.

Then I heard my mother's voice. Her cry rose well above the noise. It turned into a scream when she saw me. "What is it, mother?" I asked, embracing her out of a vaguely despairing sense of terror. But she pushed me away with an hysterical violence that astounded me.

"What misery have I brought you, my child?" she cried. At that point many women in the room began to cry too. Soon, there was much wailing in the room, and then all over the house. The sound of it! The anguish! Understanding, yet eager for knowledge, I became desperate. I had to hold onto something. The desire to embrace my mother no longer had anything to do with comforting her; for whatever she had done, whatever its magnitude, had become inconsequential. I needed to embrace her for all the anguish that tied everyone in the house into a knot. I wanted to be part of that knot, yet I wanted to know what had brought it about.

Eventually, we found each other, my mother and I, and clasped each other tightly. When I finally released her, I looked around at the neighbors and suddenly had a vision of how that anguish had to be turned into a simmering kind of indignation. The kind of indignation that had to be kept at bay only because there was a higher purpose at that moment: the sharing of concern.

Slowly and with a calmness that surprised me, I began to gather the details of what had happened. Instinctively, I seemed to have been gathering notes for a news report.

It happened during the day, when the soldiers and the police that had been patrolling the township in their Casspirs° began to shoot in the streets at random. Need I describe what I did not see? How did the child come to die just at that moment when the police and the soldiers began to shoot at random, at any house, at any moving thing? That was how one of our windows was shattered by a bullet. And that was when my mother, who looked after her grandchild when we were away at work, panicked. She picked up the child and ran to the neighbors. It was only when she entered the neighbor's house that she noticed the wetness of the blanket that covered the child she held to her chest as she ran for the sanctuary of neighbors. She had looked at her unaccountably bloody hand, then she noted the still bundle in her arms, and began at that moment to blame herself for the death of her grandchild . . .

Later, the police, on yet another round of shooting, found people gathered at our house. They stormed in, saw what had happened. At first, they dragged my mother out, threatening to take her away unless she agreed not to say what had happened. But then they returned and, instead, took the body of the child away. By what freak of logic did they hope that by this act their carnage would never be discovered?

That evening, I looked at Buntu closely. He appeared suddenly to have grown older. We stood alone in an embrace in our bedroom. I noticed, when I kissed his face, how his once lean face had grown suddenly puffy.

At that moment, I felt the familiar impulse come upon me once more, the impulse I always felt when I sensed that Buntu was in some kind of

Casspirs: armoured vehicles used by the South African security services danger, the impulse to yield something of myself to him. He wore the look of someone struggling to gain control of something. Yet, it was clear he was far from controlling anything. I knew that look. Had seen it many times. It came at those times when I sensed that he faced a wave that was infinitely stronger than he, that it would certainly sweep him away, but that he had to seem to be struggling. I pressed myself tightly to him as if to vanish into him; as if only the two of us could stand up to the wave.

"Don't worry," he said. "Don't worry. I'll do everything in my power to right this wrong. Everything. Even if it means suing the police!" We went silent.

I knew that silence. But I knew something else at that moment: that I had to find a way of disengaging myself from the embrace.

Suing the police? I listened to Buntu outlining his plans. "Legal counsel. That's what we need," he said. "I know some people in Pretoria°," he said. As he spoke, I felt the warmth of intimacy between us cooling. When he finished, it was cold. I disengaged from his embrace slowly, yet purposefully. Why had Buntu spoken?

Later, he was to speak again, when all his plans had failed to work: "Over my dead body! Over my dead body!"

He sealed my lips. I would wait for him to feel and yield one day to all the realities of misfortune.

Ours was a home, it could be said. It seemed a perfect life for a young couple: I, a reporter; Buntu, a personnel officer at an American factory manufacturing farming implements. He had traveled to the United States and returned with a mind fired with dreams. We dreamed together. Much time we spent, Buntu and I, trying to make a perfect home. The occasions are numerous on which we paged through *Femina, Fair Lady, Cosmopolitan, Home Garden, Car,* as if somehow we were going to surround our lives with the glossiness in the magazines. Indeed, much of our time was spent window-shopping through the magazines. This time, it was different from the window-shopping we did that Saturday when we courted. This time our minds were consumed by the things we saw and dreamed of owning: the furniture, the fridge, TV, videocassette recorders, washing machines, even a vacuum cleaner and every other imaginable thing that would ensure a comfortable modern life.

Especially when I was pregnant. What is it that Buntu did not buy then? And when the boy was born Buntu changed the car. A family, he would say, must travel comfortably.

The boy became the center of Buntu's life. Even before he was born Buntu had already started making inquiries at white private schools. That was where he would send his son, the bearer of his name.

Dreams! It is amazing how the horrible findings of my newspaper reports often vanished before the glossy magazines of our dreams, how I easily forgot that the glossy images were concocted out of the keys of typewriters, made by writers whose business was to sell dreams at the very

Pretoria: South Africa's then-administrative capital

moment that death pervaded the land. So powerful are words and pictures that even their makers often believe in them.

Buntu's ordeal was long. So it seemed. He would get up early every morning to follow up the previous day's leads regarding the body of our son. I wanted to go with him, but each time I prepared to go he would shake his head.

"It's my task," he would say. But every evening he returned, empty-handed, while with each day that passed and we did not know where the body of my child was, I grew restive and hostile in a manner that gave much pain. Yet Buntu always felt compelled to give a report on each day's events. I never asked for it. I suppose it was his way of dealing with my silence.

One day he would say: "The lawyers have issued a court order that the body be produced. The writ of *habeas corpus*."

On another day he would say: "We have petitioned the Minister of Justice."

On yet another he would say: "I was supposed to meet the Chief Security Officer. Waited the whole day. At the end of the day they said I would see him tomorrow if he was not going to be too busy. They are stalling."

Then he would say: "The newspapers, especially yours, are raising the hue and cry. The government is bound to be embarrassed. It's a matter of time."

And so it went on. Every morning he got up and left. Sometimes alone, sometimes with friends. He always left to bear the failure alone.

How much did I care about lawyers, petitions and Chief Security Officers? A lot. The problem was that whenever Buntu spoke about his efforts, I heard only his words. I felt in him the disguised hesitancy of someone who wanted reassurance without asking for it. I saw someone who got up every morning and left not to look for results, but to search for something he could only have found with me.

And each time he returned, I gave my speech to my eyes. And he answered without my having parted my lips. As a result, I sensed, for the first time in my life, a terrible power in me that could make him do anything. And he would never ever be able to deal with that power as long as he did not silence my eyes and call for my voice.

And so, he had to prove himself. And while he left each morning, I learned to be brutally silent. Could he prove himself without me? Could he? Then I got to know, those days, what I'd always wanted from him. I got to know why I have always drawn him into me whenever I sensed his vulnerability.

I wanted him to be free to fear. Wasn't there greater strength that way? Had he ever lived with his own feelings? And the stress of life in this land: didn't it call out for men to be heroes? And should they live up to it even though the details of the war to be fought may often be blurred? They should.

Yet it is precisely for that reason that I often found Buntu's thoughts lacking in strength. They lacked the experience of strife that could only come from a humbling acceptance of fear and then, only then, the need to fight it.

Me? In a way, I have always been free to fear. The prerogative of being a girl. It was always expected of me to scream when a spider crawled across the ceiling. It was known I would jump onto a chair whenever a mouse blundered into the room.

Then, once more, the Casspirs came. A few days before we got the body back, I was at home with my mother when we heard the great roar of truck engines. There was much running and shouting in the streets. I saw them, as I've always seen them on my assignments: the Casspirs. On five occasions they ran down our street at great speed, hurling tear-gas canisters at random. On the fourth occasion, they got our house. The canister shattered another window and filled the house with the terrible pungent choking smoke that I had got to know so well. We ran out of the house gasping for fresh air.

So, this was how my child was killed? Could they have been the same soldiers? Now hardened to their tasks? Or were they new ones being hardened to their tasks? Did they drive away laughing? Clearing paths for their families? What paths?

And was this our home? It couldn't be. It had to be a little bird's nest waiting to be plundered by a predator bird. There seemed no sense to the wedding pictures on the walls, the graduation pictures, birthday pictures, pictures of relatives, and paintings of lush landscapes. There seemed no sense anymore to what seemed recognizably human in our house. It took only a random swoop to obliterate personal worth, to blot out any value there may have been to the past. In desperation, we began to live only the moment. I do feel hunted.

It was on the night of the tear gas that Buntu came home, saw what had happened, and broke down in tears. They had long been in the coming . . .

My own tears welled out too. How much did we have to cry to refloat stranded boats? I was sure they would float again.

A few nights later, on the night of the funeral, exhausted, I lay on the bed, listening to the last of the mourners leaving. Slowly, I became conscious of returning to the world. Something came back after it seemed not to have been there for ages. It came as a surprise, as a reminder that we will always live around what will happen. The sun will rise and set, and the ants will do their endless work, until one day the clouds turn gray and rain falls, and even in the township, the ants will fly out into the sky. Come what may.

My moon came, in a heavy surge of blood. And, after such a long time, I remembered the thing Buntu and I had buried in me. I felt it as if it had just entered. I felt it again as it floated away on the surge. I would be ready for another month. Ready as always, each and every month, new beginnings.

And Buntu? I'll be with him, now. Always. Without our knowing, all the trying events had prepared for us for new beginnings. Shall we not prevail?

Bapsi Sidhwa

*t*he author of four novels as well as numerous short stories and essays, Bapsi Sidhwa is the recipient of many awards and grants including the Sitari-I-Imtiaz, the highest honour in the arts in Pakistan. In 1985 she moved to the United States, where she has worked as writer-in-residence and English professor at a number of colleges and universities. She received a Bunting Fellowship from Harvard and a National Endowment of the Arts grant in 1986 and 1987 and, in 1993, the $100,000 Lila Wallace–Reader's Digest Award. In 1991, she received the German *Literaturepreis* and a nomination for Notable Book of the Year from the American Library Association, for *Cracking India* (the American title of *Ice-Candy-Man*), which was also listed as a *New York Times* Notable Book of the Year.

Born in Karachi in 1938 and raised in Lahore, Pakistan, Sidhwa grew up in the turbulent period of Partition (the subcontinent of India was divided into largely Hindu India and predominately Muslim Pakistan in 1947). It is this experience that forms the backdrop for her third novel, *Ice-Candy-Man* (1991), the source of the selection that follows. Like Rohinton Mistry (see "Lend Me Your Light"), Sidhwa is a member of the Parsi or Zoroastrian community and she has used the Parsi perspective from what she calls "the borderline of a few cultures" (*Interviews* 214) to give her narrators a sense of objectivity. The Parsi community, Sidhwa has explained, being neither Hindu nor Muslim (nor Sikh, another group involved in the riots), was largely spared the violent attacks which took such a toll on the other groups. In a discussion of *Ice-Candy-Man*, she described the process whereby Hindus and Muslims separated into "'others' when the Partition movement gather[ed] steam":

> Suddenly, Hindus are being more obviously Hindu, Muslims more obviously Muslims, and they're showing their differences, their prejudices, much more strongly. The normally congenial people are, because of their religious and political differences, turning into something a little monstrous.
> (*Interviews* 203)

In Lahore, where Muslims are in the majority, the violence expressed itself largely in Muslim attacks on Hindus and Sikhs but, Sidhwa explained, "to give a fair picture of it, I had to also show the atrocities committed in East Punjab, which is now in India, against the Muslims. The Muslims were peasants there—a majority—and suddenly it [India] was divided and the Sikhs and Hindus drove them out." She describes the tension between Hindus and Muslims as comparable to "the splitting up of a family and of course the tearing apart of one country" (*Interviews* 199). Her novel is an attempt at an even-handed portrayal of both the anguish and the cruelty of each side of the division and it is informed by her own memories of the period:

> I was a child then. Yet the ominous roar of distant mobs was a constant of my awareness, alerting me, even at age seven, to a palpable sense of the evil that was taking place in various parts of Lahore. The glow of fires beneath the press of smoke, which bloodied the horizon in a perpetual sunset, wrenched at my heart. For many of us, the departure of the British and longed-for independence of the subcontinent were overshadowed by the ferocity of partition. (*Time* 1)

Though her first language is Gujarati and her second Urdu, Sidhwa has always written in English. From early childhood, it has been her literary language. Because she had polio (like the female narrator of *Ice-Candy-Man*), she was educated at home until the age of fifteen, which gave her the opportunity to read intensively, beginning with Louisa May Alcott's *Little Women* (*College Street Journal* 1). "English," she says, "is a world language, a language of communication not only between different countries, but between different provinces in Pakistan . . . in India . . . I think writers from our part of the world are twisting it, changing its inner structure to suit their new expressions" (*Interviews* 215). Like other multilingual writers, she believes that her access to other languages gives her writing greater freshness and interest, just as she believes her awareness of other cultures—Hindu, Sikh, Muslim, British and American—gives her a richer and less biased perspective.

Works Cited

Jassawalla, Feroza, and Reed Way Dasenbrock. *Interviews with Writers of the Post-Colonial World*. Jackson: University of Misssissippi Press, 1992.
_____. "New Neighbors." *Time*. 11 Aug. 1997. Vol.150. No.6.
"Writer-in-Residence Bapsi Sidhwa Takes Laughter Seriously." (28 Mar. 1997) *The College Street Journal*. Internet: 2 Apr. 1997.
www.mtholyoke.edu/offices/comm/csj/970328/sidhwa.html

Ice-Candy-Man

[excerpt]

Late that afternoon the clamour of the monsoon° downpour suddenly ceased. Chidda raised her hands from the dough she was kneading and, squatting before the brass tray, turned to her mother-in-law. Sitting by his grandmother Ranna sensed their tension as the old woman stopped chaffing the wheat. She slowly pushed back her age-brittle hair and, holding her knobbly fingers immobile, grew absolutely still.

Chidda stood in their narrow doorway, her eyes nervously scouring the courtyard. Ranna clung to her shalwar° peering out. His cousins, almost naked in their soaking rags, were shouting and splashing in the slush in their courtyard. 'Shut up. Oye!' Chidda shouted in a voice that rushed so violently from her strong chest that the children quietened at once and leaned and slid uneasily against the warm black hides of the buffaloes tethered to the rough stumps. The clouds had broken and the sun shot beams that lit up the freshly bathed courtyard.

The other members of the household, Ranna's older brothers, his uncles, aunts and cousins were quietly filing into the courtyard. When she saw Khatija and Parveen, Chidda strode to her daughters and pressed them fiercely to her body. The village was so quiet it could be the middle of the night: and from the distance, buffeting the heavy, moisture-laden air, came the wails and the hoarse voices of men shouting.

Already their neighbours' turbans skimmed the tall mud ramparts of their courtyard, their bare feet squelching on the path the rain had turned into a muddy channel.

I can imagine the old mullah°, combing his faded beard with trembling fingers as he watches the villagers converge on the mosque° with its uneven green dome. It is perched on an incline; and seen from there the fields, flooded with rain, are the same muddy colour as the huts. The mullah

monsoon: a South Asian wind that is wet in summer and dry in winter

shalwar: (or salwar) loose, light oriental trousers

mullah: religious leader, learned in Islamic theology and sacred law

mosque: Muslim place of worship

drags his cot forward as the villagers, touching their foreheads and greeting him sombrely, fill the prayer ground. The *chaudhry*° joins the mullah on his charpoy°. The villagers sit on their haunches in uneven rows lifting their confused and frightened faces. There is a murmur of voices. Conjectures. First the name of one village and then of another. The Sikhs° have attacked Kot-Rahim.° No, it sounds closer . . . It must be Makipura.°

The *chaudhry* raises his heavy voice slightly: 'Dost Mohammad and his party will be here soon . . . We'll know soon enough what's going on.'

At his reassuring presence the murmuring subsides and the villagers nervously settle down to wait. Some women draw their veils across their faces and, shading their bosoms, impatiently shove their nipples into the mouths of whimpering babies. Grandmothers, mothers and aunts rock restive children on their laps and thump their foreheads to put them to sleep. The children, conditioned to the numbing jolts, grow groggy and their eyes become unfocused. They fall asleep almost at once.

Half an hour later the scouting party, drenched and muddy, the lower halves of their faces wrapped in the ends of their turbans, pick their way through the squatting villagers to the *chaudhry*.

Removing his wet *puggaree*° and wiping his head with a cloth the mullah hands him, Dost Mohammad turns on his haunches to face the villagers. His skin is grey, as if the rain has bleached the colour. Casting a shade across his eyes with a hand that trembles slightly, speaking in a matter-of-fact voice that disguises his ache and fear, he tells the villagers that the Sikhs have attacked at least five villages around Dehra Misri°, to their east. Their numbers have swollen enormously. They are like swarms of locusts, moving in marauding bands of thirty and forty thousand. They are killing all Muslims. Setting fires, looting, parading the Muslim women naked through the streets—raping and mutilating them in the centre of villages and in mosques. The Bias°, flooded by melting snow, and the monsoon, is carrying hundreds of corpses. There is an intolerable stench where the bodies, caught in the bends, have piled up.

'What are the police doing?' a man shouts. He is Dost Mohammad's cousin. One way or another the villagers are related.

'The Muslims in the force have been disarmed at the orders of a Hindu Sub-Inspector; the dog's penis!' says Dost Mohammad, speaking in the same flat monotone. 'The Sikh and Hindu police have joined the mobs.'

The villagers appear visibly to shrink—as if the loss of hope is a physical thing. A woman with a child on her lap slaps her forehead and begins to wail: *'Hai! Hai!'* The other women join her: *'Hai! Hai!'* Older

chaudhry: the village chief

charpoy: Urdu word meaning bedstead

Sikhs: founded in Punjab, in the fifteenth century, Sikhism is a monotheistic faith (one God) with elements drawn from both Hinduism and Islam.

Kot-Rahim, Makipura, Dehra Misri: towns or villages in Punjab

puggaree: turban

The Bias: or Beas, a river in northern India

women, beating their breasts like hollow drums, cry, 'Never mind us . . . save the young girls! The children! *Hai! Hai!*'

Ranna's two-toothed old grandmother, her frail voice quavering bitterly, shrieks: 'We should have gone to Pakistan!'

It was hard to believe that the decision to stay was taken only a month ago. Embedded in the heart of the Punjab°, they had felt secure, inviolate. And to uproot themselves from the soil of their ancestors had seemed to them akin to tearing themselves, like ancient trees, from the earth.

And the messages filtering from the outside had been reassuring. Gandhi, Nehru, Jinnah, Tara Singh° were telling the peasants to remain where they were. The minorities would be a sacred trust . . . The communal trouble was being caused by a few mischief-makers and would soon subside—and then there were their brothers, the Sikhs of Dera Tek Singh, who would protect them.

But how many Muslims can the Sikh villagers befriend? The mobs, determined to drive the Muslims out, are prepared for the carnage. Their ranks swollen by thousands of refugees recounting fresh tales of horror they roll towards Pir Pindo° like the heedless swells of an ocean.

The *chaudhry* raises his voice: 'How many guns do we have now?'

The women quieten.

'Seven or eight,' a man replies from the front.

There is a disappointed silence. They had expected to procure more guns but every village is holding on to its meagre stock of weapons.

'We have our axes, knives, scythes and staves!' a man calls from the back. 'Let those bastards come. We're ready!'

'Yes . . . we're as ready as we'll ever be,' the *chaudhry* says, stroking his thick moustache. 'You all know what to do . . .'

They have been over the plan often enough recently. The women and the girls will gather at the *chaudhry's*. Rather than face the brutality of the mob they will pour kerosene around the house and burn themselves. The canisters of kerosene are already stored in the barn at the rear of the *chaudhry's* sprawling mud house. The young men will engage the Sikhs at the mosque, and at other strategic locations, for as long as they can and give the women a chance to start the fire.

A few men from each family were to shepherd the younger boys and lock themselves into secluded back rooms, hoping to escape detection. They were peaceable peasants, not skilled in such matters, and their plans were sketchy and optimistic. Comforted by each other's presence, reluctant

---

Punjab: region in the North West of the Indian subcontinent. In 1947, it was separated into an Indian state and a Pakistani province, bearing the same name. The capital of Punjab Province in Pakistan (a Muslim state) is Lahore where Sidhwa grew up. The story takes place in the Indian Punjab, where Hindus and Sikhs are in the majority. Sikh nationalists have sought an independent Sikh state within the Punjab since Partition in 1947.

Gandhi, Nehru, Jinnah, Tara Singh: leaders representing three of India's religious communities, the Hindus (Gandhi and Nehru), Muslims (Jinnah), and Sikhs (Tara Singh)

Pir Pindo: village in the Punjab

to disperse, the villagers remained in the prayer yard as dusk gathered about them. The distant wailing and shouting had ceased. Later that night it rained again, and comforted by its seasonal splatter the tired villagers curled up on their mats and slept.

The attack came at dawn. The watch from the mosque's single minaret hurtled down the winding steps to spread the alarm. The panicked women ran to and fro screaming and snatching up their babies, and the men barely had time to get to their posts. In fifteen minutes the village was swamped by the Sikhs—tall men with streaming hair and thick biceps and thighs, waving full-sized swords and sten-guns, roaring, *'Bolay so Nihal! Sat Siri Akal!'°*

They mowed down the villagers in the mosque with the sten-guns. Shouting *'Allah-o-Akbar!°'* the peasants died of sword and spear wounds in the slushy lanes and courtyards, the screams of women from the *chaudhry's* house ringing in their ears, wondering why the house was not burning.

Ranna, abandoned by his mother and sisters halfway to the *chaudhry's* house, ran howling into the courtyard. Chidda had spanked his head and pushed him away, shrieking, 'Go to your father! Stay with the men!'

Ranna ran through their house to the room the boys had been instructed to gather in. Some of his cousins and uncles were already there. More men stumbled into the dark windowless room—then his two older brothers. There must be at least thirty of them in the small room. It was stifling. He heard his father's voice and fought his way towards him. Dost Mohammad shouted harshly: 'Shut up! They'll kill you if you make a noise.'

The yelling in the room subsided. Dost Mohammad picked up his son, and Ranna saw his uncle slip out into the grey light and shut the door, plunging the room into darkness. Someone bolted the door from inside, and they heard the heavy thud of cotton bales stacked against the door to disguise the entrance. With luck they would remain undetected and safe.

The shouting and screaming from outside appeared to come in waves: receding and approaching. From all directions. Sometimes Ranna could make out the words and even whole sentences. He heard a woman cry, 'Do anything you want with me, but don't torment me . . . For God's sake, don't torture me!' And then an intolerable screaming. 'Oh God!' a man whispered on a sobbing intake of breath. 'Oh God, she is the mullah's daughter!' The men covered their ears—and the boys' ears—sobbing unaffectedly like little children.

A teenager, his cracked voice resounding like the honk of geese, started wailing: 'I don't want to die . . . I don't want to die! Catching his fear, Ranna and the other children set to whimpering: 'I don't want to die . . . Abba, I don't want to die!'

"**Bolay so Nihal! Sat Siri Akal!**": Sikh religious call or holy cheer that translates as "Whoseoever would speak would be blessed. God is the supreme truth."
Allah-o-Akbar: "God is great," also the Muslim call to prayer

'Hush,' said Dost Mohammad gruffly. 'Stop whining like girls!' Then, with words that must have bubbled up from a deep source of strength and compassion, with infinite gentleness, he said, 'What's there to be afraid of? Are you afraid to die? It won't hurt any more than the sting of a bee.' His voice, unseasonally light-hearted, carried a tenderness that soothed and calmed them. Ranna fell asleep in his father's arms.

Someone was banging on the door, shouting: 'Open up!' 'Open up!'

Ranna awoke with a start. Why was he on the floor? Why were there so many people about in the dark? He felt the stir of men getting to their feet. The air in the room was oppressive: hot and humid and stinking of sweat. Suddenly Ranna remembered where he was and the darkness became charged with terror.

'We know you're in there. Come on, open up!' The noise of the banging was deafening in the pitch-black room, drowning the other children's alarmed cries. 'Allah! Allah! Allah!' an old man moaned non-stop.

'Who's there?' Dost Mohammad called; and putting Ranna down, stumbling over the small bodies, made his way to the door. Ranna, terrified, groping blindly in the dark, tried to follow.

'We're Sikhs!'

There was a pause in which Ranna's throat dried up. The old man stopped saying 'Allah'. And in the deathly stillness, his voice echoing from his proximity to the door, Dost Mohammad said, 'Kill us . . . Kill us all . . . but spare the children.'

'Open at once!'

'I beg you in the name of all you hold sacred, don't kill the little ones,' Ranna heard his father plead. 'Make them Sikhs . . . Let them live . . . they are so little . . .'

Suddenly the noon light smote their eyes. Dost Mohammad stepped out and walked three paces. There was a sunlit sweep of curved steel. His head was shorn clear off his neck. Turning once in the air, eyes wide open, it tumbled in the dust. His hands jerked up slashing the air above the bleeding stump of his neck.

Ranna saw his uncles beheaded. His older brothers, his cousins. The Sikhs were among them like hairy vengeful demons, wielding bloodied swords, dragging them out as a sprinkling of Hindus, darting about at the fringes, their faces vaguely familiar, pointed out and identified the Mussulmans by name. He felt a blow cleave the back of his head and the warm flow of blood. Ranna fell just inside the door on a tangled pile of unrecognisable bodies. Someone fell on him, drenching him in blood.

Every time his eyes open the world appears to them to be floating in blood. From the direction of the mosque come the intolerable shrieks and wails of women. It seems to him that a woman is sobbing just outside their courtyard: great anguished sobs—and at intervals she screams: 'You'll kill me! *Hai Allah* . . . Y'all will kill me!'

Ranna wants to tell her, 'Don't be afraid to die . . . It will hurt less than the sting of a bee.' But he is hurting so much . . . Why isn't he dead? Where are the bees? Once he thought he saw his eleven-year-old sister, Khatija, run stark naked into their courtyard: her long hair dishevelled, her boyish body bruised, her lips cut and swollen and a bloody scab where her front teeth were missing.

Later in the evening he awoke to silence. At once he became fully conscious. He wiggled backwards over the bodies and slipping free of the weight on top of him felt himself sink knee-deep into a viscous fluid. The bodies blocking the entrance had turned the room into a pool of blood.

Keeping to the shadows cast by the mud walls, stepping over the mangled bodies of people he knew, Ranna made his way to the *chaudhry's* house. It was dark inside. There was a nauseating stench of kerosene mixed with the smell of spilt curry. He let his eyes get accustomed to the dimness. Carefully he explored the rooms cluttered with smashed clay pots, broken charpoys, spilled grain and chapatis°. He had not realised how hungry he was until he saw the pile of stale bread. He crammed the chapatis into his mouth.

His heart gave a lurch. A woman was sleeping on a charpoy. He reached for her and his hand grasped her clammy, inert flesh. He realised with a shock she was dead. He walked round the cot to examine her face. It was the *chaudhry's* older wife. He discovered three more bodies. In the dim light he turned them over and peered into their faces searching for his mother.

When he emerged from the house it was getting dark. Moving warily, avoiding contact with the bodies he kept stumbling upon, he went to the mosque.

For the first time he heard voices. The whispers of women comforting each other—of women softly weeping. His heart pounding in his chest he crept to one side of the arching mosque entrance. He heard a man groan, then a series of animal-like grunts.

He froze near the body of the mullah. How soon he had become accustomed to thinking of people he had known all his life as bodies. He felt on such easy terms with death. The old mullah's face was serene in death, his beard pale against the brick plinth. The figures in the covered portion at the rear of the mosque were a dark blur. He was sure he had heard Chidda's voice. He began inching forward, prepared to dash across the yard to where the women were, when a man yawned and sighed, 'Wah Guru!'°

'Wah Guru! Wah Guru!' responded three or four male voices, sounding drowsy and replete. Ranna realised that the men in the mosque were Sikhs. A wave of rage and loathing swept his small body. He knew it was wrong of the Sikhs to be in the mosque with the village women. He could not explain why: except that he still slept in his parents' room.

chapatis: a form of Indian flatbread
"Wah Guru!": in Sikhism a divine guru and a name for God

'Stop whimpering, you bitch, or I'll bugger you again!' a man said irritably.

Other men laughed. There was much movement. Stifled exclamations and moans. A woman screamed, and swore in Punjabi. There was a loud cracking noise and the rattle of breath from the lungs. Then a moment of horrible stillness.

Ranna fled into the moonless night. Skidding on the slick wet clay, stumbling into the irrigation ditches demarcating the fields, he ran in the direction of his Uncle lqbal and his Noni chachi's° village. He didn't stop until deep inside a thicket of sugar-cane he stumbled on a slightly elevated slab of drier ground. The clay felt soft and caressing against his exhausted body. It was a safe place to rest. The moment Ranna felt secure his head hurt and he fainted.

Ranna lay unconscious in the cane field all morning. Intermittent showers washed much of the blood and dust off his limbs. Around noon two men walked into the cane field, and at the first rustle of the dried leaves Ranna became fully conscious.

Sliding on his butt to the lower ground, crouching amidst the pricking tangle of stalks and dried leaves, Ranna followed the passage of the men with his ears. They trampled through the field, selecting and cutting the sugarcane with their *kirpans*°, talking in Punjabi. Ranna picked up an expression that warned him that they were Sikhs. Half-buried in the slush he scarcely breathed as one of the men came so close to him that he saw the blue check on his lungi° and the flash of a white singlet. There was a crackling rustle as the man squatted to defecate.

Half an hour later when the men left, Ranna moved cautiously towards the edge of the field. A cluster of about sixty Sikhs in lungis and singlets, their carelessly knotted hair snaking down their backs, stood talking in a fallow field to his right. At some distance, in another field of young green shoots, Sikhs and Hindus were gathered in a much larger bunch. Ranna sensed their presence behind him in the fields he couldn't see. There must be thousands of them, he thought. Shifting to a safe spot he searched the distance for the green dome of his village mosque. He had travelled too far to spot it. But he knew where his village lay and guessed from the coiling smoke that his village was on fire.

Much later, when it was time for the evening meal, the fields cleared. He could not make out a single human form for miles. As he ran again towards his aunt's village, the red sun, as if engorged with blood, sank into the horizon.

All night he moved, scuttling along the mounds of earth protecting the waterways, running in shallow channels, burrowing like a small animal through the standing crop. When he stopped to catch his breath, he saw the glow from burning villages measuring the night distances out for him.

chachi: aunt
kirpan: a small knife or dagger carried by Sikh males
lungi: a loincloth

Ranna arrived at his aunt's village just after dawn. He watched it from afar, confused by the activity taking place around five or six huge lorries° parked in the rutted lanes. Soldiers, holding guns with bayonets sticking out of them, were directing the villagers. The villagers were shouting and running to and fro, carrying on their heads charpoys heaped with their belongings. Some were herding their calves and goats towards the trucks. Others were dumping their household effects in the middle of the lanes in their scramble to climb into the lorries.

There were no Sikhs about. The village was not under attack. Perhaps the army trucks were there to evacuate the villagers and take them to Pakistan.

Ranna hurtled down the lanes, weaving through the burdened and distraught villagers and straying cattle, into his aunt's hut. He saw her right away, heaping her pots and pans on a cot. A fat roll of winter bedding tied with a string lay to one side. He screamed: 'Noni *chachi!* It's me!'

'For a minute I thought: Who is this filthy little beggar?' Noni *chachi* says, when she relates her part in the story. *'I said: Ranna? Ranna? Is that you? What're you doing here!'*

The moment he caught the light of recognition and concern in her eyes, the pain in his head exploded and he crumpled at her feet unconscious.

'It is funny,' Ranna says. *'As long as I had to look out for myself, I was all right. As soon as I felt safe, I fainted.'*

Her hands trembling, his *chachi* washed the wound on his head with a wet rag. Clots of congealed blood came away and floated in the pan in which she rinsed the cloth. *'I did not dare remove the thick scabs that had formed over the wound,'* she says. *'I thought I'd see his brain!'* The slashing blade had scalped him from the rise in the back of his head to the top, exposing a wound the size of a large bald patch on a man. She wondered he had lived; found his way to their village. She was sure he would die in a few moments. Ranna's *chacha°*, Iqbal, and other members of the house gathered about him. An old woman, the village *dai°*, checked his pulse and his breath and, covering him with a white cloth, said: 'Let him die in peace!'

A terrifying roar, like the warning of an alarm, throbs in his ears. He sits up on the charpoy, taking in the disorder in the hastily abandoned room. The other cot, heaped with his aunt's belongings, lies where it was. He can see the bedding roll abandoned in the courtyard. Clay dishes, mugs, chipped crockery, and hand-fans lie on the floor with scattered bits of clothing. Where are his aunt and uncle? Why is he alone? And in the fearsome noise drawing nearer, he recognises the rhythm of the Sikh and Hindu chants.

Ranna leapt from the cot and ran through the lanes of the deserted village. Except for the animals lowing and bleating and wandering owner-

lorries: trucks

chacha: uncle

dai: (or da'i) a village priest or imam responsible for the spiritual well-being of the others in the community

less on the slushy paths there was no one about. Why hadn't they taken him with them?

His heart thumping, Ranna climbed to the top of the mosque minaret. He saw the mob of Sikhs and Hindus in the fields scuttling forward from the horizon like giant ants. Roaring, waving swords, partly obscured by the veil of dust raised by their trampling feet, they approached the village.

Ranna flew down the steep steps. He ran in and out of the empty houses looking for a place to hide. The mob sounded close. He could hear the thud of their feet, make out the words of their chants. Ranna slipped through the door into a barn. It was almost entirely filled with straw. He dived into it.

He heard the Sikhs' triumphant war cries as they swarmed into the village. He heard the savage banging and kicking open of doors: and the quick confused exchange of shouts as the men realised that the village was empty. They searched all the houses, moving systematically, looting whatever they could lay their hands on.

Ranna held his breath as the door to the barn opened.

'Oye! D'you think the Musslas° are hiding here?' a coarse voice asked.

'We'll find out,' another voice said.

Ranna crouched in the hay. The men were climbing all over the straw, slashing it with long sweeps of their swords and piercing it with their spears.

Ranna almost cried out when he felt the first sharp prick. He felt steel tear into his flesh. As if recalling a dream, he heard an old woman say: He's lost too much blood. Let him die in peace.

Ranna did not lose consciousness again until the last man left the barn.

And while the old city in Lahore, crammed behind its dilapidated Mogul gates, burned, thirty miles away Amritsar° also burned. No one noticed Ranna as he wandered in the burning city. No one cared. There were too many ugly and abandoned children like him scavenging in the looted houses and the rubble of burnt-out buildings.

His rags clinging to his wounds, straw sticking in his scalped skull, Ranna wandered through the lanes stealing chapatis and grain from houses strewn with dead bodies, rifling the corpses for anything he could use. He ate anything. Raw potatoes, uncooked grains, wheat-flour, rotting peels and vegetables.

No one minded the semi-naked spectre as he looked in doors with his knowing, wide-set peasant eyes as men copulated with wailing children— old and young women. He saw a naked woman, her light Kashmiri skin° bruised with purple splotches and cuts, hanging head down from a ceiling

Musslas: Muslims

Amritsar: a centre of administration in Punjab, India, as well as being an industrial city where carpets, fabrics and handicrafts are manufactured. It is the centre of the Sikh religion and contains the Golden Temple, Sikhism's most sacred place.

Kashmiri skin: people from the Indian state of Kashmir tend to have light skin.

fan. And looked on with a child's boundless acceptance and curiosity as jeering men set her long hair on fire. He saw babies, snatched from their mothers, smashed against walls and their howling mothers brutally raped and killed.

Carefully steering away from the murderous Sikh mobs he arrived at the station on the outskirts of the city. It was cordoned off by barbed wire, and beyond the wire he recognised a huddle of Muslim refugees surrounded by Sikh and Hindu police. He stood before the barbed wire screaming, 'Amma°! Amma! Noni chachi! Noni chachi!'

A Sikh sepoy°, his hair tied neatly in a khaki turban, ambled up to the other side of the wire. 'Oye! What're you making such a racket for? Scram!' he said, raising his hand in a threatening gesture.

Ranna stayed his ground. He could not bear to look at the Sikh. His stomach muscles felt like choked drains. But he stayed his ground: 'I was trembling from head to toe,' he says.

'O, me-kiya! I say!' the sepoy shouted to his cronies standing by an opening in the wire. 'This little mother-fucker thinks his mother and aunt are in that group of Musslas.'

'Send him here, someone shouted.

Ranna ran up to the men.

'Don't you know? Your mother married me yesterday,' said a fat-faced, fat-bellied Hindu, his hairy legs bulging beneath the shorts of his uniform. 'And your chachi married Makhan Singh,' he said, indicating a tall young sepoy with a shake of his head.

'Let the poor bastard be,' Makhan Singh said. 'Go on: run along.' Taking Ranna by his shoulder he gave him a shove.

The refugees in front watched the small figure hurtle towards them across the gravelly clearing. A middle-aged woman without a veil, her hair dishevelled, moved forward holding out her arms.

The moment Ranna was close enough to see the compassion in her stranger's eyes, he fainted.

With the other Muslim refugees from Amritsar, Ranna was herded into a refugee camp at Badami Baug°. He stayed in the camp, which is quite close to our Fire Temple°, for two months, queuing for the doled-out chapatis, befriended by improvident refugees, until chance—if the random queries of five million refugees seeking their kin in the chaos of mammoth camps all over West Punjab can be called anything but chance—reunited him with his Noni chachi and Iqbal chacha.

Amma: mother

sepoy: soldier

Badami Baug: a village near Srinigar, the capital of Indian-controlled Kashmir

Fire Temple: Zoroastrian/ Parsi place of worship

Critical Focus Questions

1. In his review "Turkish Stories," Ndebele emphasizes the importance of giving readers complex, emotionally engaging literature which evokes "lived experience" in contrast to fiction which is essentially simplistic propaganda. How does he achieve this in his own story? Choose any fiction in this section and demonstrate why it does or does not achieve the goal he articulates. Gates' essay is, of course, not fiction. Is it propaganda? How do you distinguish between argument and propaganda?

2. Near the end of "Sonny's Blues" Baldwin's narrator thinks: "For while the tale of how we suffer, and how we are delighted, and how we may triumph is never new, it always must be heard . . . it's the only light we've got in all this darkness." Explain the significance of this passage in terms of the story's theme. What other selections in this section (or others) can be related to this idea?

3. Focussing on two or three of the selections, discuss the role of families in the lives of individuals coping with racism. Also consider the impact racism has on the family.

4. In his poem "Multiculturalism," Dabydeen refers to a number of instances of racism. To what extent are these events the product of the same kind of thinking which can be seen in Ndebele's South Africa or Sidhwa's India?

5. In the passage from Mudrooroo's novel, Wooreddy has returned to his home island to determine whether he can live in the presence of the white intruders. What has the invasion of the Europeans caused him to lose? What strategy do you see him working out? Are there other selections in this section which present a similar approach?

6. Both Danticat and Ndebele present us with strong female characters. What is being implied by both authors about the nature of the contribution such people make to the struggle against oppression? Is bell hooks making a similar point in her essay "Homeplace" (Part V)?

7. Can you find any evidence that what Chinua Achebe ("The Novelist as Teacher" in Part I) calls "internalized racism" is a concern in any of the selections in this section? What strategies do the authors present to deal with this problem?

the
idea of home—
real and
imagined

In our various groping ways, we are all in search of that heaven, that Hawaiki, where our hearts will find meaning; most of us never find it, or, at the moment of finding it, fail to recognize it. At this stage in my life I have found it in Oceania: it is a return to where I was born, or, put another way, it is a search for where I was born.

—Albert Wendt, "Towards a New Oceania"

The condition of exile both invites and precludes nostalgia. The homeland, which increasingly in the mind of a child becomes an imagined homeland, is a place, not to which one will not return but to which one cannot return. It evokes nostalgia as an originary, fixed place of perpetual longing and belonging. But the realities of having left, the reasons for leaving—political threat or persecution, economic deprivation or war—preclude sentimental fixations.

—Abena Busia, "Re:locations"

I n the shift in the focus of world literature which Homi Bhabha has observed from "the transmission of national traditions" to "transnational histories of migrants, the colonized, or political refugees" (12), ideas concerning home and community have necessarily changed while assuming a degree of importance that they perhaps did not possess in a less mobile world. Ideas about home lie at the heart of this anthology, informing virtually every other category explored. Thinking about identity, race relations, migration, and language both shapes and is itself shaped by conceptions and experiences of home, family and community. If to some extent we are where we come from, we also interpret, define, and create our homes—both as places of origin and as the places or people of our present experience.

During the colonial period, Europe was widely viewed as the "motherland," the source of a "higher" culture that was seen as universal in a way that local (colonial) culture was not. But Europe has often been a cold mother, an unhomely home, and for postcolonial writers, offered neither cultural support nor a positive sense of identity. Increasingly, home as the source of identity, culture, and perceptual filters, has come to mean Africa, India, the West Indies, Australia, rather than London or Paris. In her discussion of the nature of postcolonial nationalism, Elleke Boehmer observes that "the effort of nationalist writers was to retrieve or invent edenic homelands, lost spiritual traditions."

The condition of placelessness—the mongrel education of the colonized, as Nehru put it—became the impulse for narratives of reconstructed belonging. Writers attempted to transform their experience of cultural schizophrenia into a restorative dream of home, a healing myth of origin, or a consolatory lyric combining diverse melodies (Boehmer 117).

Noting that a significant number of (male) Caribbean writers refer to Africa as a mother, Boehmer remarks that for Edward Kamau Brathwaite (who is well-known for his global peregrinations) it is "his home island of Barbados" that is " addressed as mother, the matrix of his connection with the past, the source of meaning and identity" (1991: 3). African playwright Matsemela Manaka, writing about home as he presents it in his 1991 play *Ekhaya—Going Home*, insists that "Ekhaya is . . . the house of one's parents in which tradition, history and memory are preserved" (Mihailovich-Dickman xiii). In choosing to locate home in their birthplaces, in asserting its cultural, emotional and spiritual richness, these writers are also affirming a positive sense of their own non-European identities. They are positioning themselves in the tradition of Martinique poet Aimé Césaire whose *Cahier d'un retour au pays natal* contains what Robert Fraser calls "the archetypal and definitive moment of return in the poetry of the Caribbean" (Mihailovich-Dickman xii). This is the moment at which Césaire, finding himself assimilating the culture and attitudes of Paris, recognizes that such an acculturation involves a rejection of his own Black, non-European identity. This epiphany leads him to return mentally and spiritually to Martinique, to accept his home, its history and culture, and in so doing, to accept himself.

To some degree we are all exiles from home and we necessarily create fictions, myths, whenever we look back at our origins. Finding or creating a positive mythology that will strengthen and support identity can be a crucial step for a people or an individual, perhaps most especially for those who have been led to devalue their "home" culture. In their essay about the fiction of Jamaica Kincaid, Jean Rhys, Paule Marshall and Michelle Cliff, Ann Morris and Margaret Dunn suggest that the idea of home or "mother-land" is a particularly important and complex one for the Caribbean woman "encompassing in its connotations her island home and its unique culture as well as the body of tropes, talismans and female bonding that is a woman's heritage through her own and other mothers. The land and one's mothers, then, are co-joined" (219). To connect positively with the land is thus, in their view, to find the means "to achieve self-realization," even in the absence of a relationship with the mother.

If the idea of home as something returned to—either physically or mentally—is especially important for writers for whom home is no longer the place of residence, there is also a sense that, in Thomas Wolfe's statement, you can't go home again. The migrant's double vision is in some ways clearer because distance yields a broader perspective, but it is also, as Salman Rushdie points out, "suspect." The home which is described by the exile is "imaginary" to a greater degree than is true for those who do not leave. It is a product of memory and imagination which have been affected by new experience elsewhere, the result of a fragmentary vision, a "broken mirror." Yet, says Rushdie, "the broken mirror may actually be as valuable as the one which is supposedly unflawed" (see "Imaginary Homelands").

Works Cited

Bhabha, Homi. *The Location of Culture*. London and New York: Routledge, 1994.

Boehmer, Elleke. "Stories of Women and Mothers: Gender and Nationalism in the Early Fiction of Flora Nwap." *Motherlands: Black Women's Writing from Africa, the Caribbean and South Asia*. Ed. Susheila Nasta. London: The Women's Press, 1991. 3–23.

———. *Colonial and Postcolonial Literature*. Oxford: Oxford University Press, 1995.

Busia, Abena. "Re:locations—Rethinking Britain from Accra, New York, and the Map Room of the British Museum." *Multicultural States*. Ed. David Bennett. London and New York: Routledge, 1998. 267–281.

Mihailovich-Dickman, Vera, ed. "Return." In *Post-Colonial Writing*. Amsterdam: Rodophi, 1994.

Morris, Ann R., and Margaret M. Dunn. "'The Bloodstream of Our Inheritance': Female Identity and the Caribbean Mothers'-Land." *Motherlands*. London: The Women's Press, 1991. 219–237.

Rushdie, Salman. *Imaginary Homelands*. London: Penguin, 1991.

Wendt, Albert. "Towards a New Oceania." *Mana Review* 1.1 (1976): 49-60 (qtd. in Juniper Ellis."Return to Exile").

social.chass.ncsu.edu/jovert/v2i2/ellis.htm

Thomas King

*i*n a short story called "Borders," Thomas King describes the efforts of a native mother and her son to cross the border from Canada into the United States. The mother refuses to identify herself to the customs official as either Canadian or American. She is Blackfoot, a category that spans the international border. For her, the border is arbitrary and meaningless, as are the identities it has created. This story, like the poem included here, demonstrates King's belief that for "[n]ative people identity comes from community"(Kamboureli 233), not from an accident of geography or a political construct.

Possessing both American and Canadian citizenships, King is the son of a Cherokee father and a mother of German and Greek descent. He was born in Oklahoma, grew up in California and earned a Ph.D. in English and American studies at the University of Utah before coming to Canada to teach Native Studies at the University of Lethbridge, where he began writing fiction. He has worked as the Chair of the American Indian Studies program at the University of Minnesota and, following a move to Southern Ontario, as a story editor for the CBC, for which he produced *The Dead Dog Café Comedy Hour*. King's first novel, *Medicine River*, was published in 1990 but his stories began to appear in small magazines in the eighties. Both his children's book, *A Coyote Columbus Story* (1992), and his highly regarded novel *Green Grass, Running Water* (1993), were nominated for Governor General's Awards. He currently teaches in the English Department at Guelph University.

From an assortment of possible ethnic identities ("I could have gone either way," he remarked in an interview) and a lifetime of movement and border-crossing, he has chosen to define himself "as a Native writer and a Canadian writer" (Rooke 413). For King, home is both a place and a community. When asked where he locates his own home, he replied, "If I think of any place as home, it's the Alberta prairies, where I spent ten years with the Blackfoot people" (Kamboureli 233).

All of my material, for the most part, is centred in that Albertan landscape and around that reserve life, that small-town life. For whatever reason, I found that stimulating, more so than I find the landscape in Southern Ontario, or in California where I lived most of my youth. It feels as though you're on the edge of almost a dangerous kind of place, on the edge of an anvil. It's appealing. It's as though you can see forever . . . there are no signs of ownership. It's not that there's nothing. There's everything. (*Northwest Passages: Author Profiles* 2)

King's fiction is notable for its sly, "subversive" humour and its incorporation of native myth and folklore—the coyote is a trickster figure, which he uses in many of his stories. In an article called "A Double-Bladed Knife" that deals with humour in Thomas King's fiction, Margaret Atwood observes that King's stories:

ambush the reader. They get the knife in, not by whacking you over the head with their own moral righteousness, but by being funny. Humour can be aggressive and oppressive, as in keep-'em-in-their-place sexist and racist jokes. But it can also be a subversive weapon, as it has often been for people who find themselves in a fairly tight spot without other, more physical, weapons (New 244).

King himself says "Comedy is simply my strategy." He frequently uses it to satirize the weaknesses and arrogance of non-native society.

Works Cited

Atwood, Margaret. "Double-Bladed Knife: Subversive Laughter in Two Stories by Thomas King." *Canadian Literature*. 124–125 (Mar. 1990): rpt. in *Native Writers*. 243–250.

Kamboureli, Smaro, ed. "Thomas King." *Making a Difference: Canadian Multicultural Literature*. Toronto: Oxford University Press, 1996. 233.

Rooke, Constance, and Leon Rooke, eds. *The Writer's Path: An Introduction to Short Fiction*. Toronto: ITP Nelson, 1998. 413.

"Thomas King: Biography." *Northwest Passages: Author Profiles*.
    www.nwpassages.com/bios/king.asp

Other Sources and Weblinks

Hager, Barbara. "Thomas King."
    www.honoursong.com/profiles/bios/king.htm

King, Thomas, ed. *All My Relations: An Anthology of Contemporary Canadian Native Fiction*. Toronto: McClelland & Stewart, 1990.

King, Thomas. "Coyote Goes to Toronto." In *Native Writers Canadian Writing*. Ed. W.H. New. Vancouver: UBC Press, 1990. 252–3.

_____. Canton, Jeffrey. "Interview with Thomas King." *Par.* 16.1. 1994: 2–6.

King, Thomas. "Shooting the Lone Ranger." *Hungry Mind Review*.
    www.bookwire.com/hmr/Review/tking34.html

"Thomas King."
    www.ipl.org/cgi/ref/native/browse.pl/A44

Coyote Goes to Toronto

Coyote went to Toronto
    to become famous.
It's TRUE
    that's what she said.

She walked up and down those
    FAMOUS streets.
And she stood on those
    FAMOUS corners.

Waiting.

But nothing happened.

so.
Coyote got hungry and went
    into a restaurant
    to EAT.

But there was a long line
    and Coyote could see it was
    because the restaurant was
    painted a BEAUTIFUL green.

so.
Coyote painted herself GREEN
    and she went back to the rez°
    to show the people what an
    UP-TO-DATE Coyote she was.

And she STOOD on the rez
    and waited.
So that RAIN came along.
So that WIND came along.
So that HAIL came along.
So that SNOW came along.

rez: reservation

And that PAINT began to peel
    and pretty soon the people
    came along and says,
HEY, that's Coyote, by golly
    she's not looking too good.

And the women brought her FOOD.
And the men brushed her COAT
    until it was shiney.
And the children PLAYED with
    their friend.

I been to Toronto Coyote tells
    the people.
Yes, everybody says,
We can SEE that.

Neil Bissoondath

For a long time now, I have thought of Trinidad as simply the place where I was born; the place where I got my early education; the place where my parents died. After half a lifetime away from the island, I have no emotional attachment left, and my interest in its events is no different from my interest in events in China or Russia or Botswana: analytical, intellectual. I miss nothing, am prey to no nostalgia . . .

My history, my past, my 'roots'— the people, places and events that have shaped me—are an integral part of myself. Just as no one can take them away, so I cannot rid myself of them. This does not mean, though, that I must be their prisoner.

—Neil Bissoondath, *Selling Illusions*

Widely praised for his novels and short stories, Neil Bissoondath has probably attracted more attention as the author of *Selling Illusions*, his controversial 1994 critique of Canada's multiculturalism policy. Arguing that the effect of the federal policy is the ghettoization of ethnic groups, and what he calls "a gentle and insidious form of cultural apartheid," he emphasized the value of un-hyphenated Canadianism, the creation of a country in which "every individual is Canadian, undiluted and undivided" (224).

Born in 1955 in Arima, Trinidad, of East Indian descent, Bissoondath arrived in Canada in 1973 to attend York University, graduating in 1977 with a B.A. in French. A scholarship from the Banff School of Fine Arts enabled him to complete his first book, *Digging Up the Mountains* (1986), a collection of short stories dealing with exile and alienation, from which the selection that follows is taken. In succeeding books, Bissoondath has continued to explore the themes of "identity, of imagination, of rootlessness, of that searching for a safe haven" (Kim 2). *A Casual Brutality* (1988), winner of the W.H. Smith/Books in Canada First Novel Award, deals with a Canadian-educated Caribbean doctor who returns to his West Indian home only to find it devastated by corruption and racial violence. A second collection of short stories, also dealing with the pain and difficulty of immigration, *On the Eve of Uncertain Tomorrows*, followed in 1990. Bissoondath's most recent work, the novel *The Worlds within Her*, which was nominated for a Governor General's Award in 1999, deals with the return of Trinidad-born Yasmin to her birthplace, in order to inter her mother's ashes. In an interview about the book, Bissoondath remarked:

> A human being is shaped by not only his past, or his parents' past, or his family's past, but also by the present of where he or she lives. That's why I think the term Canadian or American is a useful one because, certainly in North America, we have the opportunity to be so many things at the same time. Race is meaning less and less. (Kim 2)

For Bissoondath, then, ideas about home and identity seem more closely related to present choices and experiences than to looking back to a point of origin.

Works Cited

Bissoondath, Neil. *Selling Illusions: The Cult of Multiculturalism in Canada*. Toronto: Penguin, 1994.
Kim, Jin David. "The Worlds Within Neil."
www.schoolnet.ca/greatquestions/e/bio_q2_bissoondath.html

Other Sources and Weblinks

www.chaptersglobe.com/author/authorbio.asp?authid=1437
www.vehiculepress.com/montreal/gallery/bissoondath.html
Downey, Fiona. "Neil Bissoondath Returns to an Old Love: The Novel." 27 Nov. 1998.
**www.infoculture.cbc.ca/archives/bookswr/bookswr-11271998_
bisoondath.html**
Hutcheon, Linda, and Marian Richmond, eds. "Interview by Aruna Srivastava." *Other Solitudes*. Toronto: Oxford University Press, 1990. 313–320.
Kureishi, Hanif
www.Nytimes.com/books/97/11/09/home/kureishi._bissoondath.htmt

There Are a Lot of Ways to Die

It was still drizzling when Joseph clicked the final padlocks on the door. The name-plate, home-painted with squared gold letters on a black background and glazed all over with transparent varnish to lend a professional tint, was flecked with water and dirt. He took a crumpled handkerchief from his back pocket and carefully wiped the lettering clean: JOSEPH HEAVEN: CARPET AND RUG INSTALLATIONS. The colon had been his idea and he had put it in over his wife's objections. He felt that it provided a natural flow from his name, that it showed a certain reliability. His wife, in the scornful voice she reserved for piercing his pretensions, had said, "That's all very well and good for Toronto, but you think people here care about that kind of thing?" But she was the one people accused of having airs, not him. As far as he was concerned, the colon was merely good business; and as the main beneficiary of the profits, she should learn to keep her mouth shut.

He had forgotten to pick up his umbrella from just inside the door where he had put it that morning. Gingerly, he extended his upturned palm, feeling the droplets, warm and wet, like newly spilled blood. He decided they were too light to justify reopening the shop, always something of an event because of the many locks and chains. This was another thing she didn't like, his obsession, as she called it, with security. She wanted a more open store-front, with windows and showcases and well-dressed mannequins smiling blankly at the street. She said, "It look just like every other store around here, just a wall and a door. It have nothing to catch the eye." He replied, "You want windows and showcases? What we going to show? My tools? The tacks? The cutter?" Besides, the locks were good for business, not a week went by without a robbery in the area. Displaying the tools would be a blatant invitation, and a recurrent nightmare had developed in which one of his cutters was stolen and used in a murder.

Across the glistening street, so narrow after the generosity of those he had known for six years, the clothes merchants were standing disconsolately in front of their darkened stores, hands in pockets, whistling and occasionally examining the grey skies for the brightening that would signal the end of the rain and the appearance of shoppers. They stared blankly at him. One half-heartedly jabbed his finger at a stalactitic line of umbrellas and dusty raincoats, inviting a purchase. Joseph showed no interest. The merchant shrugged and resumed his tuneless whistling, a plaintive sound from between clenched front teeth.

Joseph had forgotten how sticky the island could be when it rained. The heat, it seemed, never really disappeared during the night. Instead, it retreated just a few inches underground, only to emerge with the morning rain, condensing, filling the atmosphere with steam. It put the lie to so much he had told his Canadian friends about the island. The morning rain wasn't as refreshing as he'd recalled it and the steam had left his memory altogether. How could he have sworn that the island experienced no humidity? Why had he, in all honesty, recalled tender tropical breezes when the truth, as it now enveloped him, was the exact, stifling opposite? Climate was not so drastically altered, only memory.

He walked to the end of the street, his shirt now clinging to his shoulders. The sidewalk, dark and pitted, seemed to glide by under his feet, as if it were itself moving. He squinted, feeling the folds of flesh bunching up at the corner of his eyes, and found he could fuzzily picture himself on Bloor Street, walking past the stores and the bakeries and the delicatessens pungent with Eastern European flavors, the hazy tops of buildings at Bloor and Yonge far away in the distance. He could even conjure up the sounds of a Toronto summer: the cars, the voices, the rumble of the subway under the feet as it swiftly glided towards downtown.

Joseph shook himself and opened his eyes, not without disappointment. He was having this hallucination too often, for too long. He was ashamed of it and couldn't confess it even to his wife. And he mistrusted it, too: might not even this more recent memory also be fooling him, as the other had done? Was it really possible to see the tops of buildings at Yonge from Bathurst? He wanted to ask his wife, pretending it was merely a matter of memory, but she would see through this to his longing and puncture him once more with that voice. She would call him a fool and not be far wrong. Were not two dislocations enough in one man's lifetime? Would not yet a third prove him a fool?

Their return had been jubilant. Friends and relatives treated it as a victory, seeking affirmation of the correctness of their cloistered life on the island, the return a defeat for life abroad. The first weeks were hectic, parties, dinners, get-togethers. Joseph felt like a curiosity, an object not of reverence but of silent ridicule, his the defeat, theirs the victory. The island seemed to close in around him.

They bought a house in the island's capital. The town was not large. Located at the extreme north-western edge of the island, having hardly expanded from the settlement originally established by Spanish adventurers as a depot in their quest for mythic gold, the town looked forever to the sea, preserving its aura of a way-station, a point at which to pause in brief respite from the larger search.

At first, Joseph had tried to deny this aspect of the town, for the town was the island and, if the island were no more than a way-station, a stopover from which nothing important ever emerged, then to accept this life was to accept second place. A man who had tasted of first could accept second only with delusion: his wife had taken on airs, he had painted his black-and-gold sign.

Then the hallucination started, recreating Bloor Street, vividly recalling the minute details of daily life. He caught himself reliving the simple things: buying milk, removing a newspaper from the box, slipping a subway token into the slot, sitting in a park. A chill would run through him when he realized they were remembrances of things past, possibly lost forever. The recollected civility of life in Toronto disturbed him, it seemed so distant. He remembered what a curious feeling of well-being had surged through him whenever he'd given directions to a stranger. Each time was like an affirmation of stability. Here, in an island so small that two leisurely hours in a car would reveal all, no one asked for directions, no one was a stranger. You didn't claim the island: it claimed you.

The street on which their house stood used to be known all over the island. It was viewed with a twinge of admired notoriety and was thought of with the same fondness with which the islanders regarded the government ministers and civil servants who had fled the island with pilfered cash: an awed admiration, a flawed love. The cause of this attention was a house, a mansion in those days, erected, in the popular lore, by a Venezuelan general who, for reasons unknown, had exiled himself to a life of darkly rumored obscurity on the island. As far as Joseph knew, no one had ever actually seen the general: even his name, Pacheco, had been assumed. Or so it was claimed; no one had ever bothered to check.

Eventually the house had became known as Pacheco House, and the street as Pacheco Street. It was said that the house, deserted for as long as anyone could remember and now falling into neglect, had been mentioned passingly in a book by an Englishman who had been looking into famous houses of the region. It was the island's first mention in a book other than a history text, the island's first mention outside the context of slavery.

The house had become the butt of schoolboys' frustration. On their way home after school, Joseph and his friends would detour to throw stones at the windows. In his memory, the spitting clank of shattering glass sounded distant and opaque. They had named each window for a teacher, thus adding thrust and enthusiasm to their aim. The largest window, high on the third floor—the attic, he now knew, in an island which had no attics—they named LeNoir, after the priest who was the terror of all students unblessed by fair skin or athletic ability. They were more disturbed by the fact that the priest himself was black; this seemed a greater sin than his choice of vocation. They had never succeeded in breaking the LeNoir window. Joseph might have put this down to divine protection had he not lost his sense of religion early on. It was a simple event: the priest at his last try at communion had showered him with sour breath the moment the flesh of Christ slipped onto Joseph's tongue. Joseph, from then on, equated the wafer with decaying flesh.

The LeNoir window went unscathed for many years and was still intact when, after the final exams, Joseph left the island for what he believed to be forever.

The raindrops grew larger, making a plopping sound on the sidewalk. A drop landed on his temple and cascaded down his cheek. He rubbed at it, feeling the prickly stubble he hadn't bothered to shave that morning.

Pacheco House was just up ahead, the lower floors obscured by a jungle of trees and bush, the garden overgrown and thickening to impenetrability. Above the treeline, the walls—a faded pink, pockmarked by the assault of stones and mangoes—had begun disintegrating, the thin plaster falling away in massive chunks to reveal ordinary grey brick underneath. The remaining plaster was criss-crossed by cracks and fissures created by age and humidity.

During his schooldays, the grounds had been maintained by the government. The house had been considered a tourist attraction and was displayed in brochures and on posters. An island-wide essay competition had been held, "The Mystery of Pacheco House", and the winning essay, of breathless prose linked by words like *tropical* and *verdant* and *lush* and *exotic*, was used as the text of a special brochure. But no tourists came. The mystery withered away to embarrassment. The government quietly gave the house up. The Jaycees, young businessmen who bustled about in the heat with the added burden of jackets and ties, offered to provide funds for the upkeep. The offer was refused with a shrug by the Ministry of Tourism, with inexplicable murmurings of "colonial horrors" by the Ministry of Culture. The house was left to its ghosts.

From the street Joseph could see the LeNoir window, still intact and dirt-streaked. He was surprised that it still seemed to mock him.

Joseph had asked his nephew, a precocious boy who enjoyed exhibiting his scattered knowledge of French and Spanish and who laughed at Joseph's clumsy attempts to resurrect the bits of language he had learnt in the same classes, often from the same teachers, if the boys still threw stones at Pacheco House. No, his nephew had informed him, after school they went to the sex movies or, in the case of the older boys, to the whorehouses. Joseph, stunned, had asked no more questions.

The rain turned perceptibly to a deluge, the thick, warm drops penetrating his clothes and running in rivulets down his back and face. The wild trees and plants of the Pacheco garden nodded and drooped, leaves glistening dully in the half-light. The pink walls darkened as the water socked into them, eating at the plaster. The LeNoir window was black; he remembered some claimed to have seen a white-faced figure in army uniform standing there at night. The story had provided mystery back then, a real haunted house, and on a rainy afternoon schoolboys could feel their spines tingle as they aimed their stones.

On impulse Joseph searched the ground for a stone. He saw only pebbles; the gravel verge had long been paved over. Already the sidewalk had cracked in spots and little shoots of grass had fought their way out, like wedges splitting a boulder.

He continued walking, oblivious of the rain.

Several cars were parked in the driveway of his house. His wife's friends were visiting. They were probably in the living room drinking coffee and eating pastries from Marcel's and looking through *Vogue* pattern books. Joseph made for the garage so he could enter, unnoticed, through the kitchen door. Then he thought, "Why the hell?" He put his hands into his pockets—his money was soaked and the movement of his fingers ripped the edge off a bill—and calmly walked in through the open front door.

His wife was standing in front of the fake fireplace she had insisted on bringing from Toronto. The dancing lights cast multicolored hues on her caftan. She almost dropped her coffee cup when she saw him. Her friends, perturbed, stared at him from their chairs which they had grouped around the fireplace.

His wife said impatiently, "Joseph, what are you doing here?"

He said, "I live here."

She said, "And work?"

He said, "None of the boys show up this morning."

"So you just drop everything?"

"I postponed today's jobs. I couldn't do all the work by myself."

She put her cup down on the mantelpiece. "Go dry yourself off. You wetting the floor."

Her friend Arlene said, "Better than the bed."

They all laughed. His wife said, "He used to do that when he was a little boy, not so, Joseph?"

She looked at her friends, and said, "You know, we having so much trouble finding good workers. Joseph already fire three men. Looks like we're going to have to fire all these now."

Arlene said, "Good help so hard to find these days."

His wife said, "These people like that, you know, girl. Work is the last thing they want to do."

Arlene said, "They 'fraid they going to melt if rain touch their skin."

His wife turned to him. "You mean not one out of twelve turned up this morning?"

"Not one."

Arlene, dark and plump, sucked her teeth and moved her tongue around, pushing at her cheeks and making a plopping sound.

Joseph said, "Stop that. You look like a monkey."

His wife and Arlene stared at him in amazement. The others sipped their coffee or gazed blankly at the fireplace.

Arlene said witheringly, "I don't suffer fools gladly, Joseph."

He said, "Too bad. You must hate being alone."

His wife said, "Joseph!"

He said, "I better go dry off." Still dripping, he headed for the bedroom. At the door he paused and added, "People should be careful when they talking about other people. You know, glass houses . . . " He was suddenly exhausted: what was the point? They all knew Arlene's story. She had once been a maid whose career was rendered transient by rain and imagined illness; she had been no different from his employees. Her fortune had improved only because her husband—who was referred to behind his back as a "sometimes worker" because sometimes he worked and sometimes he didn't—had been appointed a minister without portfolio in the government. He had lost the nickname because now he never worked, but he had gained a regular cheque, a car and a chauffeur, and the tainted respectability of political appointment.

Joseph slammed the bedroom door and put his ear to the keyhole: there was a lot of throat-clearing; pages of a *Vogue* pattern book rustled. Finally his wife said, "Come look at this pattern." Voices oohed and ahhed and cooed. Arlene said, "Look at this one." He kicked the door and threw his wet shirt on the bed.

The rain had stopped and the sky had cleared a little. His wife and her friends were still in the living room. It was not yet midday. His clothes had left a damp patch on the bed, on his side, and he knew it would still be wet at bedtime. He put on a clean set of clothes and sat on the bed, rubbing the dampness, as if this would make it disappear. He reached up and drew the curtains open: grey, drifting sky, vegetation drooping and wet, like wash on a line; the very top of Pacheco House, galvanized iron rusted through, so thin in parts that a single drop of rain might cause a great chunk to go crashing into the silence of the house. Except maybe for the bats, disintegration was probably the only sound now to be heard in Pacheco House. The house was like a dying man who could hear his heart ticking to a stop.

Joseph sensed that something was missing. The rainflies, delicate ant-like creatures with brown wings but no sting. Defenceless, wings attached to their bodies by the most fragile of links, they fell apart at the merest touch. After a particularly heavy rainfall, detached wings, almost transparent, would litter the ground and cling to moist feet like lint to wool. As a child, he used to pull the wings off and place the crippled insect on a table, where he could observe it crawling desperately around, trying to gain the air. Sometimes he would gingerly tie the insect to one end of a length of thread, release it, and control its flight. In all this he saw no cruelty. His friends enjoyed crushing them, or setting them on fire, or sizzling them with the burning end of a cigarette. Joseph had only toyed with the insects; he could never bring himself to kill one.

There was not a rainfly in sight. The only movement was that of the clouds and dripping water. In the town, the insects had long, and casually, been eradicated. He felt the loss.

He heard his wife call her friends to lunch. He half expected to hear his name but she ignored him: he might have not been there. He waited a few more minutes until he was sure they had all gone into the dining room, then slipped out the front door.

Water was gurgling in the drains, rushing furiously through the iron gratings into the sewers. In the street, belly up, fur wet and clinging, lay a dead dog, a common sight. Drivers no longer even bothered to squeal their tires.

Joseph walked without direction, across streets and through different neighborhoods, passing people and being passed by cars. He took in none of it. His thoughts were thousands of miles away, on Bloor Street, on Yonge Street, among the stalls of Kensington Market.

He was at National Square when the rain once more began to pound down. He found a dry spot under the eaves of a store and stood, arms folded, watching the rain and the umbrellas and the raincoats. A man hurried past him, a handkerchief tied securely to his head the only protection from the rain. It was a useless gesture, and reminded Joseph of his grandmother's warnings to him never to go out at night without a hat to cover his head, "because of the dew".

National Square was the busiest part of town. Cars constantly sped by, horns blaring, water splashing. After a few minutes a donkey cart loaded with fresh coconuts trundled by on its way to the Savannah, a wide, flat park just north of the town where the horse races were held at Christmas. A line of impatient cars crept along behind the donkey cart, the leaders bobbing in and out of line in search of an opportunity to pass.

Joseph glanced at his watch. It was almost twelve-thirty. He decided to have something to eat. Just around the corner was a cheap restaurant frequented by office workers from the government buildings and foreign banks which enclosed the square. Holding his hands over his head, Joseph dashed through the rain to the restaurant.

Inside was shadowed, despite the cobwebby fluorescent lighting. The walls were lined with soft-drink advertisements and travel posters. One of the posters showed an interminable stretch of bleached beach overhung with languid coconut-tree branches. Large, cursive letters read: Welcome To The Sunny Caribbean. The words were like a blow to the nerves. Joseph felt like ripping the poster up.

A row of green metal tables stretched along one wall of the rectangular room. A few customers sat in loosened ties and shirt-sleeves, sipping beer and smoking and conversing in low tones. At the far end, at a table crowded with empty bottles and an overflowing ashtray, Joseph noticed a familiar face. It was lined and more drawn than when he'd known it, and the eyes had lost their sparkle of intelligence; but he was certain he was not mistaken. He went up to the man. He said, "Frankie?"

Frankie looked up slowly, unwillingly, emerging from a daydream. He said, "Yes?" Then he brightened. "Joseph? Joseph!" He sprang to his feet, knocking his chair back. He grasped Joseph's hand. "How you doing, man? It's been years and years. How you doing?" He pushed Joseph into a chair and loudly ordered two beers. He lit a cigarette. His hand shook.

Joseph said, "You smoking now, Frankie?"

"For years, man. You?"

Joseph shook his head.

Frankie said, "But you didn't go to Canada? I thought somebody tell me . . ."

"Went and came back. One of those things. How about you? How the years treat you?"

"I work in a bank. Loan officer."

"Good job?"

"Not bad."

Joseph sipped his beer. The situation wasn't right. There should have been so much to say, so much to hear. Frankie used to be his best friend. He was the most intelligent person Joseph had ever known. This was the last place he would have expected to find him. Frankie had dreamt of university and professorship, and it had seemed, back then, that university and professorship awaited him.

Frankie took a long pull on his cigarette, causing the tube to crinkle and flatten. He said, "What was Canada like?" Before Joseph could answer, he added, "You shouldn't have come back. Why did you come back? A big mistake." He considered the cigarette.

The lack of emotion in Frankie's voice distressed Joseph. It was the voice of a depleted man. He said, "It was time."

Frankie leaned back in his chair and slowly blew smoke rings at Joseph. He seemed to be contemplating the answer. He said, "What were you doing up there?"

"I had a business. Installing carpets and rugs. Is a good little business. My partner looking after it now."

Frankie looked away, towards the door. He said nothing.

Joseph said, "You ever see anybody from school?"

Frankie waved his cigarette. "Here and there. You know, Raffique dead. And Jonesy and Dell."

Joseph recalled the faces: boys, in school uniform. Death was not an event he could associate with them. "How?"

"Raffique in a car accident. Jonesy slit his wrists over a woman. Dell . . . who knows? There are a lot of ways to die. They found him dead in the washroom of a cinema. A girl was with him. Naked. She wasn't dead. She's in the madhouse now."

"And the others?" Joseph couldn't contemplate the death roll. It seemed to snuff out a little bit of his own life.

"The others? Some doing something, some doing nothing. It don't matter."

Joseph said, "You didn't go to university.'

Frankie laughed. "No, I didn't."

Joseph waited for an explanation. Frankie offered none.

Frankie said, "Why the hell you come back from Canada? And none of this 'It was time' crap."

Joseph rubbed his face, feeling the stubble, tracing the fullness of his chin. "I had some kind of crazy idea about starting a business, creating jobs, helping my people."

Frankie laughed mockingly.

Joseph said, "I should have known better. We had a party before we left. A friend asked me the same question, why go back. I told him the same thing. He said it was bullshit and that I just wanted to make a lot of money and live life like a holiday. We quarrelled and I threw him out. The next morning he called to apologize. He was crying. He said he was just jealous." Joseph sipped the beer, lukewarm and sweating. "Damn fool."

Frankie laughed again. "I don't believe this. You mean to tell me you had the courage to leave *and* the stupidity to come back?" He slapped the table, rocking it and causing an empty beer bottle to fall over. "You always used to be the idealist, Joseph. I was more realistic. And less courageous. That's why I never left."

"Nobody's called me an idealist for years." The word seemed more mocking than Frankie's laugh.

Frankie said, "And now you're stuck back here for good." He shook his head vigorously, drunkenly. "A big, idealistic mistake, Joseph."

"I'm not stuck here." He was surprised at how much relief the thought brought him. "I can go back any time I want."

"Well, go then." Frankie's voice was slurred, and it held more than a hint of aggressiveness.

Joseph shook his head. He glanced at his watch. He said, "It's almost one. Don't you have to get back to work?"

Frankie called for another beer. "The bank won't fall down if I'm not there."

"We used to think the world would fall down if not for us."

"That was a long time ago. We were stupid." Frankie lit another cigarette. His hand shook badly. "In this place, is nonsense to think the world, the world out there, have room for you."

Joseph said, "You could have been a historian. History was your best subject, not so?"

"Yeah."

"You still interested in history?"

"Off and on. I tried to write a book. Nobody wanted to publish it."

"Why not?"

"Because our history doesn't lead anywhere. It's just a big, black hole. Nobody's interested in a book about a hole."

"You know anything about Pacheco House?"

"Pacheco House? A little."

"What?"

"The man wasn't a Venezuelan general. He was just a crazy old man from Argentina. He was rich. I don't know why he came here. He lived in the house for a short time and then he died there, alone. They found his body about two weeks later, rotting and stinking. They say he covered himself with old cocoa bags, even his head. I think he knew he was going to die and after all that time alone he couldn't stand the thought of anyone seeing him. Crazy, probably. They buried him in the garden and put up a little sign. And his name wasn't really Pacheco either, people just called him that. They got it from a cowboy film. I've forgot what his real name was but it don't matter. Pacheco's as good as any other."

"That's all? What about the house itself?"

"That's all. The house is just a house. Nothing special." Frankie popped the half-finished cigarette into his beer bottle, it sizzled briefly. He added, "R.I.P. Pacheco, his house and every damn thing else." He put another cigarette between his lips, allowing it to droop to his chin, pushing his upper lip up and out, as if his teeth were deformed. His hands shook so badly he couldn't strike the match. His eyes met Joseph's.

Joseph couldn't hold the gaze. He was chilled. He said, "I have to go."

Frankie waved him away.

Joseph pushed back his chair. Frankie looked past him with bloodshot eyes, already lost in the confusion of his mind.

Joseph, indicating the travel poster, offered the barman five dollars for it. The man, fat, with an unhealthy greasiness, said, "No way."

Joseph offered ten dollars.

The barman refused.

Joseph understood: it was part of the necessary lie.

Grey clouds hung low and heavy in the sky. The hills to the north, their lower half crowded with the multicolored roofs of shacks, poverty plain from even so great a distance, were shrouded in mist, as if an inferno had recently burned out and the smoke not yet cleared away.

Some of his workers lived there, in tiny, crowded one-room shacks, with water sometimes a quarter-mile away at a mossy stand-pipe. There was a time when the sight of these shacks could move Joseph to pity. They were, he believed, his main reason for returning to the island. He really had said, "I want to help my people." Now the sentence, with its pomposity, its naivety, was just an embarrassing memory, like the early life of the minister's wife.

But he knew that wasn't all. He had expected a kind of fame, a continual welcome, the prodigal son having made good, having acquired skills, returning home to share the wealth, to spread the knowledge. He had anticipated a certain uniqueness but this had been thwarted. Everyone knew someone else who had returned from abroad—from England, from Canada, from the States. He grew to hate the stock phrases people dragged out: "No place like home, this island is a true Paradise, life's best here." The little lies of self-doubt and fear.

The gate to Pacheco House was chained but there was no lock: a casual locking-up, an abandonment. The chain, thick and rusted, slipped easily to the ground, leaving a trace of gritty oxide on his fingertips. He couldn't push the gate far; clumps of grass, stems long and tapering to a lancet point, blocked it at the base. He squeezed through the narrow opening, the concrete pillar rough and tight on his back, the iron gate leaving a slash of rust on his shirt. Inside, wild grass, wet and glistening, enveloped his legs up to his knees. The trees were further back, thick and ponderous, unmoving, lending the garden the heavy stillness of jungle.

Walking, pushing through the grass, took a little effort. The vegetation sought not so much to prevent intrusion as to hinder it, to encumber it with a kind of tropical lassitude. Joseph raised his legs high, free of the tangle of vines and roots and thorns, and brought his boots crashing down with each step, crushing leaves into juicy blobs of green and brown, startling underground colonies of ants into frenzied scrambling. Ahead of him, butterflies, looking like edges of an artist's canvas, fluttered away, and crickets, their wings beating like pieces of stiff silk one against the other, buzzed from tall stalk to tall stalk, narrowly avoiding the grasshoppers which also sought escape. A locust, as long as his hand and as fat, sank its claws into his shirt, just grazing the surface of his skin. He flicked a finger powerfully at it, knocking off its head; the rest of the body simply relaxed and fell off.

Once past the trees, Joseph found himself at the house. The stone foundation, he noticed, was covered in green slime and the wall, the monotony of which was broken only by a large cavity which must once have been a window, stripped of all color. He made his way to the cavity and peered through it into the half-darkness of a large room. He carefully put one leg through, feeling for the floor. The boards creaked badly but held.

The room was a disappointment. He didn't know what he had expected—he hadn't really thought about it—but its emptiness engendered an atmosphere of uncommon despair. He felt it was a room that had always been empty, a room that had never been peopled with emotion or sound, like a dried-up old spinster abandoned at the edge of life. He could smell the pungency of recently disturbed vegetation but he didn't know whether it came from him or through the gaping window.

He made his way to another room, the floorboards creaking under the wary tread of his feet; just another empty space, characterless, almost shapeless in its desertion. A flight of stairs led upwards, to the second floor and yet another empty room, massive, dusty, cobwebs tracing crazy geometric patterns on the walls and the ceiling. In the corners the floorboards had begun to warp. He wondered why all the doors had been removed and by whom. Or had the house ever had doors? Might it not have been always a big, open, empty house, with rooms destined to no purpose, with a façade that promised mystery but an interior that took away all hope?

He had hoped to find something of Pacheco's, the merest testament to his having existed, a bed maybe, or a portrait, or even one line of graffiti. But were it not for the structure itself, a vacuous shell falling steadily to ruin, and the smudges of erroneous public fantasy fading like the outer edges of a dream, Pacheco might never have existed. Whatever relics might have been preserved by the government had long been carted away, probably by the last workmen, those who had so cavalierly slipped the chain around the gate, putting a period to a life.

Joseph walked around the room, his footsteps echoing like drumbeats. Each wall had a window of shattered glass and he examined the view from each. Jumbled vegetation, the jungle taking hold in this one plot of earth in the middle of the town: it was the kind of view that would have been described in the travel brochures as *lush* and *tropical*, two words he had grown to hate. Looking through the windows, recalling the manicured grounds of his youth, he felt confined, isolated, a man in an island on an island. He wondered why anyone would pay a lot of money to visit such a place. The answer came to him: for the tourist, a life was not to be constructed here. The tourist sought no more than an approximation of adventure; there was safety in a return ticket and a foreign passport.

There was no way to get to the attic, where the LeNoir window was. Another disappointment: the object of all that youthful energy was nothing more than an aperture to a boxed-in room, airless and musty with age and probably dank with bat mess.

He made his way back down the stairs and out the gaping front door. The air was hot and sticky and the smell of vegetation, acrid in the humidity, was almost overpowering.

Frankie had said that Pacheco was buried in the garden and that a marker had been erected. Joseph knew there was no hope of finding it. Everything was overgrown: the garden, the flowers, the driveway that had once existed, Pacheco's grave, Pacheco himself, the mysterious South American whose last act was to lose his name and his life in sterile isolation.

Joseph began making his way back to the gate. Over to the left he could see the path he had made when going in, the grass flat and twisted, twigs broken and limp, still dripping from the morning rain. He felt clammy, and steamy perspiration broke out on his skin.

At the gate, he stopped and turned around for a last look at the house: he saw it for what it was, a deceptive shell that played on the mind. He looked around for something to throw. The base of the gate-pillars was cracked and broken and moss had begun eating its way to the centre. He broke off a piece of the concrete and flung it at the LeNoir window. The glass shattered, scattering thousands of slivers into the attic and onto the ground below.

His wife wasn't home when he returned. The house was dark and silent. Coffee cups and plates with half-eaten pastries lay on the side-tables. The false fireplace had been switched off. On the mantelpiece, propped against his wife's lipstick-stained cup, was a notepad with a message: "Have gone out for the evening with Arlene. We have the chauffeur and the limo coz Brian's busy in a cabinet meeting. Don't know what time I'll be back." She hadn't bothered to sign it.

He ripped the page from the notepad: he hated the word "coz" and the word "limo" and he felt a special revulsion for "Arlene" and "Brian", fictitious names assumed with the mantle of social status. As a transient domestic, Arlene had been called Thelma, the name scribbled on her birth certificate, and Brian's real name was Balthazar. Joseph avoided the entire issue by simply referring to them as the Minister and the Minister's Wife. The sarcasm was never noticed.

He took the notepad and a pencil and sat down. He wrote *Dear* then crossed it out. He threw the page away and started again. He drew a circle, then a triangle, then a square: the last disappointment, it was the most difficult act. Finally, in big square letters, he wrote, *I am going back*. He put the pad back on the mantelpiece, switched on the fireplace lights, and sat staring into their synchronized dance.

Austin Clarke

I am Barbadian by nature—the best of me is Barbadian; the best of my memories are Barbadian.

—Austin Clarke, *Other Solitudes*

In Barbados, I breathe in the smell of the soil, I taste the scandals of the landscape. The mud through which I trample and the sand that pours through my fingers are the roots and ruins I spoke about.

—Clarke, *The Globe and Mail*

This was his way of telling, in plain blunt terms, and I was proud to have apprehended his meaning and intention, that he was once more within the lap of the culture and the people from whom he had come. And it was this appreciation and this oneness with the landscape that was the fuel to his tremendous facility in reproducing the essence of West Indian-ness.

—Clarke, *A Passage Back Home*

born in St. James Parish, Barbados, in 1934, Austin Ardinel Chesterfield Clarke came to Toronto in 1955, on leave from his job as a high school teacher to study economics and political science at the University of Toronto. He dropped out of his university program and began to write while supporting himself with a series of jobs, eventually working as a freelance broadcaster for the CBC. In this capacity, he produced interviews and documentaries dealing with social and cultural issues of the West Indies and of the Black diaspora° in Britain and North America.

Critical acclaim for Clarke's first two novels, *The Survivors of the Crossing* (1964) and *Among Thistles and Thorns* (1965), led to appointments

diaspora: literally means the dispersal of a people—communities established in countries other than the "original" homeland

as visiting professor of Black studies at several American universities including Duke, Brandeis and Yale, and as writer-in-residence at a number of universities in Canada. Between 1973 and 1976, Clarke worked for the government of Barbados, first as cultural attaché at the Embassy of Barbados in Washington (1974–75) and then as general manager of the Caribbean Broadcasting Corporation in Barbados (1975–76). Returning to Toronto in 1977, Clarke ran (unsuccessfully) as a Progressive Conservative candidate in the provincial elections. He has served as vice-chairman of the Ontario Film Review Board (1983–85) and on the Immigration and Refugee Board of Canada (1988–93).

Throughout this period, he continued to publish both fiction and non-fiction works. His trilogy of novels about Toronto, *The Meeting Point* (1967), *Storm of Fortune* (1971) and *The Bigger Light* (1975), brought him significant critical and popular acclaim, while the first volume of his memoirs, *Growing Up Stupid Under the Union Jack* (1980), was awarded the Casa de las Americas Prize for Literature. His most recent novel, *The Origin of Waves*, published in 1997, was the first recipient of the Rogers Communications Writers' Trust Fiction Prize in 1998.

An outspoken critic of racism in Canada, Clarke has focussed on the difficulty of the immigrant experience in his stories and novels. But, as the following story makes clear, home itself is not without complications. It remains, however, as geography and as culture, imbued with profound emotion and intimately connected to his sense of identity. In his memoir about his friendship with Trinidad-born author Samuel Selvon, Clarke recalls listening to the Caribbean Voices series on the BBC and hearing writers, who, like Selvon, had been born in the Caribbean and were now living in England, read their work. Their evocations of home (where Clarke as a child was still living) were affirmations of the value of Caribbean culture: "But to hear, all of a sudden . . . the names of flowers we had passed earlier that very Sunday, to and from Sin-Matthias° or Sin-Barnabas° . . . to hear these symbols of words, greater than words; greater than our recognition of them in everyday life, all this was to make us feel 'we was people, too'" (*A Passage Back Home* 8).

Sin-Matthias, Sin-Barnabas: Clarke is giving the word "Saint" a Caribbean pronunciation.

Works Cited

Clarke, Austin. *A Passage Back Home: A Personal Reminiscence of Samuel Selvon.* Toronto: Exile Editions, 1994.

_____. "A Stranger in a Strange Land." *The Globe and Mail.* 15 Aug. 1990 (qtd. in *Pens of Many Colours.* Ed. Eva C. Karpinski and Ian Lea. Toronto: Harcourt Brace Javanovich Canada, 1993).

Hutcheon, Linda, and Marion Richmond, eds. *Other Solitudes: Canadian Multicultural Fictions.* Toronto: Oxford University Press, 1990. 69.

Other Sources and Weblinks

Clarke, Austin
infoculture.cbc.ca/archives/bookswr/bookswr_06021999_ mitchellprize.html

Clarke, Austin
www.nwpassages.com/canlit/authors/clarke.asp

Clarke, Austin. "A Black Man Talks About Race Prejudice in White Canada." *Maclean's* 20 April 1963: 18, 55–8.

Dance, Daryl Cumber. "Austin Clarke." In *New World Adams: Conversations with Contemporary West Indian Writers.* Leeds: Peepal Tree, 1992. 65–78.

Leaving This Island Place

The faces at the grilled windows of the parish almshouse° were looking out, on this hot Saturday afternoon, on a world of grey-flannel and cricket and cream shirts, a different world, as they had looked every afternoon from the long imprisonment of the wards. Something in those faces told me they were all going to die in the almshouse. Standing on the cricket field I searched for the face of my father. I knew he would never live to see the sun of day again.

It is not cricket, it is leaving the island that makes me think about my father. I am leaving the island. And as I walk across the green playing field and into the driveway of the almshouse, its walkway speckled with spots of tar and white pebbles, and walk right up to the white spotless front of the building, I know it is too late now to think of saving him. It is too late to become involved with this dying man.

In the open verandah I could see the men, looking half-alive and half-dead, lying on the smudged canvas cots that were once white and cream as

---

almshouse: a home or, in this case, a hospital for those too poor to pay for the care they need. The word "alms" means charity.

the cricketers' clothes, airing themselves. They have played, perhaps, in too many muddy tournaments, and are now soiled. But I am leaving. But I know before I leave there is some powerful tug which pulls me into this almshouse, grabbing me and almost swallowing me to make me enter these doors and slap me flat on the sore-back canvas cot beside a man in dying health. But I am leaving.

'You wasn't coming to visit this poor man, this poor father o' yourn?' It is Miss Brewster, the head nurse. She knew my father and she knew me. And she knew that I played cricket every Saturday on the field across the world from the almshouse. She is old and haggard. And she looks as if she has looked once too often on the face of death; and now she herself resembles a half-dead, dried-out flying fish, wrapped in the grease-proof paper of her nurse's uniform. 'That man having fits and convulsions by the hour! Every day he asking for you. All the time, day in and day out. And you is such a poor-great, high-school educated bastard that you now acting *too proud* to come in here, because it is a almshouse and not a *private ward*, to see your own father! And you didn't even have the presence o' mind to bring along a orange, not even one, or a banana for that man, *your father!*'

She was now leading me through a long dark hallway, through rows of men on their sides, and some on their backs, lying like soldiers on a battle field. They all looked at me as if I was dying. I tried to avoid their eyes, and I looked instead at their bones and the long fingernails and toenails, the thermometers of their long idle illness. The matted hair and the smell of men overdue for the bed-pan: men too weary now to raise themselves to pass water even in a lonely gutter. They were dying slowly and surely, for the almshouse was crowded and it did not allow its patients to die too quickly. I passed them, miles out of my mind: the rotting clothes and sores, men of all colours, all ages, dressed like women in long blue sail-cloth-hard shirts that dropped right down to the scales on their toothpick legs. One face smiled at me, and I wondered whether the smile meant welcome.

'Wait here!' It was Miss Brewster again who had spoken. She opened the door of a room and pushed me inside as you would push a small boy into the headmaster's office for a caning; and straightway the smell of stale urine and of sweat and faeces whipped me in the face. When the door closed behind me I was alone with the dead, with the smells of the almshouse.

I am frightened. But I am leaving. I find myself thinking about the trimmed sandwiches and the whiskey-and-sodas waiting for me at the farewell party in honour of my leaving. Something inside me is saying I should pay some respect in my thoughts for this man, this dying man. I opened my eyes and thought of Cynthia. I thought of her beautiful face beside my father's face. And I tried to hold her face in the hands of my mind, and I squeezed it close to me and kept myself alive with the living outside world of cricket and cheers and 'tea in the pavilion.' There is death in this room and I am inside it. And Cynthia's voice is saying to me, Run run run! back through the smells, through the fallen lines of the men, through the front door and out into the green sunlight of the afternoon and the cricket and shouts; out into the applause.

'That's he laying-down there. Your father,' the voice said. It was Miss Brewster. She too must have felt the power of death in the room, for she spoke in a whisper.

This is my father: more real than the occasional boundary hit by the cricket bat and the cheers that came with the boundary only. The two large eyeballs in the sunset of this room are my father.

'Boy?' It was the skeleton talking. I am leaving. He held out a hand to touch me. Dirt was under his fingernails like black moons. I saw the hand. A dead hand, a dirty hand, a hand of quarter-moons of dirt under the claws of its nails. ('You want to know something, son?' my godmother told me long ago. 'I'll tell you something. That man that your mother tell you to call your father, he isn't your father, in truth. Your mother put the blame of your birth on him because once upon a time, long long ago in this island, that man was a man.')

I do not touch the hand. I am leaving this place.

And then the words, distant and meaningless from this departure of love because they came too late, began to turn the room on a side. Words and words and words. He must have talked this way each time he heard a door open or shut; or a footstep . . . is a good thing you going away, son, a good thing. I hear you going away, and that is a good thing . . . because I am going away . . . from this place . . . Miss Brewster, she . . . but I am sorry . . . cannot go with you . . .' (Did my mother hate this man so much to drive him here? Did she drive him to such a stick of love that it broke his heart; and made him do foolish things with his young life on the village green of cricket near his house, that made him the playful enemy of Barrabas the policeman, whose delight, my godmother told me, was to drag my father the captain of the village team away drunk from victory and pleasure to throw him into the crowded jail to make him slip on the cold floor fast as a new cricket pitch with vomit . . . ('And it was then, my child, after all those times in the jail, that your father contract that sickness which nobody in this village don't call by name. It is so horrible a sickness.') . . . and I remember now that even before this time I was told by my mother that my father's name was not to be mentioned in her house which her husband made for me as my stepfather. And she kept her word. For eighteen years. For eighteen years, his name was never mentioned; so he had died before this present visit. And there was not even a spasm of a reminiscence of his name. He was dead before this. But sometimes I would risk the lash of her hand and visit him, in his small shack on the fringe of Rudders Pasture where he lived out the riotous twenty-four years of middle life. ('Your mother never loved that bastard' my godmother said.) But I loved him, in a way. I loved him when he was rich enough to give me two shillings for a visit, for each visit. And although my mother had said he had come 'from no family at-all, at-all,' had had 'no background,' yet to me in those laughing days he held a family circle of compassion in his heart. I see him now, lying somewhere on a cot, and I know I am leaving this island. In those days of cricket when I visited him, I visited him in his house: the pin-up girls of the screen, white and naked; and the photographs of black women he had taken with a box camera (because 'Your father is some kind o' genius, but in this island we call him a blasted madman, but he may be a real genius'), black women always dressed in their Sunday-best after church, dressed in too much clothes, and above them all, above all those pin-ups and photographs, the photographs of me, caught running in a record time, torn from the island's newspapers. And there was one of me he had framed, when I passed my examinations at Harrison College. And once, because in those days he was my best admirer, I gave him a silver cup which I had won for winning a race in a speed which no boy had done in twenty-five years, at the same school, in the history of the school. And all those women on the walls, and some in real life, looking at me, and whispering under their breath so I might barely hear it, 'That's his *son!*'; and some looking at me as if I had entered their bedroom of love at the wrong moment of hectic ecstasy; and he, like a child caught stealing, would hang his father's head in shame and apologize for them in a whisper, and would beg the women in a loud voice, 'You don't see I am with *my son?* You can't behave yourself in his presence?' And once, standing in his house alone, when he went to buy a sugar cake for me, I was looking at the photograph of a naked woman on the wall and my eyes became full of mists and I saw coming out of the rainwater of vision my mother's face, and her neck and her shoulders and her breasts and her navel. And I shut my eyes tight, tight, tight and ran into him returning with the sugar cake and ran screaming from his house. That was my last visit. This is my first visit after that. And I am leaving this island place. After that last visit I gave myself headaches wondering if my mother had gone to his shack before she found herself big and heavy with the burden of me in her womb. ('Child, you have no idea what he do to that poor pretty girl, your mother, that she hates his guts even to this day!') . . . and the days at Harrison College when the absence of his surname on my report card would remind me in the eyes of my classmates that I might be the best cricketer and the best runner, but that I was after all, among this cream of best blood and brains, only a bas—) '. . . this island is only a place, one place,' his voice was saying. 'The only saving thing is to escape.' He was a pile of very old rags thrown around a stunted tree. Then he was talking again, in a new way. 'Son, do not leave before you get somebody to say a prayer for me . . . somebody like Sister Christopher from the Nazarene Church . . .'

But Sister Christopher is dead. Dead and gone five years now, 'When she was shouting at the Lord one night at a revival,' my godmother said.

'She's dead.'

'Dead?'

'Five years.'

'But couldn' you still ask her to come, ask Miss Christo, Sister Christopher to come . . .'

There is no point listening to a dying man talk. I am going to leave. No point telling him that Sister Christopher is alive, because he is beyond that, beyond praying for, since he is going to die and he never was a Catholic. And I am going to leave, For I cannot forget the grey-flannel and the cream of the cricket field just because he is dying, and the sharp smell of the massage and the cheers of the men and women at the tape, which I have now made a part of my life. And the Saturday afternoon matinees with the wealthy middle-class girls from Queen's College, wealthy in looks and wealthy in books, with their boyfriends the growing-up leaders of the island. Forget all that? And forget the starched white shirt and the blue-and-gold Harrison College tie? Forget all this because a man is dying and because he tells you he is going to die?

Perhaps I should forget them. They form a part of the accident of my life, a life which—if there were any logic in life—ought to have been spent in the gutters round the Bath Corner, or in some foreign white woman's rose garden, or fielding tennis balls in the Garrison Savannah Tennis Club where those who played tennis could be bad tennis players but had to be white.

Let him die. I am leaving this island place. And let him die with his claim on my life. And let the claim be nailed in the coffin, which the poor authorities for the poor will authorize out of plain dealboard, without a minister or a prayer. And forget Sister Christopher who prefers to testify and shout on God; and call somebody else, perhaps, more in keeping with the grey-flannel and the cream of the cricket field and Saturday afternoon walks in the park and matinees at the Empire Theatre. Call a canon. Call a canon to bury a pauper, call a canon to bury a pauper, ha-ha-haaaa! . . .

Throughout the laughter and the farewell speeches and the drinks that afternoon, all I did hear was the slamming of many heavy oak doors of the rectory when I went to ask the canon to bury the pauper. And I tried to prevent the slamming from telling me what it was telling me: that I was out of place here, that I belonged with the beginning in the almshouse. Each giggle, each toast, each rattle of drunken ice cubes in the whirling glass pointed a finger back to the almshouse. 'Man, you not drinking?' a wealthy girl said. 'Man, what's wrong with you, at all?' And someone else was saying, 'Have any of you remember Freddie?' But Briggs said, 'Remember that bitch? The fellar with the girl with the biggest bubbies in the whole Caribbean? And who uses to . . . man, Marcus! Marcus, I calling you! God-blummuh, Marcus we come here to drink rum and you mean to tell me that you selling we *water*, instead o' rum?' And Joan Warton said, 'But wait, look this lucky bastard though, saying he going up in Canada to university! Boy, you real lucky, in truth. I hear though that up there they possess some real inferior low-class rum that they does mix with water. Yak-yak-yak! From now on you'd be drinking Canadian rum-water, so stop playing the arse and drink this Bajan rum, man. We paying for this, yuh know!' I was leaving. I was thinking of tomorrow, and I was climbing the BOAC gangplank on the plane bound for Canada, for hope, for school, for glory; and the sea and the distance had already eased the pain of conscience; and there was already much sea between me and the cause of conscience . . .

And when the party was over, Cynthia was with me on the sands of Gravesend Beach. And the beach was full of moonlight and love. There was laughter too; and the laughter of crabs scrambling among dead leaves and skeletons of other crabs caught unawares by someone running into the sea. And there was a tourist ship in the outer harbour. 'Write! write, write, write, write me everyday of the week, every week of the year, and tell me what Canada is like, and think of me always, and don't forget to say nice things in your letters, and pray for me every night. And write poems, love poems like the ones you write in the college magazine; and when you write don't send the letters to the Rectory, because father would, well . . . send them to Auntie's address. You understand? You know how ministers and canons behave and think. I have to tell father, I have to tell him I love you, and that we are getting married when you graduate. And I shall tell him about us . . . when you leave tomorrow.' Watching the sea and the moonlight on the sea; and watching to see if the sea was laughing; and the scarecrows of masts on the fishing boats now lifeless and boastless, taking a breather from the depths and the deaths of fishing; and the large incongruous luxury liner drunk-full of tourists. And all the time Cynthia chatting and chattering, '. . . but we should have got married, even secretly and eloped somewhere, even to Trinidad, or even to Tobago. Father won't've known, and won't've liked it, but we would've been married . . . Oh hell, man! this island stifles me, and I wish I was leaving with you. Sometimes I feel like a crab in a crab hole with a pile o' sand in front . . .'

'Remember how we used to build sandcastles on bank holidays?'

'And on Sundays, far far up the beach where nobody came . . .'

'Cynthia?'

'Darling?'

'My Old Man, my Old Man is dying right now . . .'

'You're too philosophical! Anyhow, where? Are you kidding? I didn't even know you had an Old Man.' And she laughs.

'I was at the almshouse this afternoon, before the party.'

'Is he really in the almshouse?'

'St Michael's almshouse, near . . .'

'You must be joking. You *must* be joking!' She turned her back to me, and her face to the sea. 'You aren't pulling my leg, eh?' she said. And before I could tell her more about my father, who he was, how kind a man he was, she was walking from me and we were in her father's Jaguar and speeding away from the beach.

And it is the next day, mid-morning, and I am sitting in the Seawell Airport terminal, waiting to be called to board the plane. I am leaving. My father, is he dead yet? A newspaper is lying on a bench without a man, or woman, Something advises me to look in the obituary column and see if . . . But my mother had said, as she packed my valises, making sure that the fried fish was in my briefcase which Cynthia had bought for me as a going-away present, my mother had said, 'Look, boy, leave the dead to live with the blasted dead, do! Leave the dead in this damn islan' place!'

And I am thinking now of Cynthia who promised ('I promise, I promise, I promise. Man, you think I going let you leave this place, *leave Barbados?* and I not going be there at the airport?') to come to wave goodbye, to take a photograph waving goodbye from the terminal and the plane, to get her photograph taken for the social column waving goodbye at the airport, to kiss, to say goodbye and promise return in English, and say *'au revoir'* in French because she was the best student in French at Queen's College.

A man looks at the newspaper, and takes it up, and gives it to a man loaded-down as a new-traveller for a souvenir of the island. And the friend wraps two large bottles of Goddards Gold Braid rum in it, smuggling the rum and the newspaper out of the island, in memory of the island. And I know I will never find out how he died. Now there are only the fear and the tears and the handshakes of other people's saying goodbye and the weeping of departure. 'Come back real soon again, man!' a fat, sweating man says, 'and next time I going take you to some places that going make your head *curl!* Man, I intend to show you the whole islan', and give you some dolphin steaks that is more bigger than the ones we eat down in Nelson Street with the whores last night!' An old woman, who was crying, was saying goodbye to a younger woman who could have been her daughter, or her daughter-in-law, or her niece. 'Don't take long to return back, child! Do not tarry too long. Come back again soon . . . and don't forget that you was borned right here, pon this rock, pon this island. This is a good decent island, so return back as soon as you get yuh learning, come back again soon, child . . .'

The plane is ready now. And Cynthia is not coming through the car park in her father's Jaguar. She has not come, she has not come as she promised. And I am leaving the island.

Below me on the ground are the ants of people, standing at an angle, near the terminal. And I can see the architect-models of houses and buildings, and the beautiful quiltwork patches of land under the plough . . . and then there is the sea, and the sea, and then the sea.

bell
hooks

It's exciting to think, write, talk about, and create art that reflects passionate engagement with popular culture, because this may very well be "the" central future location of resistance struggle, a meeting place where new and radical happenings can occur.

—bell hooks, "Postmodern Blackness"

In January of 1995, Michael Berube announced "Something new is happening in American cultural history." He was talking about the emergence of a group of African-American intellectuals who were achieving public popularity as well as academic recognition, writers and thinkers whose work "has become a fixture of mall bookstores, talk shows, elite universities, and black popular culture." Observing that a mere ten years earlier one of this number, Cornel West, had deplored the absence of a vital, Black intellectual exchange that was "organically linked with African-American cultural life," Berube remarks on the extent to which the situation has changed and "a new African-American intelligentsia has become part of this country's cultural landscape" (73).

Prominent among this emergent group (which includes Henry Louis Gates, Jr.) is bell hooks, a university professor at the City College of New York who writes for a general audience rather than simply for her academic peers, and who has addressed herself to a broad spectrum of cultural phenomena.

She is interested not only in academic theory, but also in the elements and movements within contemporary mass culture. She writes analyses of current films and of popular icons such as Madonna and has conducted interviews with performers such as rapper Ice Cube.

From the first, hooks has been a controversial figure, bringing together concerns about racism, feminism and class in ways that seem at times contradictory and often inflammatory (Berube calls her review of Spike

Lee's *Malcolm X* "gnarled and skewed" and "outrageously unfair"), and in language that combines the critical discourse of academia with the popular argot of the street. Deborah Coen remarks:

> bell hooks makes herself difficult to talk about: Is she bell hooks, the revolutionary black feminist? Bell Hooks, the respected critic and professor of English? Can she belong to the white-male-dominated halls of academia when she is teaching, but reunite herself with the working-class black world of her youth during a sabbatical? Rather than shrinking uncomfortably from such ambiguities, hooks makes them a foundation for her thinking about popular culture. By refusing to be anything but an outsider, she speaks in one of today's clearest voices against the injustices inflicted on marginalized groups. (1)

What consistently characterizes hooks' work is her refusal to accept conventional boundaries: between the struggle for racial equality and feminism, between "high" and popular culture, between intellectuals and the community. Rejecting the belief that any criticism of Black culture or its products undermines the struggle for racial equality, hooks attacks sexism and racial stereotyping wherever she finds them—as much (or more, since it is more important, its consequences more insidious) in the work of Black filmmaker Spike Lee as in films by "Spielberg, or any other white filmmaker exploiting black subject matter" (hooks 176). She has also refused to maintain a united front with feminist spokeswomen, arguing that much of the contemporary feminist agenda is driven by the needs of privileged, white, middle-class women who are utterly unconcerned with the experience of economically disadvantaged women of colour. A response to a remark from widely publicized, white, feminist author Camille Paglia epitomizes hooks' wit and combative style. Describing herself as "very loud," Paglia complained, "I've had a hell of a time in academe. This is why I usually get along with African Americans. I mean, when we're together, 'Whoo!' It's like I feel totally myself—we just let everything go!" hooks rejoined: "Naturally, all black Americans were more than pleased to have Miss Camille give us this vote of confidence, since we live to make it possible for white girls like herself to have a place where they can be 'totally' themselves " (Berube 75).

Born Gloria Watkins, into a segregated Black community in Hopkinsville, Kentucky, bell hooks has written about both the pain of racism and the cultural richness of her childhood. From a background of poverty in the agrarian south, she has gone on to achieve academic success and professional recognition. She received her Ph.D. from the University of California at Santa Cruz in 1983, producing a dissertation on the work of Toni Morrison, and has become a leading figure in the struggle against racial, sexual and economic inequality. hooks' assumption of her grandmother's name reflects a desire to honour the women in her own family who have gone before her and the vital contribution made by generations of Black women. Her ability to cross boundaries allows her to find important intellectual work being done in the community outside the academy, as well as within its often repressive structures. And it allows her to move between the language of formal academic theory and the language of the street because, as she points out in an essay in *Outlaw Culture*, "[t]alking sex in meta-language and theoretical prose, does not capture the imagination of masses of folks who are working daily to understand how their lives have been affected by shifting gender roles and expectations and how sexism fucks us all up."

Works Cited

Berube, Michael. "Public Academy." *The New Yorker*. 9 Jan.1995. 73–80.

Coen, Deborah. "The Back Page." Rev. of *Outlaw Culture*.
www.digitas.harvard.edu/~perspy/issues/1995/Feb/bell.html

hooks, bell. "Postmodern Blackness." *Yearning: Race, Gender, and Cultural Politics*. Boston: South End Press, 1990. 23–33.

Other Sources and Weblinks

"hooks, bell." altculture.
www.altculture.com/aentries/b/bxhooks.html

Hua, Julie. "Voices from the Gaps: bell hooks."
voices.cla.umn.edu/authors/bellhooks.html

Kerr, Jody F. "Biography: Bell Hooks." *Writing & Resistance*.
www.public.asu.edu/~metro/aflit/hooks/index.html"

"There's No Place To Go But Up: Maya Angelou in Conversation with bell hooks." *Shambhala Sun*.
www.shambhalasun.com/Archives/Features/1998/Jan98/Angelou.htm

Homeplace:
A Site of Resistance

When I was a young girl the journey across town to my grandmother's house was one of the most intriguing experiences. Mama did not like to stay there long. She did not care for all that loud talk, the talk that was usually about the old days, the way life happened then—who married whom, how and when somebody died, but also how we lived and survived as black people, how the white folks treated us. I remember this journey not just because of the stories I would hear. It was a movement away from the segregated blackness of our community into a poor white neighborhood. I remember the fear, being scared to walk to Baba's (our grandmother's house) because we would have to pass that terrifying whiteness—those white faces on the porches staring us down with hate. Even when empty or vacant, those porches seemed to say "danger," "you do not belong here," "you are not safe."

Oh! that feeling of safety, of arrival, of homecoming when we finally reached the edges of her yard, when we could see the soot black face of our grandfather, Daddy Gus, sitting in his chair on the porch, smell his cigar, and rest on his lap. Such a contrast, that feeling of arrival, of homecoming, this sweetness and the bitterness of that journey, that constant reminder of white power and control.

I speak of this journey as leading to my grandmother's house, even though our grandfather lived there too. In our young minds houses belonged to women, were their special domain, not as property, but as places where all that truly mattered in life took place—the warmth and comfort of shelter, the feeding of our bodies, the nurturing of our souls. There we learned dignity, integrity of being; there we learned to have faith. The folks who made this life possible, who were our primary guides and teachers, were black women.

Their lives were not easy. Their lives were hard. They were black women who for the most part worked outside the home serving white folks, cleaning their houses, washing their clothes, tending their children—black women who worked in the fields or in the streets, whatever they could do to make ends meet, whatever was necessary. Then they returned to their homes to make life happen there. This tension between service outside one's home, family, and kin network, service provided to white folks which took time and energy, and the effort of black women to conserve enough of themselves to provide service (care and nurturance) within their own families and communities is one of the many factors that has historically distinguished the lot of black women in patriarchal white supremacist society from that of black men. Contemporary black struggle must honor this history of service just as it must critique the sexist definition of service as women's "natural" role.

Since sexism delegates to females the task of creating and sustaining a home environment, it has been primarily the responsibility of black women to construct domestic households as spaces of care and nurturance in the face of the brutal harsh reality of racist oppression, of sexist domination. Historically, African-American people believed that the construction of a homeplace, however fragile and tenuous (the slave hut, the wooden shack), had a radical political dimension. Despite the brutal reality of racial apartheid, of domination, one's homeplace was the one site where one could freely confront the issue of humanization, where one could resist. Black women resisted by making homes where all black people could strive to be subjects, not objects, where we could be affirmed in our minds and hearts despite poverty, hardship, and deprivation, where we could restore to ourselves the dignity denied us on the outside in the public world.

This task of making homeplace was not simply a matter of black women providing service: it was about the construction of a safe place where black people could affirm one another and by so doing heal many of the wounds inflicted by racist domination. We could not learn to love or respect ourselves in the culture of white supremacy, on the outside; it was there on the inside, in that "homeplace," most often created and kept by black women, that we had the opportunity to grow and develop, to nurture our spirits. This task of making a homeplace, of making home a community of resistance, has been shared by black women globally, especially black women in white supremacist societies.

I shall never forget the sense of shared history, of common anguish, I felt when first reading about the plight of black women domestic servants in South Africa, black women laboring in white homes. Their stories evoked vivid memories of our African-American past. I remember that one of the black women giving testimony complained that after traveling in the wee hours of the morning to the white folks' house, after working there all day, giving her time and energy, she had "none left for her own." I knew this story. I had read it in the slave narratives of African-American women who, like Sojourner Truth, could say, "When I cried out with a mother's grief none but Jesus heard." I knew this story. I had grown to womanhood hearing about black women who nurtured and cared for white families when they longed to have time and energy to give to their own.

I want to remember these black women today. The act of remembrance is a conscious gesture honoring their struggle, their effort to keep something for their own. I want us to respect and understand that this effort has been and continues to be a radically subversive political gesture. For those who dominate and oppress us benefit most when we have nothing to give our own, when they have so taken from us our dignity, our humanness that we have nothing left, no "homeplace" where we can recover ourselves. I want us to remember these black women today, both past and present. Even as I speak there are black women in the midst of racial apartheid in South Africa, struggling to provide something for their own. "We . . . know how our sisters suffer" (Quoted in the petition for the repeal of the pass laws, August 9, 1956). I want us to honor them, not because they suffer but because they continue to struggle in the midst of suffering, because they continue to resist. I want to speak about the importance of homeplace in the midst of oppression and domination, of homeplace as a site of resistance and liberation struggle. Writing about "resistance," particularly resistance to the Vietnam war, Vietnamese Buddhist monk Thich Nhat Hahn says:

> . . . . resistance, at root, must mean more than resistance against war. It is a resistance against all kinds of things that are like war . . . So perhaps, resistance means opposition to being invaded, occupied,

assaulted and destroyed by the system. The purpose of resistance, here, is to seek the healing of yourself in order to be able to see clearly . . . I think that communities of resistance should be places where people can return to themselves more easily, where the conditions are such that they can heal themselves and recover their wholeness.

Historically, black women have resisted white supremacist domination by working to establish homeplace. It does not matter that sexism assigned them this role. It is more important that they took this conventional role and expanded it to include caring for one another, for children, for black men, in ways that elevated our spirits, that kept us from despair, that taught some of us to be revolutionaries able to struggle for freedom. In his famous 1845 slave narrative, Frederick Douglass tells the story of his birth, of his enslaved black mother who was hired out a considerable distance from his place of residence. Describing their relationship, he writes:

> I never saw my mother, to know her as such more than four or five times in my life; and each of these times was very short in duration, and at night. She was hired by Mr. Stewart, who lived about twelve miles from my house. She made her journeys to see me in the night, traveling the whole distance on foot, after the performance of her day's work. She was a field hand, and a whipping is the penalty of not being in the field at sunrise . . . I do not recollect of ever seeing my mother by the light of day. She was with me in the night. She would lie down with me and get me to sleep, but long before I waked she was gone.

After sharing this information, Douglass later says that he never enjoyed a mother's "soothing presence, her tender and watchful care" so that he received the "tidings of her death with much the same emotions I should have probably felt at the death of a stranger." Douglass surely intended to impress upon the consciousness of white readers the cruelty of that system of racial domination which separated black families, black mothers from their children. Yet he does so by devaluing black womanhood, by not even registering the quality of care that made his black mother travel those twelve miles to hold him in her arms. In the midst of a brutal racist system, which did not value black life, she valued the life of her child enough to resist that system, to come to him in the night, just to hold him.

Now I cannot agree with Douglass that he never knew a mother's care. I want to suggest that this mother, who dared to hold him in the night, gave him at birth a sense of value that provided a groundwork, however fragile, for the person he later became. If anyone doubts the power and significance of this maternal gesture, they would do well to read psychoanalyst Alice Miller's book, *The Untouched Key: Tracing Childhood Trauma in Creativity and Destructiveness*. Holding him in her arms, Douglass's mother provided, if only for a short time, a space where this black child was not the subject of dehumanizing scorn and devaluation but was the recipient of a quality of care that should have enabled the adult Douglass to look back and reflect on the political choices of this black mother who resisted slave codes, risking her life, to care for her son. I want to suggest that devaluation of the role his mother played in his life is a dangerous oversight. Though Douglass is only one example, we are currently in danger of forgetting the powerful role black women have played in constructing for us homeplaces that are the site for resistance. This forgetfulness undermines our solidarity and the future of black liberation struggle.

Douglass's work is important, for he is historically identified as sympathetic to the struggle for women's rights. All too often his critique of male domination, such as it was, did not include recognition of the particular circumstances of black women in relation to black men and families. To me one of the most important chapters in my first book, *Ain't I A Woman: Black Women and Feminism*, is one that calls attention to "Continued Devaluation of Black Womanhood." Overall devaluation of the role black women have played in constructing for us homeplaces that are the site for resistance undermines our efforts to resist racism and the colonizing mentality which promotes internalized self-hatred. Sexist thinking about the nature of domesticity has determined the way black women's experience in the home is perceived. In African-American culture there is a long tradition of "mother worship." Black autobiographies, fiction, and poetry praise the virtues of the self-sacrificing black mother. Unfortunately, though positively motivated, black mother worship extols the virtues of self-sacrifice while simultaneously implying that such a gesture is not reflective of choice and will, rather the perfect embodiment of a woman's "natural" role. The assumption then is that the black woman who works hard to be a responsible caretaker is only doing what she should be doing. Failure to recognize the realm of choice, and the remarkable re-visioning of both woman's role and the idea of "home" that black women consciously exercised in practice, obscures the political commitment to racial uplift, to eradicating racism, which was the philosophical core of dedication to community and home.

Though black women did not self-consciously articulate in written discourse the theoretical principles of decolonization, this does not detract from the importance of their actions. They understood intellectually and intuitively the meaning of homeplace in the midst of an oppressive and dominating social reality, of homeplace as site of resistance and liberation struggle. I know of what I speak. I would not be writing this essay if my mother, Rosa Bell, daughter to Sarah Oldham, granddaughter to Bell Hooks, had not created homeplace in just this liberatory way, despite the contradictions of poverty and sexism.

In our family, I remember the immense anxiety we felt as children when mama would leave our house, our segregated community, to work as a maid in the homes of white folks. I believe that she sensed our fear, our concern that she might not return to us safe, that we could not find her (even though she always left phone numbers, they did not ease our worry). When she returned home after working long hours, she did not complain. She made an effort to rejoice with us that her work was done, that she was home, making it seem as though there was nothing about the experience of working as a maid in a white household, in that space of Otherness, which stripped her of dignity and personal power.

Looking back as an adult woman, I think of the effort it must have taken for her to transcend her own tiredness (and who knows what assaults or wounds to her spirit had to be put aside so that she could give something to her own). Given the contemporary notions of "good parenting" this may seem like a small gesture, yet in many post-slavery black families, it was a gesture parents were often too weary, too beaten down to make. Those of us who were fortunate enough to receive such care understood its value. Politically, our young mother, Rosa Bell, did not allow the white supremacist culture of domination to completely shape and control her psyche and her familial relationships. Working to create a homeplace that affirmed our beings, our blackness, our love for one another was necessary resistance. We learned degrees of critical consciousness from her. Our lives were not without contradictions, so it is not my intent to create a romanticized portrait. Yet any attempts to critically assess the role of black women in liberation struggle must examine the way political concern about the impact of racism shaped black women's thinking, their sense of home, and their modes of parenting.

An effective means of white subjugation of black people globally has been the perpetual construction of economic and social structures that deprive many folks of the means to make homeplace. Remembering this should enable us to understand the political value of black women's resistance in the home. It should provide a framework where we can discuss the development of black female political consciousness, acknowledging the political importance of resistance effort that took place in homes. It is no accident that the South African apartheid regime systematically attacks and destroys black efforts to construct homeplace, however tenuous, that small private reality where black women and men can renew their spirits and recover themselves. It is no accident that this homeplace, as fragile and as transitional as it may be, a makeshift shed, a small bit of earth where one rests, is always subject to violation and destruction. For when a people no longer have the space to construct homeplace, we cannot build a meaningful community of resistance.

Throughout our history, African-Americans have recognized the subversive value of homeplace, of having access to private space where we do not directly encounter white racist aggression. Whatever the shape and direction of black liberation struggle (civil rights reform or black power movement), domestic space has been a crucial site for organizing, for forming political solidarity. Homeplace has been a site of resistance. Its structure was defined less by whether or not black women and men were conforming to sexist behavior norms and more by our struggle to uplift ourselves as a people, our struggle to resist racist domination and oppression.

That liberatory struggle has been seriously undermined by contemporary efforts to change that subversive homeplace into a site of patriarchal domination of black women by black men, where we abuse one another for not conforming to sexist norms. This shift in perspective, where homeplace is not viewed as a political site, has had negative impact on the construction of black female identity and political consciousness. Masses of black women, many of whom were not formally educated, had in the past been able to play a vital role in black liberation struggle. In the contemporary situation, as the paradigms for domesticity in black life mirrored white bourgeois norms (where home is conceptualized as politically neutral space), black people began to overlook and devalue the importance of black female labor in teaching critical consciousness in domestic space. Many black women, irrespective of class status, have responded to this crisis of meaning by imitating leisure-class sexist notions of women's role, focusing their lives on meaningless compulsive consumerism.

Identifying this syndrome as "the crisis of black womanhood" in her essay, "Considering Feminism as a Model for Social Change," Sheila Radford-Hill points to the mid-sixties as that historical moment when the primacy of black woman's role in liberation struggle began to be questioned as a threat to black manhood and was deemed unimportant. Radford-Hill asserts:

> Without the power to influence the purpose and the direction of our collective experience, without the power to influence our culture from within, we are increasingly immobilized, unable to integrate self and role identities, unable to resist the cultural imperialism of the dominant culture which assures our continued oppression by destroying us from within. Thus, the crisis manifests itself as social dysfunction in the black community—as genocide, fratricide, homicide, and suicide. It is also manifested by the abdication of personal responsibility by black women for themselves and for each other . . . The crisis of black womanhood is a form of cultural aggression: a form of exploitation so vicious, so insidious that it is currently destroying an entire generation of black women and their families.

This contemporary crisis of black womanhood might have been avoided had black women collectively sustained attempts to develop the latent feminism expressed by their willingness to work equally alongside black men in black liberation struggle. Contemporary equation of black liberation struggle with the subordination of black women has damaged collective black solidarity. It has served the interests of white supremacy to promote the assumption that the wounds of racist domination would be less severe were black women conforming to sexist role patterns.

We are daily witnessing the disintegration of African-American family life that is grounded in a recognition of the political value of constructing homeplace as a site of resistance; black people daily perpetuate sexist norms that threaten our survival as a people. We can no longer act as though sexism in black communities does not threaten our solidarity; any force which estranges and alienates us from one another serves the interests of racist domination.

Black women and men must create a revolutionary vision of black liberation that has a feminist dimension, one which is formed in consideration of our specific needs and concerns. Drawing on past legacies, contemporary black women can begin to reconceptualize ideas of homeplace, once again considering the primacy of domesticity as a site for subversion and resistance. When we renew our concern with homeplace, we can address political issues that most affect our daily lives. Calling attention to the skills and resources of black women who may have begun to feel that they have no meaningful contribution to make, women who may or may not be formally educated but who have essential wisdom to share, who have practical experience that is the breeding ground for all useful theory, we may begin to bond with one another in ways that renew our solidarity.

When black women renew our political commitment to homeplace, we can address the needs and concerns of young black women who are groping for structures of meaning that will further their growth, young women who are struggling for self-definition. Together, black women can renew our commitment to black liberation struggle, sharing insights and awareness, sharing feminist thinking and feminist vision, building solidarity.

With this foundation, we can regain lost perspective, give life new meaning. We can make homeplace that space where we return for renewal and self-recovery, where we can heal our wounds and become whole.

Jamaica Kincaid

this is how you smile to someone you don't like too much; this is how you smile to someone you don't like at all; this is how you smile to someone you like completely; this is how you set a table for tea; this is how you set a table for dinner; this is how you set a table for dinner with an important guest; this is how your set table for lunch; this is how you set a table for breakfast; this is how to behave in the presence of men who don't know you very well, and this way they won't recognize immediately the slut I have warned you against becoming . . .

—Jamaica Kincaid, *At the Bottom of the River*

amaica Kincaid began life in 1949 as Elaine Potter Richardson on the West Indian island of Antigua. The child of a poor family, she grew up without electricity or running water. With the arrival of other children, financial constraints on the family became acute. In 1966, at the suggestion of her parents, Kincaid left Antigua at the age of seventeen to work in the United States. There, she provided live-in childcare for a family in Scarsdale, New York. She did not return to the West Indies for nineteen years.

Virtually all of Kincaid's fiction is informed by her relationship with her mother. It constitutes what Leslie Garis calls the "mystery at the center of her work." The relationship had been extremely close until Kincaid was nine, when the first of her three brothers arrived and her mother began to withdraw her affection. The profound sense of betrayal and anger she felt then has never left her, and she has continued to explore the powerful and corrosive effects of her resultant emotional isolation in her work.

When she left her first job in Scarsdale to work for a family in New York City, she didn't inform her family: "That's how I really left my mother . . . Because I never told her where I was going and I ended up not seeing her for 19 years" (Garis 6). While working in New York, she completed high school and began to take college courses, eventually receiving a full scholarship to Franconia College in New Hampshire, where she remained for only a year before returning to New York. She began writing articles for *Ingenue* and in 1973 she changed her name to Jamaica Kincaid. The name change liberated her, providing what she calls "a way for me to do things with being the same person who couldn't do them—the person who had all these weights" (Garis 7).

Through her friendship with George Trow, who wrote for *The New Yorker*, she began to write for the magazine, becoming a regular contributor. Four years later she produced her first work of fiction, which *The New Yorker* published. "Girl" is a page-long sentence reproducing her memory of the direction and criticism she had received from her mother. It became part of her first book, *At the Bottom of the River*. With the 1983 publication of this collection of thematically related short fiction, Jamaica Kincaid instantly established her reputation as an important and exciting author. She followed it with the publication of two novels, *Annie John* (1985) and *Lucy* (1990), and two personal memoirs: *The Autobiography of My Mother* (1996) and *My Brother* (1997). Her 1988 publication, *A Small Place*, is an extended essay in which she furiously attacks colonialism and corruption in Antigua, a British dependency until 1967, when it finally became an independent nation joining the Commonwealth in 1981.

Kincaid's prose often has a dream-like quality, what Garis calls "almost hallucinatory." She has been praised for her "highly poetic literary style" and the "rhythms, imagery and characterization" of her writing ("The Writer, Jamaica Kincaid"). Like Ben Okri ("Incidents at the Shrine"), Kincaid blends mythic and fantastic elements with an often painful realism. In describing her tormented relationship with a cold and abusive mother, Kincaid has been brutally honest, employing what Elizabeth Manus, in a review of *My Brother*, refers to as an "incantatory style" in her searing indictment.

Scholars have argued that Kincaid's explorations of her relationship with her mother deal with more than family dynamics. In a real sense, her mother is related to the forces of colonialism—in "Girl" the mother is clearly attempting to enforce the norms of the British colonial culture. But the mother figure in Kincaid's fiction also expresses her larger view of her homeland—initially warm and sustaining, ultimately coldly repressive. Describing her feelings when she first left Antigua, she told Leslie Garis:

> When I left home I never wanted to know another Antiguan. Of course I thought about Antigua all the time. But I did not know any Antiguans . . . I just wanted to . . . To be something other. I didn't want to be somebody important, I just wanted not to have that thing choking me all the time."
> (3)

In *My Brother*, Kincaid writes, "I could not have become a writer while living among the people I knew best, I could not have become myself" (qtd. in Manus 2). If she blames the British for depriving Antiguans of a culture

and language of their own, asserting that "nothing can erase [her] rage . . .
for this wrong can never be made right" (*A Small Place* 32), she also blames
Antiguans for their failure to discard the worst aspects of colonialism.
"Mother" and "home" are both complex realities, which ultimately require
her escape. Yet both remain at the centre of her work.

Works Cited

Garis, Leslie. "Through West Indian Eyes." *The New York Times*. 7 Oct. 1990. Final
    Section 6: 42. Available Online at *The New York Times* Archives.
Kincaid, Jamaica. *At the Bottom of the River*. New York: Farrar, Straus, Giroux,. 1996.
———. *A Small Place*. New York: Farrar, Straus, Giroux,. 1988.
Manus, Elizabeth. "Jamaica Kincaid, My Brother."
    www.weeklywire.com/ww/10-20-97/boston_books_1.html

Other Sources and Weblinks

Jamaica Kincaid.
    www.emory.edu/English/Bahril/Kincaid.html
Lichtenstein, David. A Brief Biography of Jamaica Kincaid.
    landow.stg.brown.edu/post/caribbean/bio.html
Morris, Ann R., and Margaret M. Dunn. "'The Bloodstream of Our Inheritance':
    Female Identity and the Caribbean Mother's-Land." In *Motherlands: Black
    Women's Writing from Africa, the Caribbean and South Asia*. Ed. Susheila Nasta.
    London: The Women's Press, 1991. 219–237.
"The Writer, Jamaica Kincaid."
    www/albany.edu/writers-inst/kincaid.html

My Mother

Immediately on wishing my mother dead and seeing the pain it caused her,
I was sorry and cried so many tears that all the earth around me was
drenched. Standing before my mother, I begged her forgiveness, and I
begged so earnestly that she took pity on me, kissing my face and placing
my head on her bosom to rest. Placing her arms around me, she drew my
head closer and closer to her bosom, until finally I suffocated. I lay on her
bosom, breathless, for a time uncountable, until one day, for a reason she
has kept to herself, she shook me out and stood me under a tree and I
started to breathe again. I cast a sharp glance at her and said to myself,
"So." Instantly I grew my own bosoms, small mounds at first, leaving a
small, soft place between them, where, if ever necessary, I could rest my

own head. Between my mother and me now were the tears I had cried, and I gathered up some stones and banked them in so that they formed a small pond. The water in the pond was thick and black and poisonous, so that only unnamable invertebrates could live in it. My mother and I now watched each other carefully, always making sure to shower the other with words and deeds of love and affection.

I was sitting on my mother's bed trying to get a good look at myself. It was a large bed and it stood in the middle of a large, completely dark room. The room was completely dark because all the windows had been boarded up and all the crevices stuffed with black cloth. My mother lit some candles and the room burst into a pink-like, yellow-like glow. Looming over us, much larger than ourselves, were our shadows. We sat mesmerized because our shadows had made a place between themselves, as if they were making room for someone else. Nothing filled up the space between them, and the shadow of my mother sighed. The shadow of my mother danced around the room to a tune that my own shadow sang, and then they stopped. All along, our shadows had grown thick and thin, long and short, had fallen at every angle, as if they were controlled by the light of day. Suddenly my mother got up and blew out the candles and our shadows vanished. I continued to sit on the bed, trying to get a good look at myself.

My mother removed her clothes and covered thoroughly her skin with a thick gold-colored oil, which had recently been rendered in a hot pan from the livers of reptiles with pouched throats. She grew plates of metal-colored scales on her back, and light, when it collided with this surface, would shatter and collapse into tiny points. Her teeth now arranged themselves into rows that reached all the way back to her long white throat. She uncoiled her hair from her head and then removed her hair altogether. Taking her head into her large palms, she flattened it so that her eyes, which were by now ablaze, sat on top of her head and spun like two revolving balls. Then, making two lines on the soles of each foot, she divided her feet into crossroads. Silently, she had instructed me to follow her example, and now I too traveled along on my white underbelly, my tongue darting and flickering in the hot air. "Look," said my mother.

My mother and I were standing on the seabed side by side, my arms laced loosely around her waist, my head resting securely on her shoulder, as if I needed the support. To make sure she believed in my frailness, I sighed occasionally—long soft sighs, the kind of sigh she had long ago taught me could evoke sympathy. In fact, how I really felt was invincible. I was no longer a child but I was not yet a woman. My skin had just blackened and cracked and fallen away and my new impregnable carapace had taken full hold. My nose had flattened; my hair curled in and stood out straight from my head simultaneously; my many rows of teeth in their retractable trays were in place. My mother and I wordlessly made an arrangement—I sent out my beautiful sighs, she received them; I leaned ever more heavily on her for support, she offered her shoulder, which shortly grew to the size of a thick plank. A long time passed, at the end of which I had hoped to see my mother permanently cemented to the seabed. My mother reached out to pass a hand over my head, a pacifying gesture, but I laughed and, with great agility, stepped aside. I let out a horrible roar, then a self-pitying whine. I had grown big, but my mother was bigger, and that would always be so. We walked to the Garden of Fruits and there ate to our hearts' satisfaction. We departed through the southwesterly gate, leaving as always, in our trail, small colonies of worms.

With my mother, I crossed, unwillingly, the valley. We saw a lamb grazing and when it heard our footsteps it paused and looked up at us. The lamb looked cross and miserable. I said to my mother, "The lamb is cross and miserable. So would I be, too, if I had to live in a climate not suited to my nature." My mother and I now entered the cave. It was the dark and cold cave. I felt something growing under my feet and I bent down to eat it. I stayed that way for years, bent over eating whatever I found growing under my feet. Eventually, I grew a special lens that would allow me to see in the darkest of darkness; eventually, I grew a special coat that kept me warm in the coldest of coldness. One day I saw my mother sitting on a rock. She said, "What a strange expression you have on your face. So cross, so miserable, as if you were living in a climate not suited to your nature." Laughing, she vanished. I dug a deep, deep hole. I built a beautiful house, a floorless house, over the deep, deep hole. I put in lattice windows, most favored of windows by my mother, so perfect for looking out at people passing by without her being observed. I painted the house itself yellow, the windows green, colors I knew would please her. Standing just outside the door, I asked her to inspect the house. I said, "Take a look. Tell me if it's to your satisfaction." Laughing out of the corner of a mouth I could not see, she stepped inside. I stood just outside the door, listening carefully, hoping to hear her land with a thud at the bottom of the deep, deep hole. Instead, she walked up and down in every direction, even pounding her heel on the air. Coming outside to greet me, she said, "It is an excellent house. I would be honored to live in it," and then vanished. I filled up the hole and burnt the house to the ground.

My mother has grown to an enormous height. I have grown to an enormous height also, but my mother's height is three times mine. Sometimes I cannot see from her breasts on up, so lost is she in the atmosphere. One day, seeing her sitting on the seashore, her hand reaching out in the deep to caress the belly of a striped fish as he swam through a place where two seas met, I glowed red with anger. For a while then I lived alone on the island where there were eight full moons and I adorned the face of each moon with expressions I had seen on my mother's face. All the expressions favored me. I soon grew tired of living in this way and returned to my mother's side. I remained, though glowing red with anger, and my mother and I built houses on opposite banks of the dead pond. The dead pond lay between us; in it, only small invertebrates with poisonous lances lived. My mother behaved toward them as if she had suddenly found herself in the same room with relatives we had long since risen above. I cherished their presence and gave them names. Still I missed my mother's close company and cried constantly for her, but at the end of each day when I saw her return to her house, incredible and great deeds in her wake, each of them singing loudly her praises, I glowed and glowed again, red with anger. Eventually, I wore myself out and sank into a deep, deep sleep, the only dreamless sleep I have ever had.

One day my mother packed my things in a grip and, taking me by the hand, walked me to the jetty, placed me on board a boat, in care of the captain. My mother, while caressing my chin and cheeks, said some words of comfort to me because we had never been apart before. She kissed me on the forehead and turned and walked away. I cried so much my chest heaved up and down, my whole body shook at the sight of her back turned toward me, as if I had never seen her back turned toward me before. I started to make plans to get off the boat, but when I saw that the boat was encased in a large green bottle, as if it were about to decorate a mantelpiece, I fell asleep, until I reached my destination, the new island. When the boat stopped, I got off and I saw a woman with feet exactly like mine, especially around the arch of the instep. Even though the face was completely different from what I was used to, I recognized this woman as my mother. We greeted each other at first with great caution and politeness, but as we walked along, our steps became one, and as we talked, our voices became one voice, and we were in complete union in every other way. What peace came over me then, for I could not see where she left off and I began, or where I left off and she began.

My mother and I walk through the rooms of her house. Every crack in the floor holds a significant event: here, an apparently healthy young man suddenly dropped dead; here a young woman defied her father and, while riding her bicycle to the forbidden lovers' meeting place, fell down a precipice, remaining a cripple for the rest of a very long life. My mother and I find this a beautiful house. The rooms are large and empty, opening on to each other, waiting for people and things to fill them up. Our white muslin skirts billow up around our ankles, our hair hangs straight down our backs as our arms hang straight at our sides. I fit perfectly in the crook of my mother's arm, on the curve of her back, in the hollow of her stomach. We eat from the same bowl, drink from the same cup; when we sleep, our heads rest on the same pillow. As we walk through the rooms, we merge and separate, merge and separate; soon we shall enter the final stage of our evolution.

The fishermen are coming in from sea; their catch is bountiful, my mother has seen to that. As the waves plop, plop against each other, the fishermen are happy that the sea is calm. My mother points out the fishermen to me, their contentment is a source of my contentment. I am sitting in my mother's enormous lap. Sometimes I sit on a mat she has made for me from her hair. The lime trees are weighed down with limes—I have already perfumed myself with their blossoms. A hummingbird has nested on my stomach, a sign of my fertileness. My mother and I live in a bower made from flowers whose petals are imperishable. There is the silvery blue of the sea, crisscrossed with sharp darts of light, there is the warm rain falling on the clumps of castor bush, there is the small lamb bounding across the pasture, there is the soft ground welcoming the soles of my pink feet. It is in this way my mother and I have lived for a long time now.

Pauline Melville

ew York Times reviewer Jay Parini has called Pauline Melville "one of the most inventive younger writers currently at work." Born in the former British colony of Guyana, in South America, Melville is the product of a marriage between a British mother and a Guyanese father of mixed ancestry. She currently lives in London, where she has worked as a standup comic and an actress, appearing in television shows such as *The Young Ones* and *Black Adder*. But it is for her writing that she is becoming increasingly well known, attracting favourable reviews from such literary luminaries as Salman Rushdie who has remarked, "Pauline Melville writes with an unusually dispassionate lushness that is both intellectual and sensual" and refers to her as "one of the few genuinely original writers to emerge in recent years" (Stanciu 3).

In her fiction, Melville focusses on the experience of immigration and the complexity and difficulties associated with the intersection of diverse cultures. Her background has provided her with ample experience upon which to draw. Guyana is remarkable for its cultural diversity, with Europeans, Amerindians, Africans and East Indians coexisting, sometimes uneasily, within its borders. It achieved independence from Britain only recently (in 1966) and memories of colonialism and cultural domination by the British remain fresh.

Melville's first novel, *The Ventriloquist's Tale* (1997), won the Whitbread First Novel Award. It charts the conflict between European and native American cultures in Guyana over three generations. The life of the central character, Chofy, a Wapisianan Indian of mixed ancestry, is haunted by a past that begins before his birth and includes an incestuous relationship between his aunt and uncle. Like the narrator of "Eat Labba and Drink Creek Water," he is shaped by both his ancestral past and present choice. As Parini points out, Melville's novel gives us a deep appreciation of the native people of Guyana but "[h]er point is not just to praise one culture at the expense of another; rather, she dwells on the mutual incomprehension that makes relations between cultures extremely difficult, if not impossible" (2).

The story which follows is from Melville's first short story collection, *Shape-Shifter* (1990), for which she received the Guardian Fiction Prize and the Macmillan Silver Pen Award. Gerd Bayer suggests that the stories are connected by "one theme: all characters are alike in their struggle to find a home, an identity and a past they can both live with and from" (1). The title of the collection suggests the fluidity of identity in a world in which the need to accommodate change is the only constant. It also can be seen to suggest something about the nature of perception: if you look at something long enough, at different times, and from various perspectives, alternate versions of its reality emerge. In *The Ventriloquist's Tale*, the narrator tells us about the way his grandmother presents variant versions of the same story, "variety being so much more important than truth in her opinion. More reliable, she says. Truth changes. Variety remains constant" (Jardine 3). As "Eat Labba and Drink Creek Water" demonstrates, this is true of both family history and home. Returning provides no easy solutions, for, as the narrator reflects: "We do return and leave and return again, criss-crossing the Atlantic, but whichever side of the Atlantic we are on, the dream is always on the other side."

Works Cited

Bayer, Ged. "Pauline Melville: Shape-Shifter."
      www.phil.uni_erlangen.de/~p2engphil/eccel/authors/melville.htm
Jardine, Lisa. "Pauline Melville: *The Ventriloquist's Tale*."
      www.prize.co/pauline_melville.html
Parini, Jay. "A Handful of Guyana." *The New York Times Book Review*. 11 Oct. 1998.
      Online at *The New York Times* on the Web.
Postlethwaite, Diana. "Flight Patterns."
      www.nytimes.com/books/99/05/23reviews/990523.23posthet.html
Stanciu, Tanya. "Tales of Love and Disaster: A British Writer's Original Fiction."
      www.gadfly.org/1999-03/melville.htm

Weblink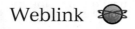

Postlethwaite, Diana. "Flight Patterns."
      www.nytimes.com/books/99/05/23reviews/990523.23posthet.html

Eat Labba and Drink Creek Water

Loma fled from Jamaica and came to live in my London flat for a year, recovering from Philip who had gone back to his wife. She arrived with two bulging suitcases and chickenpox:

'I can't bear to live on the island while he's there with her.' The tears were extraordinary. They spouted from the outermost corners of her eyes. When she blinked they squirted out. She consumed quantities of Frascati wine and swallowed all the pills my doctor could provide. Sometimes I heard her shouting in her sleep. Every so often she managed to haul herself by train to the provincial university where she was completing a thesis on the sugar riots of the thirties. I imagined her, this white-looking creole girl, jolting along in a British Rail compartment that smelled of stale smoke, weeping and puffing at cigarettes and staring out at the grey English weather which she hated. In the end:

'I'm going back,' she said.

'I'm going back too, to Guyana.'

'Why?'

'I don't know. I want to see my aunts before they die. They're old. And I want to spend some time in Georgetown, in the house with Evelyn and the others. I miss the landscape. Perhaps I'll buy a piece of land there. I don't know why. I just want to go back.'

'Eat labba° and drink creek water and you will always return', so the saying goes.

Once I dreamed I returned by walking in the manner of a high-wire artist, arms outstretched, across a frail spider's thread suspended sixty feet above the Atlantic attached to Big Ben at one end and St George's Cathedral, Demerara, at the other. It took me twenty-two days to do it and during the whole of that time only the moon shone.

Another time, my dream blew me clean across the ocean like tumbleweed. That took only three days and the sun and the moon shone alternately as per usual.

We do return and leave and return again, criss-crossing the Atlantic, but whichever side of the Atlantic we are on, the dream is always on the other side.

I am splashing in the waters of the lake at Suddie. The waters are a strange reddish colour, the colour of Pepsi-Cola and the lake is fenced in with reeds. The sky is a grey-blue lid with clouds in it—far too big for the lake. Opposite me on the far side, an Amerindian woman sits motionless in the back of a canoe wedged in the reeds. She is clutching a paddle.

Labba: Guyanese name for a form of rodent, eaten as game

They say that the spirit of a pale boy is trapped beneath the waters of one of the creeks near by. You can see him looking up when sunlight penetrates the overhanging branches and green butterfly leaves, caught between the reflections of tree roots that stretch like fins from the banks into the water.

'So you're going back to the West Indies,' says the man at the party, in his blue and white striped shirt. 'I was on holiday in Montego Bay last year. How I envy you. All those white beaches and palm trees.'

But it's not like that, I think to myself. It's not like that at all. I think of Jamaica with its harsh sunlight and stony roads. Everything is more visible there, the gunmen, the politics, the sturdy, outspoken people. And I think of the Guyanese coast, with its crab-infested mud-flats and low trees dipping into the water.

'You've got all that wonderful reggae music too,' the man is saying. But I don't bother to put him right because the buzz of conversation is too loud.

The pale boy's name is Wat. He is standing on the deck of a ship at anchor in the estuary of a great river, screwing up his eyes to scan the coast. The boards of the deck are burning hot underfoot. The sun pulverizes his head. His father, leader of the expedition, comes over to him and puts his hand on the boy's shoulder:

'At last we have found entry into the Guianas,' he says.

Wat's heart beats a little faster. This is it. Somewhere in the interior they will find Manoa which the Spaniards call El Dorado. They will outdo the feats of Cortes and Pizarro. They will discover

The mountain of crystal

The empire where there is more abundance of gold than in Peru

The palaces that contain feathered fish, beasts and birds, all fashioned in gold by men with no iron implements

The pleasure gardens with intricate replicas of trees, herbs and flowers, all wrought in silver and gold.

He gazes eagerly ahead. There is mud, green bush, river and more bush stretching as far as the eye can see. And there are no seagulls. Unlike the coast of England where the birds had shrieked them such a noisy farewell, this coast is utterly silent.

The body of an Amerindian is falling through the mists, a brown leaf curling and twisting downwards until it reaches the earth with a thud like fruit.

A low mournful hoot signals the departure of the SS *Essequibo* as it steams out of the Demerara° into the Atlantic.

A young man of twenty-one braces himself against the rail taking deep breaths of the future. There is not much of the African left in his appearance,

Demerara: a river in the Guiana Highlands, in Guyana, it is navigable for ocean-going ships

a hint of it perhaps in the tawny colour of a complexion mixed over generations with Scottish, Amerindian and Portuguese. He lets go of the rail and strolls towards the prow of the ship. His eyes never leave the horizon. Not once does he look back as the land recedes away behind him, because

In England there is a library that contains all the books in the world, a cathedral of knowledge the interior of whose dome shimmers gold from the lettering on spines of ancient volumes.

In England there are theatres and concert halls and galleries hung from ceiling to floor with magnificent gold-framed paintings and all of these are peopled by men in black silk opera hats and women with skins like cream of coconut.

In England there are museums which house the giant skeletons of dinosaurs whose breastbones flute into a ribcage as lofty and vast as the stone ribs inside Westminster Abbey, which he has seen on a post-card.

This is what will happen.

He will disembark in the industrial docks of Liverpool to the delicious shock of seeing, for the first time, white men working with their hands.

For a year he will study law at the Inns of Court in London.

In the Great War of Europe, two of the fingers of his left hand will be torn off by shrapnel. A bluish wound will disfigure the calf of his leg. The thundering of the artillery will render him stone deaf in one ear and after a period of rehabilitation in Shorncliffe, Kent, he will be returned to his native land where his mother, brothers and sisters wait for him on the veranda. He brings with him a letter signed by the King of England which his mother frames and hangs in the living-room. It says:

'A Grateful Mother Country Thanks You For Your Sacrifice.'

They are drenched with spray, Wat, his father and six of the crew, clinging to the rocks at the base of the giant falls of Kaeitur, a waterfall so enormous that it makes the sound of a thousand bells as the column of water falls thousands of feet to the River Potaro below. Each one of them is exhausted, but above all, perplexed. For two weeks they have travelled upriver led by an Arawak° guide. Before they set off they explained carefully to him through an interpreter that they were seeking the mountain of crystal. And this is where he has brought them.

'I'm coming on November the sixth,' I yell down the phone to Evelyn. 'I'll go to see my aunts in New Amsterdam for a couple of days then I'll come and stay with you.'

'That is good.' Evelyn's voice is faint and crackly. 'Bring a Gestetner machine with you. They need one at the party headquarters. Really we need

Arawak: indigenous people found mostly in tropical rain forested areas north of the Amazon

a computer but that costs thousands of dollars. We'll pay you for it when you reach.'

'OK Evelyn. I'll see you in two weeks' time. I can't wait. Bye.'

'Bye. Don't forget ink and paper.'

I lie back on the bed wiggling my toes and thinking of Evelyn. She is a stockily built black woman of thirty-six, a financial wizard in the pin-ball economy of the country. She will never leave. Her house is set back a little from the road. On every side of its white-painted exterior, tiers of Demerara shutters open, bottom out, stiff sails designed to catch the last breath of wind. I try to imagine whereabouts she is in the house. She has a cordless telephone now so she could be anywhere—in the kitchen perhaps or wandering about upstairs. When the trade winds blow the upper floors of the house are full of air encrusted with salt and at night the house creaks like a ship resting at anchor in the city of wooden dreams, a city built on stilts, belonging neither to land nor to sea but to land reclaimed from the sea.

Beneath his father's framed certificate from the King of England, a slim youth of nineteen leans his back against the dresser thinking:

'If I don't get out of this colony I shall suffocate.'

A problem has arisen over his leaving. His father and Mr. Wilkinson, his employer, are discussing it in the stifling inertia of midday. His father is frowning and flexing the stubs of his two fingers, as if they have pins and needles. Mr. Wilkinson is one of those gingery, peppery Englishmen whose long stay in the tropics has sucked all the moisture from him, leaving a dry sandy exterior. He too is frowning at the piece of paper in his hand.

'The trouble is with this damn birth certificate. The transfer to London went through all right. The Booker-McConnell people in London agreed to it, then, out of the blue, they ask for his birth certificate. Just a formality I suppose. All the same . . .'

His voice tails off into silence.

On the birth certificate, under the section marked 'Type' are written the words: 'Coloured. Native. Creole.'

The young man's eyes are solemn and watchful as he waits for his elders to find a solution. He has a recurring nightmare which is this: that Crab Island, the chunk of mud and jungle in the estuary of the Berbice River, grows to such enormous proportions that it blocks for ever his escape from New Amsterdam; that he is forced to stay in the stultifyingly dull town with its straggly cabbage palms and telegraph poles whose wires carry singing messages from nowhere to nowhere. He awakes from the dream sweating and in a claustrophobic panic.

In London there is jazz and the Café Royal.

In London you can skate across the Thames when it is frozen and there is snow snow snow in a million crystal flakes.

In London there are debonair, sophisticated, cosmopolitan men. It is impossible to *be* a real man until you have been to London.

He watches them sip their rum punches by the window. In the silence, music drifts up from the phonograph playing in the bottom-house:

The music goes round and round

Oh oh oh, Oh oh oh

And it comes out here.

Gazing at the three of them with blank disdainful eyes is the portrait of an Amerindian.

Mr. Wilkinson continues, embarrassed:

'Frankly, I don't expect it will make any difference, but I wouldn't like there to be any foul-up at this late stage. I'll tell you what we'll do. Have you got his baptism certificate? They don't put all this rubbish on the baptism certificate. I'll write a letter to London saying the birth certificate was destroyed by a fire in the records office. I'll enclose the baptism certificate instead. That should fix it. They won't bother once he's there.' He takes another swallow of his drink. 'I suppose they have to be careful. It is the City of London after all, where they set the Gold Standard for the world.' He winks.

The great and golden city is to be discovered in the heart of a large, rich and beautiful empire. The city is well proportioned and has many great towers. Throughout, there are laid out goodly gardens and parks, some of them containing ponds of excellent fish. There are, too, many squares where trading is done and markets are held for the buying and selling of all manner of wares: ornaments of gold, silver, lead, brass and copper; game, birds of every species, rabbits, hares and partridges; vegetables, fish and fruit.

In all the districts of this great city are many temples or houses for their idols.

In one part of the city they have built cages to house large numbers of lions, tigers, wolves, foxes and cats of various kinds.

There are yet other large houses where live many men and women with deformities and various maladies. Likewise there are people to look after them.

In some of these great towers are hollow statues of gold which seem giants and all manner of gold artefacts, even gold that seems like wooden logs to burn. Here dwell men who deal in markets of coffee and sugar and vast numbers of other like commodities. They have eyes in their shoulders, mouths in the middle of their breasts, a long train of hair grows backwards between their shoulders. They sit on finely made leather cushions and there are also men like porters to carry food to them on magnificent plates of gold and silver.

In the uppermost rooms of these towers, which are as we would call palaces, sit stockbrokers, their bodies anointed with white powdered gold blown through hollow canes until they are shining all over. Above their heads hang the skulls of dead company directors, all hung and decked with feathers. Here they sit drinking, hundreds of them together, for as many as six or seven days at a time.

I am squatting on the veranda in the hot yellow afternoon making spills for my grandfather. I tear strips from the *Berbice Advertiser* as he's shown me and fold them carefully into tiny pleats. In the yard is the Po' Boy tree which is supposed to be lucky. Children late for school stop to touch it and recite:

> Pity pity Po' Boy
>
> Sorry fi me
>
> If God don' help me
>
> The devil surely will.

My grandfather rests in his chair, one foot up on the long wooden arm. I want to please him so I place four spills for his pipe on the wicker table at his side but he hardly notices. I try to peek at the hand that has two fingers missing but it is folded in his lap in such a way that I can't see properly.

Aunt Rosa comes out of the living-room to give me a glass of soursop: 'Tomorrow your daddy is coming to take you back to England.'

'England. England. England,' I dance along the veranda.

'Come in out of the sun, chile. You're gettin' all burnt up. I will take you over to the da Silvas to play one last time.'

I stop short, filled with apprehension and start to scuff my shoe on the floor.

'I don' want to go.' I follow her inside where it is darker and cooler: 'What is this foolishness? Why you don' want to go?'

I don't want to tell her. I try to distract her attention from the da Silvas: 'What does my daddy do in London?'

'He works for Booker-McConnell, of course, in a big building called Plantation House in the City of London.' There is a note of pride in her voice which encourages me to lead her further away from the subject of the da Silvas:

'Will you show me the photograph of the men in London again?'

Aunt Rosa goes over to the large, carved oak dresser. She is darker than my father but with the same large creole eyes. Her black hair is in a roll at the front. On top of the dresser are some of my favourite objects: a tumbler full of glass swizzle sticks, a bell jar, glass goblets and, best of all, a garishly painted wooden Chinese god with a face like a gargoyle and a chipped nose. I hang around the edge fingering the carved roses while Aunt Rosa rummages in the drawer:

'Here it is. These men are very important. They are the men who meet every day to fix the price of sugar on the world market.'

She shows a photograph of dull, sombre-suited men with white faces gathered round a table and points to one of them:

"This is the man who owns the company your daddy works for.'

I try to look interested but I can feel the time running out. I am right.

'Now what is all this nonsense about the da Silvas?' she asks.

'I hate the da Silvas. They keep callin' me "ice-cream face".' And I burst into tears.

Later that night I lie in bed under a single sheet. The doors to the adjoining room are fixed back and I can hear Aunt Rosa talking to Mrs. Hunter:

'Look how she fair-skinned, Frank's daughter. No one would ever know. An' she complainin' about it.' They laugh and lower their voices, but I can still hear fragments. Mrs. Hunter is talking in a troubled voice about her brother:

'. . . the first coloured officer in the British Army . . . imagine how proud . . . other officers would not speak to him . . . the men refused to obey his orders . . . Some incident . . . trumped up, I tell you . . . an excuse . . . cashiered . . . the shock that ran through the family.' I hear the sob in her voice and Aunt Rosa hush-hushing her.

I creep out of bed towards the open doors. Moonlight floods over the leaves of the Molucca pear tree and spills through the jalousies on to the floor, a dark lake of polished wood. Stepping delicately over it is Salamander, the pale, golden gazelle of a cat, thin with pointy ears. He seems to be dancing some sort of minuet, extending each paw, then with a hop tapping the floor. Delighted, I move to take a closer look. And then I see it. Between his paws is a huge cockroach, a great black ugly thing lying on its back, its feelers moving this way and that. I must have squawked because there is a pause in the conversation, then Aunt Rosa says:

'Get back to bed, chile. If you look out of the window on a night like this you will see Moongazer at the cross-roads.'

'Hello, ice-cream face.' It is my father and he is laughing as he lifts me way up into the sky and sing-chants:

> Molasses, molasses
>
> Sticky sticky goo
>
> Molasses, molasses
>
> Will always stick to you.

My aunts, uncles and cousins are standing round by the wooden lattice at the front of the house. Everyone is laughing and I laugh too.

Some time afterwards, in England, I am playing with my doll Lucy in a garden full of browns and greys. Lucy's face is cracked like crazy paving because I left her out in the rain but I love her because her hair is the colour of golden syrup. The cockney boy who lives next door has climbed into the pear tree on his side of the fence and is intoning in a sneery voice:

'Your fahver looks like a monkey. Your fahver looks like a monkey.'

I go inside and tell my mother.

'Mum, Keith says Daddy looks like a monkey. And I think so too.'

My mother stops beating the cake mixture. She looks sad but not the way she looks when she is sad herself. It is the way she looks when she is teaching me what to be sad about:

'Ahh,' she says, as if I have grazed my knee. 'Well don't tell Daddy, you know he would be so hurt.'

They are lost, Wat, his father and the ragged remnants of the crew. They are paddling the small craft which the Arawaks have named 'the eight-legged sea-spider', and they are lost in a labyrinth of rivers, a confluence of streams that branch into rapids and then into more billowing waters all crossing the other, ebbing and flowing. They seem to travel far on the same spot so that it takes an hour to travel a stone's cast. The sun appears in the sky in three places at once and whether they attempt to use the sun as a guide or a compass they are carried in circles amongst a multitude of islands.

I am fourteen and back from England for the summer. My friend Gail Fraser has pestered and pestered her mother to cook labba for me before I return.

Now we sit at the dinner table, Gail's great-aunt Bertha, her mother, her brother Edmund, and me and Gail. Great-aunt Bertha is a yellow-skinned woman whose face is all caught up in leathery pouches under her white wavy hair. Gail's mother is square-jawed with iron-grey crinkly hair and she is too practical for my liking as I judge everybody by how much 'soul' they have. My friend Gail is honey-coloured and round as a butterball. She has brown almond eyes and curly brown hair and scores about eight out of ten for soul. We have spent most of the holiday lying on her bed exchanging passionate secrets and raiding the rumbly old fridge for plum-juice. My deepest secret is that I am so in love with her brother Edmund that I could die. Edmund has what I call a *crème de cacao* complexion, tight black curls, full lips with the first black hairs of a moustache. He is slim and has black eyes that are brimful of soul. I know he would respond to me if he would stop talking about cricket for ONE minute. As it is, I have to be content to breathe the same air as him, which is pretty nice in itself.

Gail and I are trying desperately not to scream out loud with laughter as great-aunt Bertha chides Edmund for not wearing his jacket:

'My father would not see the boys at dinner without their jackets.'

Dreadful snorts are coming out of Gail and Edmund is pulling faces. I can't look up. Gail is heaving and shaking next to me. Great-aunt Bertha turns to me:

'When I was in London I used to look after a sick. She was a real lady. I was her companion. I would have liked to stay in England. I asked to stay but they wouldn't let me.'

Gail explodes and runs out of the room. Her mother looks disapproving. I manage to hang on to myself.

That evening Edmund takes Gail and me in the rowing-boat to the middle of Canje Creek because Gail insists that I drink creek water and I won't drink from the edge because it's too muddy and slimy. We row out on to the midnight black and glittering waters of the creek. It is silent apart from a goat-sucker bird calling 'hoo yoo, hoo yoo' in the distance.

'This time tomorrow I'll be in London.'

'What will you be doing?' asks Gail.

'I don't know. I might be in a coffee bar with my friends playing the juke-box.'

'Play something for me.'

'What?'

'"Blue-suede shoes" by Elvis Presley.'

'Oh phooey that's old. They won't still have it.' I can tell that she is hurt. I am sitting behind Edmund. I kiss him on the back of his shoulder so lightly he doesn't notice. Gail grasses me up:

'She kissin' you, Edmund.' He ignores me.

I lean over the edge of the boat, cup my hands and scoop up some of the water. It is clear and refreshing.

'Now you must come back,' says Gail. 'Now you're bound to come back.' And her voice is full of spite.

Wearied and scorched, they bury Wat as best they can in the muddy bank of the creek. His father's demeanour is grim and he says no prayers. They just sit around for a bit. After they have gone, dead leaves, twigs, bark and moss begin to float and fall on to the burial spot, the first signs of rain. Seed-pods plummet and burst on the water and heavy raindrops start to pock the surface of the creek. Out on the lake torrential rains flatten the reeds at the water's edge. Everything turns grey. Wat's body, loosened from its grave, begins a quest of its own through the network of creeks and streams and rivers.

A month later, Wat's father gives up his search for the tantalizing city of El Dorado and writes in his log:

'It's time to leave Guiana to the sun whom they worship and steer northwards.'

I am back at last. The old metal bucket of a ferry dips in the sweet brown waters of the Berbice River, passes Crab Island and ties up at the stelling.

I walk through the town to the house. The Po' Boy tree is still there but the house looks ramshackle, sagging on its rigid wooden stilts, the wood where the paint has peeled, grey from the sun.

I haven't told my aunts I'm coming. I'm going to surprise them. I go up the steps to the front door and announce myself through the open slats of the jalousies. There is no sign of life.

'It's me. Frank's daughter,' I say, in case in their old age they have forgotten my name.

Through the slatted door I see a shape. It is one of my aunts. She doesn't open the door. I peer through. She is swaying and wringing her hands.

'Avril. It's me. Open the door.'

I can hear her moaning softly:

'Oh this is disastrous. Oh this is disastrous. Deep trouble. We in deep trouble.'

Finally she opens the door. I hear Aunt Rosa's voice on the telephone, shriller than I remembered it:

'I tell you it's a plot, Laura. They're lying to you. They're all on drugs. Don' believe them.' She hangs up and turns around. Both of them are neatly dressed in blouses and slacks. Aunt Rosa's hair is still in the same black roll at the front but her face has shrunk with age and her eyes are blazing:

'So you've come back. I suppose you want our money. Well you're unlucky. We haven't got any.'

We go into the living-room. The place is in dusty disorder. Aunt Rosa stands by the window, angry and troubled:

'I didn't want you to see us like this. Why did you come? We all busted up over here. The family is all busted up. Laura is in the hospital with some kinda sclerosis. She's twisted up in the bed like a hermit crab and all the doctors and nurses are on drugs, I can see it in their eyes.'

Avril is moving about, muttering, picking up things and putting them down again, pulling at the frizzy hair round her dark impassive face:

'STOP STILL FOR ONE MINUTE WILL YOU, AVRIL?' screams Aunt Rosa. 'Your niece is here from England. Don't you remember her? We raised her and then she left.'

'Where's Auntie Florence?' I asked timidly.

'We had to send her up to Canada to your Uncle Bertie's. She livin' in the past. She talkin' to the dead. She thinks they're still alive. She anxious and upset all the time. She thought everything in the house was on fire. Even us, her sisters. She saw us burnin' up burnin' up like paper, black with a red edge. Paper sisters. She's turned into a screwball.'

She moves over to the sofa and sits there gripping her walking-stick and turning it round and round. I try to think of somebody who could help:

'What about the Frasers? Do you still see them?'

'Oh they left a long time ago, Toronto, New Orleans, somewhere. They all left. I didn't think my brothers would leave but they did. They all left and married white, street-walkin' bitches. They left us behind because we were too dark.'

She leans forward and speaks passionately:

'I loved my brothers. My brothers are innocent. It's their wives that keep them from us. Especially that red-headed bitch that stole Bertie. Mind you, Bertie could charm a cobra. Bertie could charm a camoodie. She drugs Bertie, you know, so that he can't come back.'

She sniffs the air:

'I can smell somethin',' she says suddenly.

'What?'

'Somethin' I shouldn't be smellin',' she snaps. She is glaring at me suspiciously:

'You don' look like you used to.'

'How not?'

'You used to have brown eyes.'

'No I didn't. Look, there's a photo of me on the dresser. I always had blue eyes.' I go and get it. It's dusty like everything else. The sight of it throws her into a venomous rage:

'Just because you've got white skin and blue eyes you think you haven't got coloured blood in you. But you have. Just like me. It's in your veins. You can't escape from it. There's mental illness in the family too.'

I am shocked. She continues in an unstoppable outburst:

'You sent your father's ashes back here because he had mixed blood. You were too ashamed to let him stay in England. And you're black-mailing your cousin over there for the same reason. If anyone finds out he'll lose his job! Why do you do these terrible things? You were a nice chile. Why do you do all these terrible things?'

'Do you have anything to drink in the fridge?' My stomach is churning.

'I don't know. Go and look. Everything's gone middly-muddly over here.'

I open the fridge door and recoil. Inside, the contents are webbed with mould from all the electricity cuts. I go back to the living-room:

'Tomorrow I'll fix for somebody to come in and help you.'

'We don' want strangers pokin' their noses in, seeing what's happened to us.' She lowers her head then jerks it up:

'Your father's skin was whiter than mine. If he'd been my colour your mother never would have married him!'

'Rosa. We're in the nineteen-eighties. Nobody cares about that sort of thing any more.'

'You think I'm crazy?' she sneers. I go over to Avril to give her a hug. She pushes me away:

'I'm not the affectionate type,' she says. 'Oh, this is terrible. This is awful.'

'AVRIL YOU'RE A DONKEY,' shouts Aunt Rosa. 'She's mentally ill too. She's ashamed of her illness. She hasn't left the house for a year. She too frighten'. I do the shopping. Everything was fine until January the fifth, then it all stopped.' Avril starts to mumble a litany of potential disasters:

'What will happen when she leaves? There will be all those people in the street. What will she do? And it might rain. She might get wet.'

'I hope she melts,' snarls Aunt Rosa.

Suddenly, she puts her head in her hands:

'I don' know what's happened to us,' she says.

That night I try and sleep. The room is musty. The sheet is damp with humidity. The mosquito net has holes all over. Through the night I hear one or other of them pacing the house. I half-sleep and doze because it gets into my head that they might set fire to my room.

It is evening when I reach Georgetown. The great house is just as I remember it.

The sight of Evelyn at the door fills me with relief. I notice the fine net of grey over the coarse tight curls.

'Goodness, Evelyn. My aunts have gone crazy in New Amsterdam.'

'So I hear. Well you know what they say. All the mad people are in Berbice. You should come back here for good. Not just for your aunts. There is so much to do here to turn this country round.'

I follow her up the old circular wooden staircase. Sitting on the steps half-way up is a black woman in a loose skirt. Next to her are two sacks marked: "US Famine Aid. Destination Ethiopia.' Evelyn sees my curious stare:

'You are shocked? She's a smuggler from the Corentyne°. We past shame in this country. There are people for whom crime is still a shock. We way past that stage. Way past. That is wheat flour she tryin' to sell.'

We go into the large kitchen and Evelyn fetches me a glass of freshly squeezed grapefruit juice. It tastes deliciously bitter and cool after the hot journey.

'Have you got a match, Evelyn?' I'm waving a cigarette in the air.

'You din' bring matches?' She laughs. 'You have forgotten what it is like to live in a country that is bankrupt. There is no milk in the country. Dried milk costs twelve US dollars a bag. Money has left the banks. Money is dancin' around in the streets. The black market rules here now. Come and I will show you which room you are staying in. The others are in a political meeting downstairs. They said they will see you in the morning.'

In my room I fix the mosquito net. Evelyn is leaning against the door jamb:

'You have everything you need?'

'Yes. Thanks. I'm going to bed, now. I'm exhausted. We'll talk in the morning.'

'You know,' says Evelyn, 'you should stay. If the party could get hold of two hundred thousand US dollars we could turn this country round. I will get it somehow. I am telling you, this place could be a paradise.'

After she has gone I peer through the jalousies. Outside is a sugar-apple tree and dragon-tongue shrubs by the brick path below. In the yard I can see the rusted shells of two cars.

Corentyne: the river which separates Guyana from Surinam

Ben Okri

born in Minna, Nigeria, Ben Okri has lived and worked in England since he was eighteen. He began his post-secondary education in Nigeria (at Urhobo College) and went on to attend the University of Essex in Colchester, England. Although he says his childhood has exercised a substantial influence on his writing, he has declined to furnish details about it, referring readers instead to his fiction.

The author of three novels in addition to a number of poetry and short story collections, Okri is considered one of Africa's foremost contemporary writers. In 1991 he received Britain's most prestigious literary award, the Booker Prize, for his novel *The Famished Road*, firmly establishing his international reputation and, as Jane Bryce observes, marking "a new direction in the evaluation and reception of African writing by the British public and literary establishment" (1).

Okri's focus on the narratives of "the dispossessed and disenfran-chised," together with his combining of African and European elements (the "hybrid" nature of his fiction), place him in the context of postmodernism. Henry Louis Gates, Jr. points to the experimental nature of Okri's writing as a departure in African fiction in which formal or aesthetic experimentation has historically been eschewed in favour of the exploration of politically important themes such as identity, the affirmation of native culture and the struggle against colonialism and its aftermath. Okri's agenda remains emphatically political but he has also "experiment[ed] with literary forms" in his pursuit of it.

The Famished Road is characterized by a number of elements which can also be found in "Incidents at the Shrine": the movement between realism and the depiction of a mythic world; the contrast between an urban environment and a rural one which is "the site of otherness, of magic, the supernatural, the unconscious, the spirit world on the margins of human existence yet interconnected with it" (Bryce 2); and the positive, life-affirming nature of the story's resolution. Lying at the heart of both works is the struggle of the poor and victimized to make sense of lives which are constantly deformed by disaster.

Any consideration of Okri as an African writer inevitably raises the question of authenticity. Jane Bryce wonders if *The Famished Road*, "written and published outside Africa, in a colonial language, for an audience which cannot be narrowly defined, [can] be considered 'African'?" Her conclusion—that the novel must be seen within the context of other fiction being written by immigrant and second-generation writers—springs from a recognition that "the post-modern, post-colonial condition, of which the novel is so clearly a marker, is one of fluid cross-cultural interconnection and dissolution of boundaries" (1) in which concepts such as identity and home are constantly being redefined. In such a context, perhaps the question of "authenticity" no longer has any meaning.

Works Cited

Bryce, Jane. "Review of The Famished Road."
   www.bbc.co.uk/education/archive/windrush.famished.shtml

Gates, Henry Louis, Jr. "Between the Living and the Unborn." *The New York Times Book Review* 13 Aug. 1989: 3, 20.
   www.uwev.ucsb.edu/rbbo/academic/projects/okri/gates.html

Other Sources and Weblinks

Ben Okri.
   www.uweb.ucsb.edu/rbbo/academic/projects/okri/life.html

Wambu, Onyekachi, ed. *Hurricane Hits England: An Anthology of Writing About Black Britain*. New York: Continuum, 2000.

Incidents at the Shrine

Anderson had been waiting for something to fall on him. His anxiety was such that for the first time in several years he went late to work. It was just his luck that the Head of Department had chosen that day for an impromptu inspection. When he got to the museum he saw that his metal chair had been removed from its customary place. The little stool on which he rested his feet after running endless errands was also gone. His official messenger's uniform had been taken off the hook. He went to the main office and was told by one of the clerks that he had been sacked, and that the supervisor was not available. Anderson started to protest, but the clerk got up and pushed him out of the office.

He went aimlessly down the corridors of the Department of Antiquities. He stumbled past the visitors to the museum. He wandered amongst the hibiscus and bougainvillea. He didn't look at the ancestral stoneworks in the museum field. Then he went home, dazed, confused by objects, convinced that he saw many fingers pointing at him. He went down streets he had never seen in his life and he momentarily forgot where his compound was.

When he got home he found that he was trembling. He was hungry. He hadn't eaten that morning and the cupboard was empty of food. He couldn't stop thinking about the loss of his job. Anderson had suspected for some time that the supervisor had been planning to give his job to a distant relation. That was the reason why the supervisor was always berating him on the slightest pretext. Seven years in the city had begun to make Anderson feel powerless because he didn't belong to the important societies, and didn't have influential relatives. He spent the afternoon thinking about his condition in the world. He fell asleep and dreamt about his dead parents.

He woke up feeling bitter. It was late in the afternoon and he was hungry. He got out of bed and went to the market to get some beef and tripe for a pot of stew. Anderson slid through the noise of revving motors and shouting traders. He came to the goatsellers. The goats stood untethered in a small corral. As Anderson went past he had a queer feeling that the goats were staring at him. When he stopped and looked at them the animals panicked. They kicked and fought backwards. Anderson hurried on till he found himself at the meat stalls.

The air was full of flies and the stench was overpowering. He felt ill. There were intestines and bones in heaps on the floor. He was haggling the price of tripe when he heard confused howls from the section where they sold generators and videos. The meat-seller had just slapped the tripe down on the table and was telling him to go somewhere else for the price he offered, when the fire burst out with an explosion. Flames poured over the stalls. Waves of screaming people rushed in Anderson's direction. He saw the fire flowing behind them, he saw black smoke. He started to run before the people reached him.

He heard voices all around him. Dry palm fronds crackled in the air. Anderson ducked under the bare eaves of a stall, tripped over a fishmonger's basin of writhing eels, and fell into a mound of snailshells. He struggled back up. He ran past the fortune-tellers and the amulet traders. He was shouldering his way through the bamboo poles of the lace-sellers when it struck him with amazing clarity that the fire was intent upon him because he had no power to protect himself. And soon the fire was everywhere. Suddenly, from the midst of voices in the smoke, Anderson heard someone calling his names. Not just the one name, the ordinary one which made things easier in the city—Anderson; he heard all the others as well, even the ones he had forgotten: Jeremiah, Ofuegbu, Nutcracker, Azzi. He was so astonished that when he cut himself, by brushing his thigh against two rusted nails, he did not know how profusely he bled till he cleared out into the safety of the main road. When he got home he was still bleeding. When the bleeding ceased, he felt that an alien influence had insinuated itself into his body, and an illness took over.

He became so ill that most of the money he had saved in all the years of humiliation and sweat went into the hands of the quack chemists of the area. They bandaged his wound. They gave him tetanus injections with curved syringes. They gave him pills in squat, silvery bottles. Anderson was reduced to creeping about the compound, from room to toilet and back again, as though he were terrified of daylight. And then, three days into the illness, with the taste of alum stale in his mouth, he caught a glimpse of himself in the mirror. He saw the gaunt face of a complete stranger. Two days later, when he felt he had recovered sufficiently, Anderson packed his box and fled home to his village.

The Image-Maker

Anderson hadn't been home for a long time. When the lorry driver dropped him at the village junction, the first things he noticed were the ferocity of the heat and the humid smell of rotting vegetation. He went down the dirt track that led to the village. A pack of dogs followed him for a short while and then disappeared. Cowhorns and the beating of drums sounded from the forest. He saw masks, eaten by insects, along the grass verge.

He was sweating when he got to the obeche tree where, during the war, soldiers had shot a woman thought to be a spy. Passing the well which used to mark the village boundary, he became aware of three rough forms running after him. They had flaming red eyes and they shouted his names.

"Anderson! Ofuegbu!"

He broke into a run. They bounded after him.

"Ofuegbu! Anderson!"

In his fear he ran so hard that his box flew open. Scattered behind him were his clothes, his medicines, and the modest gifts he had brought to show his people that he wasn't entirely a small man in the world. He discarded the box and sped on without looking back. Swirls of dust came towards him. And when he emerged from the dust, he saw the village.

It was sunset. Anderson didn't stop running till he was safely in the village. He went on till he came to the pool office with the signboard that read: MR. ABAS AND CO. LICENSED COLLECTOR. Outside the office, a man sat in a depressed cane chair. His eyes stared divergently at the road and he snored gently. Anderson stood panting. He wanted to ask directions to his uncle's place, but he didn't want to wake the owner of the pool office.

Anderson wasn't sure when the man woke up, for suddenly he said: "Why do you have to run into our village like a madman?"

Anderson struggled for words. He was sweating.

"You disturb my eyes when you come running into our village like that."

Anderson wiped his face. He was confused. He started to apologize, but the man looked him over once, and fell back into sleep, with his eyes still open. Anderson wasn't sure what to do. He was thirsty. With sweat dribbling down his face, Anderson tramped on through the village.

Things had changed since he'd been away. The buildings had lost their individual colours to that of the dust. Houses had moved several yards from where they used to be. Roads ran diagonally to how he remembered them. He felt he had arrived in a place he had almost never known.

Exhausted, Anderson sat on a bench outside the market. The roadside was full of ants. The heat mists made him sleepy. The market behind him was empty, but deep within it he heard celebrations and arguments. He listened to alien voices and languages from the farthest reaches of the world. Anderson fell asleep on the bench and dreamt that he was being carried through the village by the ants. He woke to find himself inside the pool office. His legs itched.

The man whom he had last seen sitting in the cane chair, was now behind the counter. He was mixing a potion of local gin and herbs. There was someone else in the office: a stocky man with a large forehead and a hardened face.

He stared at Anderson and then said: "Have you slept enough?"

Anderson nodded. The man behind the counter came round with a tumbler full of herbal mixtures.

Almost forcing the drink down Anderson's throat, he said: "Drink it down. Fast!"

Anderson drank most of the mixture in one gulp. It was very bitter and bile rushed up in his mouth.

"Swallow it down!"

Anderson swallowed. His head cleared a little and his legs stopped itching.

The man who had given him the drink said: "Good." Then he pointed to the other man and said: "That's your uncle. Our Image-maker. Don't you remember him?"

Anderson stared at the Image-maker's face. The lights shifted. The face was elusively familiar. Anderson had to subtract seven years from the awesome starkness of the Image-maker's features before he could recognize his own uncle.

Anderson said: "My uncle, you have changed!"

"Yes, my son, and so have you," his uncle said.

"I'm so happy to see you," said Anderson.

Smiling, his uncle moved into the light at the doorway. Anderson saw that his left arm was shrivelled.

"We've been expecting you," his uncle said.

Anderson didn't know what to say. He looked from one to the other. Then suddenly he recognized Mr. Abas, who used to take him fishing down the village stream.

"Mr. Abas! It's you!"

"Of course it's me. Who did you think I was?"

Anderson stood up.

"Greetings, my elders. Forgive me. So much has changed."

His uncle touched him benevolently on the shoulder and said: "That's all right. Now, let's go."

Anderson persisted with his greeting. Then he began to apologize for his bad memory. He told them that he had been pursued at the village boundary.

"They were strange people. They pursued me like a common criminal."

The Image-maker said: "Come on. Move. We don't speak of strange things in our village. We have no strange things here. Now, let's go."

Mr. Abas went outside and sat in his sunken cane chair. The Image-maker led Anderson out of the office.

They walked through the dry heat. The chanting of worshippers came from the forest. Drums and jangling bells sounded faintly in the somnolent air.

"The village is different," Anderson said.

The Image-maker was silent.

"What has happened here?"

"Don't ask questions. In our village we will provide you with answers before it is necessary to ask questions," the Image-maker said with some irritation.

Anderson kept quiet. As they went down the village Anderson kept looking at the Image-maker: the more he looked, the more raw and godlike the Image-maker seemed. It was as though he had achieved an independence from human agencies. He looked as if he had been cast in rock, and left to the wilds.

"The more you look, the less you see," the Image-maker said.

It sounded, to Anderson, like a cue. They had broken into a path. Ahead of them were irregular rows of soapstone monoliths. Embossed with abstract representations of the human figure, the monoliths ranged from the babies of their breed to the abnormally large ones. There were lit candles and varied offerings in front of them. There were frangipani and iroko trees in their midst. There were also red-painted poles which had burst into flower.

His uncle said: "The images were originally decorated with pearls, lapis lazuli, amethysts and magic glass which twinkled wonderful philosophies. But the pale ones from across the seas came and stole them. This was whispered to me in a dream."

Anderson gazed at the oddly elegant monoliths and said: "You resemble the gods you worship."

His uncle gripped him suddenly.

"We don't speak of resemblances in our village, you hear?"

Anderson nodded. His uncle relaxed his grip. They moved on.

After a while his uncle said: "The world is the shrine and the shrine is the world. Everything must have a centre. When you talk rubbish, bad things fly into your mouth."

They passed a cluster of huts. Suddenly the Image-maker bustled forward. They had arrived at the main entrance to a circular clay shrinehouse. The Image-maker went to the niche and brought out a piece of native chalk, a tumbler and a bottle of herbs. He made a mash which he smeared across Anderson's forehead. On a nail above the door, there was a bell which the Image-maker rang three times.

A voice called from within the hut.

The Image-maker sprayed himself forth in a list of his incredible names and titles. Then he requested permission to bring to the shrine an afflicted "son of the soil."

The voices asked if the "son of the soil" was ready to come in.

The Image-maker was silent.

A confusion of drums, bells, cowhorns, came suddenly from within. Anderson fainted.

Then the Image-maker said to the voices: "He is ready to enter!"

They came out and found that Anderson was light. They bundled him into the shrinehouse and laid him on a bed of congealed palm oil.

The Image

When Anderson came to he could smell burning candles, sweat and incense. Before him was the master Image, a hallucinatory warrior monolith decorated in its original splendour of precious stones and twinkling glass. At its base were roots, kola nuts and feathers. When Anderson gazed at the master Image he heard voices that were not spoken and he felt drowsiness come over him.

Candles burned in the mist of blue incense. A small crowd of worshippers danced and wove Anderson's names in songs. Down the corridors he could hear other supplicants crying out in prayer for their heart's desires, for their afflictions and problems. They prayed like people who are ill and who are never sure of recovering. It occurred to Anderson that it must be a cruel world to demand such intensity of prayer.

Anderson tried to get up from the bed, but couldn't. The master Image seemed to look upon him with a grotesque face. The ministrants closed in around him. They praised the master Image in songs. The Image-maker gave a sudden instruction and the ministrants rushed to Anderson. They spread out their multiplicity of arms and embraced Anderson in their hard compassions. But when they touched Anderson he screamed and shouted in hysteria. The ministrants embraced him with their remorseless arms and carried him through the corridors and out into the night. They rushed him past the monoliths outside. They took him past creeks and waterholes. When they came to a blooming frangipani tree, they dumped him on the ground.

Then they retreated with flutters of their smocks, and disappeared as though the darkness were made of their own substance.

Anderson heard whispers in the forest. He heard things falling among the branches. Then he heard footsteps that seemed for ever approaching. He soon saw that it was Mr. Abas. He carried a bucket in one hand and a lamp in the other. He dropped the bucket near Anderson.

"Bathe of it," Mr. Abas said, and returned the way he had come.

Anderson washed himself with the treated water. When he finished the attendants came and brought him fresh clothes. Then they led him back to the shrinehouse.

The Image-maker was waiting for him. Bustling with urgency, his bad arm moving restlessly like the special instrument of his functions, the Image-maker grabbed Anderson and led him to an alcove.

He made Anderson sit in front of a door. There was a hole greased with palm oil at the bottom of the door. The Image-maker shouted an instruction and the attendants came upon Anderson and held him face down. They pushed him towards the hole; they forced his head and shoulders through it.

In the pain Anderson heard the Image-maker say: "Tell us what you see!"

Anderson couldn't see anything. All he could feel was the grinding pain. Then he saw a towering tree. There was a door on the tree trunk. Then he saw a thick blue pall. A woman emerged from the pall. She was painted over in native chalk. She had bangles all the way up her arms. Her stomach and waist were covered in beads.

"I see a woman," he cried.

Several voices asked: "Do you know her?"

"No."

"Is she following you?"

"I don't know."

"Is she dead?"

"I don't know."

"Is she dead?"

"No!"

There was the merriment of tinkling bells.

"What is she doing?"

She had come to the tree and opened the door. Anderson suffered a fresh agony. She opened a second door and tried the third one, but it didn't open. She tried again and when it gave way with a crash Anderson finally came through—but he lost consciousness.

Afterwards, they fed him substantially. Then he was allowed the freedom to move round the village and visit some of his relations. In the morning the Image-maker sent for him. The attendants made him sit on a cowhide mat and they shaved off his hair. They lit red and green candles and made music around him. Then the Image-maker proceeded with the extraction of impurities from his body. He rubbed herbal juices into Anderson's shoulder. He bit into the flesh and pulled out a rusted little padlock which he spat into an enamel bowl. He inspected the padlock. After he had washed out his mouth, he bit into Anderson's shoulder again and pulled out a crooked needle. He continued like this till he had pulled out a piece of broken glass, a twisted nail, a cowrie, and a small key. There was some agitation as to whether the key would fit the padlock, but it didn't.

When the Image-maker had finished he picked up the bowl, jangled the objects, and said: "All these things, where do they come from? Who sent them into you?"

Anderson couldn't say anything.

The Image-maker went on to cut light razor strokes on Anderson's arm and he rubbed protective herbs into the bleeding marks. He washed his hands and went out of the alcove. He came back with a pouch, which he gave to Anderson with precise instructions of its usage.

Then he said: "You are going back to the city tomorrow. Go to your place of work, collect the money they are owing you, and look for another job. You will have no trouble. You understand?"

Anderson nodded.

"Now, listen. One day I went deep into the forest because my arm hurt. I injured it working in a factory. For three days I was in the forest praying to our ancestors. I ate leaves and fishes. On the fourth day I forgot how I came there. I was lost and everything was new to me. On the fifth day I found the Images. They were hidden amongst the trees and tall grasses. Snakes and tortoises were all around. My pain stopped. When I found my way back and told the elders of the village what I had seen they did not believe me. The Images had been talked about in the village for a long time but no one had actually seen them. That is why they made me the Image-maker."

He paused, then continued.

"Every year, around this time, spirits from all over the world come to our village. They meet at the marketplace and have heated discussions about everything under the sun. Sometimes they gather round our Images outside. On some evenings there are purple mists round the iroko tree. At night we listen to all the languages, all the philosophies, of the world. You must come home now and again. This is where you derive power. You hear?"

Anderson nodded. He hadn't heard most of what was said. He had been staring at the objects in the enamel bowl.

The Image-Eaters

Anderson ate little through the ceremonies that followed the purification of his body. After all the dancing and feasting to the music of cowhorns and tinkling bells, they made him lie down before the master Image. Then the strangest voice he had ever heard thundered the entire shrinehouse with its full volume.

"ANDERSON! OFEUGBU! YOU ARE A SMALL MAN. YOU CANNOT RUN FROM YOUR FUTURE. GOVERNMENTS CANNOT EXIST WITHOUT YOU. ALL THE DISASTERS OF THE WORLD REST ON YOU AND HAVE YOUR NAME. THIS IS YOUR POWER."

The ministrants gave thanks and wept for joy.

Anderson spent the night in the presence of the master Image. He dreamt that he was dying of hunger and that there was nothing left in the world to eat. When Anderson ate of the master Image he was surprised at its sweetness. He was surprised also that the Image replenished itself.

In the morning Anderson's stomach was bloated with an imponderable weight. Shortly before his departure the Image-maker came to him and suggested that he contribute to the shrine fund. When Anderson made his donation, the Image-maker gave his blessing. The ministrants prayed for him and sang of his destiny.

Anderson had just enough money to get him back to the city. When he was ready to leave, Anderson felt a new heaviness come upon him. He thanked his uncle for everything and made his way through the village.

He stopped at the pool office. Mr. Abas was in his sunken cane chair, his eyes pursuing their separate lines of vision. Anderson wasn't sure if Mr. Abas was asleep.

He said: "I'm leaving now."

"Leaving us to our hunger, are you?"

"There is hunger where I am going," Anderson said.

Mr. Abas smiled and said: "Keep your heart pure. Have courage. Suffering cannot kill us. And travel well."

"Thank you."

Mr. Abas nodded and soon began to snore. Anderson went on towards the junction.

As he walked through the heated gravity of the village Anderson felt like an old man. He felt that his face had stiffened. He had crossed the rubber plantation, had crossed the boundary, and was approaching the junction, when the rough forms with blazing eyes fell upon him. He fought them off. He lashed out with his stiffened hands and legs. They could easily have torn him to pieces, because their ferocity was greater than his. There was a moment in which he saw himself dead. But they suddenly stopped and stared at him. Then they pawed him, as though he had become allied with them in some way. When they melted back into the heat mists, Anderson experienced the new simplicity of his life, and continued with his journey.

To explain why we become attached to our birthplaces we pretend that we are trees and speak of roots. Look under your feet. You will not find gnarled growths spouting through the soles. Roots, I sometimes think, are a conservative myth, designed to keep us in our places.

—Salman Rushdie, *Shame*

I'm not interested in an idealised, romantic vision of India. I know it is the great pitfall of the exile . . . There have been many losses in this last decade but the loss of the easy return to India has been for me an absolute anguish, an inescapable anguish. I feel as if I've lost a limb . . .

—Rushdie, "A Fantasy Called India"

In the work of Salman Rushdie, a number of the themes of this book come together. One of the most eloquent tellers of what he has called "migrants' tales," he describes *The Satanic Verses* as "a novel about the act of migration and . . . about the internal effect of migration" (Kadzis 6). In stories and novels he has explored the nature of identity, particularly for those who have immigrated, and thus "come unstuck . . . floated upwards from history from memory, from Time."(*Shame* 91). A native speaker of Urdu, he has defended the use of English, a colonial language, in India and argued that Indian English (the literary use of which he has pioneered) is as valid a dialect as Irish or American or Caribbean English. In numerous essays and articles he has attacked prejudice and racism both in England and in India, where there is considerable support for the idea of a homogenous, Hindu nation. There is scarcely an idea or a theme discussed by cultural critics and theorists upon which Rushdie has not touched.

Rushdie's fame has, unfortunately, more to do with the banning of his 1988 novel, *The Satanic Verses*, by a number of Islamic countries which deemed it blasphemous, and the issuing of a fatwa, or edict, by the Iranian leader Ayatollah Khomeini, calling for his death. For several years Rushdie was forced to live in hiding and only gradually began to make unannounced appearances and to grant a few interviews. He has resumed a more public life since the lifting of the fatwa by the Iranian government in 1998, but there remain religious groups who consider it still in effect and it has taken a great deal of courage for him to live as openly as he does.

Rushdie certainly didn't need the religious controversy that developed around *The Satanic Verses* to acquire the attention of critics and the reading public. His second novel, *Midnight's Children* (1981), won him three literary awards, including the prestigious Booker Prize, and rave reviews from critics. Writing in *The New York Times*, Clarke Blaise announced that with its publication, "[t]he literary map of India is about to be redrawn" and commented, "*Midnight's Children* sounds like a continent finding its voice" (3).

Rushdie's writing is notable for its epic range, and its combining of surrealistic fantasy with historical and mythic allusion. His style has been described as "pungent," "coarse, knowing . . . and, above all, aggressive" (Kadzis 2). In his use of Indian English in his writing and his abandonment of the "cool" tone of restraint characteristic of much Anglo-Indian literature, his inclusion of elements of "pop" culture in serious literature, he has been tremendously influential for a whole generation of Indian writers. As Anita Desai comments, "*Midnight's Children* . . . seemed to set tongues free in India in an odd way. Suddenly, younger writers realized that they didn't need to write correct and perfect English in the English tradition, but they could use Indian English . . . a whole crop of younger [writers] . . . have all written I'm sure, whether they acknowledge it or not, under the influence of Rushdie" (Desai 172).

Works Cited

Blaise, Clarke. "A Novel of India's Coming of Age."
　　www.nytimes.com/books/99/04/18/specials/rushdie.html

Jussawalla, Feroza, and Reed Way Dasenbrock. "Interview with Anita Desai." *Interviews with Writers of the Post-Colonial World*. Jackson and London: University Press of Mississippi, 1992.

Kadzis, Peter. "Salman Speaks."
　　www.bostonphoenix.com/archive/books/99/05/06/SALMAN.
　　RUSHDIE.html

Rushdie, Salman. *Shame*. New York: Aventura/Vintage, 1984.

———, ed. *The Vintage Book of Indian Writing, 1947–1997*. London: Random House, 1997.

Other Sources and Weblinks

Rushdie, Salman. "A Fantasy Called India."
    www.india_today.com/itody/18081997/rushdie.html
"The Salon Interview: Salman Rushdie."
    www/salon.com/06/features/interview.html

Imaginary Homelands

An old photograph in a cheap frame hangs on a wall of the room where I work. It's a picture dating from 1946 of a house into which, at the time of its taking, I had not yet been born. The house is rather peculiar—a three-storeyed gabled affair with tiled roofs and round towers in two corners, each wearing a pointy tiled hat, 'The past is a foreign country,' goes the famous opening sentence of L.P. Hartley's novel *The Go-Between*, 'they do things differently there.' But the photograph tells me to invert this idea; it reminds me that it's my present that is foreign, and that the past is home, albeit a lost home in a lost city in the mists of lost time.

A few years ago I revisited Bombay, which is my lost city, after an absence of something like half my life. Shortly after arriving, acting on an impulse, I opened the telephone directory and looked for my father's name. And, amazingly, there it was; his name, our old address, the unchanged telephone number, as if we had never gone away to the unmentionable country across the border°. It was an eerie discovery. I felt as if I were being claimed, or informed that the facts of my faraway life were illusions, and that this continuity was the reality. Then I went to visit the house in the photograph and stood outside it, neither daring nor wishing to announce myself to its new owners. (I didn't want to see how they'd ruined the interior.) I was overwhelmed. The photograph had naturally been taken in black and white; and my memory, feeding on such images as this, had begun to see my childhood in the same way, monochromatically. The colours of my history had seeped out of my mind's eye; now my other two eyes were assaulted by colours, by the vividness of the red tiles, the yellow-edged green of cactus-leaves, the brilliance of bougainvillaea creeper. It is probably not too romantic to say that that was when my novel *Midnight's Children* was really born; when I realized how much I wanted to restore the past to myself, not in the faded greys of old family-album snapshots, but whole, in CinemaScope and glorious Technicolor.

the unmentionable country across the border: Pakistan

Bombay is a city built by foreigners upon reclaimed land; I, who had been away so long that I almost qualified for the title, was gripped by the conviction that I, too, had a city and a history to reclaim.

It may be that writers in my position, exiles or emigrants or expatriates, are haunted by some sense of loss, some urge to reclaim, to look back, even at the risk of being mutated into pillars of salt. But if we do look back, we must also do so in the knowledge—which gives rise to profound uncertainties—that our physical alienation from India almost inevitably means that we will not be capable of reclaiming precisely the thing that was lost; that we will, in short, create fictions, not actual cities or villages, but invisible ones, imaginary homelands, Indias of the mind.

Writing my book in North London, looking out through my window on to a city scene totally unlike the ones I was imagining on to paper, I was constantly plagued by this problem, until I felt obliged to face it in the text, to make clear that (in spite of my original and I suppose somewhat Proustian ambition to unlock the gates of lost time so that the past reappeared as it actually had been, unaffected by the distortions of memory) what I was actually doing was a novel of memory and about memory, so that my India was just that: 'my' India, a version and no more than one version of all the hundreds of millions of possible versions. I tried to make it as imaginatively true as I could, but imaginative truth is simultaneously honourable and suspect, and I knew that my India may only have been one to which I (who am no longer what I was, and who by quitting Bombay never became what perhaps I was meant to be) was, let us say, willing to admit I belonged.

This is why I made my narrator, Saleem, suspect in his narration; his mistakes are the mistakes of a fallible memory compounded by quirks of character and of circumstance, and his vision is fragmentary. It may be that when the Indian writer who writes from outside India tries to reflect that world, he is obliged to deal in broken mirrors, some of whose fragments have been irretrievably lost.

But there is a paradox here. The broken mirror may actually be as valuable as the one which is supposedly unflawed. Let me again try and explain this from my own experience. Before beginning *Midnight's Children*, I spent many months trying simply to recall as much of the Bombay of the 1950s and 1960s as I could; and not only Bombay—Kashmir, too, and Delhi and Aligarh, which, in my book, I've moved to Agra to heighten a certain joke about the Taj Mahal. I was genuinely amazed by how much came back to me. I found myself remembering what clothes people had worn on certain days, and school scenes, and whole passages of Bombay dialogue verbatim, or so it seemed; I even remembered advertisements, film-posters, the neon Jeep sign on Marine Drive, toothpaste ads for Binaca and for Kolynos, and a footbridge over the local railway line which bore, on one side, the legend 'Esso puts a tiger in your tank' and, on the other, the curiously contradictory admonition: 'Drive like Hell and you will get there.' Old songs came back to me from nowhere: a street entertainer's version of 'Good Night, Ladies', and, from the film *Mr 420* (a very appropriate source for my narrator to have used), the hit number 'Mera Joota Hai Japani'° which could almost be Saleem's theme song.

I knew that I had tapped a rich seam; but the point I want to make is that of course I'm not gifted with total recall, and it was precisely the partial nature of these memories, their fragmentation, that made them so evocative for me. The shards of memory acquired greater status, greater resonance, because they were *remains*; fragmentation made trivial things seem like symbols, and the mundane acquired numinous qualities. There is an obvious parallel here with archaeology. The broken pots of antiquity, from which the past can sometimes, but always provisionally, be reconstructed, are exciting to discover, even if they are pieces of the most quotidian objects.

It may be argued that the past is a country from which we have all emigrated, that its loss is part of our common humanity. Which seems to me self-evidently true; but I suggest that the writer who is out-of-country and even out-of-language may experience this loss in an intensified form. It is made more concrete for him by the physical fact of discontinuity, of his present being in a different place from his past, of his being 'elsewhere.' This may enable him to speak properly and concretely on a subject of universal significance and appeal.

But let me go further. The broken glass is not merely a mirror of nostalgia. It is also, I believe, a useful tool with which to work in the present.

John Fowles begins *Daniel Martin* with the words: 'Whole sight: or all the rest is desolation.' But human beings do not perceive things whole; we are not gods but wounded creatures, cracked lenses, capable only of fractured perceptions. Partial beings, in all the senses of that phrase. Meaning is a shaky edifice we build out of scraps, dogmas, childhood injuries, newspaper articles, chance remarks, old films, small victories, people hated, people loved; perhaps it is because our sense of what is the case is constructed from such inadequate materials that we defend it so

Mera joota hai Japani
Mera joota hai Japani
Yé patloon Inglistani
Sar pé lal topi Rusi—
Phir bhi dil hai Hindustani
—which translates roughly as:
O, my shoes are Japanese
These trousers English, if you please
On my head, red Russian hat—
My heart's Indian for all that

[This is also the song sung by Gibreel Farishta as he tumbles from the heavens at the beginning of *The Satanic Verses*.]—Rushdie's original footnote

fiercely, even to the death The Fowles position seems to me a way of succumbing to the guru-illusion. Writers are no longer sages, dispensing the wisdom of the centuries. And those of us who have been forced by cultural displacement to accept the provisional nature of all truths, all certainties, have perhaps had modernism forced upon us. We can't lay claim to Olympus, and are thus released to describe our worlds in the way in which all of us, whether writers or not, perceive it from day to day.

In *Midnight's Children,* my narrator Saleem uses, at one point, the metaphor of a cinema screen to discuss this business of perception: 'Suppose yourself in a large cinema, sitting at first in the back row, and gradually moving up, . . . until your nose is almost pressed against the screen. Gradually the stars' faces dissolve into dancing grain; tiny details assume grotesque proportions . . . it becomes clear that the illusion itself is reality.' The movement towards the cinema screen is a metaphor for the narrative's movement through time towards the present, and the book itself, as it nears contemporary events, quite deliberately loses deep perspective, becomes more 'partial.' I wasn't trying to write about (for instance) the Emergency in the same way as I wrote about events half a century earlier. I felt it would be dishonest to pretend, when writing about the day before yesterday, that it was possible to see the whole picture. I showed certain blobs and slabs of the scene.

I once took part in a conference on modern writing at New College, Oxford. Various novelists, myself included, were talking earnestly of such matters as the need for new ways of describing the world. Then the playwright Howard Brenton suggested that this might be a somewhat limited aim: does literature seek to do no more than to describe? Flustered, all the novelists at once began talking about politics.

Let me apply Brenton's question to the specific case of Indian writers, in England, writing about India. Can they do no more than describe, from a distance, the world that they have left? Or does the distance open any other doors?

These are of course political questions, and must be answered at least partly in political terms. I must say first of all that description is itself a political act. The black American writer Richard Wright once wrote that black and white Americans were engaged in a war over the nature of reality. Their descriptions were incompatible. So it is clear that redescribing a world is the necessary first step towards changing it. And particularly at times when the State takes reality into its own hands, and sets about distorting it, altering the past to fit its present needs, then the making of the alternative realities of art, including the novel of memory, becomes politicized. 'The struggle of man against power,' Milan Kundera has written, 'is the struggle of memory against forgetting.' Writers and politicians are natural rivals. Both groups try to make the world in their own images; they fight for the same territory. And the novel is one way of denying the official, politicians' version of truth.

The 'State truth' about the war in Bangladesh, for instance, is that no atrocities were committed by the Pakistani army in what was then the East Wing. This version is sanctified by many persons who would describe themselves as intellectuals. And the official version of the Emergency in India was well expressed by Mrs Gandhi in a recent BBC interview. She said that there were some people around who claimed that bad things had happened during the Emergency, forced sterilizations, things like that; but, she stated, this was all false. Nothing of this type had ever occurred. The interviewer, Mr Robert Kee, did not probe this statement at all. Instead he told Mrs Gandhi and the *Panorama* audience that she had proved, many times over, her right to be called a democrat.

So literature can, and perhaps must, give the lie to official facts. But is this a proper function of those of us who write from outside India? Or are we just dilettantes in such affairs, because we are not involved in their day-to-day unfolding, because by speaking out we take no risks, because our personal safety is not threatened? What right do we have to speak at all?

My answer is very simple. Literature is self-validating. That is to say, a book is not justified by its author's worthiness to write it, but by the quality of what has been written. There are terrible books that arise directly out of experience, and extraordinary imaginative feats dealing with themes which the author has been obliged to approach from the outside.

Literature is not in the business of copyrighting certain themes for certain groups. And as for risk: the real risks of any artist are taken in the work, in pushing the work to the limits of what is possible, in the attempt to increase the sum of what it is possible to think. Books become good when they go to this edge and risk falling over it—when they endanger the artist by reason of what he has, or has not, *artistically* dared.

So if I am to speak for Indian writers in England I would say this, paraphrasing G.V. Desani's H. Hatterr: The migrations of the fifties and sixties happened. 'We are. We are here.' And we are not willing to be excluded from any part of our heritage; which heritage includes both a Bradford-born Indian kid's right to be treated as a full member of British society, and also the right of any member of this post-diaspora community to draw on its roots for its art, just as all the world's community of displaced writers has always done. (I'm thinking, for instance, of Grass's Danzig-become-Gdansk, of Joyce's abandoned Dublin, of Isaac Bashevis Singer and Maxine Hong Kingston and Milan Kundera and many others. It's a long list.)

Let me override at once the faintly defensive note that has crept into these last few remarks. The Indian writer, looking back at India, does so through guilt-tinted spectacles. (I am of course, once more, talking about myself.) I am speaking now of those of us who emigrated. . . and I suspect that there are times when the move seems wrong to us all, when we seem, to ourselves, post-lapsarian men and women. We are Hindus who have crossed the black water; we are Muslims who eat pork°. And as a result—as

Hindus who have crossed . . . Muslims who eat pork: In traditional Hindu belief, it is taboo for Hindus to leave India—to cross the ocean—just as Islam forbids the eating of pork.

my use of the Christian notion of the Fall indicates—we are now partly of the West. Our identity is at once plural and partial. Sometimes we feel that we straddle two cultures; at other times, that we fall between two stools. But however ambiguous and shifting this ground may be, it is not an infertile territory for a writer to occupy. If literature is in part the business of finding new angles at which to enter reality, then once again our distance, our long geographical perspective, may provide us with such angles.

Or it may be that that is simply what we must think in order to do our work.

Midnight's Children enters its subject from the point of view of a secular man. I am a member of that generation of Indians who were sold the secular ideal. One of the things I liked, and still like, about India is that it is based on a non-sectarian philosophy. I was not raised in a narrowly Muslim environment; I do not consider Hindu culture to be either alien from me or more important than the Islamic heritage. I believe this has something to do with the nature of Bombay, a metropolis in which the multiplicity of commingled faiths and cultures curiously creates a remarkably secular ambience. Saleem Sinai makes use, eclectically, of whatever elements from whatever sources he chooses. It may have been easier for his author to do this from outside modern India than inside it.

I want to make one last point about the description of India that *Midnight's Children* attempts. It is a point about pessimism. The book has been criticised in India for its allegedly despairing tone. And the despair of the writer-from-outside may indeed look a little easy, a little pat. But I do not see the book as despairing or nihilistic. The point of view of the narrator is not entirely that of the author. What I tried to do was to set up a tension in the text, a paradoxical opposition between the form and content of the narrative. The story of Saleem does indeed lead him to despair. But the story is told in a manner designed to echo, as closely as my abilities allowed, the Indian talent for non-stop self-regeneration. This is why the narrative constantly throws up new stories, why it 'teems'. The form—multitudinous, hinting at the infinite possibilities of the country—is the optimistic counterweight to Saleem's personal tragedy. I do not think that a book written in such a manner can really be called a despairing work.

England's Indian writers are by no means all the same type of animal. Some of us, for instance, are Pakistani. Others Bangladeshi. Others West, or East, or even South African.

And V. S. Naipaul, by now, is something else entirely. This word 'Indian' is getting to be a pretty scattered concept. Indian writers in England include political exiles, first-generation migrants, affluent expatriates whose residence here is frequently temporary, naturalized Britons, and people born here who may never have laid eyes on the subcontinent. Clearly, nothing that I say can apply across all these categories. But one of the interesting things about this diverse community is that, as far as Indo-British fiction is concerned, its existence changes the ball game, because that fiction is in future going to come as much from addresses in London, Birmingham and Yorkshire as from Delhi or Bombay.

One of the changes has to do with attitudes towards the use of English. Many have referred to the argument about the appropriateness of this language to Indian themes. And I hope all of us share the view that we can't simply use the language in the way the British did; that it needs remaking for our own purposes. Those of us who do use English do so in spite of our ambiguity towards it, or perhaps because of that, perhaps because we can find in that linguistic struggle a reflection of other struggles taking place in the real world, struggles between the cultures within ourselves and the influences at work upon our societies. To conquer English may be to complete the process of making ourselves free.

But the British Indian writer simply does not have the option of rejecting English, anyway. His children, her children, will grow up speaking it, probably as a first language; and in the forging of a British Indian identity the English language is of central importance. It must, in spite of everything, be embraced. (The word 'translation' comes, etymologically, from the Latin for 'bearing across.' Having been borne across the world, we are translated men. It is normally supposed that something always gets lost in translation; I cling, obstinately, to the notion that something can also be gained.)

To be an Indian writer in this society is to face, every day, problems of definition. What does it mean to be 'Indian' outside India? How can culture be preserved without becoming ossified? How should we discuss the need for change within ourselves and our community without seeming to play into the hands of our racial enemies? What are the consequences, both spiritual and practical, of refusing to make any concessions to Western ideas and practices? What are the consequences of embracing those ideas and practices and turning away from the ones that came here with us? These questions are all a single, existential question: How are we to live in the world?

I do not propose to offer, prescriptively, any answers to these questions; only to state that these are some of the issues with which each of us will have to come to terms.

To turn my eyes outwards now, and to say a little about the relationship between the Indian writer and the majority white culture in whose midst he lives, and with which his work will sooner or later have to deal:

In common with many Bombay-raised middle-class children of my generation, I grew up with an intimate knowledge of, and even sense of friendship with, a certain kind of England: a dream-England composed of Test Matches at Lord's presided over by the voice of John Arlott, at which Freddie Trueman bowled unceasingly and without success at Polly Umrigar; of Enid Blyton and Billy Bunter, in which we were even prepared to smile indulgently at portraits such as 'Hurree Jamset Ram Singh,' 'the dusky nabob of Bhanipur.' I wanted to come to England. I couldn't wait. And to be fair, England has done all right by me; but I find it a little difficult to be properly grateful. I can't escape the view that my relatively easy ride is not the result of the dream-England's famous sense of tolerance and fair play, but of my social class, my freak fair skin and my 'English' English accent. Take away any of these, and the story would have been very different. Because of course the dream-England is no more than a dream.

Sadly, it's a dream from which too many white Britons refuse to awake. Recently, on a live radio programme, a professional humorist asked me, in all seriousness, why I objected to being called a wog°. He said he had always thought it a rather charming word, a term of endearment. 'I was at the zoo the other day,' he revealed, 'and a zoo keeper told me that the wogs were best with the animals; they stuck their fingers in their ears and wiggled them about and the animals felt at home.' The ghost of Hurree Jamset Ram Singh walks among us still.

As Richard Wright found long ago in America, black and white descriptions of society are no longer compatible. Fantasy, or the mingling of fantasy and naturalism, is one way of dealing with these problems. It offers a way of echoing in the form of our work the issues faced by all of us: how to build a new, 'modern' world out of an old, legend-haunted civilization, an old culture which we have brought into the heart of a newer one. But whatever technical solutions we may find, Indian writers in these islands, like others who have migrated into the north from the south, are capable of writing from a kind of double perspective: because they, we, are at one and the same time insiders and outsiders in this society. This stereoscopic vision is perhaps what we can offer in place of 'whole sight.'

There is one last idea that I should like to explore, even though it may, on first hearing, seem to contradict much of what I've so far said. It is this: of all the many elephant traps lying ahead of us, the largest and most dangerous pitfall would be the adoption of a ghetto mentality. To forget that there is a world beyond the community to which we belong, to confine ourselves within narrowly defined cultural frontiers, would be, I believe, to go voluntarily into that form of internal exile which in South Africa is called the 'homeland.' We must guard against creating, for the most virtuous of reasons, British-Indian literary equivalents of Bophuthatswana or the Transkei°.

This raises immediately the question of whom one is writing 'for'. My own, short, answer is that I have never had a reader in mind. I have ideas, people, events, shapes, and I write 'for' those things, and hope that the completed work will be of interest to others. But which others? In the case

---

wog: British derogatory word for people of colour—sometimes used to refer to anyone foreign (e.g., "The wogs begin at Calais")

'homeland' . . . Bophuthatswana . . . Transkei: Black homelands in South Africa (see note in Miriam Tlali, "Metamorphosis")

of *Midnight's Children* I certainly felt that if its subcontinental readers had rejected the work, I should have thought it a failure, no matter what the reaction in the West. So I would say that I write 'for' people who feel part of the things I write 'about', but also for everyone else whom I can reach. In this I am of the same opinion as the black American writer Ralph Ellison, who, in his collection of essays *Shadow and Act*, says that he finds something precious in being black in America at this time; but that he is also reaching for more than that. 'I was taken very early,' he writes, 'with a passion to link together all I loved within the Negro community and all those things I felt in the world which lay beyond.'

Art is a passion of the mind. And the imagination works best when it is most free. Western writers have always felt free to be eclectic in their selection of theme, setting, form; Western visual artists have, in this century, been happily raiding the visual storehouses of Africa, Asia, the Philippines. I am sure that we must grant ourselves an equal freedom.

Let me suggest that Indian writers in England have access to a second tradition, quite apart from their own racial history. It is the culture and political history of the phenomenon of migration, displacement, life in a minority group. We can quite legitimately claim as our ancestors the Huguenots, the Irish, the Jews; the past to which we belong is an English past, the history of immigrant Britain. Swift, Conrad, Marx are as much our literary forebears as Tagore or Ram Mohan Roy. America, a nation of immigrants, has created great literature out of the phenomenon of cultural transplantation, out of examining the ways in which people cope with a new world; it may be that by discovering what we have in common with those who preceded us into this country, we can begin to do the same.

I stress this is only one of many possible strategies. But we are inescapably international writers at a time when the novel has never been a more international form (a writer like Borges speaks of the influence of Robert Louis Stevenson on his work; Heinrich Böll acknowledges the influence of Irish literature; cross-pollination is everywhere); and it is perhaps one of the more pleasant freedoms of the literary migrant to be able to choose his parents. My own—selected half consciously, half not—include Gogol, Cervantes, Kafka, Melville, Machado de Assis; a polyglot family tree, against which I measure myself, and to which I would be honoured to belong.

There's a beautiful image in Saul Bellow's latest novel, *The Dean's December*. The central character, the Dean, Corde, hears a dog barking wildly somewhere. He imagines that the barking is the dog's protest against the limit of dog experience. 'For God's sake,' the dog is saying, 'open the universe a little more!' And because Bellow is, of course, not really talking about dogs, or not only about dogs, I have the feeling that the dog's rage, and its desire, is also mine, ours, everyone's. 'For God's sake, open the universe a little more!'

Critical Focus Questions

1. Pauline Melville, Austin Clarke and Neil Bissoondath all present the Caribbean as being in some sense "home." Compare/contrast their visions of home. What does the Caribbean represent to each?

2. The idea of the return home is a frequent theme in the literature of the late twentieth century. Identify the authors in this section who explore this theme. What do their presentations of the return home imply about the nature of identity?

3. Ben Okri's story emphasizes the power of home to nurture and restore the individual, while Salman Rushdie focusses on the advantages of leaving home. Are there ways in which their definitions of home and what it offers are similar?

4. In her essay, bell hooks emphasizes the idea of home as something created by strong nurturing women to support and protect families confronting a hostile world. Compare her vision of home with that of Ben Okri.

5. Pauline Melville presents home as being, like the individual, subject to change. Consider the nature of the change that overtakes the home presented in "Eat Labba and Drink Creek Water." Is this change the result of leaving and returning home or is it simply an inevitable part of life?

6. Some of the fiction contained in this section is "naturalistic" (e.g., Neil Bissoondath) in that it attempts to present a realistic or believable view of the world. Other pieces are more overtly allegorical or even dream-like. What is the difference in terms of the effect on the reader? What advantages are there to each approach? Consider also the differences between the effect of an essay such as Rushdie's and that of a short story.

7. The dynamics of home and family often change when a child becomes more educated than the parent, particularly in more traditional cultures. Examine the ways in which the family in Clarke's "Leaving This Island Place" has been affected by altered roles within the family.

8. Both Thomas King and bell hooks present home as a community of people with a shared experience, a "site of resistance" to a hostile or oppressive surrounding culture. Discuss how, while using very different styles (and genres) King and hooks effectively communicate their ideas about the nature and power of home.

credits

Chinua Achebe. "The Novelist as Teacher," from *New Statesman, 2000*. Copyright © New Statesman, 2000.

Anthony Akerman. "The Exile," from *The Penguin Book of Contemporary South African Short Stories*, ed. Stephen Gray (London: Penguin, 1993). Copyright © 1987 by Anthony Akerman. First published in *Contrast*, 1987, and reprinted in *The Penguin Book of Contemporary South African Short Stories* (ed. Stephen Gray, 1993). Used by permission of the author.

James Baldwin. "Sonny's Blues," from *Going To Meet the Man* (New York: The Dial Press, 1965; Toronto: Random House of Canada, 1995). Copyright © 1965 by James Baldwin. Copyright renewed. Collected in *Going To Meet the Man*, published by Vantage Books. Reprinted by arrangement with the James Baldwin Estate.

Louise Bennett. "Colonisation in Reverse," from *Sisters of Caliban* (Sangster Books); orginal copyright date 1962. "Colonisation in Reverse" by Louise Bennett. Copyright © by Louise Bennett. Reprinted by permission of the Jamaican Ministry of Culture.

Neil Bissoondath. "There Are a Lot of Ways to Die," from *Digging Up the Mountains* (Toronto: MacMillan of Canada, 1985). Permission granted by author.

Clark Blaise. "North," from *Resident Alien* (Markham: Penguin Canada, 1986). From *Resident Alien* by Clark Blaise. Copyright © 1986 by Clark Blaise. Reprinted by permission of Penguin Books Canada Limited.

Dionne Brand. Excerpt from *No Language is Neutral* (Coach House Press, 1990; McClelland & Stewart, 1998).

Austin Clarke. "Leaving This Island Place," from *When he was free and young and used to wear silks* (Toronto: House of Anansi, 1971). "Leaving This Island Place" by Austin Clarke from *When he was free and young and used to wear silks*, copyright © 1971 by House of Anansi. Published in Canada by Pearson Education Canada.

George Elliot Clarke. "Blank Sonnet," from *Whylah Falls* (Polestar Book Publishers, 1990; tenth anniversary ed., 2000). "Blank Sonnet" by George Elliot Clarke reprinted from the book *Whylah Falls* (1999), published by Polestar Book Publishers.

Michelle Cliff. "If I Could Write This in Fire, I Would Write This in Fire," from *The Land of Look Behind* (Ithaca, NY: Firebrand Books, 1985). Copyright © Michelle Cliff. Printed by permission.

Lucille Clifton. "at the cemetery, walnut grove plantation, south carolina, 1989," from *Quilting: Poems, 1987–1990* (Brookport, New York: BOA Editions, 1989). LUCILLE CLIFTON: "at the cemetery, walnut grove plantation, south carolina, 1989," © 1991 by Lucille Clifton. Reprinted from QUILTING: POEMS 1987–1990, by Lucille Clifton, with the permission of BOA Editions, Ltd.

Matt Cohen. "Racial Memories," from *Living on Water* (Toronto: McClelland & Steward, 1988). From *Living on Water* by Matt Cohen. Copyright © 1988 by Matt Cohen. Reprinted by permission of Penguin Books Canada Limited.

Cyril Dabydeen. "Multiculturalism," from *Making a Difference* (Oxford). Used by permission of the author.

Edwidge Danicat. "Nineteen Thirty-Seven," from *Kric? Krac!* (New York: Soho Press, 1996). Reprinted by permission of Soho Press.

Henry Louis Gates, Jr. "What's in a Name? Some Meanings of Blackness," from *Loose Canons: Notes From the Culture Wars* (New York: Oxford University Press, 1992). "What's in a Name? Some Meanings of Blackness" from LOOSE CANONS: NOTES ON THE CULTURAL WARS by Henry Louis Gates, Jr., copyright © 1992 by Henry Louis Gates, Jr. Used by permission of Oxford University Press, Inc.

Jack Hodgins. "The Lepers' Squint," from *The Barclay Family Theatre* (Toronto: Macmillan Canada, 1981). Copyright © Jack Hodgins 1978; reprinted here by arrangement with Bella Pomer Agency.

Eva Hoffman. "Life in a New Language," from *Lost in Translation* (New York: E. P. Dutton, 1989; New York: Penguin Books, 1990). From LOST IN TRANSLATION by Eva Hoffman, copyright © 1989 by Eva Hoffman. Used by permission of Dutton, a division of Penguin Putnam Inc.

bell hooks. "Homeplace," from *Yearning: Race, Gender, and Cultural Politics* (Toronto: Between the Lines, 1990). Reprinted by permission of Between the Lines.

Michael Ignatieff. "Quebec," from *Blood and Belonging: Journeys into the New Nationalism* (Toronto: Penguin, 1994). From *Blood and Belonging* by Michael Ignatieff. Copyright © 1993 by Michael Ignatieff. Reprinted by permission of Penguin Books Canada Limited.

Colin Johnson. Excerpt from *Dr. Wooreddy's Prescription for Enduring the World* (Melbourne: Hyland House, 1983). From *Dr. Wooreddy's Prescription for Enduring the World* by Mudrooroo (Colin Johnson). Copyright © by Mudrooroo (Colin Johnson). Reprinted by permission of Hyland House Publishing, P.O. Box 122 Flemington, Victoria 3031, Australia.

Basil Johnston. "One Generation from Extinction," from *Canadian Literature (124-25) 10-15*. "One Generation from Extinction" by Basil Johnston. Copyright © Basil Johnston.

Jamaica Kincaid. "My Mother," from *At the Bottom of the River* (New York: Plume, 1992). "My Mother" from AT THE BOTTOM OF THE RIVER by Jamaica Kincaid. Copyright © 1983 by Jamaica Kincaid. Reprinted by permission of Farrar, Straus and Giroux, LLC.

Thomas King. "Coyote Goes to Toronto," from *Native Canadian Writers*, ed. W. H. New (Vancouver: University of British Columbia Press, 1990), 252-3. Copyright © Thomas King, 1990. Originally published in *Canadian Literature*, Vol. 124-125, Spring/Summer 1990. Reprinted with permission.

Hanif Kureishi. "We're Not Jews," from *Love in a Blue Time* (Faber & Faber, 1997). Copyright © Hanif Kureishi, 1997. Reproduced by permission of the author c/o Rogers, Coleridge & White Ltd., 20 Powis Mews, London, W11 1JN.

Earl Lovelace. "Joebell and America," from *A Brief Conversation and Other Stories* (Oxford: Heinemann Educational Publishers, 1988). From *A Brief Conversation and Other Stories* by Earl Lovelace. Reprinted by permission of Heinemann Educational Publishers.

E. A. Markham. "Higuamota's Monserratian Lover," from *Ten Stories* (PAVIC, 1994). "Higuamota's Monserratian Lover" by E. A. Markham. Copyright © by E. A. Markham. First published in *Cross Cultures No. 12: Readings in Post-Colonial*

index

Page numbers in **boldface** indicate terms defined in footnotes.

Outlaw Culture (hooks), 356